Lecture Notes in
Computer Science

Lecture Notes in Computer Science

Vol. 379: A. Kreczmar, G. Mirkowska (Eds.), Mathematical Foundations of Computer Science 1989. Proceedings, 1989. VIII, 605 pages. 1989.

Vol. 380: J. Csirik, J. Demetrovics, F. Gécseg (Eds.), Fundamentals of Computation Theory. Proceedings, 1989. XI, 493 pages. 1989.

Vol. 381: J. Dassow, J. Kelemen (Eds.), Machines, Languages, and Complexity. Proceedings, 1988. VI, 244 pages. 1989.

Vol. 382: F. Dehne, J.-R. Sack, N. Santoro (Eds.), Algorithms and Data Structures. WADS '89. Proceedings, 1989. IX, 592 pages. 1989.

Vol. 383: K. Furukawa, H. Tanaka, T. Fujisaki (Eds.), Logic Programming '88. Proceedings, 1988. VII, 251 pages. 1989 (Subseries LNAI).

Vol. 384: G. A. van Zee, J. G. G. van de Vorst (Eds.), Parallel Computing 1988. Proceedings, 1988. V, 135 pages. 1989.

Vol. 385: E. Börger, H. Kleine Büning, M. M. Richter (Eds.), CSL '88. Proceedings, 1988. VI, 399 pages. 1989.

Vol. 386: J.E. Pin (Ed.), Formal Properties of Finite Automata and Applications. Proceedings, 1988. VIII, 260 pages. 1989.

Vol. 387: C. Ghezzi, J. A. McDermid (Eds.), ESEC '89. 2nd European Software Engineering Conference. Proceedings, 1989. VI, 496 pages. 1989.

Vol. 388: G. Cohen, J. Wolfmann (Eds.), Coding Theory and Applications. Proceedings, 1988. IX, 329 pages. 1989.

Vol. 389: D.H. Pitt, D. E. Rydeheard, P. Dybjer, A.M. Pitts, A. Poigné (Eds.), Category Theory and Computer Science. Proceedings, 1989. VI, 365 pages. 1989.

Vol. 390: J.P. Martins, E.M. Morgado (Eds.), EPIA 89. Proceedings, 1989. XII, 400 pages. 1989 (Subseries LNAI).

Vol. 391: J.-D. Boissonnat, J.-P. Laumond (Eds.), Geometry and Robotics. Proceedings, 1988. VI, 413 pages. 1989.

Vol. 392: J.-C. Bermond, M. Raynal (Eds.), Distributed Algorithms. Proceedings, 1989. VI, 315 pages. 1989.

Vol. 393: H. Ehrig, H. Herrlich, H.-J. Kreowski, G. Preuß (Eds.), Categorical Methods in Computer Science. VI, 350 pages. 1989.

Vol. 394: M. Wirsing, J.A. Bergstra (Eds.), Algebraic Methods: Theory, Tools and Applications. VI, 558 pages. 1989.

Vol. 395: M. Schmidt-Schauß, Computational Aspects of an Order-Sorted Logic with Term Declarations. VIII, 171 pages. 1989 (Subseries LNAI).

Vol. 396: T. A. Berson, T. Beth (Eds.), Local Area Network Security. Proceedings, 1989. IX, 152 pages. 1989.

Vol. 397: K. P. Jantke (Ed.), Analogical and Inductive Inference. Proceedings, 1989. IX, 338 pages. 1989 (Subseries LNAI).

Vol. 398: B. Banieqbal, H. Barringer, A. Pnueli (Eds.), Temporal Logic in Specification. Proceedings, 1987. VI, 448 pages. 1989.

Vol. 399: V. Cantoni, R. Creutzburg, S. Levialdi, G. Wolf (Eds.), Recent Issues in Pattern Analysis and Recognition. VII, 400 pages. 1989.

Vol. 400: R. Klein, Concrete and Abstract Voronoi Diagrams. IV, 167 pages. 1989.

Vol. 401: H. Djidjev (Ed.), Optimal Algorithms. Proceedings, 1989. VI, 308 pages. 1989.

Vol. 402: T. P. Bagchi, V. K. Chaudhri, Interactive Relational Database Design. XI, 186 pages. 1989.

Vol. 403: S. Goldwasser (Ed.), Advances in Cryptology – CRYPTO '88. Proceedings, 1988. XI, 591 pages. 1990.

Vol. 404: J. Beer, Concepts, Design, and Performance Analysis of a Parallel Prolog Machine. VI, 128 pages. 1989.

Vol. 405: C. E. Veni Madhavan (Ed.), Foundations of Software Technology and Theoretical Computer Science. Proceedings, 1989. VIII, 339 pages. 1989.

Vol. 406: C. J. Barter, M. J. Brooks (Eds.), AI '88. Proceedings, 1988. VIII, 463 pages. 1990 (Subseries LNAI).

Vol. 407: J. Sifakis (Ed.), Automatic Verification Methods for Finite State Systems. Proceedings, 1989. VII, 382 pages. 1990.

Vol. 408: M. Leeser, G. Brown (Eds.), Hardware Specification, Verification and Synthesis: Mathematical Aspects. Proceedings, 1989. VI, 402 pages. 1990.

Vol. 409: A. Buchmann, O. Günther, T. R. Smith, Y.-F. Wang (Eds.), Design and Implementation of Large Spatial Databases. Proceedings, 1989. IX, 364 pages. 1990.

Vol. 410: F. Pichler, R. Moreno-Diaz (Eds.), Computer Aided Systems Theory – EUROCAST '89. Proceedings, 1989. VII, 427 pages. 1990.

Vol. 411: M. Nagl (Ed.), Graph-Theoretic Concepts in Computer Science. Proceedings, 1989. VII, 374 pages. 1990.

Vol. 412: L. B. Almeida, C. J. Wellekens (Eds.), Neural Networks. Proceedings, 1990. IX, 276 pages. 1990,

Vol. 413: R. Lenz, Group Theoretical Methods in Image Processing. VIII, 139 pages. 1990.

Vol. 414: A.Kreczmar, A. Salwicki, M. Warpechowski, LOGLAN '88 – Report on the Programming Language. X, 133 pages. 1990.

Vol. 415: C. Choffrut, T. Lengauer (Eds.), STACS 90. Proceedings, 1990. VI, 312 pages. 1990.

Vol. 416: F. Bancilhon, C. Thanos, D. Tsichritzis (Eds.), Advances in Database Technology – EDBT '90. Proceedings, 1990. IX, 452 pages. 1990.

Vol. 417: P. Martin-Löf, G. Mints (Eds.), COLOG-88. International Conference on Computer Logic. Proceedings, 1988. VI, 338 pages. 1990.

Vol. 418: K.H. Bläsius, U. Hedtstück, C.-R. Rollinger (Eds.), Sorts and Types in Artificial Intelligence. Proceedings, 1989. VIII, 307 pages. 1990. (Subseries LNAI).

Vol. 419: K. Weichselberger, S. Pöhlmann, A Methodology for Uncertainty in Knowledge-Based Systems. VIII, 136 pages. 1990 (Subseries LNAI).

Vol. 420: Z. Michalewicz (Ed.), Statistical and Scientific Database Management, V SSDBM. Proceedings, 1990. V, 256 pages. 1990.

Vol. 421: T. Onodera, S. Kawai, A Formal Model of Visualization in Computer Graphics Systems. X, 100 pages. 1990.

Vol. 422: B. Nebel, Reasoning and Revision in Hybrid Representation Systems. XII, 270 pages. 1990 (Subseries LNAI).

Vol. 423: L. E. Deimel (Ed.), Software Engineering Education. Proceedings, 1990. VI, 164 pages. 1990.

Vol. 424: G. Rozenberg (Ed.), Advances in Petri Nets 1989. VI, 524 pages. 1990.

Vol. 425: C. H. Bergman, R. D. Maddux, D. L. Pigozzi (Eds.), Algebraic Logic and Universal Algebra in Computer Science. Proceedings, 1988. XI, 292 pages. 1990.

Vol. 426: N. Houbak, SIL – a Simulation Language. VII, 192 pages. 1990.

Vol. 427: O. Faugeras (Ed.), Computer Vision – ECCV 90. Proceedings, 1990. XII, 619 pages. 1990.

Vol. 428: D. Bjørner, C. A. R. Hoare, H. Langmaack (Eds.), VDM '90. VDM and Z – Formal Methods in Software Development. Proceedings, 1990. XVII, 580 pages. 1990.

Vol. 429: A. Miola (Ed.), Design and Implementation of Symbolic Computation Systems. Proceedings, 1990. XII, 284 pages. 1990.

Vol. 430: J. W. de Bakker, W.-P. de Roever, G. Rozenberg (Eds.), Stepwise Refinement of Distributed Systems. Models, Formalisms, Correctness. Proceedings, 1989. X, 808 pages. 1990.

Vol. 431: A. Arnold (Ed.), CAAP '90. Proceedings, 1990. VI, 285 pages. 1990.

Vol. 432: N. Jones (Ed.), ESOP '90. Proceedings, 1990. IX, 436 pages. 1990.

Vol. 433: W. Schröder-Preikschat, W. Zimmer (Eds.), Progress in Distributed Operating Systems and Distributed Systems Management. Proceedings, 1989. V, 206 pages. 1990.

Vol. 434: J.-J. Quisquater, J. Vandewalle (Eds.), Advances in Cryptology – EUROCRYPT '89. Proceedings, 1989. X, 710 pages. 1990.

Vol. 435: G. Brassard (Ed.), Advances in Cryptology – CRYPTO '89. Proceedings, 1989. XIII, 634 pages. 1990.

Vol. 436: B. Steinholtz, A. Sølvberg, L. Bergman (Eds.), Advanced Information Systems Engineering. Proceedings, 1990. X, 392 pages. 1990.

Lecture Notes in Computer Science

Edited by G. Goos and J. Hartmanis

491

A. Yonezawa   T. Ito (Eds.)

Concurrency: Theory, Language, and Architecture

UK/Japan Workshop
Oxford, UK, September 25–27, 1989
Proceedings

Springer-Verlag
Berlin Heidelberg New York London Paris
Tokyo Hong Kong Barcelona Budapest

Volume Editors

Akinori Yonezawa
Department of Information Science, The University of Tokyo
Hongo, Bunkyo-ku, Tokyo 113, Japan

Takayasu Ito
Department of Information Engineering
Faculty of Engineering, Tohoku University
Sendai 980, Japan

CR Subject Classification (1991): F.1.1, F.3.2, C.1.3, D.1.3, D.3.3

ISBN 3-540-53932-8 Springer-Verlag Berlin Heidelberg New York
ISBN 0-387-53932-8 Springer-Verlag New York Berlin Heidelberg

Printing and binding: Druckhaus Beltz, Hemsbach/Bergstr.
2145/3140-543210 – Printed on acid-free paper

Foreword

Japan's period as a closed society terminated abruptly in 1868, and Japan has played an increasingly important role in the world of business and technology. But communication between Japan and Europe on scientific matters, including Computer Science, is still quite limited. Japanese researchers are well read in the international literature, but barriers of language and culture have restricted their participation at a more personal level, and meant that Europeans are often unaware of Japanese work and unsure how to conduct themselves in personal encounters with Japanese whom they meet at a conference, or who may visit their workplace.

The situation is improving as many Japanese spend time abroad, and some Europeans visit Japan. Particularly it has been noticeable over the last ten years that many more Japanese researchers are able to converse in English with some facility. Sadly our efforts to learn Japanese and understand Japanese social conventions have been much less intensive.

This series of Japan-UK workshops, the first at Sendai in 1987 and the second at Oxford in 1989, is in some sense the fruit of almost twenty years of growing friendship between Professor Ito and myself, since 1967 when he was doing a PhD at Stanford with John McCarthy and I was a young lecturer in "Machine Intelligence" at Edinburgh.

It seemed to me that, beside the technical outcome of exchanging research results, we should try to get a group of Japanese and British researchers to feel comfortable together and begin the long process of sharing the unspoken assumptions about what is worth finding out - assumptions which underly all our research efforts. This was made easier by the warmth and generosity of Japanese hospitality at Sendai, a welcome which, with the help of Bill McColl, we tried to repay in some small measure at Oxford.

The first workshop was on Logic, Proof and Specification; there were no published proceedings, but the list of participants and talks is included at the end of this volume. The second Workshop on Concurrency gave rise to this volume. The first section reflects the UK concentration on the theory of concurrency with just one Japanese contribution, and the second emphasises the strong Japanese interest in the object oriented approach to programming and in particular to concurrent programming. The third section on architectures and VLSI is more evenly matched with contributions from a variety of researchers in both countries. The abstracts at the end of the book cover some other talks which were not submitted for publication.

We hope to continue this series and further encourage amiable conversation amongst this community of researchers.

Edinburgh University, January 1991   Rod Burstall

Preface

Concurrency has grown into one of the most active and prolific research areas in Computer Science. The second UK/Japan Workshop in Computer Science was held at Wadham College, Oxford, September 25-27, 1989, and focused its topics on Concurrency to exchange ideas emerging in the two countries. The workshop was organized by Rodney M. Burstall, Takayasu Ito, and Akinori Yonezawa with the help of William F. McColl (Oxford) for local arrangements at Oxford. At the workshop, 18 UK and 13 Japanese talks were given on various topics in concurrency, ranging from theories and languages to architectures and applications.

This volume, which contains the papers based on the research works presented at the workshop, is organized into four parts. Part I contains the papers on theoretical aspects of concurrency which reflect the flourishing research activities in UK, and Part II contains the papers on object-orientation and concurrent languages which reflect major research activities on concurrency in Japan. Part III contains a number of papers on parallel architectures and VLSI logic. Part IV gives an overview of the workshop including the abstracts of the talks and the list of the participants. The Appendix gives a brief report of the first UK/Japan Workshop in Computer Science, held at Sendai, Japan, July 6-9, 1987. The major topics of the first workshop, which was organized by R. M. Burstall and T. Ito, were Logic, Proof, and Specification in Computer Science. The idea of holding the Workshop on Concurrency was one of the major outcomes at this workshop.

This second UK/Japan Workshop at Oxford was sponsored by SERC (Science and Engineering Research Council of the British Government) and JSPS (Japanese Society for the Promotion of Science). It was held with the great help of Oxford people. In particular, we would like to express our cordial thanks to W. F. McColl of Oxford Computing Laboratory for his efforts on local arrangements of the workshop held at Wadham College. Also our special thanks go to Eleanor Kerse who served as the conference secretary during the workshop.

For the publication of this proceedings, we thank Hans Wössner of Springer-Verlag for his assistance and encouragement. Finally, we thank all those who helped organize the workshop and made this publication possible.

Hongo, Tokyo   Akinori Yonezawa
January 1991   Takayasu Ito

Table of Contents

PART III : Parallel Architectures and VLSI Logic

PART IV : Overview of UK/Japan Workshop, Oxford, 1989

APPENDIX :

PART I

Theoretical Aspects of Concurrency

An Introduction to
Modal and Temporal Logics for CCS

Colin Stirling
Dept. of Computer Science
University of Edinburgh
Edinburgh EH9 3JZ, UK

1 Motivation

Consider two non-equivalent CCS agents:

$$a.0 + \tau.b.0 \not\approx a.0 + b.0$$

Unlike the second agent, the first may silently evolve to the agent $b.0$ which is unable to respond to a. Generally, when two agents are not equivalent (either in the strong or weak sense) we would like to exhibit a *property* that one agent has but the other lacks. To do this we need to formalize suitable notions of property. Logic provides the framework for such an enterprise. Below a *modal* logic, a slight extension of Hennessy-Milner logic [5, 6], is presented whose formulas express properties of agents. The discriminating power of the logic is tied to bisimulation equivalence: two equivalent processes have precisely the same modal properties, and two non-equivalent image-finite agents do not.

More generally practitioners have found it useful to be able to express *temporal* properties of concurrent systems, especially *liveness* and *safety* properties (see [10, 4] for two recent survey articles). A safety property amounts to *nothing bad ever happens* while a liveness property expresses *something good does eventually happen*. The crucial safety property of a mutual exclusion algorithm is that no two processes are ever in their critical sections at the same time. And an important liveness property is that whenever a process requests execution of its critical section then eventually it is granted. Cyclic properties of systems are also salient. An example is a CCS specification of a scheduler (p.113 [9]) part of which is that it must perform a sequence of actions $a_1, \ldots, a_n$ cyclically starting with a_1. A logic expressing temporal notions provides a framework for the precise formalization of such specifications.

Formulas of the modal logic are not rich enough to express such temporal properties. So an extra operator, a fixed point operator, is added to it. The result is a very expressive temporal logic, (a slight extension of) the modal mu-calculus (see [7, 3, 8, 12]) which preserves the important feature that two equivalent agents have exactly the same temporal properties.

The modal and temporal logics provide a repository of useful properties. However it is also very important to be able to *verify* that an agent has or lacks a particular property.

When an agent is finitary this can be done automatically (and has been implemented in the *Concurrency Workbench* [2], a prototype system for analysing CCS processes). Below a tableau decision procedure, a *local* model checker from [13], is presented.

2   Hennessy-Milner logic

Processes of CCS generate labelled transition systems, structures which encapsulate their potential behaviour. These have the form $(\mathcal{P}, \{\xrightarrow{a} \mid a \in \mathcal{A}\})$ where $\mathcal{P}$ is a non-empty set of agents; $\mathcal{A}$ is an action set; and $\xrightarrow{a}$ the a transition relation for each $a \in \mathcal{A}$. Modal logics are interpreted on such systems. Let K range over subsets of an action set $\mathcal{A}$ then the following abstract syntax definition specifies formulas of (a slightly generalized) Hennessy-Milner logic, a particular modal logic.

$$A ::= \text{tt} \mid \neg A \mid A_1 \wedge A_2 \mid [K]A$$

A formula is either the constant true formula tt; or a negated formula $\neg A$; or a conjunction of formulas $A_1 \wedge A_2$; or a *modalized* formula $[K]A$ whose intended meaning is: A holds after every (performance of any) action in K. Notice that the set of formulas is parameterized on the action set $\mathcal{A}$. So each transition system has a Hennessy-Milner logic associated with it. The slight generalization is that sets of actions appear in the modalities instead of single actions.

Assume a fixed transition system $(\mathcal{P}, \{\xrightarrow{a} \mid a \in \mathcal{A}\})$. For any formula A of its associated Hennessy-Milner logic we define when a process $E \in \mathcal{P}$ has, or satisfies, the property A. We use $E \models A$ to denote this; and if E fails to have the property A we write $E \not\models A$. The satisfaction relation $\models$ is defined inductively on the structure of formulas:

$$
\begin{aligned}
&E \models \text{tt} \\
&E \models \neg A && \text{iff} && E \not\models A \\
&E \models A \wedge B && \text{iff} && E \models A \text{ and } E \models B \\
&E \models [K]A && \text{iff} && \forall E' \in \mathcal{P}. \forall a \in K. \text{ if } E \xrightarrow{a} E' \text{ then } E' \models A
\end{aligned}
$$

Every process in $\mathcal{P}$ has the property tt. A process has the property $\neg A$ when it fails to have the property A, while it has the property $A \wedge B$ when it has both properties A and B. Finally a process satisfies $[K]A$ if after every performance of any action in K all the resulting processes have the property A.

A valuable derived operator is $\langle K \rangle$, the *dual* of $[K]$:

$$\langle K \rangle A \stackrel{def}{=} \neg[K]\neg A$$

This operator expresses: after (a performance of) an action in K.

$$E \models \langle K \rangle A \quad \text{iff} \quad \exists E' \in \mathcal{P}. \exists a \in K. E \xrightarrow{a} E' \text{ and } E' \models A$$

Other helpful derived operators are disjunction, $\vee$, and the constant false formula, ff defined as follows:

$$
\begin{aligned}
\text{ff} &\stackrel{def}{=} \neg\text{tt} \\
A \vee B &\stackrel{def}{=} \neg(\neg A \wedge \neg B)
\end{aligned}
$$

Finally, three useful abbreviations are:

$$[a_1, \ldots, a_n] \text{ for } [\{a_1, \ldots, a_n\}]$$
$$[-K] \text{ for } [\mathcal{A} - K]$$
$$[-] \text{ for } [\mathcal{A}]$$

Their diamond versions are similarly condensed.

An alternative semantics of Hennessy-Milner logic inductively defines for each formula A the subset of processes $\|A\| \in \mathcal{P}$ having the property A as follows:

$$\begin{aligned}
\|true\| &= \mathcal{P} \\
\|\neg A\| &= \mathcal{P} - \|A\| \\
\|A \wedge B\| &= \|A\| \cap \|B\| \\
\|[K]A\| &= \overline{[K]}\,\|A\|
\end{aligned}$$

Here $\overline{[K]}$ is the following agent transformer: for any $\mathcal{P}' \subseteq \mathcal{P}$

$$\overline{[K]}\mathcal{P}' = \{E \in \mathcal{P} \mid \forall E' \in \mathcal{P}. \forall a \in K. \text{ if } E \xrightarrow{a} E' \text{ then } E' \in \mathcal{P}'\}$$

Clearly, $E \models A$ iff $E \in \|A\|$. The dual transformer $\overline{\langle K \rangle}$ associated with $\langle K \rangle$ is defined as follows:

$$\overline{\langle K \rangle}\mathcal{P}' = \{E \in \mathcal{P} \mid \exists E' \in \mathcal{P}'. \exists a \in K. E \xrightarrow{a} E'\}$$

3   Capacity and necessity

What kinds of properties are expressible within Hennessy-Milner logic? First consider the simple modal formula $\langle K \rangle \mathrm{tt}$ which expresses a *capacity* to perform an action in K:

$$E \models \langle K \rangle \mathrm{tt} \text{ iff } \exists E'. \exists a \in K. E \xrightarrow{a} E'$$

In sharp contrast $[K]\mathrm{ff}$ expresses an *inability* to perform any action in K. And when K is the full action set $\mathcal{A}$ it therefore expresses *deadlock*, an inability to perform any action. Consider a simple vending machine:

$$V \stackrel{def}{=} 2p.big.collect.V + 1p.little.collect.V$$

Here $V \models \langle 2p \rangle \mathrm{tt}$, that is V can accept $2p$. But a button can not yet be depressed (before money is deposited), so $V \models [big, little]\mathrm{ff}$. V has more interesting properties too.

- $V \models [2p]([little]\mathrm{ff} \wedge \langle big \rangle \mathrm{tt})$: after $2p$ is deposited the little button cannot be depressed whereas the big one can.

- $V \models [1p, 2p][1p, 2p]\mathrm{ff}$: after a coin is entrusted no other coin ($2p$ or $1p$) may be deposited.

- $V \models [1p, 2p][big, little]\langle collect \rangle \mathrm{tt}$: after a coin is deposited and then a button is depressed, a chocolate can be collected.

Verifying that V has these properties is undemanding. Their proofs appeal to the meaning of formulas on the transition system for V. For instance, a proof of the first of these properties is:

$$V \models [2p]([little]\text{ff} \land \langle big \rangle \text{tt})$$
iff $big.collect.V \models [little]\text{ff} \land \langle big \rangle \text{tt}$ as $\{big.collect.V\} = \{E \mid V \xrightarrow{2p} E\}$
iff $big.collect.V \models [little]\text{ff}$ and
$big.collect.V \models \langle big \rangle \text{tt}$

And clearly $big.collect.V$ is able to perform big but not $little$. Similarly, verifying that V lacks a property, such as $\langle 1p \rangle \langle 1p \rangle \text{tt}$, is equally routine. Notice that it is not necessary to *compute*, or even to know, the transition system for V in advance of checking a property. The above proof remains valid for any vending machine V of the form $V \stackrel{def}{=} 2p.big.E_1 + 1p.E_2$ irrespective of the processes E_1 and E_2.

Actions in the modal operators may contain values. For instance the simple cell:

$$C \stackrel{def}{=} in(x).\overline{out}(x).C$$

has the property $[in(v)]\langle \overline{out}(v) \rangle \text{tt}$. Proofs may now become more demanding, depending on additional reasoning. A simple example is the following cell which (assuming $x : \mathbb{N}$) inputs a number and outputs its square:

$$SQ \stackrel{def}{=} in(x).\overline{out}(x^2).SQ$$

Verifying that $SQ \models [in(3)]\langle \overline{out}(9) \rangle \text{tt}$ requires a modest calculation.

More demanding are proofs that depend on induction. Consider the following family of processes CT_n, for $n \in \mathbb{N}$:

$$
\begin{aligned}
CT_0 &= up.CT_1 + around.CT_0 \\
CT_{n+1} &= up.CT_{n+2} + down.CT_n
\end{aligned}
$$

Let $[up]^n \Phi$ be the formula Φ when $n = 0$ and $[up]^{n-1}[up]\Phi$ when $n > 0$ (and similarly for $\langle down \rangle^n$). Using induction we can then show that whatever goes up may come down in equal proportions:

$$CT_m \models [up]^n \langle down \rangle^n \text{tt}$$

The modal logic can also express *necessity*. The property that E can only perform a, that it *must* perform a, is given by:

$$E \models \langle - \rangle \text{tt} \land [-a]\text{ff}$$

The formula $\langle - \rangle \text{tt}$ affirms that some action can happen while $[-a]\text{ff}$ says that every action but a is impossible. For instance, after $2p$ is deposited V must perform big: $V \models [2p](\langle - \rangle \text{tt} \land [-big]\text{ff})$. A further example is that the third action V performs must be *collect*:

$$V \models \langle - \rangle \text{tt} \land [-](\langle - \rangle \text{tt} \land [-](\langle - \rangle \text{tt} \land [-collect]\text{ff}))$$

4 Two modal logics for CCS

There are two labelled transition systems associated with each CCS process depending on whether or not τ is observable. They are marked by different transition relations $\longrightarrow$ and $\Longrightarrow$; differing sets of actions; and different equivalences, strong $\sim$ and weak $\approx$. If $(\mathcal{P}, \{\xrightarrow{a} \mid a \in \mathcal{A}\})$ is the transition system generated by a process when τ is observable then $(\mathcal{P}, \{\xRightarrow{a} \mid a \in \mathcal{A}'\})$ is the corresponding transition system when it is unobservable where $\mathcal{A}' = (\mathcal{A} - \{\tau\}) \cup \{\varepsilon\}$. Recall that there is not a transition relation $\xRightarrow{\tau}$ but there is the relation $\xRightarrow{\varepsilon}$ meaning zero or more τ moves.

We distinguish between the two resulting modal logics by appealing to the modality $[K]$ (when $K \subseteq \mathcal{A}$) and $[\![K]\!]$ (when $K \subseteq \mathcal{A}'$). Consequently, $E \models [\![K]\!] A$ if $E' \models A$ for every E' such that $E \xRightarrow{a} E'$ for any $a \in K$. Similarly, we use the operator $\langle\!\langle K \rangle\!\rangle$ as the dual of $[\![K]\!]$. For instance, the modal property $A = \langle\!\langle \varepsilon \rangle\!\rangle [a]\, \mathtt{ff}$ distinguishes the following two agents:

$$a.0 + \tau.b.0 \models A$$

$$a.0 + b.0 \not\models A$$

This second modal logic permits us to express capacities and incapacities of agents to perform actions with respect to the $\Longrightarrow$ transition relations. For instance we can define the useful property of being deadlocked, incapable of performing an observable action:

$$Deadlock \overset{def}{=} [\![-\varepsilon]\!]\, \mathtt{ff}$$

Expressing necessities is, however, more subtle. First any agent E has the property $\langle\!\langle - \rangle\!\rangle \mathtt{tt}$ because $E \xRightarrow{\varepsilon} E$. Moreover for the same reason no agent has the property $[\![-a]\!]\, \mathtt{ff}$ when a is observable. How can we therefore represent that E *must* perform a? We may try the formula:

$$\langle\!\langle -\varepsilon \rangle\!\rangle \mathtt{tt} \wedge [\![-\{a, \varepsilon\}]\!]\, \mathtt{ff}$$

But this is flawed. For it is true of an agent $\tau.0 + a.0$ even though it may silently terminate without performing a. So let us introduce the idea of an agent being live in the sense that it can not silently terminate:

$$Live \overset{def}{=} [\![\varepsilon]\!] \langle\!\langle -\varepsilon \rangle\!\rangle \mathtt{tt}$$

Now we can appeal to the formula:

$$Live \wedge [\![-\{a, \varepsilon\}]\!]\, \mathtt{ff}$$

But there is still a question mark over this. This property holds of an agent $U \overset{def}{=} a.U + \tau.U$ which has a capacity to engage in infinite τ-cycles (and therefore presumably need not perform a). But this capacity is not preserved by the weak equivalence $\approx$ (see p.147ff [9]): $U \approx W$ when $W \overset{def}{=} a.W$. So we shall understand necessity in a weak sense: E must perform a means that E can not silently terminate and the next observable action must be a. (This is justified if we think of the behaviour of an agent as performances of sequences of observable actions.) Later we shall see how to define a stronger necessity.

5 Properties and bisimilarity

Bisimulation equivalence is definable on arbitrary transition systems. Strong equivalence $\sim$ is given by bisimulation equivalence on transition systems when τ is observable whereas $\approx$, weak equivalence, is bisimulation equivalence on transition systems involving the $\Longrightarrow$ relations. An alternative notion of equivalence is provided by modal logic. Two agents from the same transition system are equivalent, written as $E \equiv E'$, if they have the same modal properties (drawn from the modal logic of the transition system they belong to). This is a very natural equivalence. But what is the relationship between bisimulation equivalence, written as $\simeq$, on a transition system and $\equiv$? First there is the result that bisimulation equivalence preserves modal properties.

Theorem 1 *If $E \simeq E'$ then $E \equiv E'$*

Proof By induction on modal formulas A one shows that for any agents F and F': if $F \simeq F'$ then $F \models A$ iff $F' \models A$.

The converse of this theorem holds for a restricted set of agents. An agent E in a transition system $(\mathcal{P}, \{\xrightarrow{a} \mid a \in Act\})$ is *image finite* if for each $a \in Act$ the set $\{F \mid E \xrightarrow{a} F\}$ is finite, and each member of it is also image finite.

Theorem 2 *If E and E' is image finite and $E \equiv E'$ then $E \simeq E'$*

Proof By showing that $\equiv$ is a bisimulation.

These two results together are known as the modal *characterization* of bisimulation equivalence, due to Hennessy and Milner [5, 6]. This characterization not only reinforces the naturalness of bisimulation equivalence but also suggests that modal logic is a very appropriate program logic. Two immediate corollaries are that $\sim$ and $\approx$ are characterized by their respective modal logics.

6 Temporal properties and modal equations

The behaviour of a system is its entire capability of communication. One perspective on this is given by all the possible *maximal* sequences of observable actions— maximality guarantees that if a sequence is finite then the final agent is deadlocked, unable to perform an observable action. For instance, the agent $U \overset{def}{=} a.U + b.E$ has as one sequence of observable actions the infinite sequence of as, a^ω, given by the following *run* of U:

$$U \xrightarrow{a} U \xrightarrow{a} \ldots$$

So U may always perform a. Similarly the vending machine V earlier has the property that whenever a coin ($2p$ or $1p$) is deposited then eventually a chocolate is collected. These temporal properties are not expressible by individual formulas of the modal logic. So we extend it to a richer logic. As a first step in this direction we examine recursive modal equations introduced in [8].

Consider the modal equation $Z = \langle a \rangle Z$. It can be viewed as expressing (various) properties of transition systems. Each of these properties is determined by a solution to the equation: a solution[1] is a set of agents $\mathcal{P}'$ with the feature

$$
\begin{aligned}
\mathcal{P}' &= \overline{\langle a \rangle} \mathcal{P}' \\
&= \{ E \in P \mid \exists E' \in \mathcal{P}'.\ E \xrightarrow{a} E' \}
\end{aligned}
$$

An example is an uncluttered clock $Cl \stackrel{def}{=} tick.Cl$ that perpetually ticks. Each subset of processes of the elementary transition system generated by Cl solves the modal equation $Z = \langle tick \rangle Z$. These solutions can be ordered by subset, $\emptyset \subseteq \{Cl\}$, offering a smallest and a largest solution. In the case of a clock $Cl' \stackrel{def}{=} tick.tock.Cl'$ that alternately ticks and tocks there is just one solution, the empty set. If instead we consider this modal equation on a family of counter processes, $i \in \mathbb{N}$, that can increase, decrease, or when i is even delay by ticking

$$
\begin{aligned}
Co_0 &\stackrel{def}{=} tick.Co_0 + inc.Co_1 \\
Co_{2i+1} &\stackrel{def}{=} inc.Co_{2i+2} + dec.Co_{2i} \\
Co_{2i+2} &\stackrel{def}{=} tick.Co_{2i+2} + inc.Co_{2i+3} + dec.Co_{2i+1}
\end{aligned}
$$

then every subset of $\{ Co_{2i} \mid i \in \mathbb{N} \}$ is a solution. Again the minimal solution is the empty set, whereas now this family of counters with an even index is the maximal solution.

Apparently we are at a loss as to what property Z expresses in the equation $Z = \langle K \rangle Z$. However, on any transition system (whose sort includes K) not only does this equation have solutions but also it always has a *least* and a *largest* (which may coincide as for Cl' when K is just $\{tick\}$ suggesting that we can select them as the prominent solutions. The general theorem that guarantees this is due to Tarski.

Proposition 3 *Let $\mathcal{P}$ be any set and assume that $f : 2^{\mathcal{P}} \to 2^{\mathcal{P}}$ is monotonic[2]. Then f*

    i. *has a least fixed point given by $\bigcap \{ \mathcal{E} \subseteq \mathcal{P} \mid f(\mathcal{E}) \subseteq \mathcal{E} \}$*

    ii. *has a greatest fixed point given by $\bigcup \{ \mathcal{E} \subseteq \mathcal{P} \mid \mathcal{E} \subseteq f(\mathcal{E}) \}$*

The transformer $\overline{\langle K \rangle}$ is clearly monotonic. Consequently, $Z = \langle K \rangle Z$ always has both a least and greatest solution. Relinquishing the equational format we let $\mu Z.\langle K \rangle Z$ express the property given by the least solution to $Z = \langle K \rangle Z$, and we let $\nu Z.\langle K \rangle Z$ express the property determined by the largest solution.

But what properties are expressed by these formulas, $\mu Z.\langle K \rangle Z$ and $\nu Z.\langle K \rangle Z$? The least case is of little import as it expresses the same property as $\mathtt{ff}$: irrespective of $\mathcal{P}$, we have that

$$
\emptyset = \{ F \in \mathcal{P} \mid \exists E \in \emptyset. \exists a \in K.F \xrightarrow{a} E \}
$$

Much more stimulating is $\nu Z.\langle K \rangle Z$ which expresses a capacity to endlessly perform K actions. The process E_0 has this property if there is an ω-run:

---

[1] Each solution $\mathcal{P}'$ is a *fixed point* of the function $f = \lambda X \subseteq \mathcal{P}.\overline{\langle a \rangle} X$, that is $f(\mathcal{P}') = \mathcal{P}'$.

[2] Recall that $2^{\mathcal{P}}$ is just the set of all subsets of $\mathcal{P}$, and f is monotonic when for any $\mathcal{E}, \mathcal{F} \subseteq \mathcal{P}$ if $\mathcal{E} \subseteq \mathcal{F}$ then $f(\mathcal{E}) \subseteq f(\mathcal{F})$.

$$E_0 \xrightarrow{a_1} E_1 \xrightarrow{a_2} \ldots \xrightarrow{a_i} E_i \xrightarrow{a_{i+1}} \ldots$$

with each $a_i \in K$. Clearly, if $\mathcal{E} \subseteq \mathcal{P}$ is the set of processes with this property then

$$E \in \mathcal{E} \text{ iff } \exists E' \in \mathcal{E}.\exists a \in K.E \xrightarrow{a} E'$$

This capacity is not expressible within the modal logic of Section 2. Two special cases are striking. First $\nu Z.\langle - \rangle Z$ expresses a capacity for infinite behaviour. Second $\nu Z.\langle \tau \rangle Z$ captures *Diverges*, that ability to engage in infinite internal chatter.

A more composite equation schema (where A does not contain Z) is: $Z = A \vee \langle K \rangle Z$. The least solution, $\mu Z.A \vee \langle K \rangle Z$, is now more interesting, expressing a capacity to continuously perform actions drawn from K *until* A holds. Process E_0 has this property if there is a derivation with $n \geq 0$,

$$E_0 \xrightarrow{a_1} E_1 \xrightarrow{a_2} \ldots \xrightarrow{a_n} E_n$$

where $E_n \models A$ and each $a_i : 1 \leq i \leq n$ belongs to K. The maximal solution $\nu Z.A \vee \langle K \rangle Z$ also includes that extra possibility of performing K actions endlessly. As an example consider the family of counters, Co_i, earlier. The formula $[dec]\mathsf{ff}$ characterizes that the counter is at zero, in the state Co_0. Each counter has the property that it can continuously decrease until it becomes zero, given by the formula $\mu Z.[dec]\mathsf{ff} \vee \langle dec \rangle Z$. However, only Co_0 has the variant property that it may continuously increase until zero, $\mu Z.[dec]\mathsf{ff} \vee \langle inc \rangle Z$. But $Co_i \models \nu Z.[dec]\mathsf{ff} \vee \langle inc \rangle Z$ (because of the capacity to increase for ever) for each i.

Again two special cases of $\mu Z.A \vee \langle K \rangle Z$ stand out. First is the case when K is the complete set of actions. This formula then expresses weak eventuality of A— that A may eventually hold. The other special case is $\mu Z.A \vee \langle \tau \rangle Z$, which is just $\langle\!\langle \epsilon \rangle\!\rangle A$: after some silent activity A can become true.

Another useful composite schema (assuming again that A does not contain Z) is $Z = A \wedge \langle K \rangle Z$. The least solution is of no interest as it expresses ff. But the maximal solution expresses a capacity to endlessly perform K actions with A holding throughout. It consists of all those processes E_0 having an ω-run:

$$E_0 \xrightarrow{a_1} E_1 \xrightarrow{a_2} \ldots \xrightarrow{a_i} E_i \xrightarrow{a_{i+1}} \ldots$$

with each $a_i \in K$, and where each E_i has the property A. Processes which are unable to perform K actions for ever fail to have any property $\nu Z.A \wedge \langle K \rangle Z$. So a natural generalization is that A holds throughout a maximal performance of K actions, expressed by the formula $\nu Z.A \wedge (\langle K \rangle Z \vee [K]\mathsf{ff})$.

Not every modal equation has solutions. A simple instance is $Z = \neg Z$ which can never be solved on any transition system. Other equations, such as $Z \stackrel{def}{=} \langle tick, tock \rangle \mathsf{tt} \wedge [tick]\neg Z$ sometimes do, and other times do not, have solutions depending on the structure of the transition system. Both these example equations fail the monotonicity requirement of Proposition 3. However, by restricting the form of an equation $Z = A$ we can guarantee monotonicity on every transition system. This restriction is that every free occurrence of Z in A lies within the scope of an *even* number of negations.

The binders $\nu Z.$ and $\mu Z.$ are duals of each other, and are therefore interdefinable:

$$\mu Z. A = \neg \nu Z. \neg A[Z := \neg Z]$$
$$\nu Z. A = \neg \mu Z. \neg A[Z := \neg Z]$$

Here $\neg A[Z := \neg Z]$ is the formula that is the result of replacing all free occurrences of Z in $\neg A$ with $\neg Z$. An illustration of this is the property of *convergence* of E when it is unable to perform silent actions for ever. Earlier we noted that $\nu Z. \langle \tau \rangle Z$ expresses divergence. Hence, convergence is given as $\neg \nu Z. \langle \tau \rangle Z$:

$$\neg \nu Z. \langle \tau \rangle Z = \neg \nu Z. \neg [\tau] \neg Z$$
$$= \mu Z. [\tau] Z$$

More generally, $E \models \mu Z. [K] Z$ provided that E does not have an ω-run consisting entirely of K actions. In particular, $\mu Z. [-] Z$ expresses that all behaviour is finite. Notice that this does not mean that there is an n such that the process must terminate, or deadlock, within n transition steps. For instance, if $x : \mathsf{N}$ and C is the process

$$C \stackrel{def}{=} in(x).B_x$$
$$B_0 \stackrel{def}{=} 0$$
$$B_{i+1} \stackrel{def}{=} down.B_i$$

then $C \models \mu Z. [-] Z$ even though for all n it has a run consisting of at least n transition steps. Another use of such an equation is to express important liveness properties such as *a must eventually happen*, that a occurs in every maximal sequence of observable actions given by the least solution to: $Z = Live \wedge [-\{a, \varepsilon\}] Z$.

A strong invariance property is that A holds throughout every ongoing performance of K actions. This fails precisely when a process may perform K actions continuously until $\neg A$ holds. So this invariance is given by $\neg \mu Z. \neg A \vee \langle K \rangle Z$ which is $\nu Z. A \wedge [K] Z$ in positive form. Consequently, $[\varepsilon] A$ is just the formula $\nu Z. A \wedge [\tau] Z$. More generally safety properties, that nothing bad ever happens, fall under this format. A simple example is the mutual exclusion process $Me \stackrel{def}{=} (M \mid P_1 \ldots \mid P_n) \backslash \{p, v\}$, when $n \geq 1$:

$$M \stackrel{def}{=} \bar{p}.v.M$$
$$P_i \stackrel{def}{=} p.c_i.\bar{v}.P_i$$

The critical section of each P_i is represented by the action c_i. The crucial safety property of Me is that no two components may enter their critical section at the same time, which can be expressed as: $\nu Z. [K][K] \mathtt{ff} \wedge [-] Z$ where $K = \{c_1, \ldots, c_n\}$.

To express the general property of the vending machine V that whenever a correct coin is deposited then a chocolate must eventually be collected we require two equations:

$$Z = [2p, 1p] Y \wedge [-] Z$$

$$Y = \langle - \rangle \mathtt{tt} \wedge [-collect] Y$$

the first of which should be solved maximally and the second minimally. Quickly then the equational format becomes cumbersome.

7 A modal mu-calculus

Instead of appealing to modal equations to express temporal properties we add to modal logic propositional variables ranged over by Z and *fixed point* operators νZ. The formulas of the resulting logic, a slight extension of the modal mu-calculus, are:

$$A ::= Z \mid \neg A \mid A \wedge A \mid [K]A \mid \nu Z. A$$

where as before K ranges over subsets of actions. The formula $\nu Z. A$ expresses the property given by the maximal solution to $Z = A$: the operator $\nu Z.$ is a *binder*, binding free occurrences of Z in A. There is a syntactic restriction, motivated in the previous section, on formulas of the form $\nu Z. A$, that each free occurrence of Z (not bound by a $\nu Z.$) in A lies within the scope of an even number of negations. As with modal logic, each labelled transition system has a temporal logic associated with it. The modal mu-calculus was introduced in [7, 11] for a very different purpose than its use here. The slight extension is that modalities contain sets of actions instead of individual labels.

The constant tt is now defined as $\nu Z. Z$. An important derived operator, as we noted in the previous section, is μZ:

$$\mu Z. A \stackrel{def}{=} \neg \nu Z. \neg A[Z := \neg Z]$$

where $A[Z := \neg Z]$ is the result of substituting $\neg Z$ for each free occurrence of Z in A. The formula $\mu Z. A$ expresses the property given by the minimal solution to $Z = A$.

Assume a fixed transition system $(\mathcal{P}, \{\stackrel{a}{\longrightarrow} \mid a \in Act\})$. But now to interpret formulas on this transition system we need a new component to deal with propositional variables. So we invoke valuations, functions ranged over by $\mathcal{V}$ which assign a set of agents to each variable: $\mathcal{V}(Z) \subseteq \mathcal{P}$ for each Z. Also assumed is a customary updating notation: $\mathcal{V}[\mathcal{E}/Z]$ is the valuation $\mathcal{V}'$ which agrees with $\mathcal{V}$ except that $\mathcal{V}'(Z) = \mathcal{E}$. Finally the set of agents having the property A under the valuation $\mathcal{V}$ is inductively defined as $|A|_\mathcal{V}$:

$$
\begin{aligned}
|Z|_\mathcal{V} &= \mathcal{V}(Z) \\
|\neg A|_\mathcal{V} &= \mathcal{P} - |A|_\mathcal{V} \\
|A \wedge B|_\mathcal{V} &= |A|_\mathcal{V} \cap |B|_\mathcal{V} \\
|[K]A|_\mathcal{V} &= \overline{[K]} \, |A|_\mathcal{V} \\
|\nu Z. A|_\mathcal{V} &= \bigcup \{\mathcal{E} \subseteq \mathcal{P} \mid \mathcal{E} \subseteq |A|_{\mathcal{V}[\mathcal{E}/Z]}\}
\end{aligned}
$$

The set of agents having the property $\mu Z. A$ is:

$$|\mu Z. A|_\mathcal{V} = \bigcap \{\mathcal{E} \subseteq \mathcal{P} \mid |A|_{\mathcal{V}[\mathcal{E}/Z]} \subseteq \mathcal{E}\}$$

Temporal properties, we assume, are only expressed by *closed* formulas of the logic (those without free variables). This means that the set of agents having a temporal property A is independent of valuations: as $|A|_\mathcal{V} = |A|_{\mathcal{V}'}$ for any $\mathcal{V}$ and $\mathcal{V}'$. So we can use the notation $E \models A$ to represent that E has the property A (which holds whenever $E \in |A|_\mathcal{V}$ for some, or all, $\mathcal{V}$).

Example temporal properties for CCS agents, now as formulas instead of as solutions to equations, are:

- *Diverges* $\qquad\qquad\qquad\qquad \nu Z. \langle\tau\rangle Z$

- Action a must eventually happen $\qquad \mu Z. Live \wedge [-\{a,\varepsilon\}] Z$

- Absence of deadlock $\qquad\qquad \nu Z. Live \wedge [-] Z$

The temporal property of the vending machine that whenever a correct coin is deposited then eventually a chocolate must be collected is expressed as:

$$\nu Z. \mu Y. [2p, 1p](\langle-\rangle\mathtt{tt} \wedge [-collect]Y) \wedge [-]Z$$

Also expressible are *fairness* properties. For instance, the following formula A expresses that *in every run if a and b happen infinitely often then so does c*:

$$
\begin{aligned}
A &= \nu Z. B \wedge [-]Z \\
B &= \mu X. [a](\nu Y. [b](\nu Y_1. X \wedge [-c]Y_1) \wedge [-c]Y)
\end{aligned}
$$

The important result earlier, Theorem 1, that bisimulation equivalence preserves modal properties extends to temporal properties. As before let $\simeq$ be bisimulation equivalence. But now let $E \equiv E'$ when E and E' have the same temporal properties (drawn from the temporal logic of the transition system they belong to).

Theorem 4 *If $E \simeq E'$ then $E \equiv E'$*

Proof See [12].

Notice that Theorem 2 remains true for temporal properties as they encompass modal properties. Consequently we also have a temporal characterization of bisimulation equivalence. Again immediate corollaries are that $\sim$ and $\approx$ are characterized by their respective mu-calculi.

8 One temporal logic for CCS

The transition systems when τ is unobservable abstract from those when it is observable: the relations $\overset{a}{\Longrightarrow}$ are defined in terms of $\overset{a}{\longrightarrow}$ and (the reflexive and transitive closure of) $\overset{\tau}{\longrightarrow}$. Similarly, the modalities $[\![K]\!]$ abstract from $[K - \{\varepsilon\}]$ and (the reflexive and transitive closure of) $[\tau]$. Naturally this leads us to examine whether the temporal logic employing the $[\![K]\!]$ modalities is *definable* within the logic based on the $[K]$ modalites. That is, for each formula A of the logic using $[\![K]\!]$ is there a formula A^* of the logic which appeals to the $[K]$ modalities with the property that for all CCS agents E: $E \models A$ iff $E \models A^*$? The answer to this question is yes, and moreover the translation * can be defined structurally. The only complexity is the definition of $([\![K]\!]A)^*$, the other translations are straightforward— $\mathtt{true}^*$ is just $\mathtt{true}$; Z^* is Z; $(\neg A)^*$ is $\neg A^*$; $(A \wedge B)^*$ is $A^* \wedge B^*$; and $(\nu Z. A)^*$ is $\nu Z. A^*$. We divide the modality case into two depending on whether $\varepsilon \in K$:

$$\text{if } \varepsilon \notin K \text{ then } ([\![K]\!]A)^* = \nu Y_1. [K](\nu Y_2. A^* \wedge [\tau]Y_2) \wedge [\tau]Y_1$$

if $\varepsilon \in K$ then $([K]A)^* = \nu Y_1.(A^* \wedge [K - \{\varepsilon\}]\nu Y_2. A^* \wedge [\tau]Y_2) \wedge [\tau]Y_1$

Thus, there is really only one temporal logic for CCS processes. But it is useful to have the defined operators $[K]$. This means that we can use the one logic to describe properties of CCS agents with respect to the $\Longrightarrow$ transition relations. But notice that now temporal properties are not always preserved by $\approx$. In particular stronger notions of necessity (compare Section 4) can be expressed that are not preserved by $\approx$. For instance that the observable action a must happen, which also excludes the possibility of infinite τ cycles:

$$\mu Z.(\langle - \rangle \mathtt{tt} \wedge [-\{a, \tau\}]\mathtt{ff}) \wedge [\tau]Z$$

The agent $U \stackrel{def}{=} a.U$ has this property whereas $W \stackrel{def}{=} a.W + \tau.W$ does not even though $U \approx W$.

9 Verifying that agents have/lack properties

We have seen how temporal properties of agents can be expressed. The next step is to *verify* that an agent has or lacks a property, deciding whether $E \models A$ or $E \not\models A$. When the agent is finitary, that is generates a finite transition system, this can be done automatically on the Concurrency Workbench [2]. We now give an equivalent decision procedure, presented in [13], as a proof system for property checking. The technique has been generalized in [1] to encompass infinite transition systems.

The property checker is a tableau system, a goal directed proof system. It appeals to an auxiliary notion of finite sequences of declarations. Each declaration has the form $U = B$ where U is a propositional constant and B is a fixpoint formula or the negation of one which is to be read as: U *abbreviates* B. A finite sequence of declarations has the form $(U_1 = B_1, \ldots, U_n = B_n)$[3] The rules are built from 'sequents' of the form $E \vdash_\Delta A$, where A may contain constants U declared in Δ. Each rule has the form

$$\frac{E \vdash_\Delta A}{E_1 \vdash_{\Delta_1} A_1 \ldots E_k \vdash_{\Delta_k} A_k}$$

possibly with side conditions. The premise sequent $E \vdash_\Delta A$ is the goal to be achieved (that E has the property A relative to the declarations Δ) while the consequents are the subgoals. A small piece of notation: if U is not declared in Δ then $\Delta \cdot U = A$ is the result of appending $U = A$ to Δ. Condition $\mathcal{C}$, the side-condition on the constant rules, is explained later as it is a condition on proof trees, rather than on the particular sequents of the premises.

$$\frac{E \vdash_\Delta \neg\neg A}{E \vdash_\Delta A} \qquad \frac{E \vdash_\Delta A \wedge B}{E \vdash_\Delta A \quad E \vdash_\Delta B}$$

---

[3]We assume that each U_i is distinct.

$$\frac{E \vdash_\Delta \neg(A \wedge B)}{E \vdash_\Delta \neg A} \qquad \frac{E \vdash_\Delta \neg(A \wedge B)}{E \vdash_\Delta \neg B}$$

$$\frac{E \vdash_\Delta [K]A}{E_1 \vdash_\Delta A \dots E_n \vdash_\Delta A} \quad \{E_1, \dots, E_n\} = \{E' \mid \exists a \in K. E \xrightarrow{a} E'\}$$

$$\frac{E \vdash_\Delta \neg[K]A}{E' \vdash_\Delta \neg A} \quad E \xrightarrow{a} E' \text{ where } a \in K$$

$$\frac{E \vdash_\Delta \nu Z. A}{E \vdash_{\Delta'} U} \quad \Delta' \text{ is } \Delta \cdot U = \nu Z. A$$

$$\frac{E \vdash_\Delta \neg \nu Z. A}{E \vdash_{\Delta'} U} \quad \Delta' \text{ is } \Delta \cdot U = \neg \nu Z. A$$

$$\frac{E \vdash_\Delta U}{E \vdash_\Delta A[Z := U]} \quad C \text{ and } U = \nu Z. A \in \Delta$$

$$\frac{E \vdash_\Delta U}{E \vdash_\Delta \neg A[Z := \neg U]} \quad C \text{ and } U = \neg \nu Z. A \in \Delta$$

To test if E has the property A then one tries to achieve the goal $E \vdash A$ (where the list of declarations is omitted when, as here, it is empty) by building a *tableau*, a maximal proof tree whose root is labelled with the sequent $E \vdash A$. The sequents labelling the immediate successors of a node labelled $E \vdash_\Delta A$ are determined by an application of one of the rules, dependent on the structure of A. When A has the form $\neg(B \wedge C)$ and $\neg[K]B$ then there may be a choice as to the consequent. This means that there may be more than one tableau associated with an initial sequent. Maximality means that no rule applies to a sequent labelling a leaf of a tableau. The rules for booleans and modal operators are straightforward. New constants are introduced in the case of a fixpoint formula and its negation. The rules for constants unroll the fixpoints they abbreviate when condition C holds. This condition is just that no node above the current premise, $E \vdash_\Delta U$, in the proof tree is labelled $E \vdash_{\Delta'} U$ for some Δ'. So failure of the condition, when there is a sequent $E \vdash_{\Delta'} U$ above $E \vdash_\Delta U$, enforces termination. In fact the presence of condition C guarantees that when E is finitary then any tableau for $E \vdash A$ has finite depth.

A *successful* tableau for $E \vdash A$ is a finite tableau in which every leaf is labelled by a sequent $F \vdash_\Delta B$ fulfilling one of the following requirements:

1. $B = [K]C$

2. $B = U$ and $U = \nu Z. C \in \Delta$

A leaf fulfilling one of these requirements is true— F then has the property B (relative to the declarations Δ). In the case of 1 it follows from maximality of the tableau: F can not then perform any actions in K, and so has any property $[K]C$. The other case is the most interesting and captures a version of co-induction. It follows that a tableau for $E \vdash A$ is only successful when $E \models A$. Theorem 5 affirms the correctness (soundness, completeness, and decidability) of the property checker. The constants are essential to the tableau technique: if fixed points were syntactically unfolded instead and their termination decided as above, reaching the same sequent again, then the tableau system is both unsound and incomplete.

Theorem 5 *When E is finitary*
    i. *every tableau for $E \vdash A$ is finite*
    ii. *$E \vdash A$ has a successful tableau if and only if $E \models A$*

Proof See the extended version of [13].

Tableau rules for the derived operators are just reformulations of some of the negation rules:

$$\frac{E \vdash_\Delta A \vee B}{E \vdash_\Delta A} \qquad \frac{E \vdash_\Delta A \vee B}{E \vdash_\Delta B}$$

$$\frac{E \vdash_\Delta \langle K \rangle A}{E' \vdash_\Delta A} \quad E \xrightarrow{a} E' \text{ for } a \in K$$

$$\frac{E \vdash_\Delta \mu Z. A}{E \vdash_{\Delta'} U} \quad \Delta' \text{ is } \Delta \cdot U = \mu Z. A$$

$$\frac{E \vdash_\Delta U}{E \vdash_\Delta A[Z := U]} \quad C \text{ and } U = \mu Z. A \in \Delta$$

We now illustrate the use of the property checker. Let $W \stackrel{def}{=} a.W + \tau.0$. First we show that W has the property $\nu Z. \langle a \rangle Z$. This yields the tableau:

$$\frac{\dfrac{\dfrac{W \vdash \nu Z. \langle a \rangle Z}{W \vdash_\Delta U}}{W \vdash_\Delta \langle a \rangle U}}{W \vdash_\Delta U} \Delta = (U = \nu Z. \langle a \rangle Z)$$

which is successful because its single leaf $W \vdash_\Delta U$ satisfies the third requirement above. A second example is to show that $W \not\models \mu Y. [-\varepsilon] Y$. We have to show that every tableau for $W \vdash \mu Y. [-\varepsilon] Y$ is unsuccessful. Again we start with the goal to be achieved.

$$\frac{\dfrac{\dfrac{W \vdash \mu Y. [-\varepsilon] Y}{W \vdash_\Delta U}}{W \vdash_\Delta [-\varepsilon] U}}{W \vdash_\Delta U} \Delta = (U = \mu Y. [-\varepsilon] Y)$$

But now this is not a successful tableau as its only leaf fails the requirements (by definition $\mu Y. A$ is $\neg \nu Y. \neg A[Y := \neg Y]$). Moreover this is the only tableau for the initial goal (modulo renaming the constant U).

A third example shows that the vending machine

$$V \stackrel{def}{=} 2p.big.collect.V + 1p.little.collect.V$$

has the property

$$\nu Z. \mu Y. [2p, 1p](\langle - \rangle tt \wedge [-collect]Y) \wedge [-]Z$$

Let this formula be A and let B be

$$\mu Y. [2p, 1p](\langle - \rangle tt \wedge [-collect]Y) \wedge [-]U$$

$$\cfrac{\cfrac{\cfrac{\cfrac{\cfrac{V \vdash A}{V \vdash_{\Delta} U}\Delta = (U = A)}{\cfrac{V \vdash_{\Delta} B}{V \vdash_{\Delta'} W}\Delta' = (U = A, W = B)}}{V \vdash_{\Delta'} [2p, 1p](\langle - \rangle tt \wedge [-collect]W) \wedge [-]U}}{V \vdash_{\Delta'} [2p, 1p](\langle - \rangle tt \wedge [-collect]W) \quad V \vdash_{\Delta'} [-]U}}{}$$

Let C be the formula $\langle - \rangle tt \wedge [-collect]W$. Following just the first of these goals we obtain as further subgoals:

$$\frac{V \vdash_{\Delta'} [2p, 1p]C}{big.collect.V \vdash_{\Delta'} C \quad little.collect.V \vdash_{\Delta'} C}$$

In turn the first of these reduces to the two subgoals

$$\frac{big.collect.V \vdash_{\Delta'} C}{big.collect.V \vdash_{\Delta'} \langle - \rangle tt \quad big.collect.V \vdash_{\Delta'} [-collect]W}$$

We now follow the fortunes of the second:

$$\cfrac{\cfrac{\cfrac{\cfrac{big.collect.V \vdash_{\Delta'} [-collect]W}{collect.V \vdash_{\Delta'} W}}{collect.V \vdash_{\Delta'} [2p, 1p]C \wedge [-]U}}{collect.V \vdash_{\Delta'} [2p, 1p]C \quad collect.V \vdash_{\Delta'} [-]U}}{V \vdash_{\Delta'} U}$$

The first is a successful leaf (because $collect.V$ can not perform either $2p$ or $1p$) while the second is successful because the sequent $V \vdash_{\Delta} U$ appears above it and U abbreviates a maximal fixpoint formula. The rest of the tableau is left as an exercise.

10 Applications

A more substantial example is an analysis of Knuth's mutual exclusion algorithm when translated into CCS, worked out by David Walker [14]. Knuth's algorithm is given by the concurrent composition of the two programs when $i = 1$ and $i = 2$, and where j is the index of the other program:

while true **do**
begin

⟨ noncritical section ⟩ ;
L_0: $c_i := 1$;
L_1: **if** $k = i$ **then goto** L_2 ;
if $c_j \neq 0$ **then goto** L_1 ;
L_2: $c_i := 2$;
if $c_j = 2$ **then goto** L_0 ;
$k := i$;
⟨ critical section ⟩ ;
$k := j$;
$c_i := 0$;

end ;

The variable c_1 (c_2) of program one (two) may take the values $0, 1$ or 2; initially its value is 0. When translated into CCS the algorithm, assuming the initial value of k to be 1, becomes the agent *Knuth* below. For the example we let capital letters range over CCS processes (states of the CCS transition system). Thus the variable k with current value 1 is represented as an agent $K1$ which may perform actions corresponding to the reading of the value 1 and the writing of the values 1 and 2 by the two programs. The agents are:

$$Knuth \stackrel{def}{=} (P_1 \mid P_2 \mid K1 \mid C_1 0 \mid C_2 0) \backslash L$$

where L is the union of the sorts of the variables and

$$K1 \stackrel{def}{=} kw1.\,K1 + kw2.\,K2 + \overline{kr1}.\,K1$$
$$K2 \stackrel{def}{=} kw1.\,K1 + kw2.\,K2 + \overline{kr2}.\,K2$$

$$C_10 \stackrel{def}{=} c_1w0.\,C_10 + c_1w1.\,C_11 + c_1w2.\,C_12 + \overline{c_1r0}.\,C_10$$
$$C_11 \stackrel{def}{=} c_1w0.\,C_10 + c_1w1.\,C_11 + c_1w2.\,C_12 + \overline{c_1r1}.\,C_11$$
$$C_12 \stackrel{def}{=} c_1w0.\,C_10 + c_1w1.\,C_11 + c_1w2.\,C_12 + \overline{c_1r2}.\,C_12$$

$$C_20 \stackrel{def}{=} c_2w0.\,C_20 + c_2w1.\,C_21 + c_2w2.\,C_22 + \overline{c_2r0}.\,C_20$$
$$C_21 \stackrel{def}{=} c_2w0.\,C_20 + c_2w1.\,C_21 + c_2w2.\,C_22 + \overline{c_2r1}.\,C_21$$
$$C_22 \stackrel{def}{=} c_2w0.\,C_20 + c_2w1.\,C_21 + c_2w2.\,C_22 + \overline{c_2r2}.\,C_22$$

$$P_1 \stackrel{def}{=} \tau.\,P_{11} + \tau.\,0$$
$$P_{11} \stackrel{def}{=} \overline{c_1w1}.\,req_1.\,P_{12}$$
$$P_{12} \stackrel{def}{=} kr1.\,P_{14} + kr2.\,P_{13}$$
$$P_{13} \stackrel{def}{=} c_2r0.\,P_{14} + c_2r1.\,P_{12} + c_2r2.\,P_{12}$$
$$P_{14} \stackrel{def}{=} \overline{c_1w2}.\,P_{15}$$
$$P_{15} \stackrel{def}{=} c_2r0.\,P_{16} + c_2r1.\,P_{16} + c_2r2.\,P_{17}$$
$$P_{16} \stackrel{def}{=} \overline{kw1}.\,enter_1.\,exit_1.\,\overline{kw2}.\,\overline{c_1w0}.\,P_1$$
$$P_{17} \stackrel{def}{=} \overline{c_1w1}.\,P_{12}$$

$$P_2 \stackrel{def}{=} \tau.\,P_{21} + \tau.\,0$$
$$P_{21} \stackrel{def}{=} \overline{c_2w1}.\,req_2.\,P_{22}$$
$$P_{22} \stackrel{def}{=} kr2.\,P_{24} + kr1.\,P_{23}$$
$$P_{23} \stackrel{def}{=} c_1r0.\,P_{24} + c_1r1.\,P_{22} + c_1r2.\,P_{22}$$
$$P_{24} \stackrel{def}{=} \overline{c_2w2}.\,P_{25}$$
$$P_{25} \stackrel{def}{=} c_1r0.\,P_{26} + c_1r1.\,P_{26} + c_1r2.\,P_{27}$$
$$P_{26} \stackrel{def}{=} \overline{kw2}.\,enter_2.\,exit_2.\,\overline{kw1}.\,\overline{c_2w0}.\,P_2$$
$$P_{27} \stackrel{def}{=} \overline{c_2w1}.\,P_{22}$$

Some remarks on this representation may be helpful. The critical section of process P_i, where $i = 1$ or 2, is modelled as a pair of actions $enter_i$ and $exit_i$ representing, respectively, entry to and exit from the critical section. The noncritical section of each process is modelled as a summation, one summand of which represents the possibility that the process may halt, the other that it may proceed to request execution of its critical section. An action req_i appears in the definition of P_i. Its occurrence indicates that process P_i has 'just' indicated that it wishes to execute its critical section (by setting c_i to true). The reason for including these 'probes' will become clear below. Note also the presence of the agents P_{i7} and the way in which the statement goto L_0 is represented. The reason for this choice is that only the first $\overline{c_iw1}$ action (setting c_i to 1) is considered as signifying the initiation of an attempt by process i to execute its critical section.

We examine safety and liveness properties of this algorithm. The crucial safety property is that both processes can never be in their critical sections at the same time. Process i is in its critical section if it can perform the action $exit_i$. Consequently we need to show

$$Knuth \models \nu Z. ((\neg(\langle\!\langle exit_1 \rangle\!\rangle tt \wedge \langle\!\langle exit_2 \rangle\!\rangle tt)) \wedge [-] Z)$$

An important liveness property is that if a process requests execution of its critical section it will eventually enter its critical section. This is shown by proving:

$$Knuth \models \nu Z. ([req_1] EICS1 \wedge [req_2] EICS2) \wedge [-] Z$$

where for $i = 1, 2$, EICSi ('eventually in critical section i') is the formula

$$\mu Y. [\varepsilon] ((\langle\!\langle exit_i \rangle\!\rangle tt \vee ([-\varepsilon] Y \wedge \langle\!\langle -\varepsilon \rangle\!\rangle tt))$$

Using the Concurrency Workbench David Walker has verified that Knuth's algorithm has these properties.

References

[1] J. Bradfield and C. Stirling. Verifying temporal properties of processes. To appear in *Proc. Concur* 1990.

[2] R. Cleaveland, J. Parrow, and B. Steffen. The concuurency workbench. *Proc. IFIP*, 1989.

[3] E. Emerson and C. Lei. Efficient model checking in fragments of the propositional mu-calculus. *Procs. 1st IEEE Symp. on Logic in Computer Science*, 1986.

[4] E. Emerson and J. Srinivasan. Branching time temporal logic. *Lect. Notes in Computer Science* 354, Springer, 1989.

[5] M. Hennessy and R. Milner. On observing nondeterminism and concurrency. *Lect. Notes in Computer Science* 85, Springer, 1980.

[6] M. Hennessy and R. Milner. Algebraic laws for nondeterminism and concurrency. *J. Assoc. Comput. Mach.* 32, 137-161, 1985.

[7] D. Kozen. Results on the propositional mu-calculus. *Theoret. Computer Science* 27, 1983.

[8] K. Larsen. Proof systems for Hennessy-Milner logic with recursion. *Lect. Notes in Computer Science* 299, Springer, 1988

[9] R. Milner. *Communication and Concurrency*. Prentice Hall, 1989.

[10] Z. Manna and A. Pnueli. The anchored version of the temporal framework. *Lect. Notes in Computer Science* 354, Springer, 1989.

[11] V. Pratt. A decidable mu-calculus. *Proc. 22nd IEEE Found. of Computer Science*, 1981.

[12] C. Stirling. Temporal logics for CCS. *Lect. Notes in Computer Science* 354, Springer, 1989.

[13] C. Stirling and D. Walker. Local model-checking in the modal mu-calculus. *Lect. Notes in Computer Science* 351, Springer, 1989. (Extended version to appear in *Theoret. Computer Science*)

[14] D. Walker. Automated analysis of mutual exclusion algorithms using CCS. *Formal Aspects of Computing* 1, 1989.

Some Results on the π-calculus

David Walker
Department of Computer Science
University of Edinburgh

1 Introduction

The π-calculus [MPW1,2] is a calculus of mobile processes in which one can naturally express systems which have changing structure. [MPW1] contains an introduction to the calculus through a sequence of examples, while in [MPW2] the algebraic theory of the calculus is developed. The present paper contains two further contributions to the theory.

The first is a modal characterization of the relation of strong ground bisimilarity on agents of the π-calculus. This result is analogous to the well-known modal characterization of bisimilarity on labelled transition systems [HM]. The second contribution concerns the expressive power of the π-calculus. In [MPW1] this power is illustrated through discussion of the encoding of the passing of processes as parameters, of combinator graph reduction and the λ-calculus, and of data values and data structures. Here we use the encodings of data values and data structures to encode a version of CCS with value passing in the π-calculus, and establish certain properties of the translation, principal among them being that the translation induces a simulation of an agent by its translation, and that a converse simulation obtains for translations of a restricted class of 'type-safe' agents.

2 The π-calculus

Here we give a brief summary of material drawn from [MPW1,2], principally to fix notation. For further details and explanation we refer to these papers. The results concerning the encoding of a version of CCS with value passing make use of a notion of weak bisimilarity of agents of the π-calculus and this notion is discussed briefly.

In the π-calculus, we begin with an infinite set of *names*, ranged over by x, y, z, w, v, u. We assume also a set of *agent identifiers*. Each agent identifier A has a nonnegative arity.

Definition 1 The set of *agents*, ranged over by P, Q, R, is defined as follows

$$
\begin{aligned}
P \;::=\; & \mathbf{0} \\
 & \mid\; \overline{x}y.\,P \\
 & \mid\; x(y).\,P \\
 & \mid\; \tau.\,P \\
 & \mid\; P + Q \\
 & \mid\; P \mid Q \\
 & \mid\; (x)P \\
 & \mid\; [x\!=\!y]P \\
 & \mid\; A(y_1, \ldots, y_n)
\end{aligned}
$$

In each agent of one of the forms $x(y).\,P$ and $(y)P$ the occurrence of y within parentheses is a *binding occurrence*, and in each case the *scope* of the occurrence is P. The set of names occurring free in P is denoted $\mathrm{fn}(P)$. We sometimes write $\mathrm{fn}(P, Q, \ldots, x, y, \ldots)$ as an abbreviation for $\mathrm{fn}(P) \cup \mathrm{fn}(Q) \cup \ldots \cup \{x, y, \ldots\}$. Associated with each agent identifier A is a unique *defining equation* of the form

$$
A(x_1, \ldots, x_n) \stackrel{\text{def}}{=} P
$$

where the x_i are pairwise distinct and $\mathrm{fn}(P) \subseteq \{x_1, \ldots, x_n\}$. We write $P\{y_1/x_1, \ldots, y_n/x_n\}$ or $P\{\tilde{y}/\tilde{x}\}$ for the agent obtained from P by simultaneously substituting the $\tilde{y}$ for the $\tilde{x}$ in P with change of bound names to avoid captures. The symbol $\equiv$ denotes the relation of *alpha-convertibility* on agents defined in the standard way.

Agents are given a transitional semantics in the style of CCS. There are four kinds of action: the *free actions*, $\overline{x}y$ and τ; and the *bound actions* $x(y)$ and $\overline{x}(y)$. The following notation is useful in giving the transition rules. If $\alpha = x(y)$ or $\overline{x}(y)$ then the set $\mathrm{bn}(\alpha)$ of *bound names* of α is $\{y\}$; otherwise $\mathrm{bn}(\alpha) = \emptyset$. If $\alpha = \overline{x}y$ then the set $\mathrm{fn}(\alpha)$ of *free names* of α is $\{x, y\}$; if $\alpha = x(y)$ or $\overline{x}(y)$ then $\mathrm{fn}(\alpha) = \{x\}$; $\mathrm{fn}(\tau) = \emptyset$. The set $\mathrm{n}(\alpha)$ of *names* of α is $\mathrm{fn}(\alpha) \cup \mathrm{bn}(\alpha)$. The transition rules are given in Table 1.

Analogous to the notion of strong bisimilarity of CCS we have the relation of *strong ground bisimilarity*, $\dot{\sim}$. This is the largest relation S on the set of π-calculus agents which is a strong bisimulation, where S is a *strong bisimulation* if both S and S^{-1} are strong simulations where

S is a *strong simulation* if whenever PSQ then

1. If $P \stackrel{\alpha}{\longrightarrow} P'$ and α is a free action,
   then for some Q', $\quad Q \stackrel{\alpha}{\longrightarrow} Q'$ and $P'SQ'$

2. If $P \stackrel{x(y)}{\longrightarrow} P'$ and $y \notin \mathrm{n}(P, Q)$,
   then for some Q', $\quad Q \stackrel{x(y)}{\longrightarrow} Q'$ and for all w, $P'\{w/y\}SQ'\{w/y\}$

3. If $P \stackrel{\overline{x}(y)}{\longrightarrow} P'$ and $y \notin \mathrm{n}(P, Q)$,
   then for some Q', $\quad Q \stackrel{\overline{x}(y)}{\longrightarrow} Q'$ and $P'SQ'$.

As discussed briefly in [MPW1], analogously with CCS there is a notion of weak ground bisimilarity which abstracts from τ actions. In the translation of agents of

TAU-ACT : $$\dfrac{\overline{}}{\tau.P \xrightarrow{\;\tau\;} P}$$ OUTPUT-ACT : $$\dfrac{\overline{}}{\overline{x}y.P \xrightarrow{\;\overline{x}y\;} P}$$

INPUT-ACT : $$\dfrac{\overline{}}{x(z).P \xrightarrow{\;x(w)\;} P\{w/z\}} \quad w \notin \mathrm{fn}((z)P)$$

SUM : $$\dfrac{P \xrightarrow{\;\alpha\;} P'}{P+Q \xrightarrow{\;\alpha\;} P'}$$ MATCH : $$\dfrac{P \xrightarrow{\;\alpha\;} P'}{[x=x]P \xrightarrow{\;\alpha\;} P'}$$

IDE : $$\dfrac{P\{\widetilde{y}/\widetilde{x}\} \xrightarrow{\;\alpha\;} P'}{A(\widetilde{y}) \xrightarrow{\;\alpha\;} P'} \quad A(\widetilde{x}) \stackrel{\mathrm{def}}{=} P$$

PAR : $$\dfrac{P \xrightarrow{\;\alpha\;} P'}{P \,|\, Q \xrightarrow{\;\alpha\;} P' \,|\, Q} \quad \mathrm{bn}(\alpha) \cap \mathrm{fn}(Q) = \emptyset$$

COM : $$\dfrac{P \xrightarrow{\;\overline{x}y\;} P' \quad Q \xrightarrow{\;x(z)\;} Q'}{P \,|\, Q \xrightarrow{\;\tau\;} P' \,|\, Q'\{y/z\}}$$ CLOSE : $$\dfrac{P \xrightarrow{\;\overline{x}(w)\;} P' \quad Q \xrightarrow{\;x(w)\;} Q'}{P \,|\, Q \xrightarrow{\;\tau\;} (w)(P' \,|\, Q')}$$

RES : $$\dfrac{P \xrightarrow{\;\alpha\;} P'}{(y)P \xrightarrow{\;\alpha\;} (y)P'} \quad y \notin \mathrm{n}(\alpha)$$ OPEN : $$\dfrac{P \xrightarrow{\;\overline{x}y\;} P'}{(y)P \xrightarrow{\;\overline{x}(w)\;} P'\{w/y\}} \quad \begin{array}{l} y \neq x \\ w \notin \mathrm{fn}((y)P') \end{array}$$

Table 1: Rules of Action. Rules involving the binary operators $+$ and $|$ additionally have symmetric forms.

the value passing CCS calculus into the π-calculus, a single transition of a CCS agent is mirrored by a sequence of transitions with equivalent observable content of its translation. The simulation theorems of Section 4 make use of a notion of weak ground bisimilarity which we write $\approx$. We do not develop the theory of this relation here. We assume however that it enjoys certain standard properties, in particular that it is preserved by the operators in question, including guarded summation, and that certain simple equations have solutions unique up to $\approx$.

3 A modal characterization of strong ground bisimilarity

It is well-known that the relation of bisimilarity on states of labelled transition systems may be characterized in terms of properties expressible in a suitable modal logic [HM]. Here an analogous characterization of strong ground bisimilarity on the π-calculus transition system is presented.

Definition 2 The set $\mathcal{L}_\pi$ of *formulae* of the logic is given by

$$A ::= \bigwedge_{i \in \theta} A_i \mid \neg A \mid \langle \alpha \rangle A \mid \langle x(y) \rangle \bigwedge_{i \in \theta} (y = v_i \longrightarrow A_i)$$

where α ranges over $\overline{x}y$, $\overline{x}(y)$ and τ, and θ over ordinals.

Definition 3 The *satisfaction relation* between agents of the π-calculus and formulae of $\mathcal{L}_\pi$ is given by

$$
\begin{aligned}
P \models \bigwedge_{i \in \theta} A_i \quad &\text{if for all } i \in \theta,\, P \models A_i \\
P \models \neg A \quad &\text{if not } P \models A \\
P \models \langle \alpha \rangle A \quad &\text{if for some } P',\, P \xrightarrow{\alpha} P' \text{ and } P' \models A \\
&\text{for } \alpha = \overline{x}y, \tau \\
P \models \langle \overline{x}(y) \rangle A \quad &\text{if for some } P' \text{ and some } w \notin \mathrm{fn}(A) - \{y\} \\
&P \xrightarrow{\overline{x}(w)} P' \text{ and } P' \models A\{w/y\} \\
P \models \langle x(y) \rangle \bigwedge_{i \in \theta}(y = v_i \to A_i) \quad &\text{if for some } P' \text{ and some } w,\, P \xrightarrow{x(w)} P' \\
&\text{and for all } i \in \theta,\, P'\{v_i/w\} \models A_i\{v_i/y\}.
\end{aligned}
$$

In the fourth clause of this definition $\mathrm{fn}(A)$ is the set of names occurring free in A and is defined as expected with

$$
\begin{aligned}
\mathrm{fn}(\langle \alpha \rangle A) &= \mathrm{fn}(A) \cup \{\mathrm{fn}(\alpha)\} \quad \text{if } \alpha = \overline{x}y, \tau \\
\mathrm{fn}(\langle \overline{x}(y) \rangle A) &= (\mathrm{fn}(A) - \{y\}) \cup \{x\} \\
\mathrm{fn}(\langle x(y) \rangle \textstyle\bigwedge_i (y = v_i \to A_i)) &= ((\textstyle\bigcup_i \mathrm{fn}(A_i) \cup \{v_i\}) - \{y\}) \cup \{x\}.
\end{aligned}
$$

We write $\equiv$ for alpha-convertibility of formulae. Set $\mathcal{L}_\pi(P) = \{A \in \mathcal{L}_\pi \mid P \models A\}$. Then the characterization result is as follows.

Theorem 1 For any π-calculus agents P, Q,

$$P \overset{.}{\sim} Q \quad \text{iff} \quad \mathcal{L}_\pi(P) = \mathcal{L}_\pi(Q).$$

To prove this result we first establish the following lemma.

Lemma 1 Suppose that $P \models A$, $P \stackrel{.}{\sim} Q$, $A \equiv B$, $u \notin \mathrm{fn}(P, Q, A)$ and $\sigma = \{u/v\}$. Then $Q\sigma \models B\sigma$.

Proof: By induction on the structure of A. The conjunction and negation cases are quite straightforward.

Suppose that $A \equiv \langle\alpha\rangle C$ where $\alpha = \overline{x}y$ or τ, so that $B \equiv \langle\alpha\rangle D$ where $C \equiv D$. Since $P \models A$ there is P' such that $P \stackrel{\alpha}{\longrightarrow} P'$ and $P' \models C$. Then $P\sigma \stackrel{\alpha\sigma}{\longrightarrow} \equiv P'\sigma$ and by induction hypothesis $P'\sigma \models C\sigma$. Since $P\sigma \stackrel{.}{\sim} Q\sigma$ there is Q' such that $Q\sigma \stackrel{\alpha\sigma}{\longrightarrow} Q'$ and $P'\sigma \stackrel{.}{\sim} Q'$. Then by induction hypothesis $Q' \models D\sigma$ and hence $Q\sigma \models B\sigma$.

Suppose that $A \equiv \langle\overline{x}(y)\rangle C$ so that $B\sigma \equiv \langle\overline{x}\sigma(y')\rangle D\sigma$ where $C\{y'/y\} \equiv D$ and y' is fresh. Since $P \models A$ there are P' and $w \notin \mathrm{fn}(P)\cup(\mathrm{fn}(C)-\{y\})$ such that $P \stackrel{\overline{x}(w)}{\longrightarrow} P'$ and $P' \models C\{w/y\}$. Choose a fresh w'. Then $P \stackrel{\overline{x}(w')}{\longrightarrow} \equiv P'\{w'/w\}$ and by induction hypothesis $P'\{w'/w\} \models C\{w'/y\}$. Then $P\sigma \stackrel{\overline{x}\sigma(w')}{\longrightarrow} \equiv P'\{w'/w\}\sigma$ and by induction hypothesis $P'\{w'/w\}\sigma \models C\{w'/y\}\sigma$. Since $P\sigma \stackrel{.}{\sim} Q\sigma$ for some Q', $Q\sigma \stackrel{\overline{x}\sigma(w')}{\longrightarrow} Q'$ and $P'\{w'/w\}\sigma \stackrel{.}{\sim} Q'$. Then by induction hypothesis $Q' \models D\sigma\{w'/y'\}$ since $D\sigma\{w'/y'\} \equiv C\{y'/y\}\sigma\{w'/y'\} \equiv C\{w'/y\}\sigma$. Hence $Q\sigma \models B\sigma$.

Suppose that $A \equiv \langle x(y)\rangle \bigwedge_i(y = v_i \rightarrow A_i)$ so that $B\sigma \equiv \langle x\sigma(y')\rangle \bigwedge_i(y' = v_i\sigma \rightarrow B_i\sigma)$ where y' is fresh and for each i, $A_i\{y'/y\} \equiv B_i$. Since $P \models A$ there are P' and $w \notin \mathrm{fn}(P)$ such that $P \stackrel{x(w)}{\longrightarrow} P'$ and for all i, $P'\{v_i/w\} \models A_i\{v_i/y\}$. Choose a fresh w'. Then $P \stackrel{x(w')}{\longrightarrow} \equiv P'\{w'/w\}$ and by induction hypothesis for all i, $P'\{w'/w\}\{v_i/w'\} \models A_i\{v_i/y\}$. Then $P\sigma \stackrel{x\sigma(w')}{\longrightarrow} \equiv P'\{w'/w\}\sigma$ and by induction hypothesis for all i, $P'\{w'/w\}\{v_i/w'\}\sigma \models A_i\{v_i/y\}\sigma$. Since $P\sigma \stackrel{.}{\sim} Q\sigma$ there is Q' such that $Q\sigma \stackrel{x\sigma(w')}{\longrightarrow} Q'$ and for all z, $P'\{w'/w\}\sigma\{z/w'\} \stackrel{.}{\sim} Q'\{z/w'\}$. In particular for all i, $P'\{w'/w\}\sigma\{v_i\sigma/w'\} \stackrel{.}{\sim} Q'\{v_i\sigma/w'\}$.

Fix i. We claim that $P'\{w'/w\}\sigma\{v_i\sigma/w'\} \models A_i\{y'/y\}\sigma\{v_i\sigma/y'\}$. First note that if $u = v$ then this is immediate since $P'\{v_i/w\} \models A_i\{v_i/y\}$. So suppose $u \neq v$. Then it is simple to check that $P'\{w'/w\}\sigma\{v_i\sigma/w'\} \equiv P'\{v_i/w\}\sigma$ and $A_i\{y'/y\}\sigma\{v_i\sigma/y'\} \equiv A_i\{v_i/y\}\sigma$, and the claim follows since $P'\{v_i/w\}\sigma \models A_i\{v_i/y\}\sigma$. By this claim and the induction hypothesis for all i, $Q'\{v_i\sigma/w'\} \models A_i\{y'/y\}\sigma\{v_i\sigma/y'\}$ and again by induction hypothesis for all i, $Q'\{v_i\sigma/w'\} \models B_i\sigma\{v_i\sigma/y'\}$. Hence $Q\sigma \models B\sigma$. $\qquad\square$

From this lemma it follows immediately that if $P \stackrel{.}{\sim} Q$ then $\mathcal{L}_\pi(P) = \mathcal{L}_\pi(Q)$. To prove the converse it suffices to establish the following.

Lemma 2 $S = \{(P, Q) \mid \mathcal{L}_\pi(P) = \mathcal{L}_\pi(Q)\}$ is a strong bisimulation.

Proof: Suppose that PSQ.

Suppose that $P \stackrel{\alpha}{\longrightarrow} P'$ where α is a free action, let $\langle Q_i\rangle_{i\in\theta}$ be an enumeration of $\{Q' \mid Q \stackrel{\alpha}{\longrightarrow} Q'\}$ and suppose that for all i not $P'SQ_i$. Choose $\langle A_i\rangle_{i\in\theta}$ with for all i, $A_i \in \mathcal{L}_\pi(P') - \mathcal{L}_\pi(Q_i)$. Then setting $A \equiv \langle\alpha\rangle \bigwedge_{i\in\theta} A_i$, $A \in \mathcal{L}_\pi(P) - \mathcal{L}_\pi(Q)$. Contradiction.

Suppose that $P \stackrel{\overline{x}(y)}{\longrightarrow} P'$ where $y \notin n(P, Q)$, let $\langle Q_i\rangle$ be an enumeration of $\{Q' \mid Q \stackrel{\overline{x}(y)}{\longrightarrow} Q'\}$ and suppose that for all i not $P'SQ_i$. Choose $\langle A_i\rangle$ with for all i, $A_i \in \mathcal{L}_\pi(P') - \mathcal{L}_\pi(Q_i)$. Then setting $A \equiv \langle\overline{x}(y)\rangle \bigwedge_i A_i$, $A \in \mathcal{L}_\pi(P) - \mathcal{L}_\pi(Q)$ since otherwise for some Q' and some $w \notin \mathrm{fn}(Q)\cup(\bigcup_i \mathrm{fn}(A_i) - \{y\})$, $Q \stackrel{\overline{x}(w)}{\longrightarrow} Q'$ and $Q' \models \bigwedge_i A_i\{w/y\}$, when since $y \notin n(Q)$ for some i, $Q'\{y/w\} \equiv Q_i$ and hence by Lemma 1, $Q_i \models \bigwedge_i A_i$. Contradiction.

Suppose that $P \xrightarrow{x(y)} P'$ where $y \notin n(P,Q)$, let $\langle Q_i \rangle$ be an enumeration of $\{Q' \mid Q \xrightarrow{x(y)} Q'\}$ and suppose that for all i there is v_i such that not $P'\{v_i/y\} S Q_i\{v_i/y\}$. Choose $\langle v_i \rangle$ and $\langle B_i \rangle$ so that for all i, $B_i \in \mathcal{L}_\pi(P'\{v_i/y\}) - \mathcal{L}_\pi(Q_i\{v_i/y\})$. Note that if $v_i \neq y$ then we may assume that $y \notin fn(B_i)$ since choosing a fresh u, $P'\{v_i/y\} \equiv P'\{v_i/y\}\{u/y\}$ so $B_i\{u/y\} \in \mathcal{L}_\pi(P'\{v_i/y\})$ while $B_i\{u/y\} \notin \mathcal{L}_\pi(Q_i\{v_i/y\})$ since otherwise by Lemma 1, $Q_i\{v_i/y\} \equiv Q_i\{v_i/y\}\{y/u\} \models B_i$, contradiction. For each i set $A_i \equiv B_i\{y/v_i\}$ and set $A \equiv \langle x(y) \rangle \bigwedge_i (y = v_i \rightarrow A_i)$. Then $A \in \mathcal{L}_\pi(P)$ since $P \xrightarrow{x(y)} P'$ and for all i, $P'\{v_i/y\} \models A_i\{v_i/y\}$, but $A \notin \mathcal{L}_\pi(Q)$ since if $w \notin fn(Q)$, $Q \xrightarrow{x(w)} Q'$ and for all i, $Q'\{v_i/w\} \models A_i\{v_i/y\}$ then for some i, $Q'\{y/w\} \equiv Q_i$ so $Q_i\{v_i/y\} \models B_i$. Contradiction. $\qquad\square$

Note that the need for infinite conjunction in $\mathcal{L}_\pi$ would be obviated if it could be shown that the π-calculus transition system is finite branching up to $\dot{\sim}$, i.e. that for all P and α, $\dot{\sim}$ partitions $\{P' \mid P \xrightarrow{\alpha} P'\}$ into finitely many classes. Of course if every agent identifier is guardedly defined then the transition system is finite branching.

Robin Milner has observed that by including a matching construct in the logic one obtains a characterization without the need for formulae of the form $\langle x(y) \rangle \bigwedge_i (y = v_i \longrightarrow A_i)$. The appropriate semantic clause is

$$P \models [x = y]A \text{ if } x \neq y \text{ or } P \models A.$$

A formula of the above form may be rendered as $\langle x(y) \rangle \bigwedge_i [y = v_i]A_i$.

4 Translating CCS with value passing into the π-calculus

The version of CCS with value passing which we consider is as follows. The class of *value expressions* is given by

$$e ::= a \mid f(e_1, \ldots, e_n)$$

where a ranges over variables and f over operators with $n \geq 0$ the arity of f. We assume implicitly that each variable and each operator has an associated type and consider only expressions which are well-typed. We assume further that each closed expression has an associated value of the same type as the expression. We write $e : t$ if e has type t; $\underline{e}$ denotes the value of e if e is closed and e otherwise. We assume that the boolean type bool is among the types.

We assume a class of *names* ranged over by $x, y, z, \ldots$ and a class of *agent identifiers* ranged over by A each with a nonnegative arity. The class of *agents* ranged over by P is given by

$$P \quad ::= \quad \sum_{i \in I} G_i \quad (I \text{ finite})$$
$$| \quad P \mid Q$$
$$| \quad (x)P$$
$$| \quad \text{if } e \text{ then } P \text{ else } Q \quad (e : \text{bool})$$
$$| \quad A(\tilde{e}) \quad \text{where } A(\tilde{a}) \stackrel{\text{def}}{=} P \text{ and } \tilde{a}, \tilde{e} : \tilde{t} \text{ for some } \tilde{t}$$

$$G \quad ::= \quad \overline{x}e.\, P$$
$$| \quad x(a).\, P$$
$$| \quad \tau.\, P$$

In an agent identifier definition $A(\tilde{a}) \stackrel{\text{def}}{=} P$ we require that $\text{fn}(P) \subseteq \tilde{a}$. Note that all summations are finite and guarded. We write 0 for the empty summation.

We adopt a fairly standard transitional semantics for agents given by the following rules in which α ranges over $\overline{x}e$, $x(a)$, τ.

$$\overline{x}e.\, P \xrightarrow{\overline{x}e} P \qquad \tau.\, P \xrightarrow{\tau} P \qquad x(a).\, P \xrightarrow{x(b)} P\{b/a\} \quad b \notin \text{fn}(P) - \{a\}$$

$$\frac{G_j \xrightarrow{\alpha} P'}{\sum_{i \in I} G_i \xrightarrow{\alpha} P'} \quad j \in I$$

$$\frac{P \xrightarrow{\alpha} P'}{P \mid Q \xrightarrow{\alpha} P' \mid Q} \quad \text{bn}(\alpha) \cap \text{fn}(Q) = \emptyset \qquad \frac{P \xrightarrow{\overline{x}e} P' \quad Q \xrightarrow{x(a)} Q'}{P \mid Q \xrightarrow{\tau} P' \mid Q'\{e/a\}} \quad a, e : t \text{ for some } t$$

$$\frac{P \xrightarrow{\alpha} P'}{(x)P \xrightarrow{\alpha} (x)P'} \quad x \notin \text{fn}(\alpha)$$

$$\frac{}{\text{if } e \text{ then } P \text{ else } Q \xrightarrow{\tau} P} \quad e = \text{true} \qquad \frac{}{\text{if } e \text{ then } P \text{ else } Q \xrightarrow{\tau} Q} \quad e = \text{false}$$

$$\frac{P\{\tilde{e}/\tilde{a}\} \xrightarrow{\alpha} P'}{A(\tilde{e}) \xrightarrow{\alpha} P'} \quad A(\tilde{a}) \stackrel{\text{def}}{=} P, \; \tilde{e}, \tilde{a} : \tilde{t} \text{ for some } \tilde{t}$$

Note that the input guard rule differs from the rule in the original formulation of CCS [Mil1]. The present rule is analogous to the bound-input rule in the π-calculus. The two rules for the composition operator | have symmetric forms. Note the side condition in the second of these rules, and that in this rule e is substituted in Q'. There is some freedom in choosing how to treat evaluation of expressions and the results given below do not depend on the particular choice adopted here. However in order to obtain precisely the form of simulation stated in the theorems below, the choice of rules for conditional agents is significant.

4.1 Encoding value expressions

The first step in the translation of the value passing calculus into the π-calculus involves developing an old idea of Hewitt [Cli] and encoding value expressions as π-calculus agents. We illustrate how this may be done by considering a specific language of expressions. Suppose that types are given by

$$t ::= \text{bool} \mid \text{nat} \mid t \text{ list};$$

that true and false are constants of type bool, $0, 1, 2, \ldots$ constants of type nat, and nil a constant of type t list for any t; and that $\neg : \text{bool} \to \text{bool}$, $\wedge : \text{bool} \times \text{bool} \to \text{bool}$, $= : \text{nat} \times \text{nat} \to \text{bool}$, $+ : \text{nat} \times \text{nat} \to \text{nat}$, and cons $: t \times t \text{ list} \to t \text{ list}$ for any t are the remaining operators.

To represent expressions as π-calculus agents it is convenient, though not necessary, to assume a number of constant names in the π-calculus. In this case we assume the following constant names: TRUE, FALSE, ZERO, ONE, NIL, CONS. Each expression e is then represented as a function $[e]$ from π-calculus names to π-calculus agents. In $[e]w$, w plays the role of a pointer in a way which will become clear below. To simplify notation we abbreviate $\alpha.0$ to α. The encoding is as follows.

$$
\begin{aligned}
[\text{true}]w &\stackrel{\text{def}}{=} \overline{w}\,\text{TRUE} \\
[\text{false}]w &\stackrel{\text{def}}{=} \overline{w}\,\text{FALSE} \\
[n]w &\stackrel{\text{def}}{=} (\overline{w}\,\text{ONE})^n.\,\overline{w}\,\text{ZERO} \quad (n = 0, 1, 2, \ldots) \\
[\text{nil}]w &\stackrel{\text{def}}{=} \overline{w}\,\text{NIL}
\end{aligned}
$$

for $f \in \{\neg, \wedge, =, +, \text{cons}\}$

$$[f(e_1, \ldots, e_n)]w = (v_1) \ldots (v_n)([e_1]v_1 \mid \cdots \mid [e_n]v_n \mid [f](v_1, \ldots, v_n, w))$$

where

$$
\begin{aligned}
[\neg](v_1, w) &\stackrel{\text{def}}{=} v_1(y).\,([y = \text{FALSE}]\,\overline{w}\,\text{TRUE} + [y = \text{TRUE}]\,\overline{w}\,\text{FALSE}) \\
[\wedge](v_1, v_2, w) &\stackrel{\text{def}}{=} v_1(y).\,([y = \text{FALSE}]\overline{w}\,\text{FALSE} + [y = \text{TRUE}]v_2(z).\,\overline{w}z) \\
[=](v_1, v_2, w) &\stackrel{\text{def}}{=} v_1(y).\,([y = \text{ONE}]\,v_2(z). \\
&\qquad ([z = \text{ONE}]\,[=](v_1, v_2, w) + [z = \text{ZERO}]\,\overline{w}\,\text{FALSE}) \\
&\quad + [y = \text{ZERO}]\,v_2(z).\,([z = \text{ZERO}]\,\overline{w}\,\text{TRUE} + [z = \text{ONE}]\,\overline{w}\,\text{FALSE})) \\
[+](v_1, v_2, w) &\stackrel{\text{def}}{=} v_1(y).\,([y = \text{ONE}]\,\overline{w}\,\text{ONE}.\,[+](v_1, v_1, w) + [y = \text{ZERO}]\,[+]'(v_2, w)) \\
[+]'(v_2, w) &\stackrel{\text{def}}{=} v_2(y).\,([y = \text{ONE}]\,\overline{w}\,\text{ONE}.\,[+]'(v_2, w) + [y = \text{ZERO}]\,\overline{w}\,\text{ZERO}) \\
[\text{cons}](v_1, v_2, w) &\stackrel{\text{def}}{=} \overline{w}\,\text{CONS}.\,\overline{w}v_1.\,\overline{w}v_2
\end{aligned}
$$

These examples illustrate a method which may be extended to cater for richer languages of expressions. Indeed, in [MPW1] and in greater detail in [Mil2], Milner shows how to give accurate encodings of the λ-calculus in the π-calculus. In the present encoding, values have but a transient existence. However alternative encodings in which values are longer-lived are possible. There is also a minor question as to whether the function agents $[\neg]$ etc. should buffer their input before delivering output. The results below do not depend on the answer to this question.

It remains to give the encoding of variables. To do this we regard the class of value variables as a coinfinite subclass of the class of names of the π-calculus[1] and define

$$[a]w = a(v).\,\mathrm{Copy}(v, w)$$

where $\mathrm{Copy}(v, w) \stackrel{\mathrm{def}}{=} v(y).\,\overline{w}y.\,\mathrm{Copy}(v, w)$. The reason for adopting this encoding will become apparent below.

It is straightforward to establish the following property of this encoding.

Lemma 3 For all e and w, $[e]w \approx [\underline{e}]w$.

In what follows we assume that this property holds of the expression language of the value passing calculus in question.

4.2 Encoding agents

We now proceed to the representation of value passing agents in the π-calculus. When a value is passed from one agent to another it may be substituted at several places in the receiving agent. To handle this we introduce for each expression e and name y an agent $\mathrm{Rep}(e, y)$ defined by

$$\mathrm{Rep}(e, y) \stackrel{\mathrm{def}}{=} (w)\overline{y}w.\,([e]w \mid \mathrm{Rep}(e, y))$$

which may provide at y an indefinite number of private copies of $[e]$[2].

The translation of agents $[P]$ is given as follows.

$$
\begin{aligned}
[\overline{x}e.\,P] &= (y)\overline{x}y.\,(\mathrm{Rep}(e, y) \mid [P]) \\
[x(a).\,P] &= x(a).\,[P] \\
[\tau.\,P] &= \tau.\,[P] \\
[\textstyle\sum_i G_i] &= \textstyle\sum_i[G_i] \\
[P \mid Q] &= [P] \mid [Q] \\
[(x)P] &= (x)[P] \\
[\text{if } e \text{ then } P \text{ else } Q] &= (w)([e]w \mid w(y).\,([y = \text{TRUE}]\,[P] + [y = \text{FALSE}]\,[Q])) \\
[A(e_1, \dots, e_n)] &= (a_1)\dots(a_n)([e_1]a_1 \mid \dots \mid [e_n]a_n \mid [P]) \\
&\qquad \text{where } A(\tilde{a}) \stackrel{\mathrm{def}}{=} P
\end{aligned}
$$

Note that on the right hand side of the clauses for $x(a).\,P$ and $A(\tilde{e})$, a and the a_i are understood as names in the π-calculus.

4.3 Simulation Theorems

The translation enjoys the properties described in the following theorems.

Theorem 2 For any P,

1. If $P \xrightarrow{\overline{x}e} P'$ then $[P] \xrightarrow{\overline{x}(y)} \approx \mathrm{Rep}(e, y) \mid [P']$ for a fresh y.

---

[1]This is not an essential requirement but it allows a very smooth treatment.

[2]In the notation of [Mil2], $\mathrm{Rep}(e, y)$ could be written $!(w)\overline{y}w.\,[e]w$, where the operator $!$ is defined by $\dfrac{P \mid !P \xrightarrow{\alpha} P'}{!P \xrightarrow{\alpha} P'}$.

2. If $P \xrightarrow{x(a)} P'$ then $[P] \xrightarrow{x(a)} \approx [P']$.

3. If $P \xrightarrow{\tau} P'$ then $[P] \xrightarrow{\tau} \approx [P']$.

Theorem 3 Let P be type-safe[3]. Then

1. Not $[P] \xrightarrow{\overline{x}y}$.

2. If $[P] \xrightarrow{\overline{x}(y)} Q$ then for some e and P', $P \xrightarrow{\overline{x}e} P'$ and $Q \approx \operatorname{Rep}(e,y) \mid [P']$.

3. If $[P] \xrightarrow{a(y)} Q$ then for some P', $P \xrightarrow{a(y)} P'$ and $Q \approx [P']$.

4. If $[P] \xrightarrow{\tau} Q$ then for some P', $P \xrightarrow{\tau} P'$ and $Q \approx [P']$.

In the second theorem an agent is *type-safe* if, informally, none of its derivatives has a subagent of the form $P \mid Q$ with P and Q capable of communicating along some link but with different expectations as to the type of value to be passed. To see the need for such a restriction recall the type-compatibility side condition in the communication transition rule, and note, for example, that if $a : \mathrm{bool}$ then $\overline{x}3. P \mid x(a). Q$ has no transition while

$$
\begin{aligned}
[\overline{x}3. P \mid x(a). Q] &\equiv (y)\overline{x}y. (\operatorname{Rep}(3,y) \mid [P]) \mid x(a). [Q] \\
&\xrightarrow{\tau} (y)(\operatorname{Rep}(3,y) \mid [P] \mid [Q]\{y/a\})
\end{aligned}
$$

Type-safety could be guaranteed by requiring that link names be typed so that prefix agents would be of the forms $\overline{x}e. P$ and $x(a). P$ with $x : t$ link and $e, a : t$ for some t (see also [Nie]). A less rigid approach is to extend the definition of agent sort from CCS to include type information but without requiring typing of link names. This is the approach adopted here. The problem of delimiting type-safety without imposing typing of link names when link names themselves are among the values is interesting. One can extend the transitional semantics of the value passing calculus to cater for the presence among the values of link names, with certain operations defined on them, allowing, for example, multiple changes of scope in a single transition. Analogues of the above theorems may be obtained.

We give a definition of type-safety adequate for the present purpose. A set I of pairs of links and types is said to be *tidy* if

$$\text{if } (x, t_1) \in I \text{ and } (\overline{x}, t_2) \in I \text{ then } t_1 = t_2.$$

With each agent identifier A we associate a tidy set $I(A)$. We then define what it means to say that an agent P *is type-safe*, and what the *interface* $I(P)$ of a type-safe agent P is.

A is type-safe and its interface is $I(A)$. If P is type-safe and $I(P) \cup \{(\overline{x}, t)\}$ is tidy where $e : t$, then $\overline{x}e. P$ is type-safe and $I(\overline{x}e. P) = I(P) \cup \{(\overline{x}, t)\}$. We abbreviate this to: $I(\overline{x}e. P) \simeq I(P) \cup \{(\overline{x}, t)\}$ if $e : t$. With this shorthand the remaining clauses are

---

[3]Defined below.

$$\begin{aligned}
I(x(a).\,P) &\simeq I(P) \cup \{(x,t)\} \quad \text{if } a:t \\
I(\tau.\,P) &\simeq I(P) \\
I(\textstyle\sum_i G_i) &\simeq \textstyle\bigcup_i I(G_i) \\
I(P \mid Q) &\simeq I(P) \cup I(Q) \\
I((x)P) &\simeq I(P) - (\{x,\overline{x}\} \times \text{Types}) \\
I(\texttt{if } e \texttt{ then } P \texttt{ else } Q) &\simeq I(P) \cup I(Q)
\end{aligned}$$

We require that for each agent identifier A, if $A(\tilde{a}) \stackrel{\text{def}}{=} P$ then P is type-safe and $I(P) \subseteq I(A)$. We then have the following straightforward result.

Lemma 4 If $P \stackrel{\alpha}{\longrightarrow} P'$ and P is type-safe then P' is type-safe, $I(P') \subseteq I(P)$, and if $\alpha = \overline{x}e$ (resp. $x(a)$) with $e:t$ (resp. $a:t$) then $(\overline{x},t) \in I(P)$ (resp. $(x,t) \in I(P)$). Hence every derivative of a type-safe agent is type-safe.

The proofs of the simulation theorems are of some interest. A number of lemmas are required.

Lemma 5 For any e and y,

$$\text{Rep}(e,y) \approx \text{Rep}(\varepsilon,y).$$

Proof: Since by Lemma 3 $[\![e]\!]w \approx [\![\varepsilon]\!]w$, both $\text{Rep}(e,y)$ and $\text{Rep}(\varepsilon,y)$ are solutions up to $\approx$ of the equation

$$X = (w)\overline{y}w.\,([\![e]\!]w \mid X).$$

But this equation has a solution unique up to $\approx$. $\qquad\square$

Lemma 6 For any e and y,

$$\text{Rep}(e,y) \stackrel{\cdot}{\sim} \text{Rep}(e,y) \mid \text{Rep}(e,y).$$

Proof: By examining the definition of $\text{Rep}(e,y)$ it is easy to see that

$$\{(P \mid \text{Rep}(e,y),\ P \mid \text{Rep}(e,y) \mid \text{Rep}(e,y)) \mid P \text{ arbitrary}\}$$

is a strong bisimulation up to $\stackrel{\cdot}{\sim}$. $\qquad\square$

Lemma 7 For any e, y, P and Q, if $\overline{y}$ does not occur in P or in Q then

$$(y)(\text{Rep}(e,y) \mid \text{Rep}(e,y) \mid P \mid Q) \stackrel{\cdot}{\sim} (y)(\text{Rep}(e,y) \mid P) \mid (y)(\text{Rep}(e,y) \mid Q).$$

Proof: It is straightforward to check that with P, Q as above,

$$\{((y)(\text{Rep}(e,y) \mid \text{Rep}(e,y) \mid P \mid Q),\ (y)(\text{Rep}(e,y) \mid P) \mid (y)(\text{Rep}(e,y) \mid Q)))\}$$

is a strong bisimulation up to $\stackrel{\cdot}{\sim}$. $\qquad\square$

Lemma 8 For any $e', \tilde{e}, \tilde{a}$ and u,

$$[\![e'\{\tilde{e}/\tilde{a}\}]\!]u \approx (\tilde{a})(\widetilde{\text{Rep}(e,a)} \mid [\![e']\!]u).$$

Proof: For ease of notation we omit the tildes. The proof is by induction on e'.

Suppose that $e' \equiv a$. Then $[\![e'\{e/a\}]\!]u \equiv [\![e]\!]u$ and $(a)(\text{Rep}(e,a) \mid [\![e']\!]u) \equiv (a)(\text{Rep}(e,a) \mid a(v).\text{Copy}(v,u))$. Now $(a)(\text{Rep}(e,a) \mid a(v).\text{Copy}(v,u))$ has only one transition: $\overset{\tau}{\longrightarrow} (a)(\text{Rep}(e,a) \mid (w)([\![e]\!]w \mid \text{Copy}(w,u))) \sim (a)([\![e]\!]w \mid \text{Copy}(w,u)) \approx [\![e]\!]u$, so the equivalence holds.

Suppose that $e' \equiv a' \not\equiv a$. Then clearly

$$[\![e'\{e/a\}]\!]u \equiv [\![e']\!]u \overset{\cdot}{\sim} (a)(\text{Rep}(e,a) \mid [\![e']\!]u).$$

Suppose that $e' \equiv f(e_1, \ldots, e_n)$. Then

$$
\begin{aligned}
[\![e'\{e/a\}]\!]u &\equiv (u_1)\ldots(u_n)([\![e_1\{e/a\}]\!]u_1 \mid \ldots \mid [\![e_n\{e/a\}]\!] \mid [\![f]\!](u_1,\ldots,u_n,u)) \\
&\overset{\cdot}{\sim} (u_1)\ldots(u_n)((a)\text{Rep}(e,a) \mid [\![e_1]\!]u_1) \mid \ldots \mid (a)(\text{Rep}(e,a) \mid [\![e_n]\!]u_n) \mid \\
&\qquad [\![f]\!](u_1,\ldots,u_n,u)) \\
&\overset{\cdot}{\sim} (u_1)\ldots(u_n)(a)(\text{Rep}(e,a) \mid [\![e_1]\!]u_1 \mid \ldots \mid [\![e_n]\!]u_n \mid [\![f]\!](u_1,\ldots,u_n,u)) \\
&\overset{\cdot}{\sim} (a)(\text{Rep}(e,a) \mid (u_1)\ldots(u_n)([\![e_1]\!]u_1 \mid \ldots \mid [\![e_n]\!]u_n \mid [\![f]\!](u_1,\ldots,u_n,u))) \\
&\equiv (a)(\text{Rep}(e,a) \mid [\![e']\!]u)
\end{aligned}
$$

using the preceding two lemmas. □

Using Lemma 5 we have the following corollary.

Corollary 1 $[\![e'\{\tilde{e}/\tilde{a}\}]\!] \approx [\![e'\{\tilde{e}/\tilde{a}\}]\!]$.

Lemma 9 For any $e', \tilde{e}, \tilde{a}$ and u,

$$\text{Rep}(e'\{\tilde{e}/\tilde{a}\}, u) \approx (\tilde{a})(\widetilde{\text{Rep}(e,a)} \mid \text{Rep}(e', u)).$$

Proof: Omitting the tildes for ease of reading we have that

$$
\begin{aligned}
\text{Rep}(e'\{e/a\}, u) &\overset{\text{def}}{=} (v)\overline{u}v.\,([\![e'\{e/a\}]\!]v \mid \text{Rep}(e'\{e/a\}, u)) \\
&\approx (v)\overline{u}v.\,((a)(\text{Rep}(e,a) \mid [\![e']\!]v) \mid \text{Rep}(e'\{e/a\}, u))
\end{aligned}
$$

by the preceding lemma. Also

$$
\begin{aligned}
(a)(\text{Rep}(e,a) \mid \text{Rep}(e', u)) &\overset{\cdot}{\sim} (a)(\text{Rep}(e,a) \mid (v)\overline{u}v.\,([\![e']\!]v \mid \text{Rep}(e', u))) \\
&\overset{\cdot}{\sim} (v)\overline{u}v.\,(a)(\text{Rep}(e,a) \mid [\![e']\!]v \mid \text{Rep}(e', u)) \\
&\overset{\cdot}{\sim} (v)\overline{u}v.\,((a)(\text{Rep}(e,a) \mid [\![e']\!]v) \mid \\
&\qquad (a)(\text{Rep}(e,a) \mid \text{Rep}(e', u)))
\end{aligned}
$$

by earlier lemmas. Hence both agents are solutions up to $\approx$ of the equation

$$X = (v)\overline{u}v.\,((a)(\text{Rep}(e,a) \mid [\![e']\!]v) \mid X).$$

The result follows since the solution of this equation is unique up to $\approx$. □

Hence again using Lemma 5 we have the following.

Corollary 2 $\text{Rep}(e'\{\tilde{e}/\tilde{a}\}, u) \approx \text{Rep}(e'\{\tilde{e}/\tilde{a}\}, u)$.

Lemma 10 For any $P, \tilde{e}$ and $\tilde{a}$,

$$[P\{\tilde{e}/\tilde{a}\}] \approx (\tilde{a})(\widetilde{\mathrm{Rep}(e,a)} \mid [P]).$$

Proof: We prove this by induction on the structure of P taking agent identifiers as atomic agents. We give three sample cases; the others are similar. To ease notation we omit the tildes.

Suppose $P \equiv A(\tilde{f})$ where $A(\tilde{b}) \stackrel{\text{def}}{=} R$. Then LHS $\equiv (\tilde{b})([\widetilde{[f]}b \mid [R])$ and

$$
\begin{aligned}
\mathrm{RHS} &\equiv (a)(\mathrm{Rep}(e,a) \mid (\tilde{b})([f_1]b_1 \mid \ldots \mid [f_n]b_n \mid [R])) \\
&\sim (\tilde{b})((a)(\mathrm{Rep}(e,a) \mid [f_1]b_1) \mid \ldots \mid (a)(\mathrm{Rep}(e,a) \mid [f_n]b_n) \mid [R]) \\
&\approx (\tilde{b})([f_1]b_1 \mid \ldots \mid [f_n]b_n \mid [R])
\end{aligned}
$$

using Lemma 8.

Suppose $P \equiv$ if e' then Q else R. Then

$$\mathrm{LHS} \equiv (w)([e'\{e/a\}] \mid w(v).([v = \mathrm{TRUE}]\,[Q\{e/a\}] + [v = \mathrm{FALSE}]\,[R\{e/a\}]))$$

and

$$
\begin{aligned}
\mathrm{RHS} &\equiv (a)(\mathrm{Rep}(e,a) \mid (w)([e']w \mid w(v).([y = \mathrm{TRUE}]\,[Q] + [y = \mathrm{FALSE}]\,[R]))) \\
&\approx (w)((a)\mathrm{Rep}(e,a) \mid [e']w) \mid w(v). \\
&\qquad ([y = \mathrm{TRUE}]\,(a)(\mathrm{Rep}(e,a) \mid [Q]) + [y = \mathrm{FALSE}]\,(a)(\mathrm{Rep}(e,a) \mid [R]))) \\
&\approx (w)([e'\{e/a\}]w \mid w(v).([v = \mathrm{TRUE}]\,[Q\{e/a\}] + [v = \mathrm{FALSE}]\,[R\{e/a\}]))
\end{aligned}
$$

Suppose $P \equiv \overline{x}e'.Q$. Then

$$
\begin{aligned}
\mathrm{LHS} &\equiv [\overline{x}e'\{e/a\}.Q\{e/a\}] \\
&\equiv (w)\overline{x}w.(\mathrm{Rep}(e'\{e/a\}, w) \mid [Q\{e/a\}])
\end{aligned}
$$

and

$$
\begin{aligned}
\mathrm{RHS} &\equiv (a)(\mathrm{Rep}(e,a) \mid (w)\overline{x}w.(\mathrm{Rep}(e',w) \mid [Q])) \\
&\sim (w)\overline{x}w.(((a)(\mathrm{Rep}(e,a) \mid \mathrm{Rep}(e',w)) \mid (a)(\mathrm{Rep}(e,a) \mid [Q])) \\
&\approx (w)\overline{x}w.(\mathrm{Rep}(e'\{e/a\}, w) \mid [Q\{e/a\}])
\end{aligned}
$$

by Lemma 8 and the induction hypothesis. $\qquad\square$

Corollary 3 1. $[P\{\tilde{e}/\tilde{a}\}]u \approx [P\{\tilde{e}/\tilde{a}\}]$.

2. If $A(\tilde{a}) \stackrel{\text{def}}{=} R$ then $[A(\tilde{e})] \approx [R\{\tilde{e}/\tilde{a}\}]$.

Lemma 11 If $P\{\tilde{e}/\tilde{a}\} \stackrel{\alpha}{\longrightarrow} Q$ then by an inference of no greater depth, $P \stackrel{\alpha'}{\longrightarrow} Q'$ with $\alpha'\{\tilde{e}/\tilde{a}\} = \alpha$ and $Q'\{\tilde{e}/\tilde{a}\} \equiv Q$, and for any $\tilde{f}$, by an inference of no greater depth, $P\{\tilde{f}/\tilde{a}\} \stackrel{\alpha'\{\tilde{f}/\tilde{a}\}}{\longrightarrow} Q'\{\tilde{f}/\tilde{a}\}$.

Proof: By induction on inference. We give only a sample case; the others are similar. Suppose $P \equiv A(\tilde{g})$ where $A(\tilde{b}) \stackrel{\text{def}}{=} R$. Then $P\{\tilde{e}/\tilde{a}\} \equiv A\{\tilde{g}/\tilde{b}\}\{\tilde{e}/\tilde{a}\} \equiv A\{\tilde{g}\{\tilde{e}/\tilde{a}\}/\tilde{b}\}$. Now as $R\{\tilde{g}\{\tilde{e}/\tilde{a}\}/\tilde{b}\} \equiv R\{\tilde{g}/\tilde{b}\}\{\tilde{e}/\tilde{a}\} \stackrel{\alpha}{\longrightarrow} Q$, $R\{\tilde{g}/\tilde{b}\} \stackrel{\alpha'}{\longrightarrow} Q'$ with $\alpha'\{\tilde{e}/\tilde{a}\} = \alpha$ and $Q'\{\tilde{e}/\tilde{a}\} \equiv Q$. Hence $P \stackrel{\alpha'}{\longrightarrow} Q'$. Moreover $R\{\tilde{g}/\tilde{b}\}\{\tilde{f}/\tilde{a}\} \stackrel{\alpha\{\tilde{f}/\tilde{a}\}}{\longrightarrow} \equiv Q'\{\tilde{f}/\tilde{a}\}$ and hence $P\{\tilde{f}/\tilde{a}\} \stackrel{\alpha\{\tilde{f}/\tilde{a}\}}{\longrightarrow} \equiv Q'\{\tilde{f}/\tilde{a}\}$. $\square$

Using this lemma we can obtain the following result.

Lemma 12 $[P\{^b/a\}] \approx [P]\{^b/a\}$ for b fresh.

Proof: We omit the proof which is fairly straightforward. $\square$

We may now prove the main theorems.

Proof of Theorem 2: We prove the three assertions by simultaneous induction on inference. We give only three sample cases; the others are similar.

Suppose $P \equiv x(a). P'$. Then $[P] \equiv x(a). [P']$ and the result follows from Lemma 12.

Suppose $P \equiv Q \mid R$, $Q \stackrel{\overline{x}e}{\longrightarrow} Q'$, $R \stackrel{x(a)}{\longrightarrow} R'$ so $P \stackrel{\tau}{\longrightarrow} Q' \mid R'\{e/a\}$. Then $[Q] \stackrel{\overline{x}(v)}{\longrightarrow} \approx \text{Rep}(e, y) \mid [Q']$ and $[R] \stackrel{x(v)}{\longrightarrow} \approx [R']\{v/a\}$. Hence $[P] \stackrel{\tau}{\longrightarrow} \approx [Q'] \mid (y)(\text{Rep}(e, y) \mid [R']\{v/a\}) \approx [Q'] \mid [R']\{e/a\} \approx [Q'] \mid [R]\{e/a\}$ by Lemma 10 and Corollary 3.

Suppose $P \equiv A(\tilde{f})$ where $A(\tilde{a}) \stackrel{\text{def}}{=} R$ and $R\{\tilde{f}/\tilde{a}\} \stackrel{\overline{x}e}{\longrightarrow} P'$. Then by Lemma 11, $R \stackrel{\overline{x}e'}{\longrightarrow} P''$ with $e'\{\tilde{f}/\tilde{a}\} = e$ and $P''\{\tilde{f}/\tilde{a}\} \equiv P'$. Then $[R] \stackrel{\overline{x}(v)}{\longrightarrow} \approx \text{Rep}(e', y) \mid [P'']$. Hence

$$
\begin{aligned}
[P] &\equiv (\tilde{a})(\widetilde{\text{Rep}(f, a)} \mid [R]) \\
&\stackrel{\overline{x}(v)}{\longrightarrow} \approx (\tilde{a})(\widetilde{\text{Rep}(f, a)} \mid \text{Rep}(e', y) \mid [P'']) \\
&\approx (\tilde{a})(\widetilde{\text{Rep}(f, a)} \mid \text{Rep}(e', y)) \mid (\tilde{a})(\widetilde{\text{Rep}(f, a)} \mid [P'']) \\
&\approx \text{Rep}(e'\{\tilde{f}/\tilde{a}\}, y) \mid [P''\{\tilde{f}/\tilde{a}\}] \\
&\approx \text{Rep}(e, y) \mid [P''\{\tilde{f}/\tilde{a}\}] \\
&\equiv \text{Rep}(e, y) \mid [P']
\end{aligned}
$$

by Lemma 10. The other two cases are similar. $\square$

Proof of Theorem 3: First note from the translation that for no P is $[P]$ of the form $\overline{x}y. Q$ and hence the first assertion follows. We prove the remaining three assertions by simultaneous induction on inference. We give three sample cases; the others are similar, the case $P \equiv x(a). P'$ making use of Lemma 12.

Suppose $P \equiv \overline{x}e. P'$. Then $[P] \equiv (y)\overline{x}y. (\text{Rep}(e, y) \mid [P']) \stackrel{\overline{x}(v)}{\longrightarrow} \text{Rep}(e, y) \mid [P']$ and $P \stackrel{\overline{x}e}{\longrightarrow} P'$ as repuired.

Suppose $P \equiv Q \mid R$, $[Q] \stackrel{\overline{x}(a)}{\longrightarrow} Q'$, $[R] \stackrel{x(a)}{\longrightarrow} R'$ and $[P] \stackrel{\tau}{\longrightarrow} (a)(Q' \mid R')$. Then $Q \stackrel{\overline{x}e}{\longrightarrow} Q''$ with $Q' \approx \text{Rep}(e, a) \mid [Q'']$, and $R \stackrel{x(a)}{\longrightarrow} R''$ with $R' \approx [R'']$. Hence since P

is type-safe, $e, a : t$ for some t and hence $P \xrightarrow{\tau} Q'' \mid R''\{e/a\}$ and $[Q''] \mid [R''\{e/a\}] \approx [Q''] \mid (a)(\text{Rep}(e,a) \mid [R'']) \approx (a)(\text{Rep}(e,a) \mid [Q''] \mid [R''])$.

Suppose $P \equiv A(\tilde{f})$ where $A(\tilde{b}) \overset{\text{def}}{=} R$, so that $[P] \equiv (\tilde{b})(\widetilde{[f]b} \mid [R])$, and $[R] \xrightarrow{\overline{x}(y)} Q'$ and $Q \equiv (\tilde{b})(\widetilde{[f]b} \mid Q')$. Then $R \xrightarrow{\overline{x}e} P'$ with $Q' \approx \text{Rep}(e,y) \mid [P']$. Hence by Lemma 11, $R\{\tilde{f}/\tilde{b}\} \xrightarrow{\overline{x}e\{\tilde{f}/\tilde{b}\}} P'\{\tilde{f}/\tilde{b}\}$ and so $P \xrightarrow{\overline{x}e\{\tilde{f}/\tilde{b}\}} P'\{\tilde{f}/\tilde{b}\}$. Then $Q \equiv (\tilde{b})(\widetilde{[f]b} \mid Q') \approx (\tilde{b})(\widetilde{\text{Rep}(f,b)} \mid \text{Rep}(e,y) \mid [P']) \approx (\tilde{b})(\widetilde{\text{Rep}(f,b)} \mid \text{Rep}(e,y)) \mid (\tilde{b})(\text{Rep}(f,b) \mid [P']) \approx \text{Rep}(e\{\tilde{f}/\tilde{b}\},y) \mid [P'\{\tilde{f}/\tilde{b}\}]$. $\qquad\square$

5 Acknowledgments

I would like to express here my gratitude to Robin Milner and Joachim Parrow to whom are due a number of the key ideas pursued in this paper and with whom I have enjoyed innumerable valuable conversations about the π-calculus, and to Professor Rod Burstall and Professor Takayasu Ito for inviting me to participate in the Japan/U.K. Workshop.

6 References

[Cli] W. Clinger, *Foundations of Actor Semantics*, AI-TR-633, MIT Artificial Intelligence Laboratory, 1981.

[HM] M. Hennessy and R. Milner, *Algebraic Laws for Non-determinism and Concurrency*, Journal of the ACM, 32 (1985) 137–161.

[Mil1] R. Milner, *A Calculus of Communicating Systems*, Springer LNCS, vol. 92, 1980.

[Mil2] R. Milner, *Functions as Processes*, typewritten paper, 1989.

[MPW1, 2] R. Milner, J. Parrow and D. Walker, *A Calculus of Mobile Processes, Parts I and II*, Reports ECS-LFCS-89-85 and -86, Laboratory for Foundations of Computer Science, University of Edinburgh, 1989.

[Nie] F. Nielson, *The typed λ-calculus with First-class Processes*, Report ID-TR:1988-43, Inst. for Datateknik, Tekniske Hojskole, Lyngby, 1988.

Analysing TM_{FS}: a Study of Nondeterminism in Real-Time Concurrency

G.M. Reed and A.W. Roscoe[1]

Oxford University Computing Laboratory
11 Keble Road, Oxford OX1 3QD, U.K.

ABSTRACT. It is well-known that nondeterminism is a consequence of concurrent computation. Modelling it correctly is one of the chief requirements of any theory. In this paper we study how nondeterminism arises in real-time concurrency. The vehicle used is TM_{FS}, the timed failures/stability model for CSP. We see both how this model is able to capture a wide range of subtle behaviours which have no direct untimed analogues, and how the axioms of the model can be justified by a detailed study of nondeterminism.

1 Introduction

Although widely used throughout the world in such critical applications as aviation and nuclear power, real-time programming is a poorly understood discipline. There are severe problems which arise in understanding the behaviour of real-time sequential code, for example relating to scheduling policies. The complexity of these problems will only intensify as we increasingly implement distributed real-time systems with the consequent possibility of nondeterministic behaviour. It is imperative that we begin now to develop the formal models on which the eventual solutions must be based. The authors have been working in this area for several years now, and have devised a number of related models for Timed CSP, a straightforward extension of Hoare's CSP notation. This paper provides a detailed study of the model which is central to their work.

Theories of concurrency can be divided into 'untimed' ones, which ignore the precise times at which events occur, concentrating only upon their relative order, and 'real-time' ones which do record these times. Untimed theories tend to be simpler to apply and are used when one is not concerned about the precise timing details of a system (or are leaving these for later) and when the system does not rely for its correct internal functioning upon time-dependent features such as timeouts. One of the major contributions of the CSP/CCS conceptual model of concurrency, with no shared memory and handshaken communication, is that it does have a rich and usable untimed theory and, until a few years ago, the literature concentrated on this side.

---

[1]The authors gratefully acknowledge that the work reported in this paper was supported by the U.S. Office of Naval Research under grant N00014-87-G-0242. Auxiliary support was provided by the ESPRIT BRA SPEC project.

Nevertheless there are occasions where timed analysis is necessary, and so a number of models and methodologies have arisen for dealing with real time. The authors' philosophy in designing real-time models has always been that the timed theory should not be separate from the untimed one, but should be a natural extension of it where there are well-understood ways of using both theories in the same development. Thus one should be able to prove properties about the untimed behaviour of a system, and be able to use this information rigorously when later refining it to meet timing constraints. Equally, if one is building a large and complex system where one needs to rely on timing only for the correctness of a few components, then there should be ways of localising the more complex timed analysis to those components.

To this end we have developed a number of timed models at different levels of abstraction in such a way that they and the untimed models form a natural hierarchy, with abstraction maps between them. Aspects of this work have already been reported and applied in a number of references, for example [RR86,RR87,Re88,Re90]. The key to getting the connection with the untimed models has been our use of the concept of *stability* (a form of observation dual to divergence) together with more obvious ones such as timed analogues of traces and refusals.

The central model in this hierarchy is the *timed failures/stability model*, TM_{FS}. Though relatively complex, it turns out to be the simplest model which both gives a fully compositional congruence for Timed CSP and which extends the standard untimed failures/divergences model of CSP. Versions of this model appeared in a number of references over the past few years, for example [RR87,Re90]. The process of development has taken the form of slight tightening of the axioms. This paper, together with a companion paper [RR90] presents what we consider to be the definitive version of the model. The other paper gives an extensive explanation of the philosophy of the model and its construction, and presents a detailed analysis of what it means to be a semantics for Timed CSP over it. The present paper concentrates more on the construction of the model, a detailed analysis of the types of nondeterminism it contains, and a justification in terms of this of why we can now claim to have the definitive model.

Comparable work on models of real-time concurrency may be found in [BG87,Z86], though generally the other authors have been concerned with a timed theory alone rather than trying to set up links with untimed ones. It might also be interesting to contrast their generally rather weaker axiomatisations with ours, particularly in the light of the work in this paper.

2   The construction of the model

2.1   The syntax of Timed CSP

It is impossible to discuss our models properly without a knowledge of Timed CSP notation, the assumptions which underlie it, and the way it is given a semantics in the model. In this section we introduce the notation and summarise the main ideas behind it. The complete standard semantics for Timed CSP is given in a later section. All of this, in particular the construction of the standard and other semantics, is discussed in more detail in the companion paper [RR90].

Timed CSP uses essentially the same notation as untimed CSP, extended as necessary to handle timing ideas. The version of untimed CSP we use is essentially that of [BHR84], [BR85] and [H85]. Additionally we will denote by ⊥ the *diverging* process which performs an infinite sequence of internal actions without communicating. Further, we will allow infinite nondeterministic choices ⊓ S and the hiding of infinite sets of events $P \setminus X$.

One might think that a wide range of additional operators would be required to reflect timed behaviour. But in fact, under the standard semantics, it is possible to produce all of the commonly needed ones as *derived* operators (i.e., combinations of standard ones) if we introduce a single extra primitive: *WAIT t* for each real number $t \geq 0$ is the process which for t units of time engages in no event visible to the environment and which then becomes able to terminate successfully. *SKIP* means the same as *WAIT 0*. The reader should consult [S90] for details of how further operators such as timeout, tireout and interrupt can be defined in terms of existing ones. Therefore we will only add this one construct to the untimed language.

In constructing the language, we assume we are given an alphabet Σ from which all communications are drawn. In the syntax below, a ranges over Σ; X, Y over subsets of Σ and f over the set of functions from Σ to Σ. $P(a)$ denotes a function from the given X to the space of processes and S ranges over nonempty subsets of the set of processes. p ranges over process variables (needed to define recursions).

$$P ::= \quad \bot \mid STOP \mid SKIP \mid WAIT\, t \mid a \to P \mid a : X \to P(a) \mid$$
$$P_1 \square P_2 \mid P_1 \sqcap P_2 \mid \sqcap S \mid P_1 \parallel P_2 \mid P_1\,_X\|_Y\, P_2 \mid P_1 \mid\mid\mid P_2 \mid$$
$$P_1; P_2 \mid P \setminus X \mid f^{-1}(P) \mid f(P) \mid p \mid \mu p.P$$

Technical notes. In order that the above syntax is properly defined we need to place a bound on the size of sets over which we allow ourselves to take nondeterministic choices. This bound can be any cardinal. We will find later that we need additional restrictions on the range of the function $P(a)$ and the members of each infinite set over which we apply ⊓. These additional restrictions will be described and discussed later.

2.2 Postulates

Timed CSP inherits more than its syntax from the untimed version of the language. Our basic understanding of what a CSP process is stays the same. It is an entity which communicates in some *alphabet* of atomic events. These communications are still thought of as instantaneous: the moment when an event occurs is the time when the handshake which is 'its essence' takes place. The fact that each sequential process performing an event actually takes some time to perform it is reflected in a delay between the instantaneous occurrence and the time when the sequential process is able to do anything else. Timed CSP also retains the postulate that any event that is observable by the environment can only occur when the environment offers it: a handshake between the process and the environment. This means that the view the environment has of a process is essentially the same as that of a another process with which it might be combined in parallel.

We now state and discuss a number of assumptions we make which are specific to the way we view time. Some we would regard as obvious and others as ones which could have been varied. Yet others turn out to be necessary for subtle reasons we seek to explain.

(1) **Continuous time domain.** The time domain consists of the nonnegative real numbers R^+, and there is no lower bound on the time difference between consecutive observable events. It will, nevertheless, be necessary to allow several events to happen at the same time since there is nothing to stop a pair of unsynchronised parallel processes communicating simultaneously.

We do not specify the units being used to model time: they might be nanoseconds, seconds or years so far as the theory is concerned. However in describing examples it is useful to follow the convention that the time consumed by the completion of an event as described above is generally much less than 1.

(2) **A global clock.** We assume that all events recorded by processes within the system relate to a *conceptual* global clock. This is time as recorded by some notional environment which interacts with the process and observes what happens and when. The environment's clock is not available in any sense to the processes comprising a network. This single thread of observed time leads to greater simplicity and abstraction.

(3) **Realism.** We postulate that no process can perform infinitely many actions in a finite time. It is necessary to build this postulate into any semantics we build for CSP. Given the language described above, one would expect it to be maintained under the condition that any unwinding of a recursion is assumed to take time bounded below by some positive constant δ.

(4) **Hiding and termination.** We wish $(a \rightarrow P)$ to denote the process that is willing at *any* time to engage in the event a and then to behave like the process P. Clearly, if $P = a \rightarrow P$, we then wish $P \setminus a = \perp$. However, consider $P = a \rightarrow (b \rightarrow STOP)$ (the process that is willing to engage in a at any time ≥ 0 and then to offer a b). What do we wish $P \setminus a$ to denote – in other words, at what time can we rely on the b becoming available?

We have already discussed the principle that, in CSP, observability is equated with external control. Given the process $a \rightarrow P$ and an environment eager to perform an a immediately, we would expect that a would indeed occur at time 0. By hiding, we remove control over the event(s) hidden. Hence, any time a process is willing to engage in a hidden action, it is permitted to do so and we would expect the hidden event to occur if no other event did. Thus, we assume that each hidden event takes place as soon as such an event becomes possible. The process $(a \rightarrow (b \rightarrow STOP)) \setminus a$ above thus executes its hidden a immediately, and thus the b becomes available after the time taken to complete a.

(5) **Stability and the treatment of divergence.** As indicated earlier, stability plays the same role in the timed models as its dual, divergence does in the untimed ones. All behaviours we record in the timed models will come from observations we can make up to some finite time. This means that they are qualitavely very different from the two types of observation recorded in the failures/divergences model for untimed CSP. There, the failure (s, X) meant that, after the trace s, the process would refuse X even if it were offered for ever after; s being a divergence means that we can watch the process performing internal actions, once again *for ever*. A process becomes *stable* when it loses the capacity to make any further progress without making some external communication. Importantly we can record the time at which stability occurs.

What does a stable process look like? For consistency with the untimed models and in order to be able to make useful deductions about the behaviour of a stable process, we take a rather severe view. We assume that once it becomes stable a process' available actions remain constant until one of them occurs, and furthermore that its subsequent behaviour does not depend on the time when the event occurred. In other words, given the initially stable process $a \rightarrow P$, the ways P can behave if we accept a at time 100 will be exactly the same as those which could have arisen if a happened at time 0, only with 100 added on the time when everything occurs. (The effect will be like 'shifting' the behaviours of P by 100 time units.)

Notice that if we have observed of a process (a) that it has become stable and (b) that it is refusing some set of events, then we know it will refuse this set for ever (until some event not in the set is accepted so the process can get out of the stable state).

For various reasons the timed models are not forced to model divergence (lack of finite stability) as severely as the untimed ones. In particular it is not necessary to treat any process which can diverge as one which is useless.

In summary, stability will give us the ability to relate the timed theory with the untimed one because the untimed theory is really a theory of non-divergent processes, in the sense that it treats any process which can perform an infinite sequence of internal actions as useless. The refusals which the failures/divergences model records are those *after stability*. The timed theory should also let us reason about processes which can perform these sequences of internal actions, because time gives us the ability to analyse their behaviour with sufficient precision.

2.3 The metric space approach

Although it is possible to place a natural refinement order on timed models (see later) it turns out that this order neither has a least element nor directed limits – both necessary for the cpo approach to fixed points to work. Fortunately, though, time gives a very natural measure for making the models into complete metric spaces: two processes are at distance 2^{-t} if t is the supremum of all times for which it is impossible to distinguish them.

Unlike the case with metrics over untimed models, it turns out that all CSP recursions over the timed models have a natural 'lack of clairvoyance' property which means that they can easily and naturally be made into contraction mappings.

2.4 The Timed Failures-Stability Model (TM_{FS})

The above discussion summarises the philosophy and framework within which we model timed CSP. The timed failures/stability model TM_{FS}, which we are analysing in this paper, models each process as the set of all observations of the form $(s, \alpha, \aleph)$ which can be made of it. Here s is a *timed trace* recording a finite sequence of events which have occurred and the times when they happened; $\aleph$ is a *timed refusal* which records the events which have been observed to be refused by the process up to some time. For reasons we have discussed extensively elsewhere, $\aleph$ records not only what is refused after the end of s but also what was refused during s. α (which may be ∞) is the supremum of all times when the process might become stable given the observation of $(s, \aleph)$. A process which diverges has stability value ∞.

Notation

A *timed event* is an ordered pair (t, a), where a is a communication and $t \in R^+$ is the time at which it occurs. The set $R^+ \times \Sigma$ of all timed events is denoted $T\Sigma$. The set of all *timed traces* is

$$(T\Sigma)^*_{\leq} = \{s \in T\Sigma^* \mid \text{if } (t, a) \text{ precedes } (t', a') \text{ in } s, \text{ then } t \leq t'\}.$$

If $s \in (T\Sigma)^*_{\leq}$, we define $\#s$ to be the length (i.e., number of events) of s and $\Sigma(s)$ to be the set of communications appearing in s (i.e., the second components of all its timed communications). $begin(s)$ and $end(s)$ are respectively the earliest and latest times of any of the timed events in s. (For completeness we define $begin(\langle\rangle) = \infty$ and $end(\langle\rangle) = 0$.)

If $X \subseteq \Sigma$, $s \upharpoonright X$ is the maximal subsequence w of s such that $\Sigma(w) \subseteq X$; $s \setminus X = s \upharpoonright (\Sigma - X)$. If $t \in [0, \infty)$, $s \upharpoonright t$ is the subsequence of s consisting of all those events which occur no later than t, while $s \upharpoonright\!\!\upharpoonright t$ is the subsequence containing the events which occur *before* t. If $t \in [-begin(s), \infty)$ and $s = \langle (t_0, a_0), (t_1, a_1), \ldots, (t_n, a_n) \rangle$,

$$s + t = \langle (t_0 + t, a_0), (t_1 + t, a_1), \ldots, (t_n + t, a_n) \rangle .$$

If $s, t \in (T\Sigma)^*_{\leq}$, we define $s \cong t$ if, and only if, t is a permutation of s (i.e., events that happen at the same time can be re-ordered). We will regard timed traces which are thus congruent as equivalent, simply different ways of writing down the same observation.[2]

If $s, w \in (T\Sigma)^*_{\leq}$, $Tmerge(s, w)$ is defined to be the set of all traces in $(T\Sigma)^*_{\leq}$ obtained by interleaving s and w. Note that this is a far more restricted set than in the untimed case, as the times of events must increase through the trace. In fact, $Tmerge(s, w)$ only contains more than one element when s and w record a pair of events at exactly the same time, and even these two traces will be equivalent ($\cong$).

Given a Timed CSP process P, $Traces(P)$ will denote the set of all timed traces which are possible for P.

The following are some more components from which our model will be built. Stability values are as described above. The time intervals we use are finite nonempty, closed at the left and open at the right. Not only do intervals of this form the most natural ones for partitioning the interval $[0, \infty) = R^+$, but this shape of interval also turns out too be the correct choice for modelling process behaviour: it reflects the idea that an event which is offered might be accepted immediately, and allows us to reason correctly about events which happen at the same time.

Notice that although refusal sets may contain infinitely many different members of Σ, they can only change finitely often in a finite time. This is essentially an assumption

---

[2] Notice that, given this assumption, the order of events in a timed trace carries no information that is not also contained in the times of the events. At first sight it might seem more natural to record process histories as sets of timed events; but the problem with this is that it is possible in CSP to have a parallel process which performs two copies of the same event at the same time. One could use multisets instead, the effect of which would be the same as our timed traces under the above congruence relation. The choice is very much a matter of taste.

that processes and the environment only undergo finitely many state-changes in a finite time.

$$
\begin{array}{llll}
\alpha: & TSTAB & = & R^+ \cup \{\infty\} & \text{(Stability values)} \\
I: & TINT & = & \{\, [l(I), r(I)) \mid 0 \le l(I) < r(I) < \infty \} & \text{(Time Intervals)} \\
T: & RTOK & = & \{I \times X \mid I \in TINT \wedge X \in P(\Sigma)\} & \text{(Refusal Tokens)} \\
\aleph: & RSET & = & \{\bigcup Z \mid Z \subseteq RTOK \wedge Z \text{ finite}\} & \text{(Refusal Sets)}
\end{array}
$$

We define various functions over $RSET$, to extract the set of communications used, times used, beginning and end, shifting and restriction.

$$
\begin{aligned}
\Sigma(\aleph) &= \{a \in \Sigma \mid \exists t.\, (t,a) \in \aleph\} \\
I(\aleph) &= \{t \in [0,\infty) \mid \exists a.\, (t,a) \in \aleph\} \\
begin(\aleph) &= inf(I(\aleph)), \ \forall \aleph \neq \emptyset \\
end(\aleph) &= sup(I(\aleph)), \ \forall \aleph \neq \emptyset \\
begin(\aleph) &= \infty, \ \text{for } \aleph = \emptyset \\
end(\aleph) &= 0, \ \text{for } \aleph = \emptyset \\
\forall t \ge -begin(\aleph), \ \aleph + t &= \{(t'+t, a) \mid (t', a) \in \aleph\} \\
\forall t \in [0,\infty), \ \aleph \upharpoonleft t &= \aleph \cap ([0,t) \times \Sigma) \\
\forall I \subseteq R^+ \ \aleph \upharpoonright I &= \aleph \cap (I \times \Sigma) \\
\forall a \in \Sigma, \ \aleph \downarrow a &= \{t \mid (t,a) \in \aleph\}.
\end{aligned}
$$

Each process will be modelled as a set of triples $(s, \alpha, \aleph)$, with $s \in (T\Sigma)^*_{\le}$, $\alpha \in TSTAB$ and $\aleph \in RSET$. The following functions are natural projections of such sets and operations to ensure (i) that there is one stability value for each trace/refusal pair and (ii) that all equivalent traces are treated the same.

$$
\begin{aligned}
Traces(S) &= \{s \mid \exists \alpha, \aleph.\, (s, \alpha, \aleph) \in S\} \\
Stab(S) &= \{(s, \alpha) \mid \exists \aleph.\, (s, \alpha, \aleph) \in S\} \\
Fail(S) &= \{(s, \aleph) \mid \exists \alpha.\, (s, \alpha, \aleph) \in S\} \\
\underline{SUP}(S) &= \{(s, \alpha, \aleph) \mid (s, \aleph) \in Fail(S) \\
&\qquad \wedge \alpha = sup\{\beta \mid (s, \beta, \aleph) \in S\}\} \\
CL_\cong(S) &= \{(s, \alpha, \aleph) \mid \exists w.\, (w, \alpha; \aleph) \in S \wedge s \cong w\}
\end{aligned}
$$

The evaluation domain TM_{FS}

We formally define TM_{FS} to be those subsets S of $(T\Sigma)^*_{\le} \times TSTAB \times RSET$ satisfying:

1. $\langle\rangle \in Traces(S)$

2. $(s.w, \aleph) \in Fail(S) \Rightarrow (s, \aleph \upharpoonleft begin(w)) \in Fail(S)$

3. $(s, \alpha, \aleph) \in S \wedge s \cong w \Rightarrow (w, \alpha, \aleph) \in S$

4. $t \in [0,\infty) \Rightarrow \exists n(t) \in N. \forall s \in Traces(S). end(s) \le t \Rightarrow \#s \le n(t)$

5. $(s, \alpha, \aleph), (s, \beta, \aleph) \in S \Rightarrow \alpha = \beta$

6. $(s, \alpha, \aleph) \in S \Rightarrow end(s) \le \alpha$

7. $\left(\begin{array}{l}(s,\alpha,\aleph) \in S \,\wedge\, (s.\langle(t,a)\rangle,\aleph) \in Fail(S) \,\wedge\, \\ t > t' \geq \alpha \,\wedge\, t \geq end(\aleph)\end{array}\right) \Rightarrow (t',a) \notin \aleph$

8. $(s,\alpha,\aleph) \in S \Rightarrow$ if $t > \alpha$, $t' \geq \alpha$, $a \in \Sigma$ and
   $w \in (T\Sigma)^*_{\leq}$ is such that $w = \langle(t,a)\rangle.w'$, then
   $(s.w,\alpha',\aleph') \in S \,\wedge\, \aleph \subseteq \aleph'\!\restriction\! t \Rightarrow$
   $\exists \gamma \geq \alpha' + (t' - t)$ such that
   $(s.(w + (t' - t)), \gamma, \aleph_1 \cup \aleph_2 \cup (\aleph_3 + (t' - t))) \in S,$
   where $\aleph_1 = \aleph'\!\restriction\!\alpha$, $\aleph_2 = [\alpha,t') \times \Sigma(\aleph' \cap ([\alpha,t) \times \Sigma))$,
   and $\aleph_3 = \aleph'\!\uparrow\![t,\infty)$.

9. $(s,\alpha,\aleph) \in S \wedge \aleph' \in RSET$ such that $\aleph' \subseteq \aleph$
   $\Rightarrow \exists \alpha' \geq \alpha$ such that $(s,\alpha',\aleph') \in S$

10. $(s,\alpha,\aleph) \in S \,\wedge\, t_1 < \alpha \,\wedge\, t_2 \geq 0 \Rightarrow$
    $\exists \aleph',\beta.\aleph \subseteq \aleph' \,\wedge\, (s,\beta,\aleph') \in S \,\wedge\, \beta \geq t_1 \,\wedge\,$
    $(t' \leq t_2 \,\wedge\, (t',a) \notin \aleph') \Rightarrow (s\!\restriction\! t'.\langle(t',a)\rangle, \aleph'\!\restriction\! t') \in Fail(S) \,\wedge\,$
    $((0 < t' \leq t_2 \wedge \neg\exists\epsilon > 0.\, ((t' - \epsilon, t') \times \{a\}) \subseteq \aleph') \Rightarrow$
    $(s\!\restriction\! t'.\langle(t',a)\rangle), \aleph'\!\restriction\! t') \in Fail(S))$

11. $(s,\alpha,\aleph) \in S \wedge I \in TINT$ such that $I \subset [\alpha,\infty)$
    $\Rightarrow (s,\alpha, \aleph \cup (I \times \Sigma(\aleph \cap ([\alpha,\infty) \times \Sigma)))) \in S$

Although some of these axioms appear complex, each reflects one or more simple healthiness properties. We will now give an intuitive explanation of each. Further intuition can be gained about the axioms from the detailed mathematical use we will make of them later.

1. Every process has initially done nothing at all.

2. If a process has been observed to communicate $s.w$ while refusing $\aleph$ then, at the time when the first event of w occurred, the pair $(s, \aleph\!\restriction\! begin(w))$ had been observed.

3. Traces which are equivalent (i.e., are the same except for the permutation of events happening at the same times) are interchangeable. Essentially, this postulates that there can be no causal dependence between simultaneous events: notice that if a process has trace $\langle(t,a),(t,b)\rangle$ then this axiom and axiom 2 show it has trace $\langle(t,b)\rangle$.

4. The process cannot perform an infinite number of visible events in a finite time.

5. There is only one stability value for each trace/refusal pair: the least time by which we can guarantee stability after the given observation.

6. The time of stability is not before the end of the trace.

7. A stable process cannot communicate an event which it has been seen to refuse since stability.

8. After stability the same set of events is available at all times. Furthermore the behaviour of a process after such an event does not depend on the exact time at

which it was executed. Thus the trace w and the corresponding part of the refusal may be translated so as to make the first event of w now occur at time t'.

The stability value γ corresponding to the translated behaviour may, in general, be greater than the obvious value because the translated behaviour may in some circumstances be possible for other reasons. Note, however, that if stability is still inferable in the new behaviour before time t', then the axiom may be used in reverse to translate the tail of the behaviour so that the beginning of w occurs back at t. This, in combination with axiom 9, can often be used to prove that the γ appearing on the right hand side of axiom 8 does equal $\alpha + t' - t$. This is true, for example, whenever $t' \geq t$.

There is a phenomenon related to this last discussion which it is worth pointing out. One can think of the way we record stability values as giving a record of by when, given the timed trace and refusal observed so far, can we guarantee that the process attains stability. Subconsciously one might think that things observed after stability give no information in this regard, but this would be wrong. It is in fact possible, by making some observation, to realise that the process must already have been stable for some time. A good example of this is provided by the process

$$(WAIT\, 1; (a \rightarrow STOP)) \sqcap STOP$$

Depending on which nondeterministic choice is made, this process either will or will not stabilise immediately. But we can only tell from refusals that it was stable at time 0 when a is refused at time 1 or later.

9. If a process has been observed to communicate s while refusing $\aleph$ then it can communicate the same trace while refusing any subset of $\aleph$. This simply reflects the fact that the environment might offer it less and so have less refused. However, because less has been observed, the stability value can, in general, be greater.

10. Given a triple $(s, \alpha, \aleph)$ and times $t_1 < \alpha$ and $t_2 \geq 0$, there exists a refusal $\aleph'$ in $RSET$ containing $\aleph$ and stability value $\beta > t_1$ such that $(s, \beta, \aleph') \in Fail(P)$ and it is consistent to believe that the (finitely many) changes in the refusals of $\aleph'$ give complete information about what the process could have refused up to time t_2 (i.e., an arbitrarily large finite time) – because it can accept anything not in the refusal set. The events in s and the changes in $\aleph$ can be thought of as the process' state changes. Notice that axiom 9 ensures that $\beta \leq \alpha$.

The construction involving t_1 and β ensures that the stability value α of $(s, \alpha, \aleph)$ is the supremum of stability values corresponding to such 'complete' behaviours – or in other words the time of stability is not increased simply though the environment failing to observe what would have been refused anyway.

The last clause of the axiom states that, if an event was not refuseable up to a given time t', then it was still possible at time t'. This means that we are assuming that any event which was on offer up to a change of state is also available at the instant of the state-change. Note that in the previous clause we state that $(s \upharpoonright t', \aleph \upharpoonright t') \in Fail(S)$ whereas in this last one we vary this to $(s \upharpoonright t', \aleph \upharpoonright t') \in Fail(S)$. Of course these two say the same in the case where s has no event happening at time t. But if there are one or more, the refusals *at* time t' refer to what the process can do *after* the event(s) at the given time, while the refusals just *before* t' allow us to reason about what it might have done *instead* of them.

This last assumption could be dropped if we wanted to consider operators which could cause a 'clean' withdrawal of an offer to communicate. It is included in our presentation because none of the CSP operators can cause such a withdrawal and because we consider it to be a property which is operationally reasonable. We will also discuss in Section 2.5 below another possible small modification to this axiom.

The concept of a complete behaviour, introduced here, will be very important later.

11. Something that is refused at one time on or after stability is refused at all such times. This axiom says the same about the end of traces that part of axiom 8 says about other points in them. Notice that these extra refusals tell us nothing more about the stability time.

Note 1. In both axioms 7 and 8, we carefully distinguish (via t' and t) between events *at* stability and events *after* stability. This is a necessary distinction. For example, the process
$$P = (a \rightarrow STOP \square WAIT\ 1); b \rightarrow STOP$$
will, in the standard semantics, become stable on the pair $(\langle\rangle, [0,1) \times (\Sigma - \{a\}))$ at time 1; however $\langle(1,a)\rangle \in Traces(P)$ (as, indeed, is forced by the last clause of axiom 10) but $\forall t > 1. \langle(t,a)\rangle \notin Traces(P)$. Events which are possible at the very moment of stability might, as in this example, result from alternatives to the stable behaviour rather than from the behaviour itself. This possibility of nondeterminism at the point of stability will cause us various difficulties later.

Note 2. The axioms above are (when taken together) strictly stronger than those we have presented in earlier papers, in the sense that they restrict further the class of processes. The difference between this set and the axioms of [Re88,Re90] is that axiom 10 above has replaced both axioms 4 (which it obviously strengthens) and 11 of the earlier paper. A discussion of this point and of our reasons for strengthening of the axioms will be found in section 2.6 below. The numbering of the axioms has also changed from earlier papers.

The complete metric on TM_{FS}

As described earlier, the metric on our model will be based on the length of time for which it is impossible to tell a pair of processes apart. To define it we need a function which gives a standard representation of a process' behaviour up to time t. If $S \subseteq (T\Sigma)^*_{\leq} \times TSTAB \times RSET$ and $t \in [0, \infty)$, we define

$$S(t) = \{(s, \alpha, \aleph) \in S \mid \alpha < t \wedge end(\aleph) < t\}$$
$$\cup \{(s, \infty, \aleph) \mid end(s) < t \wedge end(\aleph) < t \wedge \exists \alpha \geq t. (s, \alpha, \aleph) \in S\}.$$

$S(t)$ has a representative of each timed failure $(s, \aleph)$ which ends before t. Where the stability value is also less than t, it is included, and otherwise it is replaced by the standard value ∞. It is worth noting that any pair S_1 and S_2 of distinct sets of triples satisfying axiom 5 have a time t such that $S_1(t) \neq S_2(t)$: if $Fail(S_1)$ and $Fail(S_2)$ were unequal then we need only pick t after the end of some element of the symmetric difference. If $(s, \alpha, \aleph) \in S_1$ and $(s, \beta, \aleph) \in S_2$ where $\alpha \neq \beta$, then t can be any time greater than both $end(\aleph)$ and the lesser of α and β (which must be finite).

The complete metric on TM_{FS} is now defined:

$$d(S_1, S_2) = inf\{2^{-t} \mid S_1(t) = S_2(t)\}$$

Given the observation we made above about being able to distinguish S_1 and S_2, it is easy to show that this function defines an ultrametric, namely a metric satisfying the strong triangle inequality

$$d(P, R) \leq max\{d(P, Q), d(Q, R)\}.$$

The completeness of this metric is demonstrated in [RR90].

2.5   More properties of the model

The most subtle – and most powerful – of our axioms is axiom 10. This says that each observed behaviour of a process can be interpreted in terms of some 'complete' description of how it might behave. Define a t_2-complete behaviour[3] to be one satisfying the conditions on the right hand side of the implication in axiom 10. In other words it is a behaviour which, up to time t_2, gives a convincing explanation of what the process might have refused in total up to time t_2. This axiom together with axiom 9 says that, for any time t, the stability value associated with any timed failure $(s, \aleph)$ is the supremum of all those associated with its t−complete extensions (i.e., t−complete behaviours with the same timed trace, and larger timed refusal). Recall axiom 11 of [Re90]:

$$(s.w, \alpha, \aleph) \in S \wedge \aleph' \in RSET \text{ is such that } end(s) \leq begin(\aleph') \wedge$$
$$end(\aleph') \leq begin(w) \wedge (\forall(t, a) \in \aleph', (s.\langle(t, a)\rangle, \aleph \upharpoonright t) \notin Fail(S))$$
$$\Rightarrow (s.w, \alpha, \aleph \cup \aleph') \in S$$

This says that that, if the timed failure $(s.w, \aleph)$ is observable, and if $\aleph'$ contains events between the end of s and the beginning of w which were impossible, then the process would also have refused $\aleph'$ if the environment had offered it. Since this must be true in every run of the process which exhibits $(s.w, \aleph)$, no further information about stability is gained from observing the refusal of $\aleph'$, so the observed stability time is the same. (Note axiom 9.)

It is a consequence of our new axioms. Assuming the conditions on the left-hand-side then, if $t > end(s.w, \aleph \cup \aleph')$, obviously any t−complete extension $(s.w, \aleph^*)$ of $(s.w, \aleph)$ must have $\aleph^* \supseteq \aleph \cup \aleph'$, which means (by axiom 9) that $(s.w, \aleph \cup \aleph') \in Fail(S)$. It is then easy to see that any complete extension of $(s.w, \aleph)$ is one of $(s.w, \aleph \cup \aleph')$, and vice-versa. The sup property of stability values discussed above then ensures that the stability values associated with $(s.w, \aleph)$ and $(s.w, \aleph \cup \aleph')$ are the same.

---

[3]Depending on the circumstances, we will refer both to timed failures $(s, \aleph)$ of P and triples $(s, \alpha, \aleph) \in P$ as t−complete behaviours if they satisfy this condition.

For reasons discussed earlier we have not based our fixed point theory on a partial order. Nevertheless there are other reasons for wanting to have an order over TM_{FS} based (as with many of the orders over untimed CSP) on the notion of nondeterminism: $P \sqsubseteq Q$ should mean that Q is more predictable than P – any observation of Q could be taken for one of P. Such an order will turn out to be useful for understanding the structure of our model, understanding the way it treats nondeterminism, and for developing a notion of refinement. Recalling that the triple $(s, \alpha, \aleph)$ means that the timed failure $(s, \aleph)$ can be observed and that α is the supremum of the resulting stability values (i.e., any stability value less than or equal to α might occur), the order is best defined as follows. $P \sqsubseteq Q$ if and only if

$$\forall (s, \alpha, \aleph) \in Q. \exists \alpha' \geq \alpha.(s, \alpha', \aleph) \in P$$

or, in other words, if every member of $Fail(Q)$ is in $Fail(P)$ but with a possibly greater associated stability value in P.

The partial order cannot have a least element because of axiom 4 – the least one could have no bound on the number of events which can occur up to time t. It also fails to be closed under the limits of increasing sequences. In the case of Σ infinite this is easy to demonstrate, using the same examples which work for untimed CSP with unbounded nondeterminism, for example

$$P_n = \sqcap \{m \to STOP \mid m \geq n\}$$

is a sequence of processes, ordered under $\sqsubseteq$, with no upper bound – any upper bound could neither communicate nor refuse the whole of Σ in contradiction to the axioms.

It also fails to be closed under limits when Σ is finite, though here the examples are rather more subtle and rely upon time-specific arguments. It turns out that no upper bound of certain sequences of well-formed processes can satisfy axiom 10, either because they must have an infinite number of state-changes or because they fail to leave events available at the instant when they are withdrawn. As an example of the first, suppose Q_n is the process that makes the event a available during the intervals $[0, 1 - 2^{-1}]$, $[1 - 2^{-2}, 1 - 2^{-3}], \ldots, [1 - 2^{-2n}, 1 - 2^{2n+1}]$ and refuses it in the appropriate half-open intervals interleaving and following these. Let $P_n = \sqcap \{Q_m \mid m \geq n\}$. A little thought will reveal that any upper bound of the ordered sequence P_n would be obliged to change state infinitely often in the time interval $[0, 1]$ (when no communication has taken place) and that there is no 1-complete extension of the timed failure $(\langle \rangle, \emptyset)$.

One could plausibly argue for a strengthening of axiom 10 that would ban this counterexample. One of the things this axiom does is to assert that, at least as far as one can detect in some sense, processes only change state finitely often in a finite time. When we asserted in axiom 4 that processes could only *communicate* finitely often in a finite time it was done by postulating the existence, for each process, of a uniform bound function $n(t)$ on the number of events the process could perform up to time t. We could have taken this approach with axiom 10 and also postulated that each of the t-complete behaviours for a process has its number of state-changes bounded by $n(t)$ (using the process' bound function from axiom 4). The reader should be able to see that this would ban the processes P_n of the previous paragraph, since the number of state-changes they make up to time 1 is not bounded (though, for any nondeterministic choice they might make, it is finite).

The strengthening of axiom 10 would, however, neither solve the incompleteness problem with infinite alphabets, and nor would it remove the following example. Let t_n be any strictly increasing sequence converging to 1 from below, and let $Q_n = ((a \rightarrow STOP) \Box WAIT\, t_n); STOP$. Under the standard semantics, the process Q_n offers a until time t_n, whereupon the $WAIT\, t_n$ process terminates and removes the possibility of the a. If a is offered at exactly t_n, it may occur or may not – the $\Box$ operator has to arbitrate between two events which become ready simultaneously. This is precisely the situation covered by our discussion of part of axiom 10 – events which are offered are still possible at the instant from which they are refuseable when withdrawn. Now consider the processes $P_n = \sqcap \{Q_m \mid m \geq n\}$. P_n may withdraw the offer of an a at any sufficiently large t_m, but note that it cannot communicate a at time 1. It is however obliged to offer a up to t_n, and as n increases this value increases to 1. Any upper bound would be obliged to offer a up to time 1 without the possibility of performing it *at* time 1, in violation of the same aspect of axiom 10.

Infinite complete behaviours

Axiom 10 gave us the notion of a t–complete behaviour. This gives us a 'convincing explanation' of how a process might have behaved up to time t, and the axiom tells us that, for arbitrary t, we can find one of these extending any given timed failure $(s, \aleph)$ with a stability value as close as we please to that associated with $(s, \aleph)$. In technical manipulations we will be doing later it will be useful to be able to extend this to an infinite complete behaviour, which gives us a convincing explanation of how the process might behave over all time. This will be a triple $(s, \alpha, \aleph^*)$, where s is still a finite timed trace, $\alpha \in R^+ \cup \{\infty\}$, but now $\aleph$ is allowed to extend to infinity: it is a set of pairs (t, a) such that each of its restrictions $\aleph^* \upharpoonright t$ is in $RSET$ (i.e., it only changes finitely often in a finite time). Informally this triple means that the process might be observed to perform the trace s and be observed though all time to refuse $\aleph^*$, and that given this we know that it became stable at time α at the latest. Such a triple (or, where appropriate, the pair $(s, \aleph^*)$) can be said to be a complete infinite behaviour of a process P if $(s, \aleph \upharpoonright t) \in Fail(P)$ for all t, $\alpha = inf\{\alpha' \mid (s, \alpha', \aleph^* \upharpoonright t) \in P\}$ and the same conditions applied as for a t-complete behaviour, namely

$$(t, a) \notin \aleph^* \Rightarrow (s \upharpoonright t.\langle(t, a)\rangle, \aleph^* \upharpoonright t) \in Fail(P)$$

for each $t \in [0, \infty)$ and $a \in \Sigma$, and

$$(\neg \exists \epsilon > 0.(t - \epsilon, t) \times \{a\} \subseteq \aleph^*) \Rightarrow (s \upharpoonright t.\langle(t, a)\rangle, \aleph^* \upharpoonright t) \in Fail(P)$$

when $t \in (0, \infty)$ and $a \in \Sigma$.

This gives an obvious extension to all time of what axiom 10 provides us with up to any finite time – a plausible explanation of the state-changes the process went through in getting to the trace s and those which might happen after the end of s on the assumption that no event subsequently occurs. The following lemma shows that these always exist, and that it is (as we might have hoped) consistent to believe that a stable process does not change state.

Lemma 1 If $P \in TM_{FS}$, $(s, \alpha, \aleph) \in P$, and $t < \alpha$ then there is an infinite complete behaviour $(s, \beta, \aleph^*)$ of P such that $\aleph \subseteq \aleph^*$ and $t < \beta \leq \alpha$. Furthermore, if $\beta < \infty$, we can assume

$$\aleph^* \uparrow [\beta, \infty) = [\beta, \infty) \times \Sigma(\aleph^* \uparrow [\beta, \infty))$$

Proof We will first give one construction that works for the main statement above in all cases, and then give a different one which works for the second statement in its restricted case. Pick a value t' such that $t < t' < \alpha$. Starting with $(\beta_0, \aleph_0) = (\alpha, \aleph)$, we use axiom 10 iteratively, on the nth iteration starting from $(s, \beta_{n-1}, \aleph_{n-1})$ with $t_2 = t'$ and $t_1 = T + n$ where $T = end(s, \aleph)$, thereby obtaining $(s, \beta_n, \aleph_n)$. Necessarily, the β_n form a (not necessarily strictly) decreasing sequence of values between t' and α, and $\aleph_n \subseteq \aleph_{n+1}$ for all n. And $(s, \beta_n, \aleph_n)$ is a $(T+n)$-complete behaviour for $n > 0$. Now, set

$$\aleph^* = \aleph_1 \uparrow [0, T+1) \cup \bigcup_{n=2}^{\infty} \aleph_n \uparrow [T+n-1, T+n)$$

Notice that, by construction, each $\aleph^* \wedge t$ for $t \in [0, \infty)$ belongs to $RSET$. Since $\aleph \subseteq \aleph^* \wedge T + n \subseteq \aleph_n$, it follows (using axiom 9) that there is some γ_n with $\beta_n \leq \gamma_n \leq \alpha$ such that $(s, \gamma_n, \aleph^* \wedge T + n) \in P$. Clearly the γ_n form a decreasing sequence with a limit β^* satisfying $t < t' \leq \beta^* \leq \alpha$. Claim $(s, \beta^*, \aleph^*)$ is a complete infinite behaviour of P.

If $(t, a) \notin \aleph^*$, then choose $n = 1$ if $t < T + 1$ or otherwise let n be such that $T + n - 1 \leq t < T + n$. By definition of $\aleph^*$, we then know that $(t, a) \notin \aleph_n$ and hence $(s \wedge t.\langle(t, a)\rangle, \aleph_n \wedge t) \in Fail(P)$. Since $\aleph^* \wedge t \subseteq \aleph_n \wedge t$ it follows by axiom 9 that $(s \wedge t.\langle(t, a)\rangle, \aleph^* \wedge t) \in Fail(P)$. If $t > 0$ and $\neg \exists \epsilon > 0.(t - \epsilon, t) \times \{a\} \subseteq \aleph^*$ we choose $n = 1$ if $t \leq T + 1$ and otherwise n is such that $T + n - 1 < t \leq T_n$. A similar argument to the above then shows that $(s \wedge t.\langle(t, a)\rangle, \aleph_n \wedge t)$ and hence $(s \wedge t.\langle(t, a)\rangle, \aleph^* \wedge t)$ belong to $Fail(P)$. This completes the proof of the first statement.

Suppose $(s, \aleph')$ is a t-complete behaviour of P and that $(s, \beta, \aleph' \wedge t) \in P$ for some $\beta < t$. Let $A = \Sigma(\aleph' \uparrow [\beta, t))$. If $a \notin A$ we know by completeness of $(s, \aleph')$ that $(s.\langle(t, a)\rangle, \aleph' \wedge t) \in Fail(P)$. Axiom 8 (with $w = \langle(t, a)\rangle$) then tells us that, for all $t' \in [\beta, \infty)$, $(s.\langle(t', a)\rangle, \aleph' \wedge \beta \cup [\beta, t') \times A) \in Fail(P)$. It follows easily that, for all $t'' < t'$, the failure $(s, \aleph' \wedge \beta \cup [\beta, t') \times A)$ is t''-complete. Axiom 11 tells us, that for $t' \geq t$, the stability value associated with this failure is β. It follows that $(s, \beta, \aleph' \wedge \beta \cup [\beta, \infty) \times A)$ is a complete infinite behaviour of P.

Suppose that the stability value β^* produced by the first part of this result was finite. This must have been because one of the sequence γ_n which converged down to it was finite. Clearly there then exists n such that $\gamma_n < T + n$. Thus the preconditions of the previous paragraph are satisfied by the failure $(s, \aleph^* \wedge T + n + 1)$, $t = T + n$ and $\beta = \gamma_n$. The conclusions of that paragraph then give exactly what is required for the second part of the lemma. $\square$

One immediate corollary of this result is that, for any $(s, \alpha, \aleph) \in P$, α is the supremum of all the stability values α^* associated with the complete infinite extensions of $(s, \alpha, \aleph)$.

3 The semantics of Timed CSP

The construction of TM_{FS} was strongly influenced by our intuition about the semantics of Timed CSP. In this section we show how the standard semantics are actually defined. They are called the 'standard' semantics because, while they are in some sense the most straightforward and natural, it would be wrong to prescribe a single real-time semantics in a world where, for perfectly good reasons, different implementations had different timing characteristics. This issue is covered in detail in [RR90].

Without further ado we will now define the standard semantic function $\mathcal{E}_T : TCSP \rightarrow TM_{FS}$.

$$\mathcal{E}_T[\![\bot]\!] = \{(\langle\rangle, \infty, \aleph) \mid \aleph \in RSET\}$$

$$\mathcal{E}_T[\![STOP]\!] = \{(\langle\rangle, 0, \aleph) \mid \aleph \in RSET\}$$

$$\mathcal{E}_T[\![SKIP]\!] = \{(\langle\rangle, 0, \aleph) \mid \sqrt{} \notin \Sigma(\aleph)\} \cup$$
$$\{(\langle(t, \sqrt{})\rangle, t, \aleph_1 \cup \aleph_2) \mid t \geq 0 \wedge (I(\aleph_1) \subseteq [0, t) \wedge$$
$$\sqrt{} \notin \Sigma(\aleph_1)) \wedge I(\aleph_2) \subseteq [t, \infty)\}$$

$$\mathcal{E}_T[\![WAIT\ t]\!] = \{(\langle\rangle, t, \aleph) \mid \aleph \cap ([t, \infty) \times \{\sqrt{}\}) = \emptyset\}$$
$$\cup \{(\langle(t', \sqrt{})\rangle, t', \aleph_1 \cup \aleph_2 \cup \aleph_3) \mid t' \geq t \wedge I(\aleph_1) \subseteq [0, t)$$
$$\wedge (I(\aleph_2) \subseteq [t, t') \wedge \sqrt{} \notin \Sigma(\aleph_2)) \wedge I(\aleph_3) \subseteq [t', \infty)\}$$

$$\mathcal{E}_T[\![a \rightarrow P]\!] = \{(\langle\rangle, 0, \aleph) \mid a \notin \Sigma(\aleph)\} \cup$$
$$\{(\langle(t, a)\rangle.(s + (t + \delta)), \alpha + t + \delta, \aleph_1 \cup \aleph_2 \cup (\aleph_3 + (t + \delta))) \mid$$
$$t \geq 0 \wedge (I(\aleph_1) \subseteq [0, t) \wedge a \notin \Sigma(\aleph_1)) \wedge I(\aleph_2) \subseteq [t, t + \delta)$$
$$\wedge (s, \alpha, \aleph_3) \in \mathcal{E}_T[\![P]\!]\}$$

$$\mathcal{E}_T[\![a : A \rightarrow P(a)]\!] = \{(\langle\rangle, 0, \aleph) \mid A \cap \Sigma(\aleph) = \emptyset\} \cup$$
$$\{(\langle(t, a)\rangle.(s + (t + \delta)), \alpha + t + \delta, \aleph_1 \cup \aleph_2 \cup (\aleph_3 + (t + \delta))) \mid$$
$$a \in A \wedge t \geq 0 \wedge (I(\aleph_1) \subseteq [0, t) \wedge A \cap \Sigma(\aleph_1) = \emptyset) \wedge$$
$$I(\aleph_2) \subseteq [t, t + \delta) \wedge (s, \alpha, \aleph_3) \in \mathcal{E}_T[\![P(a)]\!]\}$$

$$\mathcal{E}_T[\![P \square Q]\!] = \underline{SUP}(\{(\langle\rangle, max\{\alpha_P, \alpha_Q\}, \aleph) \mid (\langle\rangle, \alpha_P, \aleph) \in \mathcal{E}_T[\![P]\!]$$
$$\wedge (\langle\rangle, \alpha_Q, \aleph) \in \mathcal{E}_T[\![Q]\!]\}$$
$$\cup \{(s, \alpha, \aleph) \mid s \neq \langle\rangle \wedge (s, \alpha, \aleph) \in \mathcal{E}_T[\![P]\!] \cup \mathcal{E}_T[\![Q]\!]$$
$$\wedge (\langle\rangle, \aleph \upharpoonright begin(s)) \in Fail(\mathcal{E}_T[\![P]\!]) \cap Fail(\mathcal{E}_T[\![Q]\!])\})$$

$$\mathcal{E}_T[\![P \sqcap Q]\!] = \underline{SUP}(\mathcal{E}_T[\![P]\!] \cup \mathcal{E}_T[\![Q]\!])$$

$$\mathcal{E}_T[\![\sqcap S]\!] = \underline{SUP}(\cup S) \qquad (S \neq \emptyset)$$

$$\mathcal{E}_T[\![P \| Q]\!] = \underline{SUP}(\{(s, max\{\alpha_P, \alpha_Q\}, \aleph_P \cup \aleph_Q) \mid$$
$$(s, \alpha_P, \aleph_P) \in \mathcal{E}_T[\![P]\!] \wedge (s, \alpha_Q, \aleph_Q) \in \mathcal{E}_T[\![Q]\!]\})$$

$$\mathcal{E}_T[\![P\ _X\|_Y\ Q]\!] = \underline{SUP}(\{(s, max\{\alpha_P, \alpha_Q\}, \aleph_P \cup \aleph_Q \cup \aleph_Z) \mid$$
$$\exists (s_P, \alpha_P, \aleph_P) \in \mathcal{E}_T[\![P]\!], (s_Q, \alpha_Q, \aleph_Q) \in \mathcal{E}_T[\![Q]\!]$$
$$\text{with } \Sigma(\aleph_P) \subseteq X \text{ and } \Sigma(\aleph_Q) \subseteq Y \text{ such that}$$
$$s \in (s_P\ _X\|_Y\ s_Q) \wedge \Sigma(\aleph_Z) \subseteq (\Sigma - (X \cup Y))\})$$
$$\text{where } v\ _X\|_Y\ w =$$
$$\{s \in (T\Sigma)^*_{\leq} \mid s \upharpoonright (X \cup Y) = s \wedge s \upharpoonright X = v \wedge s \upharpoonright Y = w\}$$

$$\mathcal{E}_T[\![P \vert\vert\vert Q]\!] = \underline{SUP}(\{(s, max\{\alpha_P, \alpha_Q\}, \aleph) \mid \exists (u, \alpha_P, \aleph) \in \mathcal{E}_T[\![P]\!]$$
$$\wedge (v, \alpha_Q, \aleph) \in \mathcal{E}_T[\![Q]\!] \text{ such that } s \in Tmerge(u, v)\})$$

$$\mathcal{E}_T[P;Q] = CL_{\cong}(\underline{SUP}(\{(s,\alpha,\aleph) \mid \checkmark \notin \Sigma(s) \land \forall I \in TINT$$
$$(s,\alpha,\aleph \cup (I \times \{\checkmark\})) \in \mathcal{E}_T[P]\}$$
$$\cup \{(s.(w+t), \alpha+t, \aleph_1 \cup (\aleph_2+t)) \mid \checkmark \notin \Sigma(s)$$
$$\land \; end(\aleph_1) \le t$$
$$\land \; (s.\langle(t,\checkmark)\rangle, \aleph_1 \cup ([0,t) \times \{\checkmark\})) \in Fail(\mathcal{E}_T[P])$$
$$\land \; (w,\alpha,\aleph_2) \in \mathcal{E}_T[Q]\}))$$

$$\mathcal{E}_T[P \setminus X] = \underline{SUP}(\{s \setminus X, \beta, \aleph) \mid \exists \alpha \ge \beta \ge end(s).$$
$$(s,\alpha,\aleph \cup ([0, max\{\beta, end(\aleph)\}) \times X)) \in \mathcal{E}_T[P]\})$$

$$\mathcal{E}_T[f^{-1}(P)] = \{(s,\alpha,\aleph) \mid (f(s), \alpha, f(\aleph)) \in \mathcal{E}_T[P]\}$$

$$\mathcal{E}_T[f(P)] = \underline{SUP}(\{(f(s),\alpha,\aleph) \mid (s,\alpha,f^{-1}(\aleph)) \in \mathcal{E}_T[P]\})$$

$\mathcal{E}_T[\mu p.F(p)] =$ The unique fixed point of the contraction mapping
$\hat{C}(Q) = C(WAIT\ \delta; Q)$, where C is the mapping on
TM_{FS} represented by F.

In order to preserve axiom 4 it is necessary to place a restriction on the use of the infinitary operators $\sqcap S$ and $x : A \to P(x)$. This is that there is a single function $n(t)$ which works (in axiom 4) for all of the processes being combined.

Provided this restriction is observed, all of the above operators preserve the axioms and are nonexpanding with respect to the metric. The first of these properties in particular requires a considerable amount of tedious checking: for a large number of the most interesting cases (for example hiding) the reader is referred to [Re88]. The fact that that reference uses a slightly weaker axiomatisation is irrelevant except when considering axiom 10 of this paper (replacing axioms 4 and 11 of the earlier work). However, just as occurred with the old axiom 4, a complete behaviour of any combination of processes is always constructed from suitable complete behaviours of an argument or arguments.

4 A study of nondeterminism in TM_{FS}

Nondeterminism is a well-known consequence of concurrency. In this section we will use the tightly-defined model we have created to study just how, and in what forms, nondeterminism appears in real-time concurrent systems. We will find that the subtleties of real-time behaviour – in particular issues relating to instants when a process can arbitrate between some internal action and an external communication – make it a rather harder subject than for untimed CSP.

One of the features of all the widely used models of untimed CSP is the way in which any process P can be identified with the set of all *deterministic*, or sometimes *pre-deterministic* processes processes Q which 'implement' it, namely $P \sqsubseteq Q$. (Where the general nondeterministic choice operator $\sqsubseteq$ was defined, this 'identification' simply amounted to saying that the set $imp(P)$ of implementations was nonempty and $\sqcap imp(P) = P$.) This idea has often been very important, notably in the development of the untimed infinite traces model [Ro88].

A deterministic process was there one which never had the choice of accepting or refusing any action, which was equivalent to being maximal in the partial order. In the models with divergence this notion had to be weakened to say that a pre-deterministic process was one which was deterministic until it diverged.

Blamey [Bl90] has written on the phenomenon of processes being determined by their (pre-)deterministic implementations, and has argued that, since the correct structure of deterministic or pre-deterministic processes is generally easier to establish and justify than that of general ones, we can say that the axioms of a CSP model are complete if we have such a property. The rationale behind this term is that, given we know what the set of 'deterministic' ones is, and what the definition of general nondeterministic composition is, we can tell exactly which objects are the nondeterministic compositions of sets of 'deterministic' ones. Thus Blamey calls a set of axioms sound if they allow all such objects, and complete if they allow no others.

Certainly this form of completeness gives powerful evidence that the way the axioms extend the notion of (pre)-deterministic processes to nondeterministic ones is correct. It also gives us a much greater level of understanding of how the model fits together and how it treats nondeterminism. The rest of this section investigates the question of a corresponding completeness result for Timed CSP, since this provides a valuable focus for our study of nondeterminism.

4.1 A taxonomy of nondeterminism

Unfortunately, it is not altogether straightforward to construct an appropriate notion corresponding to deterministic processes and which is sufficient to give us a completeness result. The resulting investigations will, however, give us a much deeper understanding of the model and of the varieties of nondeterminism it encompasses.

Fully predictable deterministic processes are sufficient for completeness in models of untimed CSP. Essentially this is because it turns out that, given any behaviour of such a process (even though that process might be genuinely nondeterministic) it is always possible to find a complete deterministic process which 'sits inside' the given one and which exhibits the given behaviour. Things turn out not to be quite as simple in the case of real-time CSP. The following list enumerates various types of 'unpredictability' which cannot, for one reason or another, be factored out in this way. The reader may note that each of them relates, in one way or another, to singular behaviour at one instant.

1. The first is connected with axiom 10, which specifies that a withdrawn event is still possible at the instant of withdrawal. This is a form of nondeterminism which we are specifying *must* be present in any process which can retract an offer of communication – and we could not hope to get a completeness result of the type above unless the class of 'deterministic' processes contained retracting ones.

2. The second concerns processes which have an event possible at an isolated time, for example

$$(a \rightarrow STOP \Box b \rightarrow STOP) \setminus b$$

which, in the standard semantics, can do a at time 0 but at no other. Since all refusals are over intervals, there is no process which can offer such a point event without also being able to refuse it if offered. We might term such an isolated event a *transient event*. No fully predictable implementation of the above process would be able to communicate an a.

3. Transient events can manifest themselves in another, yet more subtle, form at the very moment when a process is becoming stable. Up to the time when a process stabilises, our axioms allow it, for example, to make a single event available continuously but have its subsequent behaviour vary quite arbitrarily depending on when the event happens. Provided that each of these different behaviours is deterministic then the whole process is. However, once it has stabilised, axiom 8 tells us that the process' subsequent behaviour does not depend on when the event did. The problem with an event happening at the instant of stability is that it might be an *alternative* to stability rather than a manifestation of the stable configuration.

This situation is actually rather similar to the one which led us to postulate that events are still possible at the moment when they are withdrawn, in that at the moment when a process would otherwise become stable it may be possible for it to do something else. The following example illustrates this. Consider the process

$$((a \rightarrow STOP) \Box SKIP); (a \rightarrow a \rightarrow STOP)$$

In the standard semantics, the first a is possible 'transiently' at time 0; otherwise the *SKIP* terminates immediately and the second a is also available at time 0, with the process being stable at once. The result of all this is that if an a is accepted at time 0 we cannot be sure whether or not the second will occur, while if we wait beyond this time we can be sure it will. Any predictable (even modulo the questions above) implementation of this process is forced, by axiom 8, to make the second a available following one at time 0. It follows that it cannot refuse a after the time taken to complete the first. Therefore the behaviour subsequent to the 'transient' a is never reflected by any such implementation. It should be clear that we could have varied the above example so that the different behaviour introduced by the transient was delayed an arbitrary number of communications beyond it, or could have been of a different sort such as a larger stability time.

In summary, when an event happens at a time *after* stability the same subsequent behaviours are possible at whatever times the event happens *at or after* stability. But subsequent behaviours which are enabled when an event happens *at* stability need not manifest themselves when the same event happens *after* it. This type of transient is more subtle than the last because they are not apparent when they happen, only in the effects they leave behind.

4. A final source of difficulties can be found in axiom 3. Recall that this states that events which happen at the same time can be re-ordered in a trace without changing behaviour. While one order in which a set of simultaneous events occurs may be totally consistent with what is refuseable on the traces where they happen, this need not be the case with another ordering. This can either be because the occurrence of one event in the set coincides with the disabling of another, or (and this causes more problems) with the enabling of another. We will see examples of these phenomena later.

There is a sense in which difficulties 1 and 4 are more pervasive than 2 and 3. If we had a notion of 'implementation' which did not allow the forms of nondeterminism which arise under these headings, there would be processes with no implementations at all. This is not the case with the transient events of 2 and 3, which arise as alternatives 'grafted on' to otherwise well-behaved processes. One consequence of this is that forms 1 and 4 must be allowed throughout an implementation, while, if we are seeking an implementation of a process P which manifests one of P's behaviours $(s, \aleph)$, it is reasonable to restrict its transient events to ones in s.

4.2 Quasi-deterministic processes

To approach the definition we need for a completeness result, we will start out with one that is too strong for all the reasons set out above. We define a *fully deterministic* process to be one for which we can always tell whether a given (instantaneous) offer of an event will be accepted. Namely, for all timed traces s, $t \geq end(s)$ and $a \in \Sigma$, we never both have $s.\langle(t, a)\rangle \in Traces(P)$ and $(t, a) \in \aleph$ for which $(s, \aleph) \in Fail(P)$. This definition ignores stability values, though for some purposes one might wish to strengthen it accordingly.

To deal with the first, and part of the fourth, problem mentioned above we must allow an event to occur if the process was unable to refuse it in some half-open interval ending at the given time. We can define a process to be quasi-deterministic if, and only if, under the same circumstances as above, we never both have $s.\langle(t, a)\rangle \in Traces(P)$ and that there exists $\epsilon > 0$ with

$$(s', [max\{0, t - \epsilon\}, t + \epsilon) \times \{a\}) \in Fail(P)$$

If P has just started (i.e., $t = 0$), then it cannot both accept and reject a at time t. Otherwise, it must not accept a if it is able to reject it in some interval up to and including the the current time t.

If we had just wished to deal with problem 1 then we would have altered the above definition to

$$(s, [max\{end(s), t - \epsilon\}, t + \epsilon) \times \{a\}) \in Fail(P)$$

The difference between these appears in a process which has just been offering an event a, but has started to refuse it at the same moment when it has accepted an event b (there being no reason why a and b must be different). Axiom 10 does not *force* the process to be able to accept a at the same time as b – after all they may have been offered as alternatives. However there are circumstances where we would expect an a to be possible, and can deduce this from axiom 3. Consider, for example, the process

$$(((a \rightarrow STOP) \square WAIT\, 1); STOP) \,|||\, (b \rightarrow STOP)$$

which is forced, by axiom 10, to have the trace $\langle(1, a), (1, b)\rangle$ and hence, by axiom 3, has the trace $\langle(1, b), (1, a)\rangle$. The second and stronger definition above would have disallowed the a after the b, whereas the first allows it. A subtle variation on this example appears if a and b are replaced by the same event.

This still does not deal with the second and third problems discussed above of transient events. In dealing with these there are two things to notice. Firstly, a given recorded trace might have a number of transients in it. Thus we need to allow for at least any finite number of transients being possible for a given process. Second, it is quite possible for a transient of either sort to appear after the process has previously been stable (i.e., on a proper prefix of the current trace), as occurs in the process

$$a \to (a \to STOP \square b \to STOP) \setminus a$$

Since we know that the behaviour of a stable process does not depend on the time at which the next event happens (axiom 8), it follows that if a transient is possible at some later time if the next event happens at one time then it must also be possible at suitably shifted later times when the next event occurs at some other time. Of course this means that sometimes, though in rather special circumstances, a process must have an uncountable infinity of transients if it has one. Given this discussion and the existence of the 'at stability' type of transient it is obviously important for us to understand the nature of stability in the class of quasi-deterministic processes. It will also allow us to find an appropriate strengthening of the definition to deal with stability.

The following result shows that quasi-deterministic processes actually have much in common with the deterministic and pre-deterministic processes of untimed CSP.

Lemma 2 Suppose $P \in TM_{FS}$ is quasi-deterministic. Then

1. If $(s, \alpha^*, \aleph^*)$ is a complete infinite extension of $(s, \emptyset)$, for $s \in Traces(P)$, then $(s, \aleph) \in Fail(P)$ if and only if $\aleph \subseteq \aleph^*$ (for all $\aleph \in RSET$).

2. The complete infinite extension $(s, \alpha^*, \aleph^*)$ of any $(s, \alpha, \aleph) \in P$ is unique.

3. If $(s, \alpha, \aleph)$ and $(s, \alpha', \aleph')$ are both in P then $\alpha = \alpha'$.

4. P is the only quasi-deterministic process with its trace/stability set $Stab(P)$.

5. If $Q \sqsupseteq P$ then Q is quasi-deterministic.

6. Over quasi-deterministic processes, the inequality in axiom 8 becomes an equality (i.e., the stability value of the shifted behaviour is also shifted by the same amount) provided that the time t' is strictly greater than α.

Proof Suppose s is any trace of P, and that $(s, \alpha, \aleph^*)$ is a complete infinite extension of the timed failure $(s, \emptyset)$. Now suppose $(s \upharpoonright t, \aleph) \in Fail(P)$ is such that $end(\aleph) \leq t$. Claim that $\aleph \subseteq \aleph^*$. If not, since the result is trivial if $t = 0$, there would be times $t_1 < t_2 < t$ such that no event of s occurs in $[t_1, t_2]$ and an event a such that $[t_1, t_2) \times \{a\} \subseteq \aleph$ and $[t_1, t_2) \times \{a\} \cap \aleph^* = \emptyset$. For all $t_1 < t' < t_2$ there thus exists ϵ with $(s \upharpoonright t_1, [t'-\epsilon, t'+\epsilon) \times \{a\}) \in Fail(P)$ though the completeness of $(s, \alpha, \aleph^*)$ ensures that $s \upharpoonright t_1.\langle (t', a) \rangle \in Traces(P)$. This contradicts our assumption of quasi-determinacy, and so the claim is established, proving part 1.

Part 2 follows easily from part 1, since if $(s, \alpha_1, \aleph_1)$ and $(s, \alpha_2, \aleph_2)$ were different complete extensions of $(s, \aleph)$ (and hence of $(s, \emptyset)$) there would be a time t such that either $\aleph_1 \upharpoonright t \not\subseteq \aleph_2$ or $\aleph_2 \upharpoonright t \not\subseteq \aleph_1$. We know that the stability value associated with any failure of the form $(s, \aleph)$ is the supremum of those associated with its complete infinite extensions. It follows that that stability value is the one belonging to the *only* complete infinite extension. Since this complete infinite extension is common to all failures $(s, \aleph')$ with the given trace, we have proved part 3.

In order to prove part 4 it is enough, by part 3, to prove that if P and Q are quasi-deterministic and $Traces(P) = Traces(Q)$ then $Fail(P) = Fail(Q)$. If not then, without loss of generality we may assume that there is $(s, \aleph) \in Fail(P)$ but not in $Fail(Q)$. Since $s \in Traces(Q)$ we can extend $(s, \emptyset)$ to a (unique) complete infinite extension $(s, \aleph^*)$ for Q. Necessarily, as in the proof of part 1, there are times $t_1 < t_2$ such that no event of s occurs in $[t_1, t_2]$ and an event a such that $[t_1, t_2) \times \{a\} \subseteq \aleph$ and $[t_1, t_2) \times \{a\} \cap \aleph^* = \emptyset$. For all $t_1 < t' < t_2$ there thus exists ϵ with $(s {\upharpoonright} t_1, [t' - \epsilon, t' + \epsilon) \times \{a\}) \in Fail(P)$ though the completeness of $(s, \aleph^*)$ ensures that $s {\upharpoonright} t_1.\langle(t', a)\rangle \in Traces(Q) = Traces(P)$. Thus part 4 is proved.

The proof of part 5 follows immediately from the relevant defintions. It is worth noting that quasi-deterministic processes are not maximal under the order. In general we can 'improve' a quasi-deterministic process P either by decreasing its stability values or by exploiting the fact that we took the definition above which was weaker on what could happen at the same time as another event.

Axiom 8 says that, if $(s, \alpha, \aleph) \in P$ and if $t > \alpha$, $t \geq end(\aleph)$ (so that by time t we can be sure the process has been stable since time α), then any behaviour of P starting from t can be shifted back to any time $t' \geq t$. If $t' > \alpha$ and we could, in fact, have deduced that the process had been stable since α at time t', then the same axiom can be used to shift the behaviour back the other way; since the inequality then works both ways between the shifted stability values, the shift must be exact. Since, by part 3, stability values in quasi-deterministic processes depend only on the trace, this deduction can always be made for them. □

Part 4 is obviously very like the result which says that, in untimed CSP, a deterministic process is determined by its set of traces or a predeterministic process is determined by its sets of traces and divergences. One significant difference is that, in the timed case, by no means every plausible set of traces gives rise to a quasi-deterministic process. An example of this is provided by the traces of the process we used to illustrate the first type of transient above.

It is interesting what part 6 does not say – it does not say that the inequality of axiom 8 becomes an equality for $t' = \alpha$. This is because the definition of quasi-deterministic processes allows a limited form of the 'at stability' type of transient discussed earlier. Consider, for example, the process

$$(a \to \bot) \Box SKIP); (a \to STOP)$$

which, under the standard semantics is immediately stable and offers a, after which it can do nothing. If the a occurs at time $t > 0$ the subsequent stability time varies linearly with t. But an initial transient destroys this relationship for $t = 0$.

4.3 Adding transients to quasi-deterministic processes

We are now going to tackle the question of how one might add a transient event (and its subsequent consequences) to a quasi-deterministic process P. Lemma 2 and the above discussion give us a clear indication of how to deduce, once we have been told to place a transient at one point (a particular time in the closed interval between the end of a trace s and the stability time associated with s), where else it must be possible because of earlier stability. (We can ignore refusal information because of what we know from Lemma 2.)

Suppose $s = v.\langle(t,a)\rangle.w$, $t > \alpha$ where α is the stability time associated with v and $t' \geq \alpha$. Then we will write $s \xLongrightarrow{t'-t}_1 v.\langle(t',a)\rangle.(w + (t' - t)) (= s')$ and observe that any transient added after s must be added after s', shifted through $t' - t$. The subscript 1 here denotes the 'one-step' nature of the relation. (The time of the shifted transient is guaranteed to be in range by axiom 8.) If $t' > t$, we will write $s \xLongleftrightarrow{t'-t}_1 s'$ and observe that if $s_1 \xLongleftrightarrow{t}_1 s_2$ then (i) $s_2 \xLongleftrightarrow{-t}_1 s_1$ and (ii) (by Lemma 2 (6)) the stability times of all traces beyond the shifted event in s_1 and s_2 are also shifted by precisely the same amount t. Since, if $s_1 \xLongrightarrow{t}_1 s_2$, the first shifted event of s_1 occurs strictly later than any predecessor, if $s'_1 \cong s_1$ then there is $s'_2 \cong s_2$ such that $s'_1 \xLongrightarrow{t}_1 s'_2$.

We can form transitive closures of these relations to take account of the fact that several events in a trace might happen after stability, adding in the re-ordering congruence, as follows:

- If $s \cong s'$ then $s \xLongrightarrow{0} s'$ and $s \xLongleftrightarrow{0} s'$.

- If $s \xLongrightarrow{t}_1 s'$ and $s' \xLongrightarrow{t'} s''$, then $s \xLongrightarrow{t+t'} s''$.

- If $s \xLongleftrightarrow{t}_1 s'$ and $s' \xLongleftrightarrow{t'} s''$, then $s \xLongleftrightarrow{t+t'} s''$.

- $\xLongleftrightarrow{t}$ and $\xLongrightarrow{t}$ are the smallest relations consistent with the above.

Both these relations are transitive (adding the times) and reflexive (with time 0). We also have that $s \xLongleftrightarrow{t} s'$ implies $s' \xLongleftrightarrow{-t} s$ and that, in this case, the order in which the various shifts are carried out to get from s to s' is irrelevant. In relation to $\cong$, it is easy to see that if $s \xLongrightarrow{t} s'$ then the groups of simultaneous events in s remain together in s' and keep their relative order except that some might be amalgamated (in a process which can become stable instantly after some communication), and that if $s \xLongleftrightarrow{t} s'$ then the integrity and order of these groups is preserved completely.

Suppose P is a quasi-deterministic process, that s is one of its traces with associated stability value α, $a \in \Sigma$ and $t \in [end(s), \alpha]$. Let us consider what the version of P would look like which had the additional (and nondeterministic) possibility of communicating the initial events of a process Q at time t, and then continuing to behave like Q. For various reasons it appears to be sufficient to consider only cases where no events have happened already in s at time t, namely when $s = \langle\rangle$ or $t > end(s)$. The various sorts of transient which might co-incide with events at the end of s either cannot arise at all because of the axioms, become duplicated by stability so that they are not transients at all, or can be dealt with by including the events of s with which they co-incide as transients as well (essentially by absorbing part of P into Q). So let Q be any element of TM_{FS} which can communicate at time 0. We can construct the element of TM_{FS} which behaves as indicated above:

$$\underline{SUP}(P \cup \{(s'.w + t' + t, \alpha'' + t' + t, (\aleph' \upharpoonright t + t') \cup (\aleph'' + t' + t)) \mid$$
$$(s', \aleph') \in Fail(P) \wedge s \xLongrightarrow{t'} s' \wedge (w, \alpha'', \aleph'') \in Q \wedge begin(w) = 0\})$$

We can denote this combination by $P \xrightarrow{s,t} Q$.

4.4 Instant enabling

In our definition of quasi-determinism we only claimed to have dealt with one aspect of the difficulties arising from axiom 3. The concept of one event instantly enabling another, so that a process becomes unable to refuse one event *because* it has performed another *at the same time*, is another source of problems relating to the interplay of that axiom with the others. At first sight it is difficult to see how one might realise such a situation, especially if we assume that all events take non-zero time to complete. It is interesting to note that axioms 2 and 3 together state that if two events are possible at one time then either may appear without the other – meaning that any absolute causal dependance between two simultaneous events is impossible. But in fact it turns out that we can get close enough to this instant enabling to have problems with our definition of quasi-determinism.

Consider the process

$$P = ((a \rightarrow STOP \,|||\, b \rightarrow STOP) \Box SKIP); STOP$$

Here, the occurrence of either a or b at time 0 instantly enables the other, in the sense that the process cannot then refuse the other event – even though the original process could refuse both events at time 0 (and all later times) on the empty trace. Though the a or b which appear here are transients (of the first type discussed earlier) this is not the case if we offer the choice between this way of offering a and another:

$$P \Box (a \rightarrow c \rightarrow STOP) \Box \bot$$

Here, things become rather difficult to disentangle. It gets worse if we replace P by the process Q which works in essentially the same way except that it cannot perform an a after time 0:

$$Q = ((((a \rightarrow STOP) \Box SKIP); STOP) \,|||\, b \rightarrow STOP) \Box SKIP); STOP$$

The process

$$R = Q \Box (a \rightarrow c \rightarrow STOP) \Box \bot$$

cannot refuse a on its first step but may, when it performs $(0, a)$, instantly lose the ability to refuse b[4]. If, on the other hand, it performs $(0, b)$ then it can and must instantly begin refusing a. Thus the trace $\langle (0, a), (0, b) \rangle$ is very much allowed by our definition of quasi-determinacy, while the equivalent trace $\langle (0, b), (0, a) \rangle$ is not. We probably would not want to consider R quasi-deterministic, since it has a definite choice of what to do at time 0. Consider, however, the process which behaves like R except that when $(0, a)$ occurs it must pick the Q behaviour rather than the one with the following c. This is an element of TM_{FS} (though seemingly not one expressible in Timed CSP under its standard semantics) which would have no quasi-deterministic implementations under the current definition. The most troublesome trace any implementation must have is $\langle (0, b) \rangle$, since it is both refuseable and carries with it no explanation of why it is there (i.e., the forceable event $(0, a)$).

---

[4]The purpose of the c in the definition of R is to ensure that we cannot ignore that it might lose the ability to refuse b – since along with this it also loses the ability to perform c later.

Rather than attempt to get around this technical difficulty, we choose to simply note it and necessarily restrict the set of processes which can expect to be determined by their implementations. Define a process to be *free of instant enabling* if, whenever $t' > t$ and $(s.\langle (t,a) \rangle, \aleph)$ is t'−complete, then there is $\epsilon > 0$ and $\aleph' \subseteq \aleph$ such that $(s, \aleph')$ is $(t + \epsilon)$−complete. This simply means that any events which might become enabled (i.e., unrefuseable in a complete behaviour) instantly after a could have become enabled at that moment event if a had not occurred. Thus there is no causal relationship between the occurrence of a and the enabling of other events. Clearly the various examples in the discussion above fail to have this property.

It is interesting to note that, while 'instant enabling' seemingly describes the behaviour of the examples discussed above on an abstract level – the communication of a at time 0 instantly enables b – in fact the CSP defined examples worked by a preventing an internal action that would have stopped the b from being enabled. Although, on the surface, this might seem a very fine distinction it is in fact significant when we come to consider stability. For in the mechanism which we described second there is the implication that, when the enabling a occurred, the process had not already become stable. There is no such implication with the simple idea of instant enabling – as might for example appear in the prefixing operation $a \rightarrow P$, were it definable for actions a that take no time and P which can communicate at time 0.

In fact, our axioms prohibit instant enabling after stability as is shown by the following argument. Suppose $(s.\langle (t,a) \rangle, \aleph)$ is t'−complete, where $t' > t$, that $(s, \alpha, \aleph {\upharpoonright} t) \in P$ for $\alpha < t$ but that there is no $\aleph' \subseteq \aleph$ and $\epsilon > 0$ with $(s, \aleph')$ $(t+\epsilon)$−complete. If $(t,b) \notin \aleph$ then $(s.\langle (t,a), (t,b) \rangle, \aleph {\upharpoonright} t) \in Fail(P)$ and hence, by axioms 2 and 3, $(s.\langle (t,b) \rangle, \aleph {\upharpoonright} t) \in Fail(P)$. Axiom 7 then tells us that $(t', b) \notin \aleph$ for any $\alpha \le t' < t$. In other words

$$\{ b \mid (t,b) \in \aleph \} \supseteq \Sigma(\aleph {\upharpoonright} [\alpha, t))$$

By the structure of $RSET$ we then know that there is $\epsilon > 0$ such that

$$\aleph {\upharpoonright} [t, t + \epsilon) \supseteq [t, t + \epsilon) \times (\Sigma(\aleph {\upharpoonright} [\alpha, t)))$$

But exactly the same arguments and constructions used in the proof of Lemma 1 show that, for any $t' \ge t$ the triple $(s, \alpha, \aleph {\upharpoonright} t \cup ([t, t') \times \Sigma(\aleph {\upharpoonright} [\aleph, t))))$ is a t'−complete behaviour of P. This is exactly what we require to establish our claim.

4.5 Towards a completeness theorem

So far in this section we have presented a taxonomy of nondeterminism in our model, the class of quasi-deterministic processes which are perhaps those most analogous to the pre-deterministic ones of untimed CSP, an operator for introducing transient events into them, and discussed the phenomenon of instant enabling. In this final subsection we bring all of these things together by conjecturing a completeness theorem of the type discussed earlier, and by providing some evidence for this conjecture.

Define the class of *almost deterministic* processes to be the smallest one which contains the quasi-deterministic ones and which, whenever P is quasi-deterministic, Q is almost deterministic with communications at time 0, $(s, \alpha) \in Stab(P)$ and $t \in [end(s), \alpha]$ $(t =$

$end(s) \Rightarrow s = \langle \rangle)$, $P \xrightarrow{s,t} Q$ is almost deterministic. In other words an almost deterministic process is quasi-deterministic except for a finite number of occasions where transients are possible, which are arranged in a single unbranching sequence. We will take these as the class of processes which will form the basis of our completeness conjecture.[5]

We define an *implementation* of $P \in TM_{FS}$ to be any almost deterministic Q such that $P \sqsubseteq Q$. Let $imp(P)$ be the set of all its implementations.

Recall that general nondeterministic choice was defined

$$\sqcap S = \underline{SUP}(\bigcup S)$$

We required that there is a fixed function $n^*(t)$ such that, for each $P \in S$, the number of events up to t in P is bounded by $n^*(t)$.

Notice that the functions $n(t)$ which exist for P by axiom 4 also work for every $Q \in imp(P)$, so that providing $imp(P)$ is nonempty, the nondeterministic composition $\sqcap(imp(P))$ is well-defined. We can thus state our conjecture:

Conjecture If $P \in TM_{FS}$ is free of instant enabling, then $imp(P)$ is nonempty and $\sqcap(imp(P)) = P$. □

If S is a set of processes Q such that $P \sqsubseteq Q$ (for fixed P), then it is easy to show that $P \sqsubseteq \sqcap S$. In order to prove the conjectured result it would thus be sufficient to find, for each $(s, \alpha, \aleph) \in P$ and $t < \alpha$, an element Q of $imp(P)$ which contains $(s, \beta, \aleph)$ for some $\beta > t$.

We expect the proof of this conjecture to consist of a construction of these Q's. Such a construction will necessarily be detailed and require careful checking of the axioms. In its essence we expect it to revolve around manipulations of complete infinite behaviours of the types constructed in Lemma 1. Starting with a complete infinite extension of the target behaviour, we would pad this out to a complete description of what the implementation Q could do after every timed trace and, where this is necessary detail (after at-stability transients), timed refusal. The only events of Q which could be transients would be ones of the target behaviour.

The following result will probably be important in this construction since it says that, if in the complete infinite behaviour $(s.w, \aleph^*)$ the first events of w apparently occurred at or before stability (because $(s, \alpha, \aleph^* \restriction (begin(w))) \in P$ where $begin(w) \le \alpha$), then we can extend the initial segment of the behaviour to infinity in such a way that we can still believe this. The importance of this is that events which happen after stability need to be treated differently from ones which happen at or before it.

Lemma 3 Suppose that $(s, \alpha, \aleph) \in P$ is t−complete where $end(s) \le t \le \alpha$. Then it has a complete infinite extension $(s, \beta, \aleph^*)$ with $t \le \beta \le \alpha$ and $\aleph^* \restriction t = \aleph \restriction t$.

Proof First suppose $t < \alpha$. Then, by Lemma 1, there is a complete infinite extension $(s, \alpha', \aleph')$ of $(s, \aleph)$ such that $t < \alpha'$. Let $\aleph^* = \aleph \restriction [0, t) \cup \aleph' \restriction [t, \infty)$. The same arguments which were applied in the proof of Lemma 1 show that there is β such that $(s, \beta, \aleph^*)$ is a complete infinite behaviour of P. Axiom 9 (applied to the finite restrictions of $\aleph'$ and $\aleph^*$) shows that $\alpha' \le \beta \le \alpha$, as required.

---

[5] If desired, this class could probably be tightened somewhat. For example one could attempt to restrict the class of transients introduced to the two specific classes identified earlier.

More care is required when $t = \alpha$. We know that there is a sequence of complete infinite extensions $(s, \alpha_n, \aleph_n)$ of $(s, \aleph)$ such that α_n is an increasing sequence converging on α from below. If any of them equal α then the same construction used in the last paragraph applies, so we could assume that all α_n are strictly less than α. We can also assume, thanks to the second part of Lemma 1, that the $\aleph_n$ are all constant after the point of stability. If we set $\aleph'_n = \aleph \upharpoonright \alpha \cup \aleph_n \upharpoonright [\alpha, \infty)$, it is easy to see that there is some $\beta_n \in [\alpha_n, \alpha]$ such that $(s, \beta_n, \aleph'_n)$ is a complete infinite behaviour. Now let

$$\aleph^* = \bigcap \{\aleph'_n \mid n \in N\}.$$

Clearly $\aleph^* \upharpoonright \alpha = \aleph \upharpoonright \alpha$, $\aleph \subseteq \aleph^*$ and $\aleph^*$ is constant after α. (The fact that all the $\aleph'_n$, and hence, $\aleph^*$, are constant after α, is necessary to ensure that $\aleph^*$ has the finite variability property – $\aleph^* \upharpoonright t \in RSET$ – we require of complete infinite behaviours.) If we can show that $(s, \aleph^*)$ is a complete infinite behaviour then, since $\aleph \subseteq \aleph^* \subseteq \aleph_n$, its associated stability value must be α.

Completeness up to time α is a straightforward consequence of the α-completeness of $(s, \aleph)$. Beyond α it follows because, if $t' \geq \alpha$ and $(t', a) \notin \aleph^*$, there is some n with $(t', a) \notin \aleph'_n$. We then know that $(s.\langle(t', a)\rangle, \aleph'_n \upharpoonright t')$ belongs to $Fail(P)$ by completeness of $(s, \aleph'_n)$, and hence so does $(s.\langle(t', a)\rangle, \aleph^* \upharpoonright t')$ by axiom 9.

We have thus shown that $(s, \alpha, \aleph^*)$ is a complete infinite behaviour of P, which completes the proof. $\square$

Assuming we can indeed establish the conjecture, it might be worthwhile broadening the definition of quasi-deterministic processes to encompass instant enabling. It is possible that one might be able to prove that for any *CSP-definable* process the result stands without assuming the lack of instant enabling assumption. On the other hand one could argue that by this result and the understanding already gained of instant enabling, we would already have gained sufficient insight into nondeterminism in TM_{FS} and confidence in the completeness of the axioms.

5 Conclusions

In this paper we have simultaneously provided a study of the detailed structure of our model TM_{FS} and of the types of nondeterminism which it can model. We provided individual explanations of its various axioms and also showed how these axioms fit together by proving a series of Lemmas and other useful results about the model. Finally, we conjectured a 'completeness' result which would allow us to argue that, at least in some sense, our axioms were definitive.

We hope that the rather detailed work in this paper will provide useful insight, and a source of potential hard cases, to those engaged in more practical work using Timed CSP.

We conclude by giving a brief survey of the literature of Timed CSP which defines the current state of the subject. As we have already stated, this paper is complementary to another one [RR90] which describes our philosophy and the rationale behind the congruence used in more detail, as well as defining just what it means to be a semantics for Timed CSP over TM_{FS}. The overall hierarchy of models is described in [Re88] and

[Re90]. Proof systems derived from the semantic models and operators are described in [S90] and [DS90]. In [J90] it has been shown how a temporal logic compatible with timed CSP can be developed. The extremely useful technique of *timewise refinement* for lifting process developments and specifications from the untimed failures/divergence model to the timed models is described in [S90]. Significant case-studies in the application of Timed CSP can be found in [Re88], [J89], [S90], [Se90]and [St90].

Acknowledgements

We are very grateful to all those working in Oxford on Timed CSP for their help and enthusiasm. In particular, Steve Schneider has been of great assistance while we have been writing this paper.

6 References

[Bl90] S.R. Blamey, *The soundness and completeness of axioms for CSP processes*, Topology, Category Theory and Computer Science, (Oxford University Press, 1990), G.M. Reed, A.W. Roscoe, R.F. Wachter, editors.

[BG87] A. Boucher and R. Gerth, *A timed failures model for extended communicating sequential processes*, ICALP'87,Springer LNCS

[BHR84] S.D. Brookes, C.A.R. Hoare and A.W. Roscoe, *A theory of communicating sequential processes*, JACM 31 (1894), 560-599.

[BR85] S.D. Brookes and A.W. Roscoe, *An improved failures model for communicating processes*, Proceedings of the Pittsburgh Seminar on Concurrency, Springer LNCS 197 (1985).

[DS90] J.W. Davies and S.A. Schneider, *Factorising proofs in Timed CSP*, Proceedings of the Fifth Workshop on the Mathematical Foundations of Programming Language Semantics (April, 1989), LNCS 442 (1990), 129-159.

[H85] C.A.R. Hoare, *Communicating Sequential Processes*, Prentice-Hall International, 1985.

[J89] D.M. Jackson, *The sepcification of aircraft engine control software using Timed CSP*, Oxford University M.Sc. differtation, 1989.

[J90] D.M. Jackson, *Specifying Timed Communicating Sequential Processes using temporal logic*, Technical Report PRG-90-5, Oxford university Computing Laboratory 1990.

[Re88] G.M. Reed, *A uniform mathematical theory for real-time distributed computing*, Oxford University D.Phil thesis 1988.

[Re90] G.M. Reed, *A hierarchy of models for real-time distributed computing*, Proceedings of the Fifth Workshop on the Mathematical Foundations of Programming Language Semantics (April,1989), LNCS 442 (1990), 80-128.

[RR86] G.M. Reed and A.W. Roscoe, *A timed model for communicating sequential processes*, Proceedings of ICALP'86, Springer LNCS 226 (1986), 314-323; Theoretical Computer Science 58, 249-261.

[RR87] G.M. Reed and A.W. Roscoe, *Metric spaces as models for real-time concurrency*, Proceedings of the Third Workshop on the Mathematical Foundations of Programming Language Semantics (April, 1987), LNCS 298 (1988), 331-343.

[RR90] G.M. Reed and A.W. Roscoe, *The Timed Failures-Stability Model for CSP*, submitted for publication.

[Ro88] A.W. Roscoe, *Unbounded nondeterminism in CSP*, in 'Two papers on CSP', Technical monograph PRG-67, Oxford University Computing Laboratory 1988.

[S90] S.A. Schneider, *Correctness and communication in real-time systems*, Oxford University D.Phil. thesis 1990. Published as technical monograph PRG-88.

[Sc90] B. Scattergood, *An application of Timed CSP to robot control software*, Oxford University MSc dissertation 1990.

[St90] R. Stamper, *The specification of AGV control software using Timed CSP*, Oxford University MSc dissertation 1990.

[Z86] A.E. Zwarico, *A formal model of real-time computing*, University of Pennsylvania technical report (1986)

Using The Temporal Logic RDL for Design Specifications

Dov Gabbay, Ian Hodkinson and Anthony Hunter
Department of Computing, Imperial College, London

Abstract

In summary, RDL is an intuitionistic temporal logic for the specification of requirements and design of time-dependent systems. Coverage of RDL includes a backward chaining theorem prover for constructing a design from a requirement, and an execution mechanism for constructing a model of the design such that the model can be checked to satisfy the requirement at each point. A brief overview of executable temporal logic is presented together with a discussion of the advantages of an intuitionistic version. RDL is being developed as a formalism that would be appropriate for AI-based design support in engineering.

Introduction

Logic-based specification languages offer the opportunity to minimize errors in the whole system development process. Adopting logic-based formalisms to specify requirements allows the checking of the requirements and opens the oppportunity to prove that an appropriate representation of the design satisfies the requirements.

For a system specification, the requirement specifies <u>what</u> a system must do and the design specifies <u>how</u> the system works. Once a specification of requirements has been adopted, the design of the system is developed by assuming certain inputs, and assuming the input/output relations of certain pieces of basic design, forming a database of pieces of design, and then deriving (and thereby proving) a design that meets the properties specified in the requirements. Pieces of basic design correspond to components that can be incorporated in the global design and have certain well established properties such as an off-the-shelf semi-conductor or other electronic device, a hardware platform, a software package or utility, or an algorithm. If a design D has the properties specified by a requirement R, then D meets R.

However, it may not be sufficient to consider a system specification in isolation. It may be necessary to consider the system specification in an environment. In order to consider such an interaction, we require in addition to a system specification, an environmental specification. If both specifications use the same language, properties of the system specification within the environment are proved from the conjunction of the system and environmental specifications. Environmental specifications can include:

- agreements on system use
- definitions
- scientific theories
- non-deterministic assignment of environmental propositions

Temporal logics have been considered for issues of specification of time-dependent systems since Pneuli (1977). From this, a number of directions have been taken including executable temporal logic (Gabbay 1989). Attempts at developing languages for specification of requirements and designs include L_{4344} (Wupper 1989) which incorporates a constructive methodology for developing designs from requirements. RDL is an intutionistic executable temporal logic that is an attempt at integrating aspects of L_{4344} within an executable temporal logic framework. Coverage of RDL presented here includes a backward chaining theorem prover for developing a design from a requirement, and an execution mechanism for constructing a model of the design such that the model can be checked to satisfy the requirement at each point. A brief overview of executable temporal logic is presented together with a discussion of the advantages of an intuitionistic version. A shorter report on this appeared in (Gabbay *et al* 1990).

Requirement Specifications and Design Specifications

If a temporal logic specification is consistent, it is satisfiable by a class of models. So for example, for the temporal logic specification $\alpha \rightarrow \beta$, the class of models that can satisfy the specification can be defined by stating that for each $t \in \mathbb{N}$, in each model M on the linear structure $(\mathbb{N}, <)$, if $M \models \alpha$ at t, then $M \models \beta$ at t.

Given a set of propositions Π, we can generate a model M, of the form $(\mathbb{N}, <, h)$ by providing an assignment $h(t, \alpha)$ for each $\alpha \in \Pi$ at each $t \in \mathbb{N}$. If Π denotes a set of observations, or behaviours, we may wish to make of a system S^*, then we can consider a model M as a sequence of behaviours of S^*. In other words, at each t, $t \in \mathbb{N}$, a set of propositions Π_t are true in a model, where $\Pi_t \subseteq \Pi$, and that the model is a sequence of these sets of propositions $\Pi_0, \Pi_1, \Pi_2, \Pi_3, \ldots$

We define (1) a model M as acceptable for a specification S^* iff S^* is consistent in M; and (2) a class of models to be acceptable for a specification S^* iff each model in the class is acceptable for a specification S^*. A specification is therefore a restriction on the class of models that is acceptable for a specification.

We regard a requirement as a temporal logic specification. We can also consider a design to be a specification, where both the requirement and design specifications use the same language. We say that a design specification 'meets' a requirement if the requirement specification is a logical consequence of the design specification.

If a design meets a requirement specification then we consider a design to be a more detailed specification than a requirement. By this we mean that if a requirement defines a class of acceptable models R_m, and a design that defines a class of acceptable models D_m, then $D_m \subseteq R_m$. Therefore, a design constitutes a restriction on the set of behaviours that a system can be observed to be involved in.

For a design to meet a requirement, a proof of the requirement being a logical consequence of the design allows the design specification to comprise of more than one wff of the language. The individual wff in a design specification are termed 'pieces' of design. In this way, we view a design as being composed of pieces of design. For example, given a requirement specification $\alpha \wedge \beta$, and a set of pieces of design $\{\alpha, \beta\}$, we can compose a design that meets the requirement.

Executable Temporal Logic

The traditional view on temporal logic is of declarative statements about the world, or about possible worlds, over time. These relate the truth of propositions in the past, in the present and in the future, and so have been considered for issues of specification of time-dependent systems. An alternative view on temporal logic is to consider the logic in terms of a declarative past, and an imperative present and future, based on the intuition that a statement about the future can be an imperative, initiating steps of action to ensure it becoming true. A temporal logic specification can thus be used by translating it into an executable form:

[f1]   ANTECEDENT ABOUT THE PAST   =>

CONSEQUENT ABOUT THE PRESENT AND FUTURE

For example, if we take time as points on the line of natural numbers, then atomic propositions are true or false at points on that line. Execution is undertaken at each point in succession. Executable temporal logic statements can be executed at a point X on that line by reviewing which atomic propositions were true in the past, i.e points less than X, and then taking appropriate action to satisfy the specification. If the appropriate action is to undertake some action in the present then that action must be undertaken now, to ensure satisfaction of the specification. If the appropriate action is to undertake some action in the future then the instruction must be passed on to the points in the future. Executable temporal logic that have been developed include USF (Gabbay 1989) and MetateM (Barringer *et al* 1990a). All specifications of USF and MetateM are reducible to a finite conjunction of [f1]'s.

If we write specifications of the form [f2] and if the antecedent refers to the past, and the consequent refers to the present and future, then we can execute such specifications so as to construct a model of the specification.

[f2] $\wedge_i \alpha_i \rightarrow \vee_j \beta_j$

Suppose then that we have a specification S in the form of a finite conjunction of clauses [f2] such that each α_i and β_j is either atomic or negated atomic. The executing agent tries to execute S in such a way as to build a model of S. It must make S true dynamically at each point in time. So at any time point, it will consider each clause [f2]. If $\wedge_i \alpha_i$ is true then it must make the disjunction $\vee_j \beta_j$ true. It can do this by making any one of the disjuncts β_j true. The choosing of which β_j to make true is a subtle (though typically decidable) problem, and the agent will take into account several factors, such as its commitment to make the other clauses true, possible future deadlocks, and the environment at the time. There may be more than one valid choice at each time point, and the actual choice may vary over time.

As an example of an executing agent, if the agent is in charge of two modules that form a system that takes no environmental input, then all the executing agent has to do is to make both modules operate such that neither module fails to meet its own specification:

Module 1: α

Module 2: $\neg\alpha \vee \beta$

Given these two specifications, there is only one way to deal with the specification, and that is to make the formula α true in the model of the system. Since, module 2 has a specification of either $\neg\alpha$ or β true in the resulting module of the system, the executing agent can satisfy the specification of module 2 by making the formula β true in the model of the system.

Some disjuncts β_j may be controlled by the environment and so are outside the agent's control. Indeed, the agent may have an impossible task: some specifications cannot be realised, or may not be realisable if the environment misbehaves. Whether this is so for a given specification is again a difficult though often decidable problem (Abadi 1989)

To say that a particular β_j is under the agent's control is to say that the agent has available a piece of (basic) design that controls β_j, making it true at will. The agent is therefore a device for combining pieces of basic design in a consistent way so that the specification is satisfied.

We can also view the executing agent as employing higher-level (non-basic) pieces of designs. Seen from the outside it may be hard to predict the executing agent's choice of disjunct. So in a sense the agent can be viewed as a series of linked modules or 'black-boxes': one for each clause. From the outside each module's behaviour is non-deterministic. We cannot generally tell which β_j it will make true. We only know that - assuming a successful execution - it will make true the 'specification' [f2] at each time point.

So each module can be regarded as a higher-level piece of design, having as a specification a clause of the form [f2]. If there is only one clause [f2], the agent's task is simple: it just uses the corresponding module at each point in time.

We see that designs can be viewed at many levels of detail. Passing from low-level designs used by a sophisticated agent, to high-level designs used by a simple agent, corresponds to passing from an interpreted to a compiled program. Furthermore, we can consider the difference between the levels as levels of abstraction, as in top-down design.

Intuitionistic Temporal Logic

Why is an intuitionistic version of executable temporal logic of interest in the specification of time-dependent systems? If we adopt an intuitionistic logic for specifications the following classical theorem does not hold:

[f3] $\quad \wedge_i \alpha_i \rightarrow \vee_j \beta_j \qquad \vdash_{classical} \neg (\wedge_i \alpha_i) \vee (\vee_j \beta_j)$

Hence if a specification is stated in the form [f2], i.e. as on the l.h.s. of the turnstile, then the specification can not be changed by the executing agent to that of the form [f4], i.e. as on the r.h.s. of the turnstile.

[f4] $\quad \neg (\wedge_i \alpha_i) \vee (\vee_j \beta_j)$

What ramifications does this have? If each module of the form [f2] is such that the antecedent refers only to the past about itself, other modules and the environment, and the consequent only refers to what the module can control, then in the intuitionistic case it is only necessary to make the consequent true when the antecedent is true. Since we have considered the formula $\wedge_i \alpha_i$ to be beyond the control of the executing agent, the executing agent can only influence the truth-value of the formula $\vee_j \beta_j$. Moreover the module could just make $\vee_j \beta_j$ true at all points irrespective of the truth-value of $\wedge_i \alpha_i$. Intuitionistic logic does not stop the executing agent from just making $\vee_j \beta_j$ true at all points. However, in the classical case it is possible to re-write the specification to the form [f4], whereas the spirit of [f2] is a construction which takes us from $\wedge_i \alpha_i$ to $\vee_j \beta_j$ and hence providing an execution that will be 'minimal'.

Outline of RDL as a Language for Requirements and Design

The language of RDL is propositional with finite atoms and the usual connectives $\wedge$, $\vee$, $\rightarrow$, $\perp$, $\neg$ and and the temporal operators, $\square$ and O^n, the always and the next state operator, respectively, where n is a non-negative integer and corresponds to the power. In this version of RDL presented here, the language is restricted to a clausal form.

We define the components of a requirement, R, and a design, D, to be sets of formulae of the language RDL. From these sets we intuitionistically prove that D meets R. So given a requirement specification and a set of pieces of design, the design is constructed. The design is the specification of the components together with the proof of D meeting R. The record of the proof is via the use of indices that are computed as the proof is built. Below is the definition of the theorem prover used to prove the design meets the requirements.

Once a design has been developed, the design specification can be executed using an executable intuitionistic temporal logic model generator that can use the design and environment specifications in order to construct an intuitionistic model of the system within the environment.

The language for RDL

In this version of RDL, the language will be restricted to a clausal form.

[s1] Π is a set of atomic propositions

[s2] α is a (present) literal if $\alpha \in \Pi$
       $O^n\alpha$ is a (future) literal if $\alpha \in \Pi$ and $n \in \mathbb{N}$ and $n > 0$
       $P^n\alpha$ is a (past) literal if $\alpha \in \Pi$ and $n \in \mathbb{N}$ and $n > 0$
       $\perp \in \Pi$

[s3]   If α is a (positive) literal, then $\neg\alpha$ is a (negative) literal

[s4]   If α is a literal then α is a wff
[s5] $\wedge_i \alpha_i$ is a wff if each α_i is a wff

[s6] $\alpha \rightarrow \beta$ is a wff
         if α is a conjunction of one or more literals
         and β is a literal

[s7]   If α is a wff then $\Box\alpha$ is an ('always') wff

Using this syntax we can represent requirements, and pieces of design, in the same language. Furthermore, using the same language allows us to use theorem proving techniques directly.

For example, we may have a requirement for a system that given an input α, always provides output δ after a delay constant d:

$$\Box(\alpha \rightarrow O^d\delta)$$

Furthermore, we may have the following pieces of design: The first if given input α, always provides output β immediately: and the second if given input β, always provides output δ after a delay constant d:

$$\Box(\alpha \rightarrow \beta)$$
$$\Box(\beta \rightarrow O^d\delta)$$

We present, below, how such a requirement can be met by these pieces of design.

As stated earlier, the underlying logic of RDL is intuitionistic logic which does not use the classical notion of truth and falsity. We will not present a definition of the semantics in this paper, but instead show the meaning of RDL via first-order intuitionistic logic. However, in order to support an understanding of RDL directly, we present the following definitions, [m1] - [m5], for reading the logical symbols in RDL. We assume the flow of time to be the natural numbers:

[m1]　We have grounds for asserting $\alpha \wedge \beta$ at time n, where $n \in \mathbb{N}$, just in case we have grounds for asserting α at n, and we have grounds for asserting β at n

[m2]　We have grounds for asserting $\alpha \rightarrow \beta$ at time n, where $n \in \mathbb{N}$, just in case we have a general procedure by which grounds for asserting α at n, can be transformed into grounds for asserting β at n

[m3]　We have grounds for asserting $\neg\alpha$ at time n, where $n \in \mathbb{N}$, just in case we have grounds for asserting $\alpha \rightarrow \perp$ at time n

[m4]　We have grounds for asserting $O^m\alpha$ at time n, where $n \in \mathbb{N}$, just in case we have grounds for asserting α at time $n + m$

[m5]　We have grounds for asserting $P^m\alpha$ at time n, where $n \in \mathbb{N}$, just in case we have grounds for asserting α at time $n - m$, and $n \geqslant m$.

[m6]　We have grounds for asserting $\Box\alpha$ at time n, where $n \in \mathbb{N}$, just in case we have grounds for asserting α for all $m \in \mathbb{N}$

A definition of a semantics, and related issues, for this intuitionistic temporal logic is the subject of a subsequent paper.

RDL Theorem Prover

We shall denote the computation of a design from a requirement by $\Delta?\Gamma$, where Δ is the set of designs and Γ is the conjunction of requirements. The set Δ can be regarded as a database and the formula Γ as a goal. From the set Δ, we can form $\Delta_\Box$, where $\Delta_\Box = \{\Box\alpha|\ \Box\alpha \in \Delta\}$ which is the set of 'always' formulae in Δ. The computation proceeds by the following rules until the goal ends in success, or until no more computation rules apply:

[c1]　$\Delta ? \alpha \wedge \beta$ succeeds if $\Delta ? \alpha$ succeeds and $\Delta ? \beta$ succeeds

[c2]　$\Delta ? \neg\alpha$ succeeds if $\Delta ? \alpha \rightarrow \perp$ succeeds

[c3]　$\Delta ? \alpha \rightarrow \beta$ succeeds if $\Delta \cup \{\alpha\} ? \beta$ succeeds

[c4]　$\Delta ? \Box\alpha$ succeeds if $\Delta_\Box ? \alpha$ succeeds

[c5]　$\Delta ? \alpha$ succeeds if $\alpha \in \Delta$ or $\Box\alpha \in \Delta$

[c6]　$\Delta ? \alpha$ succeeds if there is a wff in Δ of the form $\Box(\beta \rightarrow \gamma)$
　　　　　and UNIFY($\alpha, \gamma, \beta, \delta$) and $\Delta ? \delta$ succeeds

where the predicate UNIFY is defined in definition [u6] below

[c7] Δ ? α succeeds if there is a wff in Δ of the form $\beta \to \alpha$ and Δ ? β succeeds

[c8]   If $\beta \wedge \gamma \in \Delta$, then Δ ? α succeeds if $\Delta \cup \{\beta, \gamma\}$? α succeeds

[c9]   If $\Box(\beta \wedge \gamma) \in \Delta$, then Δ ? α succeeds if $\Delta \cup \{\Box\beta, \Box\gamma\}$? α succeeds

[c10] If $\neg\beta \in \Delta$, then Δ ? α succeeds if $\Delta \cup \{\beta \to \bot\}$? α succeeds

The aim of using the theorem prover as outlined in [c1] - [c10] is to show that the goal (the requirements) logically follow from the database (the design). For this we can assume that for any arbitrary point in time, if the requirements follow from the design, then this holds for every point in time since the same database and the same goal is used for each point in time.

Unification of Temporal Literals

In RDL we have three kinds of temporal literal - past, present and future. There are equivalences that we can define between these types of literal. Firstly we can extend the definition of a wff by using the operator O^n to define the notion of a relative literal:

[u1] $O^n\alpha$ is a relative literal if $\alpha \in \Pi$ and $n \in Z$

[u2]   If α is a present literal, then the relative literal $O^0\alpha$ represents α

[u3]   If $P^n\alpha$ is a past literal, then the relative literal $O^{-n}\alpha$ represents $P^n\alpha$

Secondly we need to consider how we can unify two relative literals for the computation rule [c6] to apply. For example, for a design goal such as $O^n\alpha$, and a piece of design such as $\Box(OP\beta \to O^q\alpha)$, a unification of the goal $O^n\alpha$ with the head of the clause $O^q\alpha$, would require some adjustment of the power p of the new goal $OP\beta$. This is covered in definition [u4].

[u4]   If A is of the form $O^n\alpha$, and the clause is of the form $\Box(\wedge_i OP_i\alpha_i \to O^q\alpha)$, then the head of the clause and the goal can unify, and the antecedent requires adjustment s.t. for each $OP_i\alpha_i$ in the antecedent, an adjusted literal $O^{k_i}\alpha_i$ is formed, where $k_i = (p_i - q + n)$ and the new goal is the conjunction of the adjusted literals, $\wedge_i O^{k_i}\alpha_i$.

In order to mechanize this unification in the theorem prover the following definition [u5] for the predicate UNIFY is given. This predicate is used in the proof rule [c6] above:

[u5]   UNIFY($O^n\alpha$, $O^q\alpha$, $\wedge_i OP_i\alpha_i$, $\wedge_i O^{r_i}\alpha_i$)

$\quad\quad$ IF for each $OP_i\alpha_i$, there is an $O^{r_i}\alpha_i$, where $r_i = (p_i - q + n)$

Effectively UNIFY takes the goal literal, the head of the clause and the antecedent, and returns a substituted antecedent.

Examples of RDL Computations

1. | | | | |
|---|---|---|---|
| $\Box(\alpha \rightarrow \beta)$ | ? | $\Box(\alpha \rightarrow \beta)$ | |
| $\Box(\alpha \rightarrow \beta)$ | ? | $\alpha \rightarrow \beta$ | by [c5] |
| $\Box(\alpha \rightarrow \beta), \alpha$ | ? | β | by [c3] |
| $\Box(\alpha \rightarrow \beta), \alpha$ | ? | α | by [c6] |
| $\Box(\alpha \rightarrow \beta), \alpha$ | ? | success | by [c5] |

2. | | | | |
|---|---|---|---|
| $\Box(\alpha \rightarrow \beta), \Box(\beta \rightarrow \gamma)$ | ? | $\dot{\Box}(\alpha \rightarrow \gamma)$ | |
| $\Box(\alpha \rightarrow \beta), \Box(\beta \rightarrow \gamma),$ | ? | $\alpha \rightarrow \gamma$ | by [c4] |
| $\Box(\alpha \rightarrow \beta), \Box(\beta \rightarrow \gamma), \alpha$ | ? | γ | by [c3] |
| $\Box(\alpha \rightarrow \beta), \Box(\beta \rightarrow \gamma), \alpha$ | ? | β | by [c6] |
| $\Box(\alpha \rightarrow \beta), \Box(\beta \rightarrow \gamma), \alpha$ | ? | α | by [c6] |
| $\Box\alpha \rightarrow \Box\beta, \Box\beta \rightarrow \Box\gamma, \Box\alpha$ | ? | success | by [c5] |

3. | | | | |
|---|---|---|---|
| $\Box(\alpha \rightarrow O^2\alpha)$ | ? | $P\alpha \rightarrow O\alpha$ | |
| $\Box(\alpha \rightarrow O^2\alpha), P\alpha$ | ? | $O\alpha$ | by [c3] |
| $\Box(\alpha \rightarrow O^2\alpha), P\alpha$ | ? | $O^{-1}\alpha$ | by [c6] |
| $\Box(\alpha \rightarrow O^2\alpha), P\alpha$ | ? | $P\alpha$ | by [u3] |
| $\Box(\alpha \rightarrow O^2\alpha), P\alpha$ | ? | success | by [c5] |

FOMIL: First-order Monadic Intuitionistic Logic

In order to analyse the nature of RDL and the associated theorem prover, we will present a fragment of first-order monadic intuitionistic temporal logic (FOMIL) as a comparison. The fragment of FOMIL will be using the connectives $\wedge$, $\rightarrow$, $\neg$, $\forall$, $\exists$, and $\bot$. The non-logical symbols in FOMIL comprise:

[k1] Π^* is a set of unary predicate symbols, where if $\alpha \in \Pi$, then $\alpha^* \in \Pi^*$

[k2]   V is a set of variable symbols ·

[k3]   N is the set of constant symbols

[k4]   {R, S} is the set of function symbols, where S is the successor function and R the predecessor function, and the following conditions apply:

   (1)   Nesting can be abbreviated by a power index i, so that S^i represents the nesting of i S symbols, and similarly for R.

   (2)   No mixed nesting is allowed. In other words RS and SR are not allowed.

[k5]   The set of terms is defined as follows:

if $t \in V$ then t is a term

if $t \in N$ then t is a term

if $t \in \{ S^i(x), R^i(x) : $ if $x \in V \cup N$ and $i \in N \}$ then t is a term

[k6] The set of atoms is defined as follows:

if σ is a term and $\alpha \in \Pi^*$ then $\alpha(\sigma)$ is an atom

Below we define axiom schemas, and associated rules, for intuitionistic logic for the relevant fragment, where $\alpha[\sigma/x]$ is formed by the closed term σ in place of all free occurrences of x in α:

[a1]	$\alpha \rightarrow (\beta \rightarrow \alpha)$
[a2]	$[\alpha \rightarrow (\beta \rightarrow \gamma)] \rightarrow [(\alpha \rightarrow \beta) \rightarrow (\alpha \rightarrow \gamma)]$
[a3]	$\alpha \wedge \beta \rightarrow \alpha$
[a4]	$\alpha \wedge \beta \rightarrow \beta$
[a5]	$\alpha \rightarrow (\beta \rightarrow \alpha \wedge \beta)$
[a6]	$\forall x \alpha \rightarrow \alpha[\sigma/x]$
[a7]	$\alpha[\sigma/x] \rightarrow \exists x \alpha$

[mp]	If α and $\alpha \rightarrow \beta$, then β
[r1]	If $\beta \rightarrow \alpha[\sigma/x]$, where $\sigma \in N$ and σ is not in α or β, then $\beta \rightarrow \forall x \alpha$
[r2]	If $\alpha[\sigma/x] \rightarrow \beta$, where $\sigma \in N$ and σ is not in α or β, then $\exists x \alpha \rightarrow \beta$

We also define the following equivalence:

[n1] $\neg \alpha \equiv \alpha \rightarrow \bot$

Some explanation of FOMIL is required at this stage. For each proposition in RDL, we introduce a corresponding monadic predicate into FOMIL. The set of constants for which we allow quantification in FOMIL is the natural numbers. The function symbols S and R in FOMIL correspond to the temporal operators O and P, respectively, in RDL. The motivation behind this is for each RDL wff, we have an equivalent FOMIL wff as outlined below in [e1] and [e2]. So for example $O^2 \alpha$ at time t, in RDL, can be rewritten to $\alpha(S^2(t))$ in FOMIL, and similarly $\Box \alpha$, at time t, in RDL can be rewritten to $\forall x \alpha(x)$ in FOMIL.

[e1] If α is a formula of RDL then α^* is a formula of FOMIL

Define α^* by induction as follows where $x \in V$:

If α is atomic then $\alpha^* = \alpha(x)$

$(O^n \alpha)^*$	$= \alpha(S^n(x))$
$(P^n \alpha)^*$	$= \alpha(R^n(x))$
$(\alpha \wedge \beta)^*$	$= \alpha^* \wedge \beta^*$
$(\alpha \rightarrow \beta)^*$	$= \alpha^* \rightarrow \beta^*$

$$(\neg\alpha)^* \qquad = \neg(\alpha^*)$$
$$(\square\alpha)^* \qquad = \forall x(\alpha^*)$$

[e2]   Define $\alpha^\wedge = \alpha^*[\emptyset/x]$ where x is free in α^*
$$\forall x\alpha^\wedge = \forall x(\alpha^*)$$

Effectively, we substitute a constant $c \in \mathbb{N}$ for all the variables that are not universally quantified. The constant c is an arbitrary choice, but could be taken to denote 'now'. Here we have used the constant $\emptyset$.

Using the axiom schemas, and the equivalences defined between FOMIL and RDL wff, we can demonstrate properties of RDL in terms of FOMIL.

Comparison of RDL Theorem Prover with FOMIL

The rewrite of an RDL database Δ to a FOMIL database is denoted by $\Delta^\wedge$. Similarly a FOMIL rewrite of an RDL goal Γ, is denoted $\Gamma^\wedge$. The consequence relation for intuitionistic logic is denoted $\vdash$. In FOMIL we can define the following theorems:

Deduction Theorem for FOMIL:

$$\Delta^\wedge \vdash (\alpha \rightarrow \beta) \text{ iff } \Delta^\wedge \cup \{\alpha\} \vdash \beta$$

Proof: follows from [a1], [a2] and [mp]

Conjunction Theorem for FOMIL:

$$\Delta^\wedge \vdash \alpha \wedge \beta \text{ iff } \Delta^\wedge \vdash \alpha \text{ and } \Delta^\wedge \vdash \beta$$

Proof: follows from [a3] - [a5] and [mp]

$\forall$ Distribution Theorem for FOMIL:

$$\Delta^\wedge \vdash \forall x(\alpha \wedge \beta) \text{ iff } \Delta^\wedge \vdash \forall x \alpha \wedge \forall x \beta$$
$$\Delta^\wedge \vdash \forall x \alpha \rightarrow \forall x \beta \text{ if } \Delta^\wedge \vdash \forall x(\alpha \rightarrow \beta)$$

Proof: follows from [a6], [a7] and [r1]

Monotonicity and Reflexivity Theorems

$$\text{If } \Delta \vdash \alpha, \text{ then } \Delta \cup \{\beta\} \vdash \alpha$$
$$\text{If } \alpha \in \Delta, \text{ then } \Delta \vdash \alpha$$

Proof: follow from [a1] and [mp]

Soundness Theorem for RDL:

For any Δ and any Γ, we have $\Delta \vdash \Gamma$ if the computation $\Delta ? \Gamma$, according to rules [c1] to [c9], results in success.

Proof.　　　In order to show that the RDL Theorem Prover is sound we demonstrate that each computation rule [c1] to [c9] is sound with respect to FOMIL. The soundness of [c1] follows from the the conjunction theorem for FOMIL and [c2] follows from the equivalence $\neg\alpha \equiv \alpha \to \bot$ holding in FOMIL. For [c3] if is $A \to B$ then:

$\Delta ? \alpha \to \beta$	if	$\Delta^\wedge$	$\vdash \alpha^\wedge \to \beta^\wedge$	by definition [e1]
	if	$\Delta^\wedge \cup \{\alpha^\wedge\}$	$\vdash \beta^\wedge$	by deduction theorem
	if	$\Delta \cup \{\alpha\}$	$? \beta$	by definition [e1]

For [c4], if Γ is $\Box A$, and we define $\Delta_\Box{}^\wedge = \{\Box A^\wedge | \Box A^\wedge \in \Delta^\wedge\}$, then:

$\Delta ? \Box\alpha$	if	$\Delta^\wedge$	$\vdash \forall x \alpha^\wedge$	by definition [e1]
	if	$\Delta_\Box{}^\wedge$	$\vdash \forall x \alpha^\wedge$	
	if	$\Delta_\Box{}^\wedge$	$\vdash \alpha^\wedge$	by [a6] and [r1]
	if	$\Delta_\Box$	$? \alpha$	by definition [e1]

The soundness of [c5] follows from the reflexivity theorem. For [c6]:

$\Delta ? \alpha$	if	$\Delta^\wedge \quad \vdash \alpha^\wedge$	
	if	$\forall x(\beta \to \gamma)^\wedge \in \Delta$	
		and $\text{UNIFY}^\wedge(\alpha^\wedge, \gamma^\wedge, \beta^\wedge, \delta^\wedge)$	
		and $\Delta^\wedge \vdash \delta^\wedge$	
	if	$\Box(\beta \to \gamma) \in \Delta$	
		and $\text{UNIFY}(\alpha, \gamma, \beta, \delta)$	
		and $\Delta ? \delta$	

where $\text{UNIFY}^\wedge(\ \alpha(S^n(\emptyset)),\ \alpha(S^q(\emptyset)),\ \wedge_i\alpha_i(SP_i(\emptyset)),\ \wedge_i\alpha_i(SP_i{\sim}(\emptyset))\ )$

IF for each $\alpha_i(SP_i(\emptyset))$ there is an $\alpha_i(SP_i{\sim}(\emptyset))$ where $P_i{\sim} = (P_i - q + n)$.

The soundness of [c7] follows from [mp]. For [c8], if $B \wedge C \in \Delta$, then by the reflexivity theorem $\Delta \vdash B \wedge C$, and by the conjunction theorem $\Delta \vdash B$ and $\Delta \vdash C$, and hence by the monotonicity theorem if $\Delta \vdash A$, then $\Delta \cup \{B, C\} \vdash A$. So if $B \wedge C \in \Delta$ and $\Delta \cup \{B, C\} ? A$ succeeds, then $\Delta ? A$ succeeds. For [c9], if Γ is of the form $\Box(A \wedge B)$, then:

$\Delta ? \Box(A \wedge B)$	if	$\Delta^\wedge$	$\vdash \forall x(A \wedge B)^\wedge$	by definition [e1] & [e2]
	if	$\Delta^\wedge$	$\vdash \forall x A^\wedge \wedge \forall x B^\wedge$	by distribution
	if	Δ	$? \Box A \wedge \Box B$	by definition [e1] & [e8]

For [c10], if Γ is of the form $\neg B$, then by [n1], $B \to \bot \in \Delta$.

Issues of Indexing a Proof

As discussed earlier, a design is the set of pieces of design together with a proof of the design meeting the requirements. Maintaining a record of the design is via the use of indices on the formulae in Δ and on the formulae generated in the proof process. Instead of complicating the presentation of the theorem prover given above, an outline of how indices can be computed will be given. As an example of indices generation, we can consider modus ponens: If α and $\alpha \rightarrow \beta$, then β. If we label the wff α with the index a, and the wff $\alpha \rightarrow \beta$ with the index b, then we can generate a new index a‖b for the consequent of the application of modus ponens, where a‖b is the concatenation of the labels of the two assumptions.

We define a function τ which for each wff α, s.t. $\alpha \in \Delta$, provides a unique index i. From this we can form the indexed set $\Delta_\tau = \{ \ i{:}\alpha \mid \alpha \in \Delta \text{ and } \tau(\alpha) = i \ \}$. For each proof rule we need to define a mechanism for indexing any wff generated by the use of that proof rule. As an example, we can take the proof rule [c2]:

[c2] $\Delta ? \alpha \rightarrow \beta$ succeeds iff $\Delta \cup \{\alpha\} ? \beta$ succeeds

In this case we require an index for the proof of $\alpha \rightarrow \beta$. This could be achieved by assigning a "temporary" index to the hypothetical assumption α, say t1, so that if α is used in the proof of β, then this could be removed from the index of the proof of $\alpha \rightarrow \beta$.

The incorporation of indices as a record of the proof allows for the representation of the "connectivity" of the components of the design, and opens the oppportunity for resource analysis, fault diagnosis, cost analysis, and reliability estimation. [It is perhaps worth noting that some locational information can be represented via the notation used to represent the propositions, as considered in Wupper (1989). For example 10_volts_at_input and $\Box(10\_volts\_at\_input \rightarrow O^3 20\_volts\_at\_output)$.]

Executing a Requirement and a Design

Given a set of designs, the design can be executed by an execution mechanism such as that in the MetateM project (Barringer et al, 1990a). By definition, RDL specifications are of an executable form:

$$\wedge_i \ \alpha_i \rightarrow \beta$$

where the antecedent is a conjunction of literals and the consequent is a literal. If assumptions about the input to the design are made, the design can be executed by the interpreter. If the design is consistent with these input assumptions a model of the input and design can be constructed.

Furthermore, if two interpreters are run side-by-side, then the design can be executed on one interpreter and the requirements on the other interpreter. From these interpreters, the models generated can be checked at each point in time in order to confirm that the requirements is met. For each atom made true in the model at each point in time in the requirements model, a corresponding atom should also be found to be true at the same point in time in the design model.

More difficult is the execution of an environmental specification with the design specification. The environment may cause the design to fail. As before, we can run two interpreters side-by-side such that one interpreter runs the specification of the design and the specification of the environment, and the other interpreter runs the specification of the requirements and: the specification of the environment. From these models, the design meets the requirements at each point if for each system atom made true in the model at each point in time in the requirements model, a corresponding system atom should also be found to be true at the same point in time in the design model.

Discussion

Further consideration needs to be given to addressing the more complex issues related to top-down design proceedures for concurrent systems. In particular this includes a comparative analysis of current design languages for such applications. Other related questions include clarification of the nature of developing a design from a bag of pieces of designs.

An appropriate language for prototyping RDL would be N-PROLOG (Gabbay & Reyle 1984), which is a development of PROLOG that supports hypothetical implications in the clauses, (i.e. formulae such as (α -> β) -> δ are allowed). There is an intuitionistic version of N-PROLOG, and furthermore the language is equal to one of its own meta-languages, and hence can be used to implement the heorem prover for RDL.

A theme that is being developed in the approach of executable temporal logics, as manifested by the systems USF and MetateM, is that of "language as meta-language" (Barringer *et al* 1990b). In this theme, meta-level reasoning is concerned with treating programs, or specifications, as data, and hence provides a formal framework with which to develop interpreters, debuggers, and loop checkers for programs or specifications. Applicability of RDL could increase from the implementation of interpretation tools developed in an appropriate meta-language that could support the execution of the requirement specification concurrently with the execution of the design specification.

Further developments of RDL include extending to disjunction in the head of clauses and to more expressive temporal connectives based on 'since' and 'until'. The nature of the intuitionistic temporal semantics for RDL requires further clarification, including issues of the nature of an intuitionistic model over time, and of the nature of an intuitionistic model at a point in time. Related issues include the generation of an intuitionistic model at a point in time: One possibility being explored is an intuitionistic semantic tableau (Fitting 1983) being used to generate a kripke model for each point in time.

Acknowledgements

The authors would like to thank Hanno Wupper and his group at the University of Nijmegen for collaborating in this research. This work is supported by ESPRIT under Basic Research Action project 3096 (SPEC).

References

Abadi M, Lamport L & Wolper P (1989) Realizable and unrealizable specification of reactive systems, in Ausiello G *et al*, Proc 16th Colloquium on Automata, Languages and Programming, LNCS 372, Springer

Barringer H, Fisher M, Gabbay D, Gough G & Owens R (1990a) MetateM: A framework for programming in temporal logic, in de Bakker J *et al*, REX Workshop on Stepwise Refinement of Distributed Systems: Models, Formalisms and Correctness, LNCS 430, Springer

Barringer H, Fisher M, Gabbay D & Hunter A (1990b) Theoretical Aspects of Executing Meta-level Temporal Logic, draft paper, Department of Computing, Imperial College, London

Fitting M, (1983) Proof Methods for Modal and Intuitionistic Logics, Reidel

Gabbay D (1989) The declarative past and imperative future: Executable temporal logic for interactive systems, in Banieqbal B, Barringer H and Pneuli A (eds), Temporal Logic Specification, LNCS 398, p409 - 448, Springer

Gabbay D, Hodkinson I & Hunter A (1990) RDL: An executable temporal logic for the specification and design of real-time systems, Proc IEE Colloquium on Temporal Reasoning

Gabbay D & Reyle U (1984) N-PROLOG: An extension of PROLOG with hypothetical implication, 1, J. Logic Programming, 4, 319 - 355

Pneuli A (1977) The temporal logic of programs, in Proc. of the Eighteenth Symp. on the Foundations of Computer Science, p 46 - 57

Wupper H, Vytopil J, Wieczorek M, & Coesmans P (1989) A real-time systems specification language, Department of Informatics, University of Nijmegen

Logic of Execution: An Outline

Takayasu ITO
Department of Information Engineering
Faculty of Engineering
Tohoku University
Sendai, Japan

Abstract

Logic of Execution is a logical framework of executing sentences, and it is aimed to provide a logical basis of concurrency and parallelism.We use "$A \mapsto B$" to express that the success of execution of A produces the success of execution of B.We assume that an execution of a statement will fall into one of success,failure and pending.We consider a set of executional operators: [;] (sequential execution), [+] (disjunctive execution), [V] (execution by non-deterministic choice), [&] (conjunctive execution), [|] (concurrent execution), [#] (parallel execution), [¬] (negation) and [C] (completion). A deductive system of Logic of Success of Execution is given in a propositional level. On the basis of this Logic of Execution how to execute propositional sentences is discussed,giving a set of executional rules for a sentence composed from the logical connectives. From the standpoint of the traditional logics the logic of execution has the 2-level structures:

    (1) the logical framework of execution for the executional operators, and
    (2) the framework to execute logical sentences ; that is, a set of rules to transform
        a logical sentence into a formula of the logic of execution.

The logic of execution is more expressible than Girard's Linear Logic, since it treats various modes of execution, including [V],[|] and [#]. Some remarks are given in connection with the traditional logics, and some topics for future study are also mentioned.

1 Introduction

Logic of Execution is a logical framework of executing sentences. An execution of a sentence may

    succeed to denote and produce an effect,

or fail to denote. Since we are considering an execution on a computing machine an execution may be

    sequential,
    interleaving,

and parallel with overlapping. An execution of a sentence may neither succeed nor fail; that is, an execution of a sentence may not result in its success nor failure, allowing the case of "pendng" or "undetermined". This kind of modes of execution with three-valued possibility are inherent in Concurrency. We are interested in giving a logical framework of execution of sentences. A logical framework may be considered to consist of structural rules,

logical rules,

and proper rules for functions and relations. Consider an execution of $(A + B)$. It will be understood as follows:

"execute A and execute B , then

return the value of executing A or executing B"

Similarly, the execution of $(\neg A)$ will be understood as follws:

"execute A, then take the negation of executing A"

The value domain is {success , failure , pending} , on which the "or" and "negation" will be defined (as below).

Since we admit the case of "pending" an execution of $(A + \neg A)$ does not necessarily result in success ; that is, the law of excluded middle does not hold in our logical framework of execution. This means that our logic of execution has a taste of intuitionistic logic(see [Remark 8]). From the standpoint of Concurrency and Parallelism each sentence may be regarded as a description of a process and a resource so that the number of their occurrences and orders have some important meanings, as is seen in Petri nets and functional nets. We must be careful to accept the structural rules like Weakening rule,Contraction rule and Exchange rule.

The executional meanings of propositions,logical connectives and functions/relations that appear in a sentence may depend on a nature of an executional mechanism. Our logic of execution is a logical framework to take into consideration of these aspects of execution ,inherent in Concurrency and Parallelism. The logic of execution has the 2-level structures:

(1) the logical framework of executuion for the executional operators,

(2) the framework to execute logical sentences ; that is, a set of rules to transform
a logical sentence into a formula of the logic of execution.

In this paper we explain an outline of Logic of Execution,discussing its structural framework in Section 2, an executional deductive framework in Section 3 and how to execute a logical sentence in Section 4.

[Remark 1]

A very premature idea of a logic of execution was considered in the author's attempt to formalise a notion of "forced execution" in [2] and [3] to discuss recovery from deadlock and starvation in a logical setting. Later he has found that Girard's Linear Logic[1] attempts a similar enterprise to formalize a logic for concurrency from a purely logical standpoint.

Some relations and comparisons between Logic of Execution and Linear Logic are given in Section 4 (see [Remark 7]).

2   Logic of Execution: ⟨A Structural Framework⟩

Given a sentence A we consider its executional meaning,and we attempt to express it by a set of rules in this paper.

An execution of A may become

"success",

"failure",

or "pending".

We read the figure

$$\frac{A}{B} \ \text{<s>}$$

as "the success of execution of A produces the success of execution of B". If there is no confusion we write it as

$$\frac{A}{B} \longrightarrow$$

,abbreviating <s>, and sometimes we will write it as "$A \mapsto B$". In order to write a sequence of executions we may write as follows:

$$\frac{\dfrac{A}{B} \longrightarrow}{C} \longrightarrow$$

Any sentence will be understood from an executional standpoint in this paper, unless otherwise stated.

We donote the success,failure and pending as <s>,<f> and <p>,assuming the following ordering:

$$\text{<s>} \sqsupseteq \text{<p>} \sqsupseteq \text{<f>}$$

We have the following identity rule:

$$\frac{A}{A} \longrightarrow \text{(Id)}$$

In order to discuss the executions of sentences we introduce several typical executional operators:

A [;] B	: sequential execution
A [+] B	: disjunctive execution
A [V] B	: execution by nondeterministic choice of A or B
A [&] B	: conjunctive execution
A [|] B	: concurrent execution
A [#] B	: parallel execution
[¬] A	: execution to return the negation of A
[C] A	: execution to return the completion of A

"A [;] B" means "execute A,then execute B".
"A [+] B" means "execute A and execute B, then return the value $lub[A, B]$".
"A [V] B" means "execute A,or execute B";that is,only one of A or B will be executed.
"A [&] B" means "execute A and execute B, then return the value $glb[A, B]$".
"A [\|] B" means "execute A and B concurrently";this case corresponds to an interleaved execution of A and B.
"A [#] B" means "execute A and B in parallel".
We assume that [+] , [V] , [&] and [\|] are commutative
but [;] and [#] are not commutative.

"[¬] A" means the nagation of the result of executing A;that is,
it returns <f> if A=<s>,
it returns <s> if A=<f>,
and it returns <p> if A=<p>.
"[C] A" means the completion of the result of executing A;that is,
it returns <s> if A=<s> or A=<f>,

and   it returns $\langle f \rangle$ if $A = \langle p \rangle$.

[On Basic Properties of Executional Operators]

We have three values $\langle s \rangle$, $\langle f \rangle$ and $\langle p \rangle$, and eight basic executional operators [;], [+] , [V] , [&] , [|] , [#] , [¬] and [C]. These constants and executional operators are assumed to satisfy the following properties:

$$\langle s \rangle \sqsupseteq \langle p \rangle \qquad \langle p \rangle \sqsupseteq \langle f \rangle$$
$$\langle s \rangle \sqsupseteq A \qquad A \sqsupseteq \langle f \rangle$$
$$A \sqsupseteq A$$
$$A \sqsupseteq B, B \sqsupseteq C \Longrightarrow A \sqsupseteq C$$
$$A \sqsupseteq B, B \sqsupseteq A \Longrightarrow A = B$$
$$A \sqsupseteq A; B$$
$$A \text{ [+] } B \sqsupseteq A \qquad A \text{ [+] } B \sqsupseteq B$$
$$A \text{ [+] } B \sqsupseteq A \text{ [V] } B$$
$$A \sqsupseteq A \text{ [&] } B \qquad B \sqsupseteq A \text{ [&] } B$$
$$A \text{ [V] } B \sqsupseteq A \text{ [&] } B$$
$$A \sqsupseteq B \Longrightarrow A \text{ [*] } C \sqsupseteq B \text{ [*] } C$$
$$A \sqsupseteq B \Longrightarrow C \text{ [*] } A \sqsupseteq C \text{ [*] } C$$

where [*] is one of [;] , [+] or [&]. (Notice that [;], [+] and [&] are monotone , but other operators are not monotone.)

$$A \text{ [;] } (B \text{ [;] } C) = (A \text{ [;] } B) \text{ [;] } C$$
$$\langle s \rangle \text{ [;] } A = A$$
$$A \text{ [;] } \langle s \rangle = A$$
$$\langle f \rangle \text{ [;] } A = \langle f \rangle$$
$$\langle p \rangle \text{ [;] } A = \langle p \rangle$$
$$A \text{ [+] } A = A \qquad\qquad A \text{ [V] } A = A$$
$$A \text{ [+] } B = B \text{ [+] } A \qquad\qquad A \text{ [V] } B = B \text{ [V] } A$$
$$A \text{ [+] } (B \text{ [+] } C) = (A \text{ [+] } B) \text{ [+] } C \quad A \text{ [V] } (B \text{ [V] } C) = (A \text{ [V] } B) \text{ [V] } C$$
$$\langle s \rangle \text{ [+] } A = \langle s \rangle$$
$$\langle f \rangle \text{ [+] } A = A$$
$$A \text{ [&] } A = A$$
$$A \text{ [&] } B = B \text{ [&] } A$$
$$A \text{ [&] } (B \text{ [&] } C) = (A \text{ [&] } B) \text{ [&] } C$$
$$\langle s \rangle \text{ [&] } A = A$$
$$\langle f \rangle \text{ [&] } A = \langle f \rangle$$
$$A \text{ [&] } (B \text{ [+] } C) = (A \text{ [&] } B) \text{ [+] } (A \text{ [&] } C)$$
$$A \text{ [+] } (B \text{ [&] } C) = (A \text{ [+] } B) \text{ [&] } (A \text{ [+] } C)$$
$$\langle s \rangle \text{ [|] } A = A$$
$$A \text{ [|] } B = B \text{ [|] } A$$
$$A \text{ [|] } (B \text{ [|] } C) = (A \text{ [|] } B) \text{ [|] } C$$
$$A \text{ [#] } (B \text{ [#] } C) = (A \text{ [#] } B) \text{ [#] } C$$
$$[\neg](\langle s \rangle) = \langle f \rangle \qquad [\neg](\langle f \rangle) = \langle s \rangle \qquad [\neg](\langle p \rangle) = \langle p \rangle$$
$$[\neg]([\neg] A) = A$$
$$[\neg](A \text{ [+] } B) = [\neg]A \text{ [&] } [\neg]B$$
$$[\neg](A \text{ [&] } B) = [\neg]A \text{ [+] } [\neg]B$$

$$[C]([C]\ A) = <s>$$
$$[C]([¬]\ A) = [C]A$$
$$[C]A\ [+]\ [¬]([C]A) = <s>$$

[On Structural Rules of Logic of Execution]

In Gentzen's Sequent Calculus we have the following Exchange rules:

$$\frac{P,A,B,Q \vdash R}{P,B,A,Q \vdash R}\ \text{(Lex)} \qquad \frac{R \vdash P,A,B,Q}{R \vdash P,B,A,Q}\ \text{(Rex)}$$

We may say that these rules hold within the framework of proof-theoretic executions of sentences. But from the standpoint of Logic of Execution these rules may be understood differently; that is,

1) Commutative Cases

In case of [&] and [|] the execution of P, A, B and Q may be regarded as $(P\ [*]\ A\ [*]\ B\ [*]\ Q)$ where [*] is one of [&] or [|].

Since [*] is commutative we may accept

$$\frac{P[*]A[*]B[*]Q \mapsto R}{P[*]B[*]A[*]Q \mapsto R}$$

as a rule of Logic of Success.

Also we may accept

$$\frac{R \mapsto P[\text{o}]A[\text{o}]B[\text{o}]Q}{R \mapsto P[\text{o}]B[\text{o}]A[\text{o}]Q}$$

where [o] is one of [+] or [V].

[Remark 2]

In Sequent Calculus "$P, A, B, Q \vdash R$" means that R holds when all of P, A, B and Q hold, so that we take "$P, A, B, Q \mapsto R$" to mean that the successful executions of all of P, A, B and Q produce R. Also, "$R \mapsto P, A, B, Q$" will be taken to mean that the successful execution of R produces at least one of the successful executions of P, A, B or Q.

2) Non-Commutative Cases

In case of [;] and [#] the order and position of executions of sentences have important meanings so that we cannot have the rules like "Exchange Rule". That is, we cannot accept

$$\frac{P[x]A[x]B[x]Q \mapsto R}{P[x]B[x]A[x]Q \mapsto R}$$

where [x] is one of [;] or [#].

$(A\ [\#]\ B)$ may be regarded as a list of processes expressed by A and B so that we shall not have Exchange Rule. But in case of $(A\ [;]\ B)$ we may have Exchange Rule if there is no side-effects of executing sentences A and B.

In Sequent Calculus there are two other structural rules: Contraction rules and Weakening rules.

The Contraction rules in Sequent Calculus can be expressed as

$$\frac{P, A, A \vdash Q}{P, A \vdash Q} \text{(Lcon)} \qquad \frac{P \vdash A, A, Q}{P \vdash A, Q} \text{(Rcon)}$$

The sets of events expressed by concurrent and parallel executions may be considered as multi-sets or listed-sets (see [Remark 3]).
Hence the executional rules corresponding to the Contraction rules do not hold in case of [|] and [#].

[Remark 3]

In case of "set" we have {a,b,a,b,a}={a,b},
in case of "multi-set" we have $\ll$ a,b,a,b.a $\gg$=$\ll$ a,a,a,b,b $\gg$,
and in case of "listed-set" we cannot reduce (a,b,a,b,a) anymore.

The Weakeing rules in Sequent Calculus can be expressed as

$$\frac{P \vdash Q}{P, A \vdash Q} \text{(Lwk)} \qquad \frac{P \vdash Q}{P \vdash A, Q} \text{(Rwk)}$$

It is again easy to see that the executional rules corresponding to these rules will not hold in case of [|] and [#].
Another structural rule in Sequent Calculus is the Cut rule:

$$\frac{P_1 \vdash A, Q_1 \qquad P_2, A \vdash Q_2}{P_1, P_2 \vdash Q_1, Q_2} \text{(Cut)}$$

The executional rule corresponding to this Cut rule does not hold in case of the concurrent and parallel executions,but it holds in case of sequential execution without side-effects.
Thus in Logic of Execution most of the structural rules does not hold except the identity rule "$A \mapsto A$".
In case of the concurrent execution([|]) the Exchange rules hold,but the Contraction rules and Weakening rules do not hold in addition to the Cut rule. This case shares some basic properties of concurrency expressible by Girard's Linear Logic(see [Remark 7]). Roughly speaking,the Logic of Execution has the following framework:

1) $A \mapsto B$ to express an execution that the execution of A produces B.

2) three constants <s>,<f> and <p>.

3) a set of executional operators:
   [;], [+], [∨], [&], [|], [#], [¬], [c]

4) the basic properties of the executional operators and a set of rules for the executional operators.

More details of the structural framework of Logic of Execution will become clear in the next section.

3 Logic of Execution: ⟨Logic of Executional Operators⟩

The logic of execution can be given as a set of rules for the success of executions combined by the executional operators.
The deductive executional rules for the executional operators are given as follows:

$$\frac{A}{A} \longrightarrow \qquad \frac{\text{<s>}}{\text{<s>}} \longrightarrow \qquad \frac{[\neg](\text{<f>})}{\text{<s>}} \longrightarrow$$

$$\frac{[\neg]([\neg]\,A)}{A} \longrightarrow \qquad \frac{A}{[\neg]([\neg]\,A)} \longrightarrow \qquad \frac{[C]([C]\,A)}{\text{<s>}} \longrightarrow \qquad \frac{[C]([\neg]\,A)}{([C]\,A)} \longrightarrow$$

$$\frac{\text{<s>}\ [;]\ A}{A} \longrightarrow \qquad \frac{A\ [;]\ B}{A} \longrightarrow \qquad \frac{(A\ [;]\ B)\ [;]\ C}{A\ [;]\ (B\ [;]\ C)} \longrightarrow \qquad \frac{A\ [;]\ (B\ [;]\ C)}{(A\ [;]\ B)\ [;]\ C} \longrightarrow$$

$$\frac{A\ [+]\ A}{A} \longrightarrow \qquad \frac{A\ [+]\ B}{B\ [+]\ A} \longrightarrow \qquad \frac{(A\ [+]\ B)\ [+]\ C}{A\ [+]\ (B\ [+]\ C)} \longrightarrow \qquad \frac{A\ [+]\ (B\ [+]\ C)}{(A\ [+]\ B)\ [+]\ C} \longrightarrow$$

$$\frac{A\ [V]\ A}{A} \longrightarrow \qquad \frac{A\ [V]\ B}{B\ [V]\ A} \longrightarrow \qquad \frac{(A\ [V]\ B)\ [V]\ C}{A\ [V]\ (B\ [V]\ C)} \longrightarrow \qquad \frac{A\ [V]\ (B\ [V]\ C)}{(A\ [V]\ B)\ [V]\ C} \longrightarrow$$

$$\frac{\text{<s>}\ [+]\ A}{\text{<s>}} \longrightarrow \qquad \frac{\text{<f>}\ [+]\ A}{A} \longrightarrow \qquad \frac{A}{A\ [+]\ B} \longrightarrow \qquad \frac{B}{A\ [+]\ B} \longrightarrow$$

$$\frac{A\ [\&]\ B}{A} \longrightarrow \qquad \frac{A\ [\&]\ B}{B} \longrightarrow \qquad \frac{A\ [\&]\ B}{B\ [\&]\ A} \longrightarrow \qquad \frac{A\ [\&]\ B}{A\ [+]\ B} \longrightarrow$$

$$\frac{A\ [\&]\ B}{A\ [V]\ B} \longrightarrow \qquad \frac{\text{<s>}\ [\&]\ A}{A} \longrightarrow \qquad \frac{A}{A\ [\&]\ \text{<s>}} \longrightarrow$$

$$\frac{[\neg](A\ [+]\ B)}{[\neg]A\ [\&]\ [\neg]B} \longrightarrow \qquad \frac{[\neg](A\ [\&]\ B)}{[\neg]A\ [+]\ [\neg]B} \longrightarrow \qquad \frac{[\neg](A\ [V]\ B)}{[\neg]A\ [V]\ [\neg]B} \longrightarrow$$

$$\frac{(A\ [\&]\ B)\ [\&]\ C}{A\ [\&]\ (B\ [\&]\ C)} \longrightarrow \qquad \frac{A\ [\&]\ (B\ [\&]\ C)}{(A\ [\&]\ B)\ [\&]\ C} \longrightarrow$$

$$\frac{A\ [\&]\ (B\ [+]\ C)}{(A\ [\&]\ B)\ [+]\ (A\ [\&]\ C)} \longrightarrow \qquad \frac{(A\ [\&]\ B)\ [+]\ (A\ [\&]\ C)}{A\ [\&]\ (B\ [+]\ C)} \longrightarrow$$

$$\frac{A\ [+]\ (B\ [\&]\ C)}{(A\ [+]\ B)\ [\&]\ (A\ [+]\ C)} \longrightarrow \qquad \frac{(A\ [+]\ B)\ [\&]\ (A\ [+]\ C)}{A\ [+]\ (B\ [\&]\ C)} \longrightarrow$$

$$\frac{A\ [\,|\,]\ B}{B\ [\,|\,]\ A} \longrightarrow \qquad \frac{<s>\ [\,|\,]\ A}{A} \longrightarrow \qquad \frac{A}{A\ [\,|\,]\ <s>} \longrightarrow$$

$$\frac{(A\ [\,|\,]\ B)\ [\,|\,]\ C}{A\ [\,|\,]\ (B\ [\,|\,]\ C)} \longrightarrow \qquad \frac{A\ [\,|\,]\ (B\ [\,|\,]\ C)}{(A\ [\,|\,]\ B)\ [\,|\,]\ C} \longrightarrow$$

$$\frac{(A\ [\#]\ B)\ [\#]\ C}{A\ [\#]\ (B\ [\#]\ C)} \longrightarrow \qquad \frac{A\ [\#]\ (B\ [\#]\ C)}{(A\ [\#]\ B)\ [\#]\ C} \longrightarrow$$

$$\frac{[C]\,(A\ [;]\ B)}{([C]\,A)\ [;]\ ([C]\ B)} \longrightarrow \qquad \frac{[C]\,(A\ [\&]\ B)}{([C]\,A)\ [\&]\ ([C]\ B)} \longrightarrow \qquad \frac{[C]\,(A\ [+]\ B)}{([C]\,A)\ [+]\ ([C]\ B)} \longrightarrow$$

[Remark 4]

(1) The [#]-operator is defined as an associative operator,so that we have

$A\ [\#]\ (B\ [\#]\ C)$

$= (A\ [\#]\ B)\ [\#]\ C$

$= A\ [\#]\ B\ [\#]\ C$

$= [\#]\,(A,\ B,\ C)$ to mean a simultaneous execution of A,B and C.

Instead of a single simultaneous operation [#] we can think of the n-ary simultaneous operation $[\#_n]\,(A_1,\ A_2,...,\ A_n)$.We may assume that the following parallel executions are all different:

$A\ [\#_2]\ (B\ [\#_2]\ C)$

$(A\ [\#_2]\ B)\ [\#_2]\ C$

$[\#_3]\,(A,\ B,\ C)$

Then we will not have the law of associativity for parallel execution expressed by $[\#_n]$.

This n-ary parallelism $[\#_n]$ was introduced in [2].

(2) The [∨]-operator needs some special cares. A [∨] B means that one of A or B will be chosen,then it will be executed. In case of [¬]$(A$ [∨] $B)$ only one of the executions of A or B will be negated so that it gives one of [¬]A or [¬]B. Thus we have

$$\frac{[\neg]\,(A\ [\vee]\ B)}{[\neg]A\ [\vee]\ [\neg]B} \longrightarrow$$

However , in case of $(<s>$ [∨] $A)$

a) it gives $<s>$, when $<s>$ is chosen,

b) it gives A, when A is chosen.

Thus we <u>do not have</u> $(<s>$ [∨] $A)\ \mapsto\ <s>$.

Similar arguments should be taken into consideration for the [∨]-operator.

But there remains an important issue on the nondeterminism introduced by [∨]; that is, we may ask if the associative law for [∨] is a right assumption for the nondeterministic choice.

[Remark 5]

The logical framework considered so far is Logic of Success of Execution;

$$\frac{A}{B}\langle s\rangle$$

should be read as "the success of execution of A produces the success of execution of B" or simply "A produces B with success".

In a similar way we can think of Logic of Failure and Logic of Pending.
Let us denote

$$\frac{A}{B}\langle f\rangle$$

to mean "the failure of execution of A produces the failure of execution of B" or simply "A produces B with failure". Let us denote

$$\frac{A}{B}\langle p\rangle$$

to mean "the pending of execution of A produces the pending of execution of B" or simply "A produces B with pending".

Using these failure-execution rule and pending-execution rule it will be possible to develop some logical frameworks for failure-execution and pending-execution, called as Logic of Failure and Logic of Pending. But they are left for future study.

[Remark 6]

In a sense we considered a set of standard executional operations in Logic of Execution. But in the actual concurrent and parallel models there are several other modes of execution. For example,

future(e): to return a virtual value "future" and to create a concurrent process to compute "e". When the real value of "e" is computed the future value will be replaced by its real value. This is the construct introduced by Halstead in Multilisp(see [4] for more details).

delay(e): to return a virtual value "delay" and to create a process to compute "e" when its real value is required.

We may be able to introduce some modes of execution based on symbolic execution, partial evaluation and warping evaluation, but they are also left for future consideration.

4 Logic of Execution: ⟨Execution of Propositional Sentences⟩

So far we have considered a structural framework of execution and rules of combining executions. On the basis of the logical framework of executional operators we consider here how to execute propositional sentences composed from logical connectives.
Let us denote the logical connectives as follows:

+ : logical or
& : logical and
¬ : negation
→ : logical implication

Then we have the following executional rules:

$$\frac{A + B}{A \; [+] \; B} \rightarrow \qquad \frac{A \; \& \; B}{A \; [\&] \; B} \rightarrow \qquad \frac{\neg A}{[\neg] A} \rightarrow$$

For the logical implication "→" we have

$$\frac{A \rightarrow B}{[\neg] A \; [+] \; B} \rightarrow$$

,assuming

$$(A \rightarrow B) = (\neg A + B)$$

Let a nondeterministic choice of A or B be denoted as $(A \vee B)$. Then we have

$$\frac{A \vee B}{A \; [\vee] \; B} \rightarrow$$

Let A and B have a shared data,and let $(A \mid B)$ denote the conjunctive operation with such a shared data.Then we have

$$\frac{A \mid B}{A \; [\mid] \; B} \rightarrow$$

Let A and B have a spacio-temporal location and $(A \, \# \, B)$ be the conjunctive operation of A and B at a spacio-temporal location. Then we have

$$\frac{A \, \# \, B}{A \; [\#] \; B} \rightarrow$$

Let $(A \Rightarrow B)$ be the linear entailment to mean that it holds only when A is true and then B is true. We have

$$\frac{A \Rightarrow B}{A \; [;] \; B} \rightarrow$$

Let $(\downarrow A)$ be the well-definedness operation of A to mean that it holds when A is well-defined. Then we have

$$\frac{\downarrow A}{[C] \; A} \rightarrow$$

In this way we can express the executions of various compound logical sentences in Logic of Execution.

[Remark 7]

As was remarked several times the Logic of Execution may have some close connection with Girard's Linear Logic. But in Logic of Execution we have two structures: (1) Executional structure and (2) Logical structure,while Linear Logic has a single proof-theoretic structure.

The computational or executional meanings of Girard's operators are not clear.Roughly speaking we can give the following correspondences between two systems.

(Linear Logic)	(Logic of Execution)	
(Logical operater)	(Logical operater)	(Executional operater)
+ (intensional or)	+	[+]
∨ (extensional or)	∨	[∨]
⊗ (intensional and)	|	[|]
& (extensional and)	&	[&]
¬ (negation)	¬	[¬]
→	→	([¬] and [+])
((none))	⇒	[;]
((none))	#	[#]
↓	↓	[c]
truth values	truth values	executional values
true	true	success
false	false	failure
(undefined)	(undefined)	pending
modal operators	(modal operators)	(modes of execution and virtual values)

[Remark 8]

(1) Since we do not allow

$$\frac{A + \neg A}{\text{<s>}}$$

our logic has the taste of intuitionistic logic. But an execution of <f> always produces <f>, so that we do not have a rule like "<f> $\vdash$ A".In intuitionistic logic and minimal logic "and","or" and "implication" are the basic logical operations,but in logic of execution "and","or","negation","sequential", "concurrent" and "parallel" are the basic executional operators.

(2) "A proves B" may be considered as "proof-theoretic execution" to deduce B from A. It is easy to see that [+] and [&] keep the properties of logical "or" and "and".The implication(say,[→]) defined through [¬] and [+] also keeps the properties of logical implication. In an ordinary logic the contradiction,denoted as ⊥,is defined as a primitive entity,and the following rule is accepted as a basic proof rule:

$$\frac{\perp}{A}$$

which may be read as "any sentence A can be deduced from ⟨ABSURDITY⟩". The system with this deduction is an intuitionistic logic if the law of excluded midde does not hold. Can we think of a kind of "absurdity" in our Logic of Execution ? One prososal of such an absurdity execution is "all possible successful executions". Let [Ω] be such an absurdity execution. Then we may have a rule,called the Ω-rule:

$$\frac{[\Omega]}{A}$$

The logic of execution with this Ω-rule may be called as the strong logic of execution.

[Remark 9]

In this paper we have discussed only the executions of propositional sentences. The next step of a generalization is to consider the case of the quantificational calculus with proper functions and relations.

Again there are two aspects:

1) to introduce some executional machinery for an quantificational statement

We may introduce the following executional quantifiers:

$\langle \exists x \rangle . P(x)$ to mean that there exists an executional procedure to find x with which the execution of $P(x)$ succeeds.

$\langle \forall x \rangle . P(x)$ to mean that there exists an executional procedure by which for all x the execution of $P(x)$ succeeds.

2) to introduce some executional modes for execution of function and relation

In case of the quantificational calculus with proper functions and relations we may introduce several constructs to denote the modes of execution of functions and relations. For example,we may employ the concurrency constructs from parallel Lisp [4]:

pcall$(f; e_1, e_2, \cdots, e_n)$
future(e)
delay(e)
eager$(f; e_1, e_2, \cdots, e_n)$

These extensions and the completenss issues of the logic are also left for future study.

REFERENCES

[1] J.Y.Girard: Linear Logic,Theoretical Computer Science,vol.50,pp.1-102 (1987)

[2] T.Ito: On Behaviors of Parallel Processes with Duration,Proceedings of Conference on Information Sciences and Systems,pp.455-467(1985)

[3] T.Ito: Recovery from Deadlock and Starvation by the Forcing Method, Proceedings of Conference on Information Sciences and Systems,pp.521-527(1988){This was also presented at the first UK/Japan Workshop in Computer Science held at Sendai,July 6-7,1987.}

[4] T.Ito and R.H.Halstead: Parallel Lisp, Springer LNCS, vol.441(1990)

[5] H.Ono: Structural Rules and a Logical Hierarchy, Mathematical Logic,(ed. P.P.Petkov), pp.95-105,Plenum(1990)

[6] D.Prawitz: Natural Deduction,Almquist & Wiksell,Stockholm(1965)

PART II

Object-Orientation

and

Concurrent Languages

Exception Handling and Real Time Features in an Object-Oriented Concurrent Language

Yuuji Ichisugi   Akinori Yonezawa

Department of Information Science, Faculty of Science
University of Tokyo
Hongo, Bunkyo-ku, Tokyo 113, Japan
{ichisugi, yonezawa}@is.s.u-tokyo.ac.jp

1 Introduction

When a well-structured and robust software system needs to be constructed, linguistic mechanisms are required which facilitate communication between a program component that discovers an occurrence of an exceptional situation and the program component that copes with the exceptional situation. Modular, yet powerful exception handling mechanisms that are based on the notion of procedure invocations were designed for ADT(abstract data type)-based languages like CLU[16] and Mesa[21]. Recently, exception handling mechanisms that are based on the notions of classes and inheritance have been proposed for object-oriented languages like Smalltalk80[7]. A good survey including a new proposal in this approach is found in [6].

We are interested in exception handling mechanisms which are effective in the object-oriented paradigm where concurrency is involved [26, 2]. This paper proposes exception handling mechanisms that are designed for our object-oriented concurrent language ABCL/1[25, 28]. Though our proposal is described in the context of ABCL/1, the proposed mechanisms are generally useful for other object-oriented concurrent languages[26, 2].

As discussed in [20], the conflict between inheritance mechanisms and synchronization constraints on behavior of concurrent objects cannot be ignored and thus no consensus has been reached about which approach is most appropriate in incorporating inheritance mechanisms into object-oriented concurrent languages. Therefore, our proposed exception handling mechanisms do not rely on inheritance mechanisms.

The remainder of this paper is organized as follows. Sections 2 and 3 introduce our object-oriented concurrent computation model and its associated language ABCL/1. Section 4 describes an extension of ABCL/1 that allows us to specify realtime constraints. A point of note is that violation of realtime constraints is one of the major sources of exceptional situations. Sections 5 through 7 present and discuss our proposed exception handling mechanisms. Comparison to previous work and concluding remarks are given in Sections 8 and 9, respectively.

```
[object object name
  (state   representation of local memory... )
  (script
    (=> message pattern where constraint   ... action ...)
      ...
    (=> message pattern where constraint    ... action ...))]
```

Figure 1: Basic Object Definition

2   Concurrent Objects in ABCL/1

2.1   State and Basic Operations

In our computation model, computation or information processing is performed by a collection of abstract entities called *concurrent objects* which become active when they receive messages, and computation proceeds as message transmissions among concurrent objects. More than one message transmission may take place in parallel and more than one object may become active simultaneously.

Each *object* in our computation model has its own (autonomous) processing power and it may have its local persistent memory, the contents of which can be accessed only by itself. (It is possible for a concurrent object not to have such memory.) The state of a concurrent object at a given time is defined as the contents of its local memory at that time.

Upon receiving a message, a concurrent object executes a sequence of the following four kinds of basic actions.

- the kinds of message passing described in Section 3.

- creation of concurrent objects.

- referencing and updating of the contents of its local memory.

- various operations (such as arithmetic operations and list processing) on values that are stored in its local memory and passed around in messages.

The messages that a concurrent object can accept are determined by the message patterns, the values contained in the messages, and the current state (and mode[1]) of the object. Therefore, in order to define the behavior of a concurrent object, we must specify:

- how its local persistent memory is represented,

- on what conditions messages are accepted, and

- the sequence of actions to be performed when a message is accepted.

---

[1]See the next subsection.

```
(wait-for
    (=> message pattern where constraint ... action ...)
       ⋮
    (=> message pattern where constraint ... action ...))
```

Figure 2: Wait-for Construct

To write a definition of a concurrent object in our language ABCL/1, we use the notation in Figure 1. (state ...) declares the variables which represent the local memory and specifies their initialization. We call such variables *state* variables. *Actions* are written in a sequential programming language, Common Lisp. *Object-name* and the construct **where** *constraint* are optional. The object definition form given in Figure 1 is a basic one. The full-fledged form is found in the User's Guide in the appendix of [28].

A *wait-for*-construct, which is used in a sequence of actions, makes the object waiting for a message with specified patterns to arrive. It specifies the patterns and constraints of messages that are able to reactivate the object. The ABCL/1 notation for this construct is given in Figure 2. Upon receiving of a message that satisfies one of the message patterns and constraints specified, the object becomes active again. We call this *selective message receipt*.

3 Message Passing

3.1 Three Types

The message passing forms in ABCM/1 are abstracted from human communication conventions in such a way that parallelism can be exploited and their implementation on computer systems can be done with relative ease. In our computation model, we distinguish three types of message passing: *past*, *now*, and *future*. In what follows, we will discuss each of them in turn. Note that the basic mode of message transmission in our computation is "asynchronous" in the sense that a sender can send a message whenever the sender wants irrespective of what mode/state the receiver is in.

[Past Type Message Passing] :
   Suppose that a concurrent object O has been activated and it sends a message M to a concurrent object T. Then O does not wait for M to be received by T. It just continues its computation immediately after the transmission of M (if the transmission of M is not the last action of the current activity of O).

This type of message passing substantially increases the concurrency of activities within a system. (A variation of past type message passing will be discussed in Section 5.) We call this type of message passing *past* type because sending a message finishes before it causes the intended effects to the message receiving object. Let us denote a past type message passing in the following ABCL/1 notation.

$$[T \; \texttt{<=} \; M]$$

[Now Type Message Passing] (send and wait) :

When a concurrent object O sends a request message M to a concurrent object T, O waits not only for M to be received by T, but also waits for the reply to the request M to be sent back to O.

This is similar to ordinary function/procedure calls, but it is more general and differs in the following two points:

- T's activation does not have to end with sending the reply to O. T may continue its computation after sending the reply.

- The reply to the request does not necessarily have to be sent back by T. T can delegate the responsibility of replying to other concurrent objects.

A now type message passing is expressed by the following ABCL/1 notation:

$$[T \text{ <== } M]$$

The reply to O may be the result of the requested task or simply an acknowledgment of receiving the request message. Thus the message sending object O is able to know for certain that his message was received by the object T though he may waste time waiting. The reply (i.e., some value or an acknowledging signal) is denoted by the same notation as that of a now type message passing. That is, the above notation denotes not merely an action of sending M to T by a now type message passing, but also denotes the information returned by T. This convention is useful in expressing the assignment of the returned value to a variable. For example, $[\text{x } := [T \text{ <== } M]]$.

[Future Type Message Passing] (reply to me later) :

Suppose that a concurrent object O sends a message M to a concurrent object T expecting a certain requested result to be sent back. But O does not need the result immediately. In this situation, after the transmission of M, O does not have to wait for the result to be returned. It continues its computation immediately. Later on when O needs that result, it checks its special *private* object called a *future object* that was specified at the time of the transmission of M. If the result has been stored in the future object, it can be used.

Of course, O can check whether or not the result is available yet before the result is actually used. A future type message passing is denoted by the following ABCL/1 notation:

$$[T \text{ <= } M \text{ \$ } x]$$

where x stands for a special variable called *future variable* which binds a future object. We assume that a future object behaves like a queue. The contents of the queue can be checked or removed *solely* by the object O which performed the future type message passing. Using a special expression (**ready?** x), O can check to see if the queue is empty. O could access the first element of the queue with a special expression (**next-value** x), or all the elements with (**all-values** x). If the queue is empty in such cases, O has to wait. Message passing of a somewhat similar vein has been adopted in previous object-oriented programming languages. For example, Act1, an actor-based language developed by H. Lieberman[15] has a language feature called "future", but it is different from ours.

3.2 Reduction of Now Type and Future Type

As keen readers might have already noticed, now type and future type message passing can be reduced to past type message passing. More specifically, a now type message passing can be reduced to a past type message passing with the use of waiting mode. A future type message passing can be reduced to a past type message passing.

Instead of sending a message in now type, the message is sent in past type and immediately after the transmission, the object sending the message changes into waiting so that it waits for the reply or acknowledgment to the message to come back. A future type message passing can be viewed as a past type message passing with the reply destination object being a future object. Accesses to the future object such as (**ready?** ...) and (**next-value** ...) are realized as special now type message transmissions. Thus all now type and future type message passing can be reduced to past type message passings with the uses of waiting mode. A precise demonstration of this reduction can be found in [27, 25]. Another way of reducing the number of different types is to start with future type. Both past type and now type can be reduced to future type. The verification of this claim is left for the reader as an exercise.

4 Real Time Constraints

In order to model and describe concurrent systems where time constraints are essential, temporal frameworks with real time measures must be introduced. In general, however, temporal frameworks with real time measures are hard to incorporate in abstract computation models. Thus we are contented that our language ABCL/1 is extended to provide programmers with facilities to describe real time constraints imposed on the behavior of concurrent objects. It should be noticed that violation of realtime constraints causes exception signals to be raised.

4.1 Now Type Message Passing with Real Time Constraints

While a past type message passing does not require the sender object to suspend its activity, a now type message transmission requires the sender object to wait for a response to the message to come back. It is often useful for the programmer to be able to specify how long the sender object of a now type message passing is allowed to wait for the response. A now type message passing with such a real time constraint is expressed by the following ABCL/1 notation:

$$[T \text{ <== } M \text{ % } time \text{ } expression]$$

where the evaluation result of *time expression* indicates the limit of time within which the response message to M must come back to the object that sends M. When no response is sent to the object within the time limit, a *time-out* signal (exception) is raised. How the time-out signal is handled will be discussed in Section 6.

4.2 Waiting Mode with Real Time Constraints

As explained before, a concurrent object changes into waiting mode by executing a **wait-for**-construct. A concurrent object being in waiting mode may be in danger of perpetual waiting. This is not tolerant in realtime programming. Thus, the programmer should be able to specify how long the object is allowed to stay in the waiting mode without receiving a desired message. For this purpose, the **wait-for**-construct is extended in ABCL/1 as follows:

> (**wait-for-within** *time expression*
>   (**=>** *message pattern* **where** *constraint* ... *action* ...)
>   ⋮
>   (**=>** *message pattern* **where** *constraint* ... *action* ...)

where the evaluation result of *time expression* indicates how long the object can stay in the waiting mode. When no message acceptable in this waiting mode arrives within this time limit, a time-out signal is raised.

4.3   Other Real Time Features

As noted earlier, the contents of a future object can be accessed only by the creator of the future object. When the creator access the contents, if the contents are empty, then the creator must wait until the contents become non-empty. Again it should be possible to specify the time limit of how long the creator of the future object can wait. We extend the three primitives for accessing the contents of a future object by allowing a key word :**within** for an optional parameter that indicates the time limit.

> (**ready?** x :**within** *time expression*)
> (**next-value** x :**within** *time expression*)
> (**all-values** x :**within** *time expression*).

Furthermore, in describing real time algorithms, it is often necessary to have a primitive to suspend execution for a specified period. For this purpose, ABCL/1 has the following primitive:

> (**wait** *time expression*)

5   Reply Destination

5.1   Information Passed Around

Let us summarize the information passed around in message passing in our computation model. A message can contain tags, elements in the specified domains of values (e.g., numbers, character strings, lists, etc.), and object names. The object name sent in a message is used in various ways. For example, suppose that a concurrent object O sends a message M to a concurrent object T in order to request T to do some task and send its result of the requested task to a specified object C_1, or in order for O to request T to do the task in cooperation with another concurrent object C_2. In such cases, O sends T a message which contains the object name C_1 or C_2 accompanied with a tag indicating the purpose (e.g., [... :**reply-to** C_1 ...]).

Besides explicit information contained in a message, we assume in our computation model that a receiver object is able to know the name of the sender of the message. In other words, when a message sent from a concurrent object O is received by a concurrent object T, it is assumed that the name of the sender object O becomes known to the receiver object T. A receiver object can decide whether it accepts or rejects an incoming message on the basis of who (or what object) sent the message. Therefore, this assumption considerably reinforces the expressive power of the ABCM/1 model. Also, it is extremely easy to realize this assumption. In describing the behavior of such a receiver object, ABCL/1 provides a language construct which allows the sender name to be bound to a variable at the beginning of a script.

(=> *message pattern* **from** *sender-var* **where** *constraint*
    ... *action* ...)

The name of the sender object which sends a message that satisfies the pattern-constraint pair is bound to *sender-var*. This variable can, of course, appear in *constraint* and ... *action* ... .

5.2 Reply Destination

When requested to do some task in now type or future type message passing, the receiver must make a reply by sending either an acknowledgment of the message or the result of the requested task. Since the destination of the reply is not necessarily the sender object of the message, the receiver of the message must always know which object it must send a reply to. The name of the object to which a reply is sent is called *reply destination*. Since the reply destination is sent with a request message, it is convenient for the receiver object to be able to make the reply destination bound to a dedicated pattern variable as an extended message pattern. In ABCL/1, the extended message pattern is denoted in the following manner.

(=> *message pattern* **@** *destination variable* ...)

When such a form is included in the definition of an object O, a future type message passing:

$$[O <= M \ \$ \ x]$$

makes x bound to the *destination variable*. As explained in [27, 25], a certain object is bound to the *destination variable* in now type message passing $[O <== M]$. Moreover, in past type message passing, any object C is allowed to be sent with a message M as the reply destination in the following manner:

$$[O <= M \ @ \ C]$$

Then, of course, C will be bound to the *destination variable*.

Note that the receiver object O can learn the reply destination from the value of the *destination variable* regardless of the type of message passing — whether it is past, now, or future. This fact gives us a great advantage: If a script of a concurrent object is defined using the destination variable, then as long as arriving messages satisfy the pattern-constraint pair of the script, the same script can be used to process the messages regardless of any of the following message passing types being used:

- past type accompanied with the reply destination,

- now type, and

- future type.

This means that in writing a script of a concurrent object the programmer need not be concerned with in which type of message passing messages that trigger the execution of the script are sent.

Notice that future type differs from past type in one aspect. That is, the future object, or a special local object, is the reply destination in future type message passing while any object can be specified as the reply destination in past type message passing.

6 Complaint Destination

As discussed in the previous section, a reply destination is a concurrent object which is specified at the time of message transmission as the destination of the acknowledgment or result of the task requested by the sender object (requester). Suppose that the requested task is impossible for the receiver object to carry out, or some unexpected thing occurs during the execution of the task. In order to cope with such situations, what kinds of measures should be taken? From the view point of object-oriented concurrent programming, some object(s) should receive the report or complaint that indicates the occurrence of such a situation and take actions to deal with the situation. We call a concurrent object which receives such a complaint (or report) and take actions a *complaint destination*. A complaint destination should, of course, be specified at the time of message transmission. This section discusses what kinds of complaints are generated and how such complaints are sent to complaint destinations in the framework of the language ABCL/1.

6.1 Kinds of Complaints

We will consider four kinds of complaints:

1. unacceptable-message complaints

2. time-out complaints

3. other system-defined complaints

4. user-defined complaints

Unacceptable-message complaints are a general characteristic of object-oriented computing. When a concurrent object sends a message, if the message is not acceptable to the receiver object, this complaint is generated at the system level. The reason why the system, not the receiver object, generates it is that in our computation model a receiver object cannot handler unacceptable messages. (In order for a concurrent object to manipulate a message, first of all, the object must accept the message.) We assume that the message which indicates such a complaint is of the following form:

$$[\text{:unacceptable } M \text{ :from } S \text{ :to } R]$$

where M is the unacceptable message, and S and R are the sender object and receiver object of M, respectively.

Time-out complaints are generated in situations where real time constraints are violated. As discussed in Section 4, our language ABCL/1 allows the programmer to specify real time constraints in now type message passing, wait-for-within constructs, and access primitives for future objects. Time-out complaints are also generated at the system-level. The signal which indicates an occurrence of time-out is of the form [:time-out..], which conforms to the syntax of messages in ABCL/1.

The third kind of complaints is the class of complaints that are generated at system level but different from unacceptable-message or time-out complaints. Examples of such complaints are signals that are raised when the divisor is zero in a divide operation or the Lisp car-operation is applied to a Lisp atomic data. Another example might be a signal that is raised when disk write-operation has not successfully completed. We also assume that the form of such signals conforms to the syntax of messages in ABCL/1. For example, the signal for zero division might look like :zero-divide.

The fourth kind, namely, user-defined complaints are signals that are raised when explicit signaling primitives are executed during the activation of a concurrent object. In ABCL/1, the explicit signal primitive used in a script of a concurrent object is of the following form:

$$(\text{signal } signal\ form)$$

We assume that the syntax of *signal forms* is the same as that of message forms. As will be explained in Section 7 in connection with the ABCL/1 signal-catching construct, signals (which are raised as results of the evaluation of expressions) are often viewed as messages sent from concurrent objects.

6.2 Where to Complain

Since now type and future type message passings reduce to past type message passing, it suffices to discuss how a complaint destination is specified in a past type message passing. As noted at the beginning of this section, a complaint destination is specified at the time of message transmission. When a complaint destination needs to be specified explicitly, the following ABCL/1 notation is used:

$$[T \text{ <= } M \text{ @ } reply\ destination \text{ @@ } complaint\ destination] \qquad (*)$$

This means that a message M accompanied with a reply destination and complaint destination is sent to a concurrent object T in a past type message massing. Corresponding to this notation, in order for the message receiving object T to be able to bind the *complaint destination* to a dedicated pattern variable, we extend the syntax of the message receiving form of a script of a concurrent object as follows:

$$(\text{=> } pattern \text{ @ } destination\text{-}var \text{ @@ } complaint\text{-}var \text{ where } constraint \qquad \dots \quad action$$

In the above past type message passing (*), suppose the message receiving object T cannot handle or accept a message M. Then, the system generates a complaint message [:unacceptable M ...] as discussed in the previous subsection. This complaint message is, of course, sent to the *complaint destination*. That is the whole reason why the complaint destination is explicitly specified.

Below we will examine where complaint messages are sent in various cases where complaint destinations may or may not be explicitly specified. Our design of exception handling features in ABCL/1 is based on the following rules:

Rules for Where to Complain:

1. If a complaint destination is explicitly specified in a message passing, then the complaint message is sent to the complaint destination whether a reply destination may or may not be explicitly specified.

2. If a reply destination is explicitly specified, but no complaint destination is specified, then the complaint message is sent to the reply destination.

3. If neither a complaint destination nor a reply destination is specified, then the complaint message is sent to the sender of the original message.

The above rules are not followed when a complaint message is sent explicitly to some object. For example. if the programmer wishes, s/he can send a complaint message to the sender of the original message by explicitly describing in a script a transmission of the complaint message to the original sender object. This is always possible because the sender of a message is always known to the receiver, which is one of the assumption of our computation model.

Let us look at several representative cases.

(**Case 1**) Neither a reply destination nor a complaint destination is specified:

$$[T \mathrel{<=} M]$$

$$\Downarrow$$

$$[sender \mathrel{<=} [\text{:unacceptable } M \text{ :from } sender \text{ :to } T]]$$

Since neither a reply destination nor a complaint destination is specified, Rule 1 is followed. Thus, the sender object of the message M should be prepared to receive and handle a complaint message. When the sender object are not prepared, namely it does not have a script to handle the [:unacceptable ...] message, a complaint message [:unacceptable ...] should not be generated in response to the [:unacceptable ...] message that was sent to the original sender object *sender*. Otherwise, if the original message receiving object T does not have a script to handle a [:unacceptable ...] message, infinite exchanges of [:unacceptable ...] messages between the *sender* and T will be caused. □

(**Case 2**) *Reply destination* may or may not be explicitly specified, but *complaint destination* is explicitly specified:

$$[T <= M \text{ @@ } complaint\ destination]$$

or

$$[T <= M \text{ @ } reply\ destination \text{ @@ } complaint\ destination]$$

⇓

$$[complaint\ destination <= [\texttt{:unacceptable}\ M\ \texttt{:from}\ sender\ \texttt{:to}\ T]]$$

Since a complaint destination is explicitly specified, following Rule 1, the complaint destination should receive the complaint message [:unacceptable ...].□

(**Case 3**) Only *reply destination* is explicitly specified:

$$[T <= M \text{ @ } reply\ destination]$$

⇕

$$[T <= M \text{ @ } reply\ destination \text{ @@ } reply\ destination]$$

⇓

$$[reply\ destination <= [\texttt{:unacceptable}\ M\ \texttt{:from}\ sender\ \texttt{:to}\ T]]$$

Since a reply destination is explicitly specified, and a complaint destination is NOT explicitly specified, following Rule 2, the default complaint destination is the specified reply destination. (⇕ means the default interpretation.) Thus, the [:unacceptable ...] message is sent to the *reply destination*. □

(**Case 4**) In a future type message passing, *complaint destination* is not explicitly specified:

$$[T <= M \text{ \$ } future\ object]$$

⇕

$$[T <= M \text{ @ } future\ object]$$

⇕

$$[T <= M \text{ @ } future\ object \text{ @@ } future\ object]$$

⇓

$$[future\ object <= [\texttt{:unacceptable}\ M\ \texttt{:from}\ sender\ \texttt{:to}\ T]]$$

Since a future type message passing reduces to a past type message passing with its reply destination being the *future object*, the reply destination is specified. On the other hand, since no complaint destination is specified, following Rule 2, the reply destination (which is the *future object*) is interpreted as the default complaint destination. Thus, the *future object* should receive the complaint message [:unacceptable ...].

(**Case 5**) In a future type message passing, *complaint destination* is explicitly specified:

$$[T \text{ <= } M \text{ \$ } future\ object \text{ @@ } complaint\ destination]$$

$$\Updownarrow$$

$$[T \text{ <= } M \text{ @ } future\ object \text{ @@ } complaint\ destination]$$

$$\Downarrow$$

$$[complaint\ destination \text{ <= } [\text{:unacceptable } M \text{ :from } sender \text{ :to } T]]$$

Since a complaint destination is explicitly specified, following Rule 1, the complaint destination should receive the complaint message [:unacceptable ...]. □

(**Case 6**) Now type message passing:

$$[T \text{ <== } M]$$

$$\Updownarrow$$

```
(progn
   [T <= M @ now-normal-obj @@ now-error-obj]
   (wait-for
     (=> normal-message from S where (eq S now-normal-obj)
         normal-message )
     (=> error-message from S where (eq S now-error-obj)    (**)
         (signal error-message))))
```

By the nature of now type message passing (which expects the result or acknowledgment of the requested task to be returned), the sender object of the message should receive an error (or complaint) message as well as the normal result (or acknowledgment) message. Moreover, the sender object starts waiting for such a message immediately after the message transmission. In order to discriminate an error (complaint) message from a normal result/acknowledgment message, a now type message passing is interpreted as a past type message passing accompanied with two distinct forwarder objects: *now-normal-obj* and *now-error-obj*, which are used as *reply destination* and *complaint destination*, respectively. Note that a complaint message (such as [:unacceptable ...]) is first sent to *now-error-obj* from the original message receiver object T, and the complaint message is forwarded to the original sender object of M. This complaint message is bound to *error-message* in the second arm of the above (wait-for ...) construct (**). This message is, in turn, raised as a signal generated as the result of the original evaluation of $[T \text{ <== } M]$. □

7 Catching Signals

In this section, we will discuss how signals (which are raised during the execution of a script of a concurrent object) are caught and how they are handled. A typical example is Case 6 in the previous section where the expression [T <== M] raises a signal by executing the second arm of the (wait-for ...)

7.1 Language Construct

Signals raised during the execution of a script should usually be caught within the script. To do so, the following (catch-signal ...) construct is used in ABCL/1.

```
(catch-signal
        ... action ... ... ... action ...
    (handler
      (=> signal pattern
              handler body   )
            ⋮
      (=> signal pattern
              handler body   )))
```

When a signal is raised during the execution of ...action ...action ..., the current execution is terminated. If the signal is matched against one of *signal patterns* in the (handler ...)-clause, the corresponding *handler body* is executed. A handler body may raise a signal, which terminates the execution of the handler body and raises the signal outside the (catch-signal ...)-construct. If the signal does not match against any of the *signal patterns*, the signal is raised further outside the (catch-signal ...)-construct. Of course, no signal is raised during the execution of ...action ...action ..., the expression following the above whole (catch-signal ...)-construct is executed.

As an example, consider a concurrent object defined as follows:

```
[object A
  (state ...)
  (script
    (=> [:ask T :real-time-thing] @ reply-var @@ complaint-var
          ... action ...
      (catch-signal
              ... action ...
              [T <== M % 100] (***)
              ... action ...
        (handler
            (=> [:time-out m]     (signal [:time-out m]))
            (=> [:unacceptable m :from sender-obj :to receiver-obj]
                  ... action ...)
            (=> :zero-divide      ... action ...   ))))
        ... action ...     )
      ⋮   )]
```

Suppose that a time-out signal is raised by the now type message passing with a real time constraint 100 (indicated by (***)), it is caught by the handler body whose signal pattern is [:time-out m] and the handler body in turn raises the same signal. If the message M is not acceptable to the receiver object T, message [:unacceptable M :from A :to T] is sent back from T and a signal [:unacceptable ...] is raised by the now type message passing expression (***). Then it is caught by the second arm of the (handler ...)-construct.

When a signal :zero-divide is raised during the execution of the sequence of actions before or after [T <== M % 100], it will be caught by the third arm of the (handler ...)-construct. As will be explained in the next subsection, the expression [T <== M % 100] may also raise a signal :zero-divide. In such a case, the signal will be caught by the same arm. Note, however, the signals raised during the execution of the sequence of actions before the (catch-signal ...)-construct will not be caught by the handlers defined in the (catch-signal ...)-construct. Who will handle such signals is one of the issues discussed in the next subsection.

7.2   Where Uncaught Complaints Go

If a signal is not caught by any (catch-signal ...)-construct appearing in a script of a concurrent object, the signal cannot be handled by the object. In such a case, if a pattern variable for a complaint destination is specified in the script and a complaint destination object was bound to the variable at the beginning of the execution of the script, the signal must be sent to the complaint destination (by past type message passing). Though no complaint destination is bound, if a reply destination has been bound, the signal should be sent to the reply destination. (Recall the default interpretations discussed above for the cases where a complaint destination is not explicitly specified at the time of a message transmission.) If neither a reply destination nor a complaint destination has been bound, that signal will be sent to the sender of the message that causes the execution of the script and the execution of the script terminates.

In the above example, when a signal, say, :car-applied-to-non-atom, which cannot be caught by any arm, is raised during execution of the ... *action* ... in the (catch-signal ...) construct, the signal will be raised outside the (catch-signal ...) construct. Then if the (catch-signal ...) construct is not embraced by any (catch-signal ...) construct in the script for [:ask ...], the signal :car-applied-to-non-atom will be sent to the object bound to *complaint-var*. If no object has been bound to *complaint-var*, the signal will be sent to the object that has been bound to *reply-var*. In case where a concurrent object is bound to neither *reply-var* nor *complaint-var*, :car-applied-to-non-atom will be sent to the sender of the [:ask ...] message.

7.3   Retry and Skip

After some remedial actions are taken in response to a signal, a handler should be able to retry the action which caused the signal. For this purpose, ABCL/1 provides the following primitive which is used in handlers of (catch-signal ...)-constructs.

```
(retry)
```

In real time situations, even just waiting for a while and retrying an action is sometimes useful. In such a case, this primitive can be used in combination with the (**wait** *time expression*) primitive explained in Subsection 4.3. (See the example below.)

After having tried to deal with exceptional situations, just ignoring and skipping to the next action might be the most useful or practical thing to do. Thus, the following primitive is also provided in ABCL/1.

(skip)

The following example illustrates typical usages of (**retry**) and (**skip**):

```
(catch-signal
        ... action ...
        [T <== M % 100]
        ... action ...
    (handler
        (=> [:time-out m]  ... (wait 50) (retry)))
        (=> [:unacceptable m :from sender-obj :to receiver-obj]
            [count := (1+ count)]
            (when (> 10 count) (retry))
            (skip)))
```

The first handler which deals with a time-out signal waits for 50 units of time and then it retries the action [T <== *M* % 100]. When the second handler tries the action 10 times and if it cannot still succeed, then it will skip to the next action. (Variable **count** is assumed to be zero before entering the (**catch-signal** ...)-construct.)

8 Previous Work

To put our proposal in a proper perspective, let us review exception handling mechanisms in other parallel (or concurrent) languages. Recall that our proposal is based on the premise that message transmissions are asynchronous in the sense explained in Section 3.

In CSP[12] or Occam[13], processes communicate with each other *synchronously* and exception handling mechanisms are not included in the language design.

Ada[4] provides a process-like notion called a *task*. Tasks run concurrently, and communicate with each other by *rendezvous*. When an exception is raised during a rendezvous, if it is not handled within the callee task, the exception signal is propagated to the caller task. Though the difference of the computation models makes the exact comparison difficult, it can be said that our proposed scheme subsumes the Ada exception handling mechanism. The default action in Case 6 of Section 6.2 together the general rule described in Section 7.2 explains this fact

Argus[17] has an asynchronous remote procedure call mechanism called *promises*[18]. The design of promises was influenced by the *future* mechanism of *Multilisp*[9]. Promises allow a caller process to run in parallel with the callee process (which evaluates a promise expression) and the return value (if ready) is picked up explicitly when the caller process needs it. If an exception signal is raised by the callee process, the caller process receives it when the caller process picks up the result of the call. This mechanism corresponds to the default action explained in Case 4 of Section 6.2.

NIL[22] provides synchronous communication using the rendezvous mechanism and also provides asynchronous communication using *send and receive* primitives. Exceptions raised during rendezvous propagate in the same way as Ada does. Unlike our mechanism, however, NIL does not have a means to specify where exception signals propagate in asynchronous communication.

Our idea of using "complaint destinations" originates from Hewitt's idea of the "complaint department" in the Actor formalism[10, 1]. Since the language design for the Actor formalism has not been explored sufficiently, systematic exception handling mechanisms have not been proposed even for actor-based languages like Act-1[15] and Acore[19].

9 Concluding Remarks

We have proposed an exception handling scheme and real-time features for our object-oriented concurrent language ABCL/1.

The default actions of our exception handling scheme for *now* type and *future* type message passing are similar to Ada's *rendezvous* and Argus' *promises*, respectively. But our whole scheme subsumes such schemes and is substantially more flexible because the user can specify a complaint destination when a message is sent.

In handling exceptional situations, handlers sometimes need to manipulate the environment where an exception is raised. To deal with this in our scheme, some provision must be made. From the nature of object-orientation, concurrent objects in ABCL/1 can only be referenced to by their names and no internal structures can be accessed directly. Thus an object which handles a raised exception cannot directly access the environment (and internal structure) of the object which raised the exception. This means that an exception raising object must provide the script for a message from the exception handling object which wants to change the state of the exception raising object.

Many exception handling schemes for sequential languages allow control to exit globally. In concurrent languages, the semantics of global exiting is not well understood. In our concurrent setting, some mechanisms are needed that stop execution of the group of concurrent objects which are "related" to an object which raises an exception.

Currently, we do not consider the language support for "resumption" at the inter-object communication level. It is often intended to undo the messages sent before an exception is raised. In object-oriented concurrent languages, message passing often causes side effects: message receiving object changes its internal state. It is sometime cumbersome to write the code to restore state changes of the object for resumption. If languages have rollback mechanisms such as the one proposed by Jefferson[14], restoration can be done easily. Also this restoration can be done at the meta-level suggested in the reflective computation scheme [23, 24].

Further experiments are needed to reach the final design of exception handling scheme for our object-oriented concurrent language ABCL/1.

Acknowledgments

The second author would like to thank Professor P. S. Krishnaprasad at University of Maryland, who suggested him the necessity of real time features in ABCL/1.

References

[1] G. Agha. *Actors: A Model of Concurrent Computation in Distributed Systems*. Cambridge, Ma., The MIT Press, 1986.

[2] G. Agha. "Concurrent Object-Oriented Programming". *Communications of the ACM*, Vol.22, 9, pages 125–141, September 1990.

[3] W. C. Athas and C. L. Seitz. "Multicomputers: Message-Passing Concurrent Computers". *IEEE Computer*, 21(8), pages 9–24, 1988.

[4] G. Booch. *Software Engineering with Ada*. 2nd ed. Benjamin/Cummings, 1983.

[5] W. J. Dally. *The J-Machine: System Support for Actors*. In C. Hewitt and G. Agha, editors, *Knowledge Processing: An Actor Perspective*. The MIT Press, 1989.

[6] C. Dony. "Exception Handling and Object-Oriented Programming: Towards a Synthesis". In *Proceedings of OOPSLA/ECOOP'90*, pages 322-330, October 1990.

[7] A. Goldberg, D. Robson. *Smalltalk-80: The Language and Its Implementation*. Addison-Wesley, Reading, Ma., 1983.

[8] J. B. Goodenough. "Exception Handling: Issues and a Proposed Notation". *Communications of the ACM*, Vol.18, 12, pages 683–696, December 1975.

[9] R. H. Halstead Jr. "Multilisp: A Language for Concurrent Symbolic Computation," *ACM Transactions on Programming Languages and Systems*, Vol.7, 4, pages 501–538, October 1985.

[10] C. Hewitt. "Viewing Control Structures as Patterns of Passing Messages". *Journal of Artificial Intelligence*, Vol.8, 3, pages 323–364, 1987.

[11] A. Hill. "Exception Handling in Object-Oriented Languages". *OOCTG Working Paper SWBT-9001WP.00*, June 1990.

[12] C. A. R. Hoare. "Communicating Sequential Processes". *Communications of the ACM*, Vol.21, 8, pages 666-677, 1978.

[13] C. A. R. Hoare, editor. *OCCAM Programming Manual*. Prentice Hall International, 1984.

[14] D. R. Jefferson. "Virtual Time". *ACM Transactions on Programming Languages and Systems*, Vol.7, 3, pages 404–425, 1985.

[15] H. Lieberman. "A Preview of Act-1". *AI-Memo AIM-625*, Artificial Intelligence Laboratory, MIT, 1981.

[16] B. Liskov and A. Snyder. "Exception Handling in CLU". *IEEE Transactions on Software Engineering*, Vol.SE-5, 6, pages 546–558, November 1979.

[17] B. Liskov, et al. "Argus Reference Manual". *Technical Report MIT/LCS/TR-400, MIT. Laboratory for Computer Science*, Cambridge, Ma., 1987.

[18] B. Liskov and L. Shrira. "Promises: Linguistic Support for Efficient Asynchronous Procedure Calls in Distributed Systems". *Proceedings of the ACM SIGPLAN '88 Conference on Programming Languages Design and Implementation*, June 1988.

[19] C. R. Manning. "Acore: Design of an Actor Core Language and its Compiler". Master's thesis, MIT EECS Department, May 1987.

[20] S. Matsuoka, K. Wakita, and A. Yonezawa. "Synchronization Constraints with Inheritance: What is not possible - so what is?". *Technical Report 10, Dept. of Information Science, Univ. of Tokyo*, April 1990.

[21] J. G. Mitchell, W. Maybury, and R. Sweet. "Mesa Language Manual". Xerox Res. Cent., Palo Alto, Ca, Rep. CSL-78-1, February 1978.

[22] R. E. Strom and S. Yemini. "NIL: An integrated language and system for distributed programming." *ACM SIGPLAN Notices*, 18, 6, pages 73–82, June 1983.

[23] T. Watanabe. "Reflection in an Object-Oriented Concurrent Language". In *Proceedings of OOPSLA '88*, pages 306–315, September 1988. Revised version in [28].

[24] T. Watanabe and A. Yonezawa. "An Actor-Based Metalevel Architecture for Group-Wide Reflection". In *Proceedings of the School/Workshop on Foundations of Object-Oriented Languages*, edited by G. Rozenberg, Lecture Notes in Computer Science, Springer-Verlag. (Forthcoming.)

[25] A. Yonezawa, J.-P. Briot, and E. Shibayama. "Object-Oriented Concurrent Programming in ABCL/1". In *Proceedings of ACM Conference on Object-Oriented Programming Systems, Languages, and Applications (OOPSLA)*, pages 258–268, 1986.

[26] A. Yonezawa and M. Tokoro, editor. *Object-Oriented Concurrent Programming*. The MIT Press, 1987.

[27] A. Yonezawa, E. Shibayama, T. Takada, Y. Honda, and J.-P. Briot. "An Object-Oriented Concurrent Computation Model ABCM/1 and its Description Language ABCL/1". In [28].

[28] A. Yonezawa, editor. *ABCL: An Object-Oriented Concurrent System — Theory, Language, Programming, Implementation and Application*. The MIT Press, 1990.

Reuse of Concurrent Object Descriptions

Etsuya Shibayama

Department of Applied Mathematics and Informatics
Ryukoku University
Seta, Ootsu, Japan, 520-21
etsuya@rins.ryukoku.ac.jp

Abstract

A code sharing technique for object-oriented concurrent programming is presented, in which the behavior of an object is defined in terms of *primary, constraint,* and *transition* methods. A primary method represents the primary task to be performed in response to an incoming message. A constraint method determines whether or not an arriving message is acceptable. A transition method establishes the next context of an object. These three sorts of methods are inherited separately, i.e., two methods in different sorts do not override each other. By this way of separation, synchronization codes can be effectively shared and reused. We present two application examples to show the effectiveness of our technique.

1 Introduction

Supporting two powerful mechanisms *polymorphism* and *inheritance*, object-oriented programming is widely accepted in various application domains. It is generally agreed that an inheritance mechanism and differential style programming are useful and necessary upon development of large scale software. Even though any single inheritance mechanism could not cover all the practical requirements, the inheritance mechanisms of existing sequential object-oriented programming languages, e.g., Smalltalk-80[GR83] and CLOS[BDG+88], have succeeded in a significant degree.

Still, however, code reuse of concurrent programs is difficult. For the purposes of synchronization, messages arriving at a concurrent object do not always processed in the arrival order. For instance, if a *buffer* object, which accepts *put* and *get* messages, receives a get message when it is empty, it suspends the get message until it becomes non-empty. Note that such suspension never occurs in a sequential computation: though at a glance a sequential object which implements a FIFO queue seems similar to a concurrent object which implements a(n unbounded) buffer, the former cannot suspend execution of an arriving message; if the former receives a dequeue message when it is empty, a run-time error occurs, a signal is raised, or the like. Unfortunately, reuse techniques for sequential objects are developed without any consideration of *synchronization* mechanisms, which determine the processing order of arriving messages at an object. In order

```
(loop
 (wait-for
  (=> [:put item] where this buffer is not full
      Send back a reply for acknowledgment.
      Enqueue item at the tail of the buffer.)
  (=> [:get] where this buffer is not empty
      Remove the first element from the buffer and send it back.)))
```

Program 1.1: Behavior of a Bounded Buffer

to reuse object-oriented concurrent programs, we need an appropriate description scheme of synchronization mechanisms so that codes for synchronization can be effectively shared and reused.

In the following, as the starting point, we assume an object-based concurrent computing model ABCM/1[YSB+86], in which autonomous information processing agents called *objects* cooperate and interact with one another via *message passing*. No global memories and no global clocks are assumed in the model. Different from CCS[Mil80] and CSP[Hoa78], ABCM/1 is based on *asynchronous buffered* communication. In this respect, ABCM/1 is similar to the Actor model. However, each object in this model has at most a single execution *thread* at a time and thus no synchronization is necessary among threads within an object.

For the purposes of inter-object synchronization, the *selective message acceptance mechanism* is available. The language ABCL/1[YSB+86], which is based on ABCM/1, provides the **wait-for** construct which realizes this mechanism. For instance, using this construct, the behavior of a bounded buffer object can be described as in Program 1.1, where **loop** is a macro in Common Lisp[Ste84] and denotes infinite iterations. The **wait-for** form declares the acceptable message patterns [:put item] and [:get]. Notice that in a message pattern every symbol beginning with ":" is a constant and every other symbol is a pattern variable, which matches any value. In this case, :put and :get are pattern constants and item is a pattern variable. The *constraints* following the key word **where** describes the following synchronization conditions:

- a [:put *value*] message is acceptable only when the buffer is not full, and

- a [:get] message is acceptable only when the buffer is not empty

This **wait-for** form also describes the actions which are performed during processing put/get messages.

Using the selective message acceptance mechanism, one can describe behaviors of objects including synchronization in two different manners. One is based on *constraint specifications* and the other is based on *context transitions*. The former approach is already shown in Program 1.1, where a boolean expression called a *constraint* is associated to each sequence of actions so that it can be performed if and only if the constraint is satisfied. In the latter approach, the notion of *context*, which is an abstraction of the set of currently active action sequences, is introduced. After completing an action sequence, an object may change its context by itself. This technique is illustrated in Program 1.2 which includes three **wait-for** forms. Each occurrence has a tag (i.e., a destination of a go

```
(tagbody
 empty
   (wait-for
    (=> [:put item]
        Send back a reply for acknowledgment.
        Enqueue item at the tail of the buffer.
        (if this buffer is not full
            (go partial)
            (go full))))
 partial
   (wait-for
    (=> [:put item]
        Send back a reply for acknowledgment.
        Enqueue item at the tail of the buffer.
        (if this buffer is not full
            (go partial)
            (go full)))
    (=> [:get]
        Remove the first element from the buffer and send it back.
        (if this buffer is not empty
            (go partial)
            (go empty))))
 full
   (wait-for
    (=> [:get]
        Remove the first element from the buffer and send it back.
        (if this buffer is not empty
            (go partial)
            (go empty)))))
```

Program 1.2: Another Description of Behavior of a Bounded Buffer

form) which is either empty, partial, or full. These three occurrences represent three different contexts where:

- the buffer is empty,

- the buffer is neither full nor empty, and

- the buffer is full.

For instance, when the buffer becomes empty, the wait-for form whose tag is empty is executed and enters the context where a put request is acceptable but no get requests can. In this technique, we do not use any where constraints. Notice that those who do not like *goto-statements* and who like structured programming may prefer Program 1.3, which also include three occurrences of wait-for.

In general, for the purposes of synchronization, the set of acceptable messages by an object is varied from one to another during execution. Program 1.1 describes the set of acceptable messages by the constraints following the key word where. In contrast, in Programs 1.2 and 1.3, the set of acceptable messages is described by one of the three wait-for forms which represent contexts. A transition between contexts is represented by control flows.

```
(loop
 (wait-for
  (=> [:put item]
      (if this buffer is full
          (wait-for
           (=> [:get]
               Remove the first element from the buffer and send it back.)))
      Send back a reply for acknowledgment.
      Enqueue item at the tail of the buffer.)
  (=> [:get]
      (if this buffer is empty
          (wait-for
           (=> [:put item]
               Send back a reply for acknowledgment.
               Send back item to the requester of the suspended [:get] message))
       Remove the first element from the buffer and send it back.))))
```

Program 1.3: Yet Another Description of Behavior of a Bounded Buffer

According to our experiences, the selective message acceptance mechanism and the combination of these two techniques are sufficient to describe the behavior of a concurrent object at least when object descriptions are not too large. In our programming methodology, the behavior descriptions of a concurrent object consist of two parts:

1. descriptions of constrains and context transitions, and

2. descriptions of the actions performed in response to arriving messages.

We consider that existing inheritance mechanisms of sequential object-oriented programming languages have succeed in reuse of the second sort of description. Therefore, our primary concern in this paper is to propose mechanisms by which the first sort of description can be effectively reused.

In the following, in Section 2, we introduce an object-oriented concurrent programming language ABCL$^+$, which provides mechanisms for both inheritance and delegation. We show by example that in ABCL$^+$ we can describe object definitions in a differential manner, assuming both approaches that are based on constraint specifications and context transitions. The example in this section includes differential descriptions of semaphores, buffers and bounded buffers. In Section 3, we present a more practical example, namely, we describe three sorts of concurrently accessible height balanced trees: the first one accepts only search requests; the second one employs exclusive locks in order to cope with possible conflicts among search and insertion requests; the third one employs both read and exclusive locks.

2   The Language ABCL$^+$

In this section, we introduce the language ABCL$^+$, which is an extended version of an object-based concurrent programming language ABCL/1[Yon90] and which incorporates

```
[class buffer
  (state [contents := nil])]

[method [:put item] (buffer)
  (enqueue contents item)]

[method [:get] (buffer)
  (:reply-to r)
  [r <= (dequeue contents)]]]

[method [:get] (buffer :constraint)
  (not (empty contents))]
```

Program 2.1: A Buffer Class

program reuse mechanisms. We start introducing ABCL$^+$ by a buffer example. In this language, a buffer class is described in Program 2.1.

The first form just describes the structure of the internal persistent memory (i.e., the instance variable name contents and its initial value nil) of each buffer object. In general, a class definition form may include more information (e.g., the list of the superclasses). The other three forms together define the behavior of buffer objects. These are called *method definitions*. The first two define *primary* methods and the last one defines a *constraint* method. The primary method definitions describe the behavior of a buffer object in response to *put* and *get* requests, respectively, and the constraint method definition describes the necessary condition to accept get requests. In the definition of the primary method [:get],

(:reply-to r)

means that the *reply destination* (i.e., the destination to which the reply to the incoming message [:get] is returned) is bound to r during execution of this method, and

[r <= (dequeue contents)]

denotes message passing in which the evaluation result of (dequeue contents) is transmitted to the destination bound to r. Message passing represented in this syntax does not require any reply and the object which executes this method can resume its computation just after it performs the message passing. We do not present any definitions of sequential functions enqueue, dequeue, and empty since they are obvious.

Intuitively, an buffer object interprets the combination of the three methods as follows:

```
if an-incoming-message and [:put item] match then
  accept an-incoming-message;
  (enqueue contents item)
elseif an-incoming-message and [:get] match then
  if (not (empty contents)) is satisfied then
    accept an-incoming-message
    [r <= (dequeue contents)]
  else
    suspend an-incoming-message
  endif
```

```
[class bounded-buffer
  (super buffer)]

[method [:put item] (bounded-buffer :constraint)
  (not (full buffer))]
```

Program 2.2: A Bounded Buffer Class

```
else
    suspend an-incoming-message
endif
```

where *an-incoming-message* is the message arriving at the buffer object.

2.1 Inheritance

Inheritance among classes is described in ABCL[+]. For instance, bounded-buffer class is defined as a child of buffer as in Program 2.2. The first form of this program describes that the *superclass* of bounded-buffer is buffer. This means that bounded-buffer inherits:

- the instance variable contents,

- the primary methods [:put item] and [:get], and

- the constraint method [:get]

of buffer. These are inherited as usual except that primary methods and constraint methods are inherited independently in a separate manner. More precisely, though a primary (or constraint) method defined at a descendant class may override another primary (or constraint, respectively) method defined at an ancestor class, any primary methods do not override any constraint methods and vice versa. By this way, the differences between the behaviors of buffer and bounded buffer objects are described as the second form in Program 2.2. This means that a bounded buffer is a buffer except that it does not accept any put request when it is full. We omit the definition of full.

As a simple example, we show how common portions of the behaviors of (unbounded) buffers and semaphores are shared using inheritance in our language. Program 2.3 shows descriptions of semaphores. The behaviors of semaphores and buffers are similar: both accept two sorts of requests (*p/v* and *put/get*); while they are empty, they postpone processing *p* and *get* requests. Therefore, it can be natural to design the class hierarchy so that the semaphore class and the buffer class share the same parent (superclass) in the hierarchy.

In order to share common synchronization codes of semaphores and buffers, we define a common superclass common-sync in Program 2.4. The class common-sync has no instance variables but has a single constraint method, which assumes an internal method whose name is empty and which is defined at a subclass. The method bound to this name is determined at run-time (at least conceptually) and this late binding capability provides flexibility of class definitions.

```
[class semaphore
  (state [n := 1])]

[method [:v-op] (semaphore)
  (incf n)]

[method [:p-op] (semaphore)
  (:reply-to r)
  [r <= (values)]
  (decf n)]

[method [:p-op] (semaphore :constraint)
  (not (zerop n))]
```

Program 2.3: A Semaphore Class

```
[class common-sync]

[method [:get] (common-sync :constraint)
  (not (empty))]
```

Program 2.4: A Common Superclass of Buffers and Semaphores

```
[class buffer
  (super common-sync)
  (state [contents := nil])]

[method [:put item] (buffer)
  (enqueue contents item)]

[method [:get] (buffer)
  (:reply-to r)
  [r <= (dequeue contents)]]

[method (empty) (buffer)
  (empty contents)]
```

Program 2.5: A Buffer Class Definition using Inheritance

```
[class semaphore
  (super common-sync)
  (state [n := 1])
  (rename [[:p-op] -> [:get]])]

[method [:v-op] (semaphore)
  (incf n)]

[method [:get] (semaphore)
  (:reply-to r)
  [r <= (values)]
  (decf n)]

[method (empty) (semaphore)
  (zerop n)]
```

Program 2.6: A Semaphore Class Definition using Inheritance

On top of common-sync, buffer is defined in Program 2.5. In the class definition form, common-sync is specified as the superclass of buffer. This means that buffer inherits the constraint method of common-sync. The first two primary methods represent the actions of buffers in response to put and get requests. The last one defines an internal method empty. In ABCL⁺, a method definition form defines an internal method if its first argument, i.e., (empty) in this case, is enclosed by parenthesis "(" and ")." An internal method dose not have its associated constraint and an object can invoke its internal methods at any time during processing messages. In contrast, a method definition form defines an externally available method if its first argument is enclosed by brackets "[" and "]." This sort of method is invoked in response to a message matching the message pattern and satisfying the corresponding constraint (if it exists).

In the similar manner, semaphore is defined in Program 2.6, where common-sync is also specified as the superclass. One difference between this definition and the definition of buffer in Program 2.5 is that, in case of semaphore, the method name [:p-op] is internally renamed to [:get], which is inherited from common-sync (See the fourth argument of the class definition form). Notice that Exemplar–based Smalltalk[LaL89] and ACT++[KL89] have already employed this sort of renaming operation as a primitive.

It is natural to put a bounded buffer class in the inheritance hierarchy. Program 2.2 is also valid in this case as the differential descriptions of buffer and bounded-buffer, though the definitions of buffers in Programs 2.1 and 2.5 are quite different. This means that the descriptions in Program 2.2 is modular. Figure 1 illustrates the inheritance relation among classes presented in this subsection.

2.2 Delegation

ABCL⁺ provides a mechanism similar to the *delegation* mechanism proposed in [Lie86, US87]. Though [Ste87] claims that "delegation" is "inheritance," in this paper we consider that:

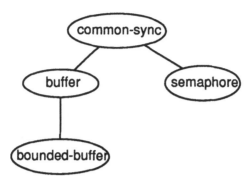

Figure 1: Inheritance Hierarchy

1. An inheritance hierarchy defines a relation among classes, whereas a delegation hierarchy defines a relation among objects.

2. An inheritance hierarchy is static, whereas a delegation hierarchy is dynamic and can be modified during execution.

3. By the inheritance mechanism, a class C inherits methods and instance variables which are defined at ancestors of C. Whereas, by the delegation mechanism, an object cannot directly refer to any instance variables of its ancestors but can borrow their methods.

Since the delegation hierarchy defines a relation among objects (not classes), it is more convenient to describe individual objects directly without using class definitions. In ABCL⁺,

```
[object buffer
  (state [contents := nil])]
```

for instance, defines an object (instead of a class) whose name is `buffer`. Its methods are defined in the same syntax as the method definitions of `buffer` class.

We introduce a new kind of option (`delegate-to` *object* ...), which specifies delegation links, into class and object definition forms. We also introduce a *become*[1] primitive to modify delegation hierarchy dynamically. Upon evaluation of (`become` *object* ...) an object discards the current list of the parents in the delegation hierarchy and adopts the new list *object* ....

Upon introduction of a delegation mechanism in a concurrent language, we have to consider one problem: in order to use delegation for sharing knowledge in a concurrent environment, delegation should be performed as an atomic and serializable operation. The notion of *atomic delegation* has already been proposed and implemented[ADT89]. However, in this paper, we get around of atomic delegations and only consider a simple case, where any object that may be a parent of an object in the delegation hierarchy does not have mutable persistent memory. In other words, a parent in the delegation hierarchy

---

[1]The Actor model[Agh87] also has a primitive whose name is *become*, which is different from our *become*. The former replaces the behavior of an object and the latter replaces the parent in the delegation hierarchy of an object. It is obvious that our *become* can simulate the *become* in the Actor model.

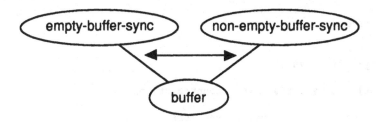

Figure 2: Context Transitions by Delegation

is only used as a *method dictionary*. In response to a delegation request, the parent does not execute any of its method by itself. Conceptually, it returns an appropriate method (if it exists) to the requester (i.e, the receiver object of the original message), which executes the returned method.

The primary reason to introduce a delegation mechanism in our language is that it can be used to represent *context transitions*. Although introduction of the delegation hierarchy for inheriting external behaviors[LaL89, DT88] might be useful even in object-oriented concurrent programming, in this paper we use the delegation mechanism to represent sole context transitions.

The basic idea to describe the behavior of buffers in terms of context transitions is as follows: first, we define two objects which represent synchronization conditions of empty and non-empty buffers, respectively; a buffer object makes the former or the latter of them as the parent in the delegation hierarchy depending on whether it is empty or not. When an empty (or a non-empty) buffer object becomes non-empty (or empty, respectively), its parent is replaced (Figure 2).

According to this idea, the two objects representing synchronization conditions are defined in Program 2.7 and a buffer object is described in Program 2.8. **empty-buffer-sync** and **non-empty-buffer-sync** represent synchronization conditions of empty and non-empty buffers. The former has a single constraint and the latter has no constraints. The initial parent of **buffer** is **empty-buffer-sync**, namely, the evaluation result of (**empty-buffer**).

In order to describe context transitions in a modular manner, we introduce a new type of methods, say *transition* methods, which are defined in the following form:

> [method *message-pattern* (*class-name* :trans)
>   *transition-description*]

The third and the fifth forms in Program 2.7 define transition methods, which in general do not override either primary or constraint methods but may override other transition methods defined at ancestors. A transition method is executed after the corresponding *primary method* is completed. Supposing for instance that an empty buffer object (e.g., a buffer object which is just born) accepts a put request, first the primary method, i.e.,

> (enqueue contents item)

is executed and then the transition method, i.e.,

> (become (non-empty-buffer))

```
;;;
;;; For empty buffers.
;;;

[object empty-buffer-sync]

[method [:get] (empty-buffer-sync :constraint) nil]

[method [:put item] (empty-buffer-sync :trans)
  (become (non-empty-buffer))]

;;;
;;; For non-empty buffers.
;;;

[object non-empty-buffer-sync]

[method [:get] (non-empty-buffer-sync :trans)
  (empty) --> (become (empty-buffer))]
```

Program 2.7: Empty and Non-empty

```
[object buffer
  (state [contents := nil])
  (delegate-to (empty-buffer))]

[method (empty-buffer) (buffer) empty-buffer-sync]

[method (non-empty-buffer) (buffer) non-empty-buffer-sync]

[method [:put item] (buffer)
  (enqueue contents item)]

[method [:get] (buffer)
  (:reply-to r)
  [r <= (dequeue contents)]]
```

Program 2.8: A Buffer Object Using Delegation

is executed, which is defined at empty-buffer-sync and is inherited by the empty buffer using the delegation mechanism. Notice that the object that executes this become form is not empty-buffer-sync but buffer, i.e., the object which accepts the original put request. In this very case,

```
(become non-empty-buffer-sync)
```

is executed and thus non-empty-buffer-sync becomes the new parent of the buffer object. Similarly, when a non-empty buffer object accepts a get request, it first executes the primary method [:get] and then the transition method [:get], where

```
(empty) --> (become (empty-buffer))
```

means that:

if (empty) *is satisfied,* (become (empty-buffer)) *is executed.*

Notice that, in this buffer case, context transitions might be described in the following:

```
[method [:put item] (buffer)
  (if (empty) (become non-empty-buffer-sync))
  (enqueue contents item)]

[method [:get] (buffer)
  (:reply-to r)
  [r <= (dequeue contents)]
  (if (empty) (become empty-buffer-sync))]
```

without using transition methods. However, for the purposes of later code sharing, it is preferable to separate codes for context transitions and those for ordinal computations.

In order to define bounded-buffer using descriptions of buffer based on context transitions, two more objects are necessary, that is, those representing synchronization conditions of *partial* and *full* buffers. A partial buffer accepts both put and get requests and a full buffer accepts sole get requests. We define partial-buffer-sync and full-buffer-sync so that both of them inherit descriptions of non-empty-buffer-sync in Program 2.9. This means that a buffer whose parent (in the delegation hierarchy) is either partial-buffer-sync or full-buffer-sync executes:

```
(become (empty-buffer))
```

after it sends back the last element in response to a get request.

Figures 3 and 4 illustrate the transition rules of bounded-buffer and buffer, respectively. Obviously, the former one is more complicated than the latter one: the latter has only two arrows, whereas the former has six[2]. Program 2.10 is a definition of a bounded buffer object based on the context transition technique.

Transition methods are inherited in a different manner from other types of methods. In case of this example, for instance, the transition method executed by a full buffer in response to a [:get] message is not the one defined at full-buffer-sync but the combination of those defined at full-buffer-sync and non-empty-buffer-sync, say,

---

[2]The situation illustrated in Figure 3 is rather artificial. This figure assumes that a bounded buffer object does not know whether or not its maximum length is one.

```
;;;
;;; For partial buffers
;;;

[object partial-buffer-sync
  (super non-empty-buffer-sync)]

;;;
;;; For full buffers
;;;

[object full-buffer-sync
  (super non-empty-buffer-sync)]

[method [:put item] (full-buffer-sync :constraint) nil]

[method [:get] (full-buffer-sync :trans)
  (not (empty)) --> (become (partial-buffer))]
```

Program 2.9: Partial and Full

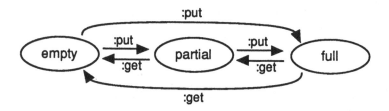

Figure 3: Context Transitions of A Bounded Buffer

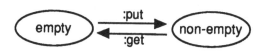

Figure 4: Context Transitions of A Buffer

```
[object bounded-buffer
  (super buffer)]

[method [:put item] (bounded-buffer :trans)
  (full) --> (become (full-buffer))]

[method (non-empty-buffer) (bounded-buffer)
  (partial-buffer)]

[method (partial-buffer) (bounded-buffer)
  partial-buffer-sync]

[method (full-buffer) (bounded-buffer)
  full-buffer-sync]
```

Program 2.10: A Bounded Buffer

```
(not (empty)) --> (become (partial-buffer))
(empty) --> (become (empty-buffer))
```

which is interpreted as :

```
if (not (empty)) then
  (become (partial-buffer))
elseif (empty) then
  (become (empty-buffer))
endif
```

In general, the body of a transition method is described in the following syntax:

$condition_1$ --> $become\text{-}form_1$

$\vdots$

$condition_n$ --> $become\text{-}form_n$

and interpreted as:

(cond ($condition_1$ $become\text{-}form_1$)

$\vdots$

($condition_n$ $become\text{-}form_n$))

If $condition_n$ is omitted, the condition part of the n-th clause is considered always satisfied.

Since non-empty-buffer-sync is inherited by both of partial-buffer-sync and full-buffer-sync, the inheritance mechanism is responsible for the two arrows in Figure 3 which direct to empty. The transition method in Program 2.10 implements the two arrows directing full in the same figure. Since bounded-buffer is defined so that its internal method non-empty-buffer returns partial-buffer-sync, the transition method represented by the arrow in Figure 4 which directs to non-empty is reused and implements the arrow in Figure 3 which directs to partial and whose label is :put. The last arrow in Figure 3 is implemented by the transition method in Program 2.9.

Delegation can support dynamic replacement of objects' behaviors. ABCL$^+$ employs delegation to represent context changes during execution. For the purposes of efficient code sharing, we separate the behavior of an object into three, which are represented by *constraint*, *primary*, and *transition* methods. These three are inherited and delegated separately.

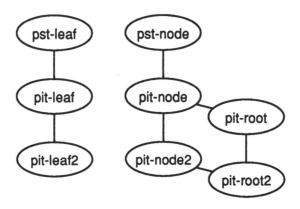

Figure 5: Inheritance Hierarchy

3   A More Practical Example

In this section, we show the expressive power of ABCL$^+$ using a more practical example. For the purposes, we describe the behaviors of a family of objects, which represent nodes of the following parallel height balanced trees:

1. those which accept concurrent search requests

2. those which accept concurrent search and insertion requests and which use exclusive locks to avoid conflicts

3. those which accept concurrent search and insertion requests and which use both exclusive and read locks to avoid conflicts

We call the first sort of tree a *parallel search tree* and the second and the third *parallel insertion trees*. We describe only 2-3 trees[AHU74] as height balanced trees but the same technique is applicable to other sorts of height balanced trees which concurrently accept search and insertion requests.

Figure 5 illustrates the inheritance hierarchy among classes which are to be presented in this section. In this figure, `pst-leaf` and `pst-node` are the classes of leaf and non-leaf node objects of parallel search trees ("pst" stands for "parallel search trees"); `pit-leaf`, `pit-node`, and `pit-root` are the classes of leaf, internal, and root node objects of parallel insertion trees which employ only exclusive locks; `pit-leaf2`, `pit-node2`, and `pit-root2` are the classes of leaf, internal, and root node objects of parallel insertion trees which employ both read and exclusive locks.

3.1   Parallel Search Trees

In the sequel, we describe a 2-3 parallel search tree each of whose nodes is implemented as a concurrent object and which as a whole can process more than one search request at a time. There are no difficulties to describe such a tree since any node does not accept any request that modify the contents of nodes. A tree always accepts search requests and does not accept any other sort of request. This means that no context transitions are required to describe the behaviors of parallel search trees.

Program 3.1 defines two classes pst-leaf and pst-node, whose instances are leaf and non-leaf nodes of a parallel search tree, respectively. A leaf node stores an *index* and a *value*. When a leaf receives a message for a search request, if the specified index in the message is equal to the stored index in the leaf, it returns its stored value. Otherwise it returns nil[3] (i.e., a void value). A non-leaf node also accepts a message for a search request. Each non-leaf node just passes both the received message and the reply destination to the appropriate child, which an internal method appropriate-child determines according to the information stored in the node. In order to forward a reply destination, the following syntax:

$$[\textit{object-name} <= \textit{message} : \texttt{reply-to} \ \textit{reply-destination}]$$

is available.

For the purposes of initialization, we add methods [:init ...]s to both classes. These methods for initialization are invoked just after instances are created using new forms. For instance, by the following form:

$$(\texttt{new 'pst-leaf} \ [\texttt{:init} \ \textit{index} \ \textit{value}])$$

an object of class pst-leaf is created and just after the creation the newly created object is forced to process an initialization message [:init *index value*]. Notice that, this form guarantees that no messages are processed earlier than [:init *index value*] by the newly created object. Using new forms, a parallel search tree in Figure 6 can be constructed as follows:

```
(new 'pst-node
     [:init [(new 'pst-node [:init [[(new 'pst-leaf [:init 1 ...]) 1]
                                    [(new 'pst-leaf [:init 2 ...]) 2]
                                    [(new 'pst-leaf [:init 3 ...]) 3]]])
             3]
            [(new 'pst-node [:init [[(new 'pst-leaf [:init 4 ...]) 4]
                                    [(new 'pst-leaf [:init 6 ...]) 6]
                                    [(new 'pst-leaf [:init 7 ...]) 7]]])
             7]
            [(new 'pst-node [:init [[(new 'pst-leaf [:init 8 ...]) 8]
                                    [(new 'pst-leaf [:init 9 ...]) 9]]])
             9]])
```

After that, if an object sends a search message (e.g., [:search 4]) to the root node, the message is passed from the root to a leaf and the leaf returns a value *directly* to the original reply destination. Although each node can execute only a single message at a time, more than one message can be processed in the whole tree simultaneously. For instance, just after the root passes a message, it can accept the next message even if the previous one is being processed by another node at that time.

---

[3]An if form in Common Lisp[Ste84] returns nil when the evaluation result of the first argument (i.e., the condition part) is nil (i.e., *false*) and the form does not have the third argument (i.e., the *else* part). We follow this convention.

```
;;;
;;; Leaves
;;;

[class pst-leaf
  (state my-index my-value)]

[method [:search index] (pst-leaf)
  (:reply-to r)
  [r <= (if (= index my-index) my-value)]]

[method [:init index value] (pst-leaf)
  [my-index := index]
  [my-value := value]]

;;;
;;; Non-leaf Nodes
;;;

[class pst-node ()
  (state my-children)]

[method [:search index] (pst-node)
  (:reply-to r)
  [(appropriate-child index) <= [:search index] :reply-to r]]

[method (appropriate-child index) (pst-node)
  (match my-children
    (is [[l-tree l-max] . _] where (<= index l-max)
      l-tree)
    (is [_ [m-tree m-max] . _] where (<= index m-max)
      m-tree)
    (is [_ _ [r-tree _]]
      r-tree))]

[method [:init children] (pst-leaf)
  [my-children := children]]
```

Program 3.1: Parallel Search Trees

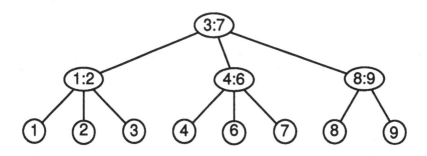

Figure 6: A 2-3 tree

3.2 Parallel Insertion Trees

Borrowing descriptions of `pst-leaf` and `pst-node`, next we describe the behaviors of leaf and internal node objects of parallel insertion trees. We use two algorithms proposed in [BS77]. The first algorithm uses only exclusive locks, whereas the second one uses both read and exclusive locks. Each node on which a read lock is placed cannot accept any other insertion requests but can accept search requests, whereas each node on which an exclusive lock is placed cannot accept any other requests.

In the sequel, we say that an insertion request is in the *search phase* if the place to insert a leaf node is being searched for by the request. Otherwise, we say that the request is in the *modification phase*. Then, the following can easily be verified:

1. when an insertion request currently in the modification phase is just modifying a node N, each node on the path from N to the first ancestor (including N itself) that has just two children will *always* be modified (and possibly split) by the request, and

2. when an insertion request currently in the search phase is just going through the node N, the same nodes as in 1 *may possibly* be modified.

The first algorithm uses a quite simple strategy: an exclusive lock is placed on each non-leaf node that may be modified by an insertion request. By using this strategy, no two requests can access the same node simultaneously if one of them might modify the node. As for the second algorithm, an exclusive lock is placed on each non-leaf node that is *always* modified by an insertion request, and a read lock is placed on each non-leaf node that *may* be modified by an insertion request. Note that the *may-be-modified* nodes turn into the *always-be-modified* nodes when the insertion request goes into the modification phase.

In the following implementation, for simplicity we assume that:

1. the number of leaves of a tree is greater than or equal to two so as to avoid the degenerate case where the root is the only leaf,

2. more than one leaf with the same index can never be inserted, and

3. the greatest index stored in a tree (i.e., the index stored in the rightmost leaf) is always greater than any index to be inserted.

The leaf nodes of the first algorithm is described as in Programs 3.2. Different from leaf nodes in a parallel search tree, leaf nodes in Program 3.2 accept insertion requests. Notice that `class` is a built-in function whose argument is an object name and which returns the class of the object referred to by the object name. `Me` is a pseudo variable, which always refers to the object evaluating it.

In response to a message matching `[:insert ...]`, a leaf node, say N, creates another leaf, say N', which is to be inserted, and returns N' and its index to the parent of N. After receiving N', the parent will make N' the immediate younger brother of N. Notice that in this implementation the index received by a leaf node as a part of an insertion request is always less than the index stored by this node. Notice that "`_`" is an anonymous pattern variable which matches every value.

```
[class pit-leaf
  (super pst-leaf)]

[method [:insert index value _] (pit-leaf)
  (:reply-to parent)
  [parent <= [:new-child [(new (class Me) [:init index value]) index]]]]]
```

Program 3.2: Leaves in Parallel Insertion Trees

```
[object unlock]

;;;
;;; Exclusive Locks
;;;

[object exclusive-lock]

[method [:release-lock] (exclusive-lock :constraint) t]

[method _ (exclusive-lock :constraint) nil]

[method [:release-lock] (exclusive-lock :trans)
  (pop-parents)]
```

Program 3.3: Objects Representing Lock and Unlock

We use the context transition technique to describe the behavior of internal node objects in parallel insertion trees. Each node object is always in either of two contexts: *unlock* and *lock* and so we define two objects unlock and exclusive-lock which represent these contexts (See Program 3.3). In general, unlock requires no constraints, whereas exclusive-lock suspends processing almost all messages. For the purposes, exclusive-lock has two constraint methods, by which a [:release-lock] message is accepted even when a node is exclusively locked and any other message cannot be accepted unless these constraint methods are overridden. Notice that the constraint method [:release-lock] has the precedence over the other constraint method "_" since the former is defined earlier. In general, the precedence among methods which are defined at the same class (or object) and which belong to the same sort are defined in terms of the definition order. A new primitive pop-parents occurring in the transition method of exclusive-lock will be explained later.

The class of internal nodes pit-node is defined in Program 3.4. It inherits descriptions of pst-node by the inheritance mechanism and each of its instance objects has the parent unlock in the delegation hierarchy at the birth time. We do not prepare as many unlock objects as the number of internal node objects but just define a single unlock since unlock is just regarded as a method dictionary.

The methods [:insert ...] and release-lock-if-necessary define the actions performed when an insertion request arrives. Roughly speaking, the former method represents the actions that are performed by both internal and root nodes and the latter

```
[class pit-node
  (super pst-node)
  (state my-parent)
  (delegate-to unlock)]

[method (lock) (pit-node) exclusive-lock]
```

```
;;;
;;; Methods for the Search Phase
;;;
```

```
[method [:insert . _] (pit-node :trans)
  (push-parents (lock))]  ;; Place an exclusive lock.

[method [:insert index value locked-ancestors] (pit-node)
  ;; locked-ancestors is the list of the locked ancestors
  (:reply-to parent)
  [(appropriate-child index)  ;; except the parent.
   <= [:insert index value (release-lock-if-necessary
                            [parent . locked-ancestors])] :reply-to Me]
  [my-parent := parent]]

[method (release-lock-if-necessary locked-ancestors) (pit-node)
  (cond (this node has two children
         [locked-ancestors <= [:release-lock]]
         ;; Release the lock on the ancestors.
         nil)
        (this node has three children
         locked-ancestors))]  ;; No locks are released.
```

```
;;;
;;; Methods for the Modification Phase
;;;
```

```
[method [:new-child . _] (pit-node :constraint) t]

[method [:new-child . _] (pit-node :trans)
  (pop-parents)]

[method [:new-child [node max]] (pit-node)  ;; This node is modified.
  Add node as a child.
  (match my-children  ;; At this stage, this node may have four children.
    (is [_ _ _])  ;; If this node has three children, there are no problems.
    (is [[n1 n1-max] [n2 n2-max] [n3 n3-max] [n4 n4-max]]
        (new-children
         (new (class Me) [:init [[n1 n1-max] [n2 n2-max]]])
         n2-max n3 n3-max n4 n4-max)))]

[method (new-children new-child new-max n3 n3-max n4 n4-max) (pit-node)
  [my-parent <= [:new-child new-child new-max]]
  [my-children := [[n3 n3-max] [n4 n4-max]]]]
```

Program 3.4: Internal Nodes of Parallel Insertion Trees

```
[class pit-root
  (super pit-node)]

[method (release-lock-if-necessary . _) (pit-root)]

[method (new-children new-child new-max n3 n3-max n4 n4-max) (pit-root)
  [my-children := [[new-child new-max]
                  [(new (class new-child)
                       [:init [[n3 n3-max] [n4 n4-max]]])
                   n4-max]]]]
```

Program 3.5: Roots of Parallel Insertion Trees

method represents the actions that are performed only by internal nodes. Later on, the descriptions of the latter is overridden at `pit-root`, whereas the descriptions of the former is reused at `pit-root`.

After executing the primary method [`:insert` ...], a node replaces its parent in the delegation hierarchy and enters the other context. `push-parents` is another primitive to modify the delegation hierarchy dynamically during execution. An object changes its parents by evaluation of `push-parents` in the similar manner to `become`. In addition, the old parents are pushed onto the *context stack* of the object. The pushed parents may be popped up and restored later in the future by execution of `pop-parents`. Now the meaning of the transition method of `exclusive-lock` becomes clear. When a node object is exclusively locked, a [`:release-lock`] message removes the lock by replacing the parent in the delegation hierarchy with the previous one (i.e., `unlock`).

The remaining parts of the descriptions concern the actions performed when an internal node becomes to have one more child. The constraint method [`:new-child` ...] overrides the constraint methods of `exclusive-lock` so that an internal node can accept a request to add a new child even when the object is locked. The transition method [`:new-child` ...] is used to escape from the exclusively locked context. Similar to the method definitions for insertion requests, the actions to add a new child is described in two separate methods: [`:new-child` ...] and `new-children`. The former represents the actions performed by both internal and root nodes and the latter represents the actions performed only by internal nodes.

The behaviors of an internal node and a root node are similar but a little different. The root node does not have any ancestor and cannot send any messages to `my-parent`. When the root becomes to have four children, it should create two new child nodes and make the old children the new grandchildren. The differences of them are described in Program 3.5.

Next, we describe the second algorithm of parallel insertion trees. An important difference between this sort of tree and the previous one is that in this case a read lock may possibly be placed on a non-leaf node object. We start with defining a `read-lock` object as in Program 3.6, which inherits descriptions from `exclusive-lock`. Two constraint methods are added to `read-lock` so that a node object accepts messages for search and/or lock requests even when a read lock is placed on the node. Constraint methods defined at `exclusive-lock` are inherited so that:

```
[object read-lock
  (super exclusive-lock)]

[method [:place-exclusive-lock] (read-lock :constraint) t]

[method [:search . _] (read-lock :constraint) t]

[method [:place-exclusive-lock] (read-lock :trans)
  (become exclusive-lock)]
```

Program 3.6: A Readlock Object

```
[class pit-leaf2
  (super pit-leaf)]

[method [:insert index value _ top] (pit-leaf2)
  [top <= [:place-exclusive-lock]]]]

[method [:place-exclusive-lock] (pit-leaf2)
  (:reply-to r)
  (call-super [:insert index value nil] :reply-to r)]
```

Program 3.7: Leaves of Parallel Insertion Trees

- a [:release-lock] message is accepted and

- any message that is neither of [:release-lock], [:place-exclusive-lock], and
  [:search ...] cannot be accepted.

Except for the the locking mechanisms, two algorithms are similar to each other. In the second algorithm, during execution of an insertion request in the search phase, read locks are placed on the nodes which may be modified in its modification phase. Just before the request turns into the modification phase, the read locks on them are converted into exclusive locks. On implementing this step, we must pay a special attention to the case where search requests transmitted to locked nodes have not yet been processed. The read lock on a node must not be converted until all of such search messages have gone through the node unless it is of the greatest height among the locked nodes. In the second algorithm, read locks placed by any insertion request are converted in the top-to-bottom order so that the conversion request goes from the locked node of the greatest height to that of the least height after these search requests.

The new leaf class pit-leaf2 is defined in Program 3.7. The first two definitions in this program are obvious. A leaf node, just after accepting an insertion request, sends to top a request for converting locks. In the last one, a new primitive call-super is used, which in this case invokes the primary method [:insert ...] defined at the superclass, i.e., pit-leaf. Notice that call-super does not invoke any constraint or transition methods. It just invokes the specified primary method as if it is an internal method. The last method is triggered by a conversion request which is born at the leaf node and which is going through the nodes on the path from top to the leaf.

```
[class pit-node2
  (super pit-node)]

[method (lock) (pit-node) read-lock]

[method [:insert index value locked-ancestors top] (pit-node2)
  (:reply-to parent)
  [(appropriate-child index)
   <= [:insert index value
              (release-lock-if-necessary [parent . locked-ancestors])
              (if (null locked-ancestors) Me top)]
   :reply-to Me]]

[method [:place-exclusive-lock] (pit-node2)
  [(appropriate-child index) <= [:place-exclusive-lock]]]]
```

Program 3.8: Internal Nodes of Parallel Insertion Trees

Figure 7: Context Transitions of `pit-node`

Program 3.8 is the descriptions of the new internal node class `pit-node2`. Figures 7 and 8 illustrate the possible context transitions of `pit-node` and `pit-node2`, respectively.

The latter one has four arrows and three of them can be implemented by reusing descriptions of the former protocol.

The descriptions of the root node class `pit-root2` is surprisingly short:

```
[class pit-root2
  (super pit-node2 pit-root)]
```

We currently assume the linearization mechanism in Flavors and CLOS to resolve possible conflicts among multiple parents. Furthermore, we assume that inheritance has a precedence over delegation. For instance, when an instance object of `pit-node2` accepts

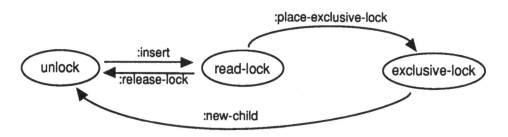

Figure 8: Context Transitions of `pit-node2`

a message, method definitions are searched for so that classes have the following precedences:

When no locks are placed:
    `pit-node2, pit-node, pst-node, unlock`

When a read lock is placed:
    `pit-node2, pit-node, pst-node, read-lock, exclusive-lock`

When an exclusive lock is placed:
    `pit-node2, pit-node, pst-node, exclusive-lock`

4 Discussion

Until now several schemes are proposed for reuse of concurrent objects [KL89, TS89]. In [TS89], synchronization conditions are described in terms of *enable sets*, which are just sets (in some sense) and so not only they can be transmitted via messages but also two or more of them can be composed into one by using the set union operator. [TS89] figured out the importance of first-class synchronization codes and their being compositional. [Rep88] also pointed out the usefulness of first-class synchronization conditions. However, in our terms, [KL89, TS89] do not use the technique based on *constraint specifications* but the one based on *context transitions*. [MWY90] reports disadvantages of this way of approach. Roughly speaking, this approach often causes troubles when a descendant class requires new contexts.

We design our language so that synchronization codes can be first-class and compositional. The delegation mechanism supports the first-class synchronization conditions since (the names of) ancestors of an object in the delegation hierarchy are the first-class values. This means that an object can send (the name of) an object representing synchronization conditions and the receiver can adopt it as an ancestor dynamically. Also, the delegation mechanism automatically composes descriptions of multiple parents. One unique point of our approach is to separate the constraint/transition methods from primary methods. We design the syntax of transition methods so that they are easily reused: the units of reuse are neither statements nor expressions but clauses (i.e., pairs of conditions and actions). As a result, even when new contexts are introduced in descendant classes, redefinitions of ancestor classes seldom occur. Without the notion of transition method, for instance, it is difficult to describe the difference between the context transitions illustrated in Figure 3 and those illustrated in Figure 4.

One may consider that our technique is similar to the daemon combination in CLOS and Flavors[Sym88]. Although the roles of constraint/transition methods seem similar to those of before/after daemons, there are many minor differences: all the before daemons are executed in Flavors and CLOS, whereas only a single constraint method is executed in ABCL$^+$; the after daemons are executed in the most-specific-last manner, whereas the most specific transition method has the highest priority; and so on. Still, however, we consider that Flavors and CLOS can be good prototyping languages of ABCL$^+$.

ABCL$^+$ provides a support for integration of two approaches which are based on constraint specifications and context transitions. For instance, a buffer object whose definition is based on context transitions can have a bounded buffer as a child whose differential descriptions are based on constraint specifications. This sort of integration is important since either of these approaches could not cover all the requirements (consult [MWY90]).

References

[ADT89]   Mehmet Aksit, Jan Willem Dijkstra, and Anand Tripathi. Atomic delega-
          tions. Technical Report INF–89–10, Un. of Twente, Department of Computer
          Science, February 1989.

[Agh87]   Gul Agha. *Actors : A Model of Concurrent Computation in Distributed Sys-
          tems*. The MIT Press, 1987.

[AHU74]   A. V. Aho, J. Hopcroft, and D. Ullman. *The Design and Analysis of Computer
          Algorithms*. Addison-Wesley, 1974.

[BDG+88] Daniel G. Bobrow, Linda G. DeMichiel, Richard P. Gabriel, Sonya E. Keene,
          Gregor Kiczales, and David A. Moon. Common lisp object system specifica-
          tion, X3J13 document 88-002R. *SIGPLAN Notices*, 23, September 1988.

[BS77]   R. Bayer and M. Schkolnick. Concurrency of operations on B-tree. *Acta
          Informatica*, 9(1):1–21, 1977.

[DT88]   Scott Danforth and Chris Tomlinson. Type theories and object-oriented pro-
          gramming. *ACM Computing Surveys*, 20(1):29–72, March 1988.

[GR83]   Adele Goldberg and David Robson. *Smalltalk-80 — The Language and its
          Implementation*. Addison-Wesley, 1983.

[Hoa78]   C. A. R. Hoare. Communicating sequential processes. *Communications of the
          ACM*, 21(8):666–677, 1978.

[KL89]   Dennis G. Kafura and Keung Hae Lee. Inheritance in actor based concurrent
          object-oriented languages. In *ECOOP'89: Proceedings of European Conference
          on Object-Oriented Programming*, pages 131–145, 1989.

[LaL89]   Wilf R. LaLonde. Designing families of data types using exemplars. *ACM
          Transactions on Programming Languages and Systems*, 11(2):212–248, April
          1989.

[Lie86]   Henry Lieberman. Using prototypical objects to implement shared behavior
          in object oriented systems. In *Proceedings of ACM Conference on Object-
          Oriented Programming Systems, Languages, and Applications, Portland OR,
          USA.*, pages 214–223, November 1986.

[Mil80]   Robin Milner. *A Calculus of Communicating Systems*, volume 92 of *Lecture
          Notes in Computer Science*. Springer-Verlag, 1980.

[MWY90] Satoshi Matsuoka, Ken Wakita, and Akinori Yonezawa. Inheritance in concurrent object-oriented languages. In *7th Conference Proceedings of Japan Society for Software Science and Technology*, pages 65–68, 1990.

[Rep88] J. H. Reppy. Synchronous operations as first-class values. In *Proceedings of ACM SIGPLAN Conference on Programming Language Design and Implementation*, pages 250–259. ACM, 1988.

[Ste84] Guy L. Steele Jr., editor. *Common Lisp — the Language*. Digital Press, 1984.

[Ste87] Lynn Andrea Stein. Delegation is inheritance. In *Proceedings of ACM Conference on Object-Oriented Programming Systems, Languages, and Applications, Orlando FL, USA.*, pages 138–155, October 1987.

[Sym88] Symbolics Inc. *Symbolics Common Lisp - Language Concepts, Symbolics Release 7.2 Document Set*, February 1988.

[TS89] Chris Tomlinson and Vineet Singh. Inheritance and synchronization with enabled-sets. In *Proceedings of ACM Conference on Object-Oriented Programming Systems, Languages, and Applications, New Orleans, USA*, pages 103–112. ACM, October 1989.

[US87] David Ungar and Randall B. Smith. Self: The power of simplicity. In *Proceedings of ACM Conference on Object-Oriented Programming Systems, Languages, and Applications, Orlando FL, USA.*, pages 227–242, October 1987.

[Yon90] Akinori Yonezawa, editor. *ABCL: An Object-Oriented Concurrent System — Theory, Language, Programming, Implementation and Application*. The MIT Press, 1990.

[YSB+86] Akinori Yonezawa, Etsuya Shibayama, Jean Pierre Briot, Yasuaki Honda, and Toshihiro Takada. An object-oriented concurrent information processing model ABCM/1 and its description language ABCL/1. *Computer Software*, 3(3):9–23, 1986. (Revised version in [Yon90]).

The Computational Field Model for Open Distributed Environments (Extended Abstract)

Mario Tokoro* and Kohei Honda
Department of Computer Science, Keio University
3-14-1 Hiyoshi, Kohoku-ku, Yokohama 223, Japan

1 Introduction

This paper presents the *computational field model*, which is a new methodological framework to capture the essence of open distributed environments. We first introduce the basic notion of the model. The underlying vision of open distributed systems is described and the essential characteristics of the model are reviewed. Then a dynamic object reconfiguration scheme in the computational field is presented as one of the fundamental functionalities of the field. We also briefly introduce the framework of the unique computational theory based on the computational field. We conclude this paper with our future view.

2 The Computational Field Model

With the advent of distributed computing age, the computational space where software systems function and interact, shows characteristics not easily understood by a simple extrapolation of the framework of single computer systems. There an application system usually consists of multiple, concurrently running subsystems, which are often scattered around in the huge geographic extension and whose existence are dynamically searched for utilization at run-time [2]. Such a subsystem has often been developed quite independently with each other, based on its own unique orientation in design and conceptualization. To combine the functionalities of these systems for accomplishing the goal of a certain application, surely results in a possible conceptual disparities among subsystems. But without this new way of composing systems, the very virtues of distributed computing environments — versatility in functions, dynamism in computation, efficiency and robustness in execution — are lost. Thus the computational space as a whole is vast geographic extensions where conceptually and physically heterogeneous systems are running and interacting with each other. New nodes and applications will be added to the space, and

*Also with Sony Computer Science Laboratory Inc. 3-14-13 Higashi Gotanda, Shinagawa-ku, Tokyo, 141, Japan

existent ones will disappear or get disconnected here and there. The computational space is huge, incomparably huge-scale as contrasted with what we have known as computing environments. In a sense, we will never know where it begins or where it ends. The space is borderless.

The computational field model(CFM for short) [14, 15] was proposed as a new conceptual scheme to capture the open distributed computational space with these unique characteristics. Instead of regarding the distributed environments as a collection of processing nodes and communication networks, the space as a whole is abstracted as horizontal, continuous extensions called the *computational field*. Entities are "floating" on it, which are concurrent objects [16, 19], and the computation proceed by their migration, interaction, and dynamic generation of new ones. The significance of CFM lies in understanding the state of computation at the higher level of abstraction, neglecting unnecessary details such as the configuration and performance of each node, network topologies, routing functionalities etc. After forgetting these details, however, we can recapture the essences of these constructs of distributed environments, such as geographic distribution, locality, work load, or communication traffics, at some abstract level, thus providing a cleaner view for design and analysis.

One notable feature of CFM is its emphasis on object migration. In general, objects are supposed to be equipped with migration capability, for the purpose of dynamically grouping objects for efficiency, balancing the workload of the field, supporting the mobility of users, and achieving robustness of the system against errors and faults. CFM even considers that message passing among objects are performed by a special kind of objects called *messengers*. In the place of sending, an object *dissimilate* a messenger. Then a messenger will migrate to the target object, and the object will *assimilate* the messenger, copying the content of the message into itself. Of course the situation becomes complex when the target object has also migration capability, for which we suppose some kind of "object chasing" functionality. This communication scheme is called *assimilation/dissimilation model*. The process can be likened to anabolism and catabolism as biological phenomena.

3   Dynamic Grouping and Diffusion of objects in the Field

CFM offers a new perspective for understanding and exploiting possibilities of open distributed environments. For example, the framework of objects floating in the field provides us with high-level scheme for load balancing strategy different from the foregoing proposals. In contrast to the traditional load balancing framework whose target is, in general, to balance the workload by task relocation, usually assuming some specific hardware configuration, the objective of CFM-based load balancing is to give the best possible framework for dynamic grouping and diffusion of objects based on factors such as workload in some local field of computation, degree of interrelationship among objects, and migration cost. The grouping is necessary, because we want to minimize the cost of frequent interaction among objects. Diffusion is inevitable, because too much concentration of objects in some local space will raise the workload , thus decreasing performance intolerably. The significance of this methodology exists that the foregoing load balancing scheme of tasks is transformed into dynamic object *reorganization* scheme.

This idea first appeared in [14] and was proposed as a concrete methodology in [17]. There the diffusion process is controlled by workload information called *repulsive force* among objects, and the grouping process is controlled by communication frequency among objects called *gravitational force*. When a repulsive force among objects in some local space is high, it means that the workload there is high, prompting diffusion. When gravitational force between two objects is large, it means that they had better come closer to each other, leading to dynamic grouping. Of course we should consider migration cost, which is abstracted as *mass* of an object, meaning the size of the object. With these three parameters, dynamic reorganization of distribution of objects is carried out. The computational field is now regarded as some kind of metric space, and this metric space and these basic parameters determine sub-optimal location of each object participating in some application. We can liken the grouping/diffusion process to Newtonian dynamics, or to a kind of process of thermo-dynamics.

While we leave the detailed formulation of this dynamic relocation scheme to [17], where several basic constructions of formulae for calculating repulsive and gravitational forces and deciding sub-optimal location in the metric space are given, we would like to note how the basic scheme of CFM is effective in conceptualization of this new perspective for distributed computing. As CFM treats computational space at the high abstraction level, details of distributed systems such as physical configuration of each processing node, network bandwidth, and communication topology are mapped to the abstract metric space, making methodological treatment quite tractable. Of course this means that pragmatics of this methodology should be established by re-mapping the abstract scheme to some concrete configurations. However, only with this abstraction can we gain the general and clear perspective for load balancing issues in open distributed environments, where we can reason about varied frameworks and concepts in more general settings..

4 Infrastructure for Computational Field Model

CFM offers us effective high-level abstraction for large-scale open distributed environments. If the foundational software architecture is based on CFM-based interfaces, this abstraction can be utilized quite effectively by programmers and users, presenting the abstract yet exact view of systems as well as hiding unnecessary details. For the kind of realization, Muse operating system [18] is being developed, where CFM provides the basic design guideline. In a sense, Muse is one of the first distributed operating systems whose target domain is not restricted to small local-area networks. Aiming at supporting dynamic computation in huge-scale open distributed environments, Muse supports concurrent objects and their migration, provision of geographical view of the computational space (at some abstract levels), and self-advancing scheme based on reflective architecture at the foundational level of operating system design. The dynamic grouping and diffusion scheme depicted above will be incorporated afterward. Muse operating system is the realization of CFM vision of computing as the basic software interface in open distributed systems.

5 The Field and Formal Theories of Concurrency

There is another research domain where CFM-related notion seems quite suggestive – formal theories of concurrency. Our argument is that we can construct an effective framework of concurrent computation *as a crystalization of the vision of distributed computation*. Here the feature of CFM which is the radical departure from the foregoing node-network framework of computation becomes essential. The point is, after the departure, we will no longer assume streams, ports, or the mail delivery system as means of communication, being synchronous or asynchronous. Instead, we will only assume that *terms* migrating to another term denote communication. The main significance here lies in *expression of pending messages as syntactic terms*, which makes the process of communication quite tractable in some formal system.

Possibly the first exposition of this idea (messages as syntactic terms) may be found in our work on the language PROTO[1][4], where the basic computational space is envisaged as horizontal or three-dimensional extension, and communication is supposed to be carried out by a "male term" swimming for a target "female term". Then atomic interaction happens, and new terms are generated, the "parent terms" disappearing from the computational space. The same "discovery" (i.e. expression of asynchronous communication by pending terms) was independently made by Nierstrasz [13] and by Meseguer [7]. Later our work on PROTO was reformulated as a small calculus of concurrent objects [5, 6], which incorporates the framework of CFM and the formalism of Milner's π-calculus [9, 11, 12].

The underlying computational framework of this small calculus is the notion of very fine-grained computational entities functioning in the field-like extension. It has several differences from the framework of CFM depicted in Section 2 of the present paper, partly because of its heritage from the language PROTO and partly because of its theoretical orientation. But the essential vision and general framework of computing is the same – the formal system is constructed as a first step to conceptualize the general concurrent computation as "condensed" open, distributed systems. We consider that distance and locality are dual essential notions even in abstract computation theories. In this regard, our orientation is in sharp contrast with Berry and Boudol's Chemical Abstract Machine [1], where global "magical mixing" plays the role of directed migration in our framework. Of course similarity is more impressive than the difference – clearly both can be characterized by their radical departure from the node-network framework for concurrent computation. But CFM view is that distribution and locality should be positioned at the foundational level of the computation theory, whose consequences are not yet clear at this stage of investigation (yet see [6]). Regarding this point, rigorous formulation of migration process as computational rules should be investigated. Also to bridge between CFM's macroscopic abstraction framework and the field-based formal theory of computation, will be a challenging research topic in future.

---

[1]named after Protozoa.

6 Conclusion

In this paper, we introduced the computational field model and related research topics. CFM offers us a high-level abstraction of computational space of open distributed environments, where we no longer have *nodes* and *networks* but the field and floating entities. The high-level abstraction enables us to concentrate on essential aspects of dynamic computation in open distributed environments, mapping detailed structures such as processor configuration and network topologies onto abstract elements such as the field and objects. Migration is positioned at the core of the framework, and we described dynamic object grouping/diffusion scheme in the computational field. We also referred to the significance of the field notion in general concurrency theory, which shows interesting similarities and differences from Berry and Boudol's Chemical Abstract Machine.

Our computational environments are undergoing radical evolution with the accelerating development of networked computers. The resulting form of computation will be quite different from what we have known until now. The new environments are both enchanting (because of its versatility and dynamism) and dangerous (because of its tremendous complexity and nondeterminism). To exploit the chances and to avoid the dangers, we need to construct a new conceptual and technological framework for software development and analysis, based on the deep understanding of the essential characteristics of the coming computer environments. Our hope is that CFM and the related works can contribute to the important methodological construction in the age of open distributed computing.

References

[1] Berry, G. and Boudol, G., *The Chemical Abstract Machine*. Proc 17 the Annual Symposium on Principles of Programming Languages, 1990.

[2] Hewitt, C., and de Jong, P., *Open Systems*. in: *On Conceptual Modeling*. Brodie, M. et al., ed. Springer-Verlag, 1984

[3] Hoare, C.A.R., *Communicating Sequential Processes*. Prentice Hall, 1985.

[4] Honda, K. and Tokoro, M., *A Report On Language PROTO and Its Underlying Computation Model*. KEIO-CS-1989-1, April 1989. With annotations in October 1990 as KEIO-CS-1990-1.

[5] Honda, K. and Tokoro, M., *A Small Calculus for Concurrent Objects*. in Proceedings of OBCS Workshop 1990, SIGPLAN NOTICES.

[6] Honda, K. and Tokoro, M., *Objects and Calculi*. 1990, submitted.

[7] Meseguer et al., *Concurrent Term Rewriting*. SRI-CSL-90-2, SRI International, February 1990.

[8] Milner, R., *Calculus of Communicating Systems*. LNCS 92, 1980.

[9] Milner, R., Parrow, J.G. and Walker, D.J., *A Calculus of Mobile Processes. Part I and II*. ECS-LFCS-89-85/86, Edinburgh University, 1989

[10] Milner, R., *Communication and Concurrency.* Prentice Hall, 1989.

[11] Milner, R., *Functions as Processes.* LNCS 443, 1990.

[12] Milner, R., *Functions as Processes.* Rapports de Recherche No.1154, INRIA-Sophia Antipolis, February 1990.

[13] Nierstrasz, O., *A Guide to Specifying Concurrent Behaviour with Abacus.* in Tsichritzis, D., ed. *Object Management.* Centre Universitaire D'informatique, Universite de Geneve, July 1990.

[14] Tokoro, M., *Issues In Object-Oriented Distributed Computing.* in: *Proceedings of 4th Conference of Japan Society for Software Science and Technology,* September 1988. (in Japanese, English version available)

[15] Tokoro, M., *Computational Field Model: Toward a New Computing Model/Methodology for Open Distributed Environment.* The 2nd IEEE Workshop on Future Trends in Distributed Computing Systems, Cairo, 1990.

[16] Tokoro, M. and Jean-Pierre Briot, *Concurrent Object-Oriented Programming.* a Tutorial given at TOOLS'90, Paris, May 1990.

[17] Uehara,M. and Tokoro,M, *An Adaptive Load Balancing Method in the Computational Field Model.* in Proceedings of OBCS Workshop 1990, SIGPLAN NOTICES.

[18] Yokote, Y., Teraoka, F., and Tokoro, M., *A Reflective Architecture for an Object-Oriented Distributed Operating System.* In Proceedings of European Conference on Object-Oriented Programming, July, 1989.

[19] Yonezawa, A. and Tokoro, M., *Object-Oriented Concurrent Programming.* MIT Press, 1986.

Concurrent Programming in COB

Kaoru Hosokawa, Hiroaki Nakamura
and Tsutomu Kamimura
IBM Research, Tokyo Research Laboratory
5-19, Sanbancho, Chiyoda-ku, Tokyo 102, Japan

Abstract

COB is a C based object oriented language. It is strongly typed and a type-safe language. It supports garbage collection of objects. COB attempts to improve the performance of the final code without sacrificing the quality of program development. As the number of COB programs increase and as more multiprocessor workstations appear, the interest in executing these COB programs concurrently on multiprocessor workstations emerge. Concurrent COB is an extension to COB that supports concurrent programming. Process with synchronous communication is introduced into COB to support concurrency. In this paper, the design of Concurrent COB and an implementation on a multiprocessor workstation are described.

1 Introduction

C based object oriented programming languages are rapidly gaining acceptance. In particular, the popularity of C++ is growing. However, certain problems have become common to many users, for example, type mismatch, memory management, unnecessary recompilation and reusability, which decrease the efficiency of programming. These problems are inherent in C++ due to its emphasis on generating efficient code more so than supporting efficient program development. COB [7] is an object oriented extension to C being developed at our laboratory. COB attempts to improve on the quality of the final executable code without sacrificing the efficiency of program development. These may seem to be two conflicting goals, but the approach taken is first to satisfy the programming efficiency during program development and then to satisfy the execution efficiency during the generation of the final code.

COB is a strongly typed and type-safe language. Type checking is performed to detect type mismatches at compile time and in some cases at runtime. Garbage collection of objects is supported to free the programmers from error prone memory management tasks. COB completely separates a class interface from its implementation. This increases the modularity of classes and also reduces the number of recompilation of classes. COB is upward compatible with C. Thus C style programming is supported in COB. COB generates efficient code by performing extensive optimizations, for example by removing runtime checks, changing indirect calls to direct calls where possible and so on.

As the number of useful COB programs increase and as more multiprocessor based workstations appear, naturally, the interest in executing these COB programs in parallel on multiprocessors emerge. Since the efficiency of developing concurrent programs can improve if a concurrent language is used instead of a sequential language, a concurrent version of COB, called Concurrent COB, is being investigated.

The concurrent programs that we intend to develop reuse much of the existing sequential programs (objects). These objects cooperate and execute in parallel to accomplish some common goals. These objects are encapsulated into processes and the processes execute concurrently and interact. The processes act as coordinators of the objects.

Concurrent COB supports the development of such concurrent programs. A process is introduced into COB that executes concurrently and interacts with other processes. A special process, called a passive process, is introduced to support sharing of objects. Since Concurrent COB is an extension of COB, the merits of COB are inherited, such as strong typing, increased modularity and so on.

The investigation into Concurrent COB was also motivated by our interest in supporting concurrent programming on a multiprocessor workstation, called TOP-1 [6], developed at our laboratory. We intend to develop applications, such as COB programming environments and tools, to run on TOP-1.

The rest of this paper is organized as follows. An overview of COB is given in Section 2. Section 3 describes the programming model of Concurrent COB. Section 4 describes the main features of Concurrent COB. They are process and its synchronous communication mechanism, passive process, and exception handling. The implementation of Concurrent COB on TOP-1 is described in Section 5. Experiences with using Concurrent COB are discussed in Section 6. Comparisons to other concurrent languages are described in Section 7. Finally, Section 8 concludes this paper.

2 Overview of COB

The design goal of COB is to increase the productivity of program development without sacrificing the performance of the final code. The main emphasis of COB can be summarized as follows.

- Provide safe language constructs
- Increase the modularity of programs
- Maintain compatibility with C
- Generate efficient final code

COB attempts to decrease the source of programming errors by providing safe language constructs. The major programming errors are type misinterpretation, illegal pointer dereferencing and memory management errors. These errors are so severe, in that in some cases result in a memory fault which even a debugger cannot help. COB constructs are designed to help in this respect. Checks are made on type conversions. Array bound check and null deference check are also supported. Garbage collection is supported to reduce memory management errors.

Most module based programming languages split the specification of a module into its interface and implementation. Usually, a module's interface contains specifications of the implementation's private data. This is because the language processor must know the size of a module to generate code. However, this complicates the interface of a module since it contains both publicly accessible data and private data. Another problem is that, whenever the interface changes due to a change in the implementation's private data, all modules accessing that interface must be recompiled, even though the public part of the interface has not changed. COB overcomes these problems by completely separating the interface and implementation of a class. The COB class interface contains only public data that the user can access and all private data are hidden, thus providing a clean interface. Recompilation of classes are also minimized in this scheme and thus improves on the efficiency of program development.

The compatibility of COB with C is maintained, so that existing C programs can be reused and that the style of programming natural to C programmers can be retained. Introducing safe language constructs without losing compatibility with C is a difficult problem. We have thus decided to confine the support of safe constructs to the COB unique parts of the language. The C parts of COB are still unsafe and allow C style programming.

To improve programming productivity usually results in a less efficient final code, for example, interpretive languages allow quick development of programs, however the final code is not efficient. To improve on both the programming productivity and final code efficiency are two conflicting goals. COB addresses these goals by achieving the first goal during development and achieving the second during final code generation by global optimizations. Conversion of indirect method calls to direct calls, removable of runtime checks such as array bound checks and so on are performed during optimization.

COB programs are organized in terms of classes. A class defines a type. An instance of a class is called an object. The definition of a class is separated into its interface part and its implementation part. The following is an example,

```
// interface
class stack {
    void init(void);           // public instance members
    void final(void);
    void push(int);
    int pop(void);
  common:
    int count;                 // public common members
};

// implementation
class impl stack {
    int empty(void);           // private instance members
    int full(void);
  definition:
    void init(void) { ... }    // member function definitions
    ...
    int full(void) { ... }
};

    stack my_stack = new@stack(); // creation of my_stack
```

Instance members (public and private) are created for each instance of a class. Common members (public and private) are created only once for a class. Common members are used to encapsulate data and operations that are common to all instances, such as constants, for example. Access to common members are treated in the same way as as to instance members. Objects are created only in the heap and unused objects are automatically garbage collected. The init function is called when an object is created by calling new. The final function is called before the destruction of an object by the garbage collector.

Multiple inheritance is supported in COB. A class may publicly and privately inherit one or more classes. A subclass inherits all public members of a superclass, except its common members. Public inheritance introduces subtyping. In other words, a superclass becomes a supertype of a class and a subclass becomes a subtype of a class. To promote the reusability of classes, every public instance function member of a superclass can be redefined in a subclass.

COB emphasizes type safety. While a type conversion from a subtype to a supertype is implicit and is always valid, the conversion from a supertype to a subtype must be explicitly made by a cast operator. If the conversion is invalid, a runtime type conversion error is raised.

Exception handling is also supported to enhance type checking. It is based on the termination model and is similar to that of CLU. The following is an example of exception declaration and use.

```
exception e1(int), e2(void);

void f(void) raises e1, e2 { raise e1(3); }
```

```
void g(void) {
    try f();
    with {
        e1(int i) => ...
        e2(void) => ...
    }
}
```

A declaration of an exception consists of its name and formal parameters. A function declaration may contain a list of exceptions that can be raised by that function. An exception is raised by a raise statement. Exception handlers are attached to statements using the try statement and exceptions are handled in the with part. An exception propagates from the inner most try statement to the outer most try statement of a runtime scope. Type checking of functions are made at translation time, to check for exceptions raised within a body but not declared in the function declaration. The propagation of an exception through functions is also checked at translation time.

To further improve programming productivity, the COB translator supports automatic inclusion of header files. The .h files which contain COB interfaces need not be explicitly included via the #include directive. Whenever a new class is encountered during a translation, the translator automatically searches the interface of that class and includes the interface when found. This support reduces the line of code and also simplifies the makefile.

The COB translator can also execute in a "server" mode. In this mode, the translator remembers the header files that were input and never rereads the same header file. This support reduces the translation time of large programs which have large header files. Examples of this type of applications are PM and Motif based applications.

3   Basic Model of Concurrent Programming

There are a number of ways to program concurrent systems by using a language like COB. One way is to provide special classes and methods in the form of a library for this purpose. In fact, we have built special classes in this direction for experimentation. This approach needs no language extension, but the programmer must fully be aware of special semantics of such classes, and needs to carefully control their use. Therefore to ease the burden of the programmer, language extension to support concurrency is more desirable.

In designing a language extension, there are a number of major issues we need to consider, such as what sort of concurrency we want to support, and how the concurrent part is related to the sequential COB program. In particular, what is the role of objects in concurrent programs? There are various existing approaches to object-oriented concurrent programming. Some languages define an object as the unit of concurrency and synchronization takes place when a message is received by an object. Other languages introduce threads as independent notion on objects, and concurrency is treated as an orthogonal notion to objects.

In designing Concurrent COB, we needed to form a basic programming model for its use. As explained in the introduction, we are motivated by the need to support programming for TOP-1. Also, compatibility with sequential COB both in language semantics and run-time performance are important factors. As a result, we have come to adopt the following model.

First, a Concurrent COB system consists of a set of global data including objects and functions, and a set of processes. Process is a new construct added to COB. The user defines a process type and the actual process is dynamically created as an instance of that type. In this respect, a process is similar to an object, but its semantics is different. First of all, a process has its own thread of control. Also, it has its own local space for data including objects. Furthermore, each process has its own heap. Each process communicates with each other through Ada-like rendezvous. Also, a process can access global data and functions. In this model, the number of processes is not expected to be very large and the granularity of concurrency is coarse. A typical example of a system we envisage is a programming environment in which each tool such as an editor, a compiler, a debugger, database of libraries, and so forth is implemented as a process, sharing a common set of objects that represents the software under development.

The detailed characteristics of the model are as follows.

Object and process coexistence. We want to be able to reuse existing COB programs with minimum modifications and loss of efficiency. This implies that the system contains both objects and processes. A model where all elements of the model are processes is a clean approach, however loss of efficiency is inevitable in cases where objects that need not be processes are converted to processes.

Server-Client model. Applications we are interested in have server-client relations and so the model supports this relation. For example, in a programming environment, an editor may request for a text to edit from a version control system. In this case the editor is the client and the version control system is the server.

Interaction on shared objects. Since objects and processes coexist, some objects become shared between processes. These objects must have serialized access. Thus, it is not allowed for a process to pass an object to another process, since the object becomes shared between two processes.

Access to global data. Access to global data is allowed to cater for existing COB programs that require access to global data. However, it is the user's responsibility to ensure that concurrent access to global data does not occur.

4 Language Features

To keep the semantics of Concurrent COB simple, few constructs as possible are introduced into COB. Of the introduced constructs, we wanted to keep the relation between COB and Concurrent COB as close as possible. Thus the language features of COB are inherited and extended to support concurrent programming where possible.

The main characteristics of COB is that of object oriented programming. An object is the main element of structuring COB programs. Extending this notion, naturally leads to the unit of concurrency to be based on objects. Thus a process is introduced as a unit of concurrency. A process is object oriented in that data encapsulation is supported. However, a class and process are similar in the sense that they both support data encapsulation, but are not similar enough, so that they can have an inheritance relation. The idea of a process inheriting a class and structuring programs based on inheritance seems plausible, but we have found that the subtyping relation between a class and process does not hold in COB.

The other characteristic of COB is that of safety. We have also incorporated safety into Concurrent COB. One of the typical concurrent programming errors is due to concurrent access to objects. This usually occurs when a process passes an object to another process and both processes access the object. In Concurrent COB, to avoid this type of concurrent access to an object, pointer types and objects to processes are not allowed to be passed as parameters and as result values.

Concurrent COB is also concerned with efficiency. Since a process is the only construct for parallel execution, it is sometimes too heavy runtime-wise and space-wise for some tasks. We have found that there are a number of degenerate processes that only serve to control concurrent access to objects. For these types of processes, a special process, called passive process, is introduced. A passive process allows the programmer to specify degenerate processes and achieve better runtime and space performance.

Concurrent COB attempts to be compatible with COB. The reasons are similar to COB's compatibility with C in that we want to reuse existing COB programs as much as possible and also promote COB style programming. We have achieved this in most respects; an object may coexist with processes without modification. However, the semantics of common members of a class was extended, to allow serialized access to common members.

4.1 Process

A process is introduced into COB. A process is a unit of concurrency. It has its own single thread of control. When a thread is created, its concurrent execution starts. Its init function executes in its own thread and continues until the init function terminates.

A process has a similar syntax to a class. It's main characteristics and difference from a class are as follows.

Single thread If multithreaded processes were adopted, existing programs must be modified to allow serialized access to data as in [4]. In our programming model, we wanted to keep the modification of existing programs to a minimum.

Synchronous communication Processes communicate via an Ada-like rendezvous. A public function call and an accept statement executes a rendezvous. Synchronous communication best fits the server-client model, since the client waits for the server until the result is returned. Another advantage of synchronous communication is its similarity to function calls. In particular, this allows the COB exception handling mechanism to be adopted for Concurrent COB.

Safety of parameters and return values The COB philosophy of type safety is applied to Concurrent COB. The parameter and result types allowed in a rendezvous may not include objects or pointer types. This is to adhere to the "interaction on shared objects" characteristics of the programming model. Checks are made at translation time to detect invalid parameters and return values.

No public variables Process communicate via rendezvous only. All process variables must be access through public function calls to the process. This is to reduce the varieties of the communication mechanisms.

No inheritance A class may not, publicly nor privately, inherit a process. Similarly, a process may not, publicly nor privately, inherit a class. Problems occur when process inheritance is introduced. In COB, a public inheritance is seen as a form of subtyping. Thus assignment of an subtype object to a supertype variable is allowed. If a process is declared as a public subclass of a class, the translator can not detect whether the variable is a process or an object. Also, when a process inherits a process, a process becomes multithreaded, which we wanted to avoid.

Since there is no inheritance in a process, the way to encapsulate an object into a process is to declare it as a private instance variable.

No common members Allowing this would either involve rendezvous with a class or serialized access to common members. Both increase the variety of communication mechanism, which we want to avoid. Common members can be seen as shared global data for classes. If sharing common global data is required, it is possible to encapsulate them into a process and achieve sharing.

Here is an example of a producer consumer system in Concurrent COB.

```
process consumer {
    void put(int i);
    void init(int n);
};

process impl consumer {
    int total;
  definition:
    void put(int i) { total += i; }
    void init(int n) {
        int i;
        total = 0;
        for (i = 1; i <= n; i++) accept put;
        printf("%d\n", total);
    }
};

process producer {
    void init(process consumer cons, int n);
};

process impl producer {
  definition:
    void init(process consumer cons, int n) {
        int i;
        for (i = 1; i <= n; i++) cons->put(i);
    }
};

void main(void) {
    process consumer cons;
    process producer prod;
    cons = new consumer(10);
    prod = new producer(cons, 10);
}
```

When prod executes cons->put(i) and cons executes accept put rendezvous occurs. During the rendezvous, put(i) is executed, and upon completion, the rendezvous also completes. The output is 55, the sum of integers from 1 to 10.

Concurrent access to objects are serialized by encapsulating the object into a process. However, process encapsulation still leaves the common members of a class unprotected from concurrent access. Therefore access to common members, both public and private, are serialized automatically to protect against concurrent access. The implementation uses locks to serialize access. Each common member has a lock, that is acquired and released, before and after access to it.

The merit of this approach is that a new construct is not introduced to control access to common members, but the demerit is that every access requires two extra lock calls. By allowing the user to define a sharable common data, increases the efficiency of the code both in time and space. However, the safety of the program can not be guaranteed since concurrent access to objects are not controlled by the language. Thus every common member automatically obtains serialized access.

4.2 Passive Process

One of the aims of Concurrent COB is to promote the reuse of existing objects. An existing object should be incorporated into a concurrent system with minimum modification. A simple and typical way of using existing objects is to allow access to it from several processes. To do this, an object is encapsulated into a process. This process simply serializes access to the object and nothing else.

These processes are called degenerate processes, since they do not interact with processes. They act as servers to other "client" processes. The programming model we adopted assumes a system consisting of clients and servers. Thus the number of these degenerate "server" processes can be large. Thus it is beneficial to improve on the performance of these processes, time and space wise.

A special process, called a passive process, is introduced for the degenerate process. Since the job of a degenerate process is to serialize access, no execution thread is created for a passive process. This reduces the size of a passive process. The current implementation on an IBM PS/2 shows a difference of about 170 bytes between the size of a passive process and a process. Since the size is smaller, the creation time is also reduced: it is about 1/6th the creation time of a process. Therefore, more passive processes can be created faster than processes.

Here is a generalized program fragment of a degenerate process.

```
process impl degenerate_process {
  definition:
    void f1(void) { ... }
    void f2(void) { ... }
    void f3(void) { ... }
    void init(void) {
        for (;;) {
            select {
                accept f1;
            or
                accept f2;
            or
                accept f3;
            }
        }
    }
};
```

This degenerate process can translate into a passive process. Thus the above example becomes,

```
passive process impl degenerate_process {
  definition:
    void f1(void) { ... }
    void f2(void) { ... }
    void f3(void) { ... }
};
```

The init function is removed from the interface, but an implicit init exists which continually accepts either f1, f2 or f3. The select statement has the same meaning as an Ada select and provides a selection mechanism of acceptable functions.

4.3 Exception Handling

In COB, when a handler for a particular exception is not found in a with block, its outer with block is searched. If the outer most with block does not contain the required handler and the function declares that this exception propagation is to be allowed, the exception is propagated to the caller of the function. This continues until the propagation reaches the outer most with block of the main function. In COB, checks are made to ensure that a handler exists for all declared exceptions. Thus if an exception is not allowed to propagate out of a function then a handler must exist for that exception within the function. If a handler does not exist a compile time error is generated.

The exception propagation rule for Concurrent COB is an extension to that of COB. We wanted the rule to be similar in concept to COB. Thus we adopted a model where a process is seen as a COB program and a rendezvous as a function call, so that the COB propagation rules can be adopted.

The exception handling rules for Concurrent COB are as follows.

- When an exception occurs during the execution of a process not engaged in a rendezvous, the propagation of the exception continues until the outer most with block of the init function; the init function of the process is considered as the main function of a COB program.

- When an exception occurs during a rendezvous, the exception is propagated until the outer with block of the rendezvous callee's init function. The exception is also propagated to the rendezvous caller and propagates to the outer with block of the caller's init function. Thus a rendezvous is considered as a function call in the exception propagation rule and both parties are involved in handling the exception. Here is an example,

```
exception error(void);

process a {
    void init(void);
    void f(void) raises error;
};

process b {
    void init(void);
};

process a proc_a;
process b proc_b;

process impl a {
  definition:
    void init(void) {
        try { accept f(void); }
        with { error(void) =>
                printf("Error handled in a\n"); }
    }
    void f(void) { raise error(); }
};

process impl b {
  definition:
    void init(void) {
        try { proc_a->f(); }
        with { error(void) =>
                printf("Error handled in b\n"); }
    }
};
```

The exception error raised in f is handled both in proc_a and in proc_b. The output is the list of messages, "Error handled in a" and "Error handled in b". Note that the raises clause specifies what exception are allowed to propagate.

- A process is in a suspended state, when it is either waiting for the caller of a rendezvous to become ready or waiting for the callee of a rendezvous to become ready. When an exception is raised when a process is in a suspended state, the process state is changed to ready and the execution of the process continues as if an exception has been raised from the function call or accept statement. This is so that the suspended process has a chance to recover from the exception. The exception raised is a system defined exception that is similar to Ada's TASK_ERROR and for example, is raised, when a caller attempts to engage in a rendezvous with a terminated process.

- When an exception is raised during a nested rendezvous and when a handler is found, the exception handling mechanism must ensure that there are no accept statement executing between the start of a try statement and the point at which the exception is raised in a runtime scope. If there is an accept statement, an exception is raised at the accept statement and the exception is propagated to the caller of the function. This can be seen as "unrolling" accept statements.

- An exception of a process can not be raised by another process. An exception is seen as an event that occurs from within a process and not initiated by another process. An exception occurs as a result of a process executing a statement. If one requires to raise an exception in another process, one simply calls a member function of that process that executes a raise statement. Also raising an exception of another process can be regarded as an asynchronous call which complicates the communication mechanism of Concurrent COB.

System defined exceptions are available; for a UNIX implementation the UNIX signals are mapped to the system defined exceptions. For example, the zero_divide system defined exception is implemented as a UNIX signal SIGTRAP. The system defined exceptions may be enabled or disabled. When a system defined exception occurs the exception is raised at the processes that enabled the exception.

5 Implementation on TOP-1

We have implemented Concurrent COB on several architectures, such as IBM RT PC, IBM PS/2 and multiprocessor workstation TOP-1. We implemented Concurrent COB on RT PC first, and modified the machine dependent part to fit PS/2. Then we restructured the PS/2 version to ease the port to TOP-1. This section describes how we implemented Concurrent COB on TOP-1.

TOP-1 is a shared-memory multiprocessor workstation. Attached to the bus are 10 processing units, each equipped with an Intel 80386, a Weitek 1167 floating-point coprocessor, 128 Kbyte snoop cache, and a system bus interface. Also 128 Mbyte (maximum) of main memory is attached to the common bus. It runs a multiprocessor operating system called TOP-1 OS, which is based on AIX [1].

There is a resemblance between Concurrent COB process and a process that TOP-1 OS provides, in the sense that they are both units of protection and concurrency. However, protection of Concurrent COB processes are ensured mainly at compile time, whereas OS processes have to be protected at execution time. Moreover we assumed that creation, suspension, resumption and destruction of Concurrent COB processes are more frequent than those of OS processes. OS processes are, in other words, much heavier than Concurrent COB processes. For the above reason, we avoided using OS processes directly to implement Concurrent COB processes.

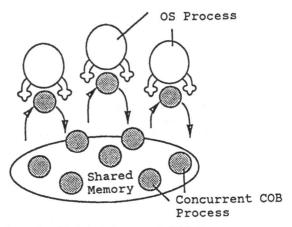

Figure 1: Execution Model of Concurrent COB Processes

The following is a sketch of our method to implement concurrency of Concurrent COB processes using OS processes. When a Concurrent COB program is invoked, a specified number of OS processes are forked, and from then on, they behave as virtual processors. Concurrent COB processes are allocated on a shared memory segment which is attached to all OS processes, so every Concurrent COB process is accessible by all OS processes. A Concurrent COB process has not only its original instance variables but also a context for its execution, including processor registers, stack area and a work area. They are used to interact with other Concurrent COB processes. Each OS process picks a Concurrent COB process up from the shared memory, executes some instructions of a method of that Concurrent COB process, and returns it to the shared memory. OS processes iterate these actions until the program terminates. From a Concurrent COB processes's point of view, on the other hand, they float from one OS process to another during execution.

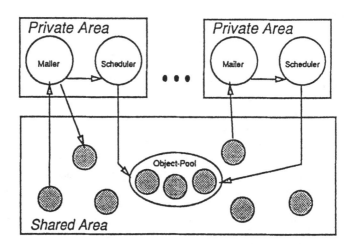

Figure 2: Structure of Runtime System

After implementing the execution mechanism of Concurrent COB processes, we have to consider the communication between them. They cannot directly invoke methods of another process because synchronization is needed in their communication. For example, a process should be suspended if it has sent a message to a busy process or a suspended process. Our solution is to put some objects that manage communication in the private area of each OS process. These objects are Mailer and Scheduler which cooperate to allow Concurrent COB processes communicate with each other. Whenever a Concurrent COB process tries to communicate with another process, it must invoke a method of Mailer which resolves the synchronization. And Scheduler ,whose methods are invoked only by Mailer, manages executable processes. Because private areas are accessed by one fixed process, synchronization is not necessary to access Mailer and Scheduler, which is an idea borrowed from [8]. Hardware-level synchronization is utilized, only when Mailer and Scheduler access shared area.

Now that Concurrent COB processes work concurrently and communicate with each other, the rest of the run-time environment of Concurrent COB can be constructed with Concurrent COB itself. Points of advantage to construct it in such a way are the following.

- To make the run-time environment simple and structured.

- To bring out internal concurrency of the environment quite naturally.

- To check the expressiveness of Concurrent COB language.

However, constructing the rest in the above manner may reduce the performance, if some system processes require a lot of communication. So we had to be careful not to bring about such performance reduction in constructing the whole system.

The following are examples of system processes.

- *memory manager* which allocates and releases memory cells

- *part of garbage collector* which interacts with memory manager

- *remote procedure call(RPC) manager* which is used to communicate with processes in another site

- *I/O manager* which serializes requests for I/O devices

Operation	Time
(1) method-call(COB)	$5.2\mu s$
(2) schedule + context-switch	$28.8\mu s$
(3) method-call(Concurrent COB)	$104\mu s$

Table 1: Execution Time of Primitives

We measured the time required for various primitive operations on TOP-1. A method call of COB (1) which is implemented as a 1-level indirect function call is much faster than that of Concurrent COB (3) which needs a context-switch with a method call. However, because synchronous communication inevitably requires rescheduling (2) twice and a method call of Concurrent COB also provides conditional synchronization, we believe that the performance of a method call of Concurrent COB is acceptable. This result implies that we have to use Concurrent COB processes where concurrency and synchronization are necessary but otherwise we should use COB objects in order to execute programs efficiently.

We were able to achieve the expected linear speedup for programs with little dependency between prosesses. However, practical programs usually have more dependency between processes, so we measured how much speedup is possible using a distributed quick sort program which has many processes connected closely with each other. The result of running the distributed quick sort program using 1-8 processor is shown in Figure 3. The speedup for 8 processors is about 3.5.

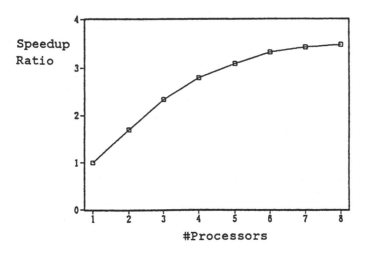

Figure 3: Speedup Ratio

6 Experience

A concurrent make program, called cake, was developed in Concurrent COB. cake is an example application of the programming model of Concurrent COB. The original source of make was utilized (object and process coexistence). The routines that perform the analysis of the dependents of a file were encapsulated into processes, so that these routines can analyze the dependents in parallel. These processes communicate to resolve questions, such as, "Is the source newer than the executable code" (server-client model). The dependence graph of the files were shared among the processes (interaction on shared objects). Some routines of make required global variables which were left as is (access to global data).

UNIX signals were handled by UNIX system calls. The problem encountered during the development of cake was that the UNIX alarm signal was caught by cake. The problem is that the alarm signal is used by the Concurrent COB run time system scheduler. The solution there was to disable and enable the alarm before and after the statement where the alarm was caught. This is obviously an inelegant solution to the problem. With the inclusion of the interrupt handling mechanism, which is currently being investigated, the enabling and disabling of the alarm will be hidden from the programmer.

7 Comparison to Other Related Work

A concurrent object oriented language of [2] allows process inheritance. Their language is C++ based with synchronous public function calls as the sole mechanism for synchronization and communication. A special function called main is executed after the creation of a process. main can be seen to be analogous in function to Concurrent COB's init. The language allows a process to inherit both class and process, and so allows the construction of an inheritance hierarchy of classes and processes. Main is protected, in other words, it can not be called from a user subclass, but may be redefined, thus allowing a subclass to change the concurrent execution behavior of its superclass (process). In Concurrent COB, we have disallowed the use of process inheritance as discussed before. By declaring objects as instance variables of a process, a hierarchy of classes and processes can be built, although calls to super classes are implemented as indirect calls to its instance objects. However, the applications that utilize existing COB programs are structured in a way that the indirect call is made once, i.e., processes directly encapsulate objects.

Concurrent C++ [3] is very similar to Concurrent COB. The steps taken to developed Concurrent C++ was to first develop Concurrent C and then merge with C++. The unit of concurrency in Concurrent C++ is a process with synchronous and asynchronous "transactions". A transaction can be thought of as a function call. The C++ object is kept as instance variable of a process and thus a process acts as a interface between other processes and the object. To increase the safety of Concurrent COB programs, checks are made to parameters and return values of process functions. This is not seen in Concurrent C++ where exchanging pointers through functions are allowed (for the purpose of developing efficient code).

A different approach is taken in Trellis/Owl [5]. Basically a function ("activity") is executed in parallel and primitives, such as locks and queues, are provided to control data access. Their approach aims at providing a minimum set of concurrency constructs and allow users to build on top of them. They have provided a number of constructs, whereas in our approach, only a process has been introduced.

The exception handling mechanisms are similar to that of Ada. However, in Concurrent COB exceptions of a process can not be raised from another process, whereas in Ada, a FAILURE exception can be raised. A FAILURE exception is a way to terminate a task in an infinite loop. The system that Concurrent COB is intended for does not require such function. If a process enters an infinite loop, the whole system is simply terminated, since the looping process is in error.

In ABCL/1 [9], the specification of propagation of exception is more general than Concurrent COB, in that an object (complaint object) to where the exception can propagate can be defined. If the complaint object is the caller object then the propagation effect is similar to Concurrent COB. Again our programming model does not require such generality, and thus such mechanism is not supported in Concurrent COB.

8 Concluding Remarks

The aim of Concurrent COB is to support the programming model discussed earlier. The characteristics of the programming model is revisited to discuss the support of Concurrent COB in what follows.

Object and process coexistence The class construct is retained and the process is introduced in Concurrent COB. Classes may contain processes as their instance variables and vice versa. Communication between processes, and between objects and processes are possible through synchronous communication.

Server-Client model A client process may call another server process to obtain some result. Objects can also act in the same manner. For a particular degenerate process, a passive process is introduced.

Interaction on shared objects Shared objects are constructed by encapsulating an object in a (passive) process. Parameters and results passed between processes are restricted, i.e., objects and pointers are not allowed.

Access to global data This is still permitted for objects and processes that require access to global data. However, the user has the responsibility to ensure the safety of concurrent access to global data.

We are currently experimenting with different implementations of exception handling. Also interrupt handling is being designed.

We are currently looking into garbage collection (GC) of processes. In a sequential program, when a variable is no longer referenced it is designated as garbage and collected. In a concurrent program, an unreferenced process can not be simply GCed, because it may still be executing some task. For example, a process calculating pi and generating the result, can be created and immediately the creator may terminate. In this situation, the pi calculating process is unreferenced, but still active. On the other hand, when a process is in an idle state and no reference is made to it, that process is terminated and GCed. A idle state implies that the process is ready to accept a communication, but if no reference is made to it, no communication will ever occur. Thus this process is GCed. GC must interact with the system scheduler to decide when a process is actually garbage.

The programming model discussed, also provides a simple frame work for garbage collection (GC) in a multiprocessor environment. If we imagine that the memory management of a process is localized, i.e., objects within a process are created in the process's local heap and use the local stack, GC is also localized. GC of the constituent objects occur when the current process is in a suspended state and sequential GC algorithms are applicable since all constituent objects are also suspended.

9 Acknowledgment

We would like to thank N. Yamanouchi for carefully reading the original paper and him and N. Suzuki for their useful suggestions.

References

[1] *IBM Advanced Interactive Executive for the Personal System/2 (AIX PS/2) General Information Manual.* International Business Machines Corporation, 1988. GC23-2055-00.

[2] P. A. Buhr, G. Ditchfield, and C. R. Zarnke. Adding concurrency to a statistically type-safe object-oriented programming language. In *Proceedings of the ACM SIGPLAN Workshop on Object-Based Concurrent Programming*, pages 18–21, Sep. 1988. SIGPLAN Notices, Vol. 24, No. 4, Apr. 1989.

[3] N. Gehani and W. D. Roome. *The Concurrent C Programming Language.* Silicon Press, 1989.

[4] P. Mehrotra and J. V. Rosendale. Concurrent object access in BLAZE 2. In *Proceedings of the ACM SIGPLAN Workshop on Object-Based Concurrent Programming*, pages 40–42, Sep. 1988. SIGPLAN Notices, Vol. 24, No. 4, Apr. 1989.

[5] J. E. B. Moss and W. H. Kohler. Concurrent features for the Trellis/Owl language. In *Proceedings of the European Conference on Object-Oriented Programming*, pages 171–180, 1987. Lecture Notes in Computer Science, Vol. 276.

[6] N. Oba, A. Moriwaki, and S. Shimizu. TOP-1: a snoop-cache-based multiprocessor. In *Proceedings of the International Pheonix Conference on Computers and Communications*, Mar. 1990.

[7] T. Onodera, K. Kuse, and K. Kamimura. *Increasing Safety and Modularity of C Based Objects.* Research Report RT0042, IBM Research, Tokyo Research Laboratory, 5-19, Sanbancho, Chiyoda-ku, Tokyo 102, Japan, 1990.

[8] J. Pallas and D. Ungar. Multiprocessor Smalltalk: a case study of a multiprocessor-based programming environment. In *Proceedings of the Conference on Programming Language Design and Implementation*, ACM, 1988.

[9] A. Yonezawa and Y. Ichisugi. Exception handling and real time features in an object-oriented concurrent language. Sep. 1989. UK-Japan Workshop, Oxford.

A Parallel Object Oriented Language FLENG++ and Its Control System on the Parallel Machine PIE64

Hidehiko Tanaka

Department of Electrical Engineering

University of Tokyo, Hongo 7-3-1, Bunkyo-ku, Tokyo, 113 JAPAN

Abstract

This paper describes the language set of PIE which is composed of three kinds of languages, Fleng++, Fleng, and Fleng--. Fleng++ is a user-level parallel language to which module facility is added through the object-oriented style. Fleng-- is a low level language used for the explicit control of execution. Fleng is the core language for this language set, on which Fleng++ and Fleng-- are based. Control features for parallel machine such as process allocation, load distribution and memory management are also discussed in relation to this language set.

1 Introduction

To realize the high level knowledge information processing, we need some nice knowledge representation languages, special processor system of super speed and memory system of large scale. We have been making our research to develop a prototype system for the large scale knowledge processing since 1987. As for the processor system of the prototype, we have been developing a parallel computer system called PIE64(Parallel Inference Engine) composed of 64 Inference Units[1].

As for the memory system, a relational database machine called SDC[2] of 8 units. We designed a committed choice language Fleng[3] as the kernel language for the prototype system. Fleng is a simple language derived from GHC[4] and easy to implement as all goals interacts only through shared variables, and implicit "AND" relation between goals is not assumed(when needed, it should be described explicitly by the form of AND predicate).

This paper describes the language set of PIE which is composed of three kinds of languages, Fleng++, Fleng, and Fleng--. Fleng++ is a user-level parallel language to which module facility is added through the object-oriented style. We describe the language features of Fleng++, and discuss its translation method into Fleng. Fleng-- is a low level language used for the target language of explicit control of execution. While the compiled code of WAM level is executed in the form of communicating parallel processes, control features for parallel machine such as process allocation, load distribution and memory management are also discussed.

2 Language set of PIE

2.1 Committed choice language, Fleng

As a parallel logic programming language, Ueda developed GHC and ICOT developed a language system KL1 based on it. However, it seems that the implementation of GHC is a little bit complicated and that the language level is too high for us to use it for the implementation of control system of parallel machine PIE. Accordingly, we developed a simplified language Fleng as the kernel language for our system.

Fleng is a kind of committed choice language, but has no guard goals. A Fleng program is a set of clauses with a head part and a body part of goals.

```
H :- G1, G2, ..., Gn.
```

A program is executed by giving it a set Q of goals. All goals are executed independently, in any order. A goal G is executed by removing it from Q, and matching it with the head of all clauses in the program. For the first clause with matching head, that clause is committed to, and the body goals of that clause are added to Q. Matching is like unification, but variable bindings is not allowed in G during the matching. If a match of a variable in G with a non-variable or an unbound variable from G is attempted, this matching is suspended, and resumes only if the variable becomes bound.

As opposed to GHC, the execution of a goal is not associated with success, failure, or any logical truth values. New goals are essentially spawned out and executed. If we do want logical truth values, they can be passed as parameters of the goals. For instance, if we have two goals g(X,R1) and h(X,R2), where R1 and R2 are bound by predicates g and h to the appropriate truth values, we can define a new predicate p(X,R3) to be the logical conjunction of g and h by:

```
p(X,R3) :- g(X,R1), h(X,R2), and(R1,R2,R3).
```

where

```
and(true,true,R) :- R=true.
and(false,_,R)   :- R=false.
and(_,false,R)   :- R=false.
```

Though the simple structure of Fleng is suitable for the role of core language, it increases the load of programmer. So, we introduced macro and library for Fleng. For example, guard macro is used to represent conditional branch, and "is" function is realized by a library. Figure 1 shows an example of macro and library.

2.2 Language set

Based on the language Fleng, we developed a language set for our system. As the programming language of application level, we developed an object oriented language Fleng++. As for the implementation language of language processor and control systems, we developed a language Fleng-- which has the capability of expressing the details of control.

```
fact(N,R) :-
    N == 0 | R = 1;
    N  > 0 | N1 is N-1,
             fact(N1,R1),
             R is R1 * N.
```

Figure 1: Example program of macro and library

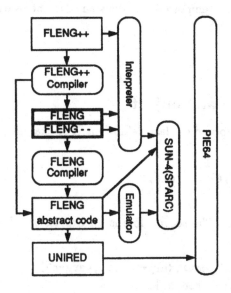

Figure 2: Language System of PIE64

The language system of PIE machine is shown in Figure 2. Application programs are written in Fleng++, translated into the programs written in Fleng--, which are compiled into programs of intermediate code. The intermediate code is of WAM(Warren Abstract Machine) level(but, not WAM itself), tuned to parallel processing and interpreted by PIE machine.

The control policy of parallel execution is not described explicitly at the level of Fleng++. Accordingly, the details of control which is expressed clearly at the level of Fleng-- should be decided by the compiler and/or programmer.

3 Fleng++

3.1 Special features of Fleng++

As a user level language, Fleng++ has special features as follows:

1. Method call of Fleng++ and predicate call of Fleng can be mixed in a program.

2. Control structure of conditional branch is the same as Fleng macro.

3. No explicit description of type and mode for variables.

4. Two kinds of variables : temporary variables and instance variables.

5. Multiple inheritance

6. Class library

3.2 Class definition and object

Program of Fleng++ is composed of class definitions. For example,

```
class ex.
  :p(Object,A) :- :q(A,1).
end.
```

ex is the name of the class. The second line is an expression of method definition, of which syntax is as follows.

```
:<method>(<object>,<arg-1>,...,<arg-n>)
        [ :- <body> ].
```

where <object> is the name of called object. :q(A,1) is a method call that message :q is sent to an object A. For example, a factorial program is described as follows.

```
class fact1.
  :do(Self,N,R) :-
        N == 0 | n = 1 ;
        N >  0 | N1 is N-1,
                    :do(Self,N1,R1),
                    R is R1 * N.
end.
```

Execution of program is performed by sending a message to an object. An object is generated by a statement such as

```
T := #fact1.
```

An instance of class fact1 is generated and assigned to T. In case of ESP, the constructor # is used to generate a class object. But, in Fleng++, # is for an instance object. To get the value of factorial 5, a statement

```
T := #fact1, :do(T,5,R).
```

or

```
:do(#fact1,5,R).
```

is used, where the result is gotten from R.

3.3 Temporary variables and instance variables

Variables of Fleng are single-assignment variables. Similarly, variables of fact1 are generated whenever it receives a message, and discarded when the execution is finished. This kind of variable is called temporary variable. We introduced the other kind of variable called instance variable which exists for the same period as the object and can be rewritten any number of times.

The instance variable is used for designating the characteristics and the internal status of the object. For example, another factorial program can be written by using an instance variable as follows.

```
class fact2
  var $n := 1.
  :do(Self,N,R) :-
        N == 0  | R := $n;
        N >  0  | $n is $n * N,
                  N1 is N - 1,
                  :do(Self,N1,R).
  end.
```

Instance variables are declared by var and shown by a prefix $.

3.4 Serialization of messages

Each goal of Fleng is executed independently. The execution order is determined only by suspension/resume mechanism through shared variables and by goal-generation process of reduction. However, as objects in Fleng++ have side effects, the arrival order of messages should be counted.

We set a principle of sequential interpretation and parallel execution. Though program can be read deterministically from right to left and in the order of depth-first, it is executed in parallel except the case where serialization is required. For example, when a method

```
:p(S) :- ..,$n is $n+1,..,$n := 0,..
```

```
class one.
  :test(Self,R) :- R = 1.
  :result1(Self,R) :- :test(Self,R).
end.

class two inherit one.
  :test(Self,R) :- R = 2.
end.
```

Figure 3: Example program of inheritance

is activated on the condition that the value of \$n is 2, the value 2 is used for the value of \$n in the goals at the left-side of "\$n is \$n+1", value 3 is between "\$n is \$n+1" and "\$n := 0", and value 0 is at the right-side of "\$n := 0".

Execution order of goals is controlled for the two kinds of method call as follows. When a method

```
:alpha(Self) :- ..,:beta(Self),.. .
```

is executed, the processing of :beta takes precedence over the reception of another message from the other object. The other is the case when multiple messages are sent in one method to an object. The messages are sent in the order of right to left and depth-first. The receive is in the same order.

3.5   Execution control facility

The syntax of conditional branch is the same as Fleng.

```
:m1(S,A,B) :-
          A > B - 1 | :m2(S);
          B > A - 1 | :m3(S).
:n1(S,A,B) :-
          A > B - 1 -> :n2(S);
          B > A - 1 -> :n3(S).
```

Conditional parts in guarded commands(|) have no priority for execution. The part whose condition is met at first is selected and executed. On the other hand, in the case of if-then-else(->), the first conditional part(A > B - 1) is tested first and the second one is tested only when the result of the first part is false.

3.6   Inheritance

Figure 3 is an example of inheritance facility of Fleng++.

Class two in Figure 3 inherits class one. All of the classes in Fleng++ inherit class "object" by default. The class "object" has methods such as :super(Object,Super) which returns a super object of Object.

Fleng++ adopts multiple inheritance. The sequence of method-traverse is determined by *"left to right up to join"*. We chose this sequence because this is natural from the view point of description.

However, for the compatibility to ESP[5], we can change the traverse order to *"depth first left to right"* by indicating it at the compile time. Instance variables can be inherited as well.

3.7 Library

We have a library to which user defined classes can be registered, from which user can pick up some objects and use them.

Other than the user defined class, we registered some system defined classes such as I/O management class and object management class.

Class which manages multiple objects is called "pool". All operations to pool are done through messages. The operations are store, take out and delete of object, and inquiry about storage status. We provided the following classes as pool.

1. list: Elements in the list have sequences. Operations are based on first-in last-out.

2. index: Same as list except that key is attached to each object and used for object-access.

3. array: The element number is fixed. Access time to each object is constant.

4. fifo: Operations are based on first-in first-out. fifo can be used to synchronize the operations of two objects by sharing a fifo pool.

4 Implementation of Fleng++

Fleng++ programs are translated into Fleng programs which in turn are compiled into an intermediate code and executed. Objects described in parallel logic programming language are implemented by recursive goal call. Internal status such as instance variables is represented explicitly by goal arguments. Followings are the major consideration points of the implementation.

4.1 Message sending

An expression of message sending :msg(A)(only an argument of destination, for the simplification of explanation) is expanded into a Fleng program,

```
A=[msg(A1)|A2], merge(A1,A3,A2)
```

where A is a stream which designates the destination object, A1 which is one of the end point of the stream is passed to the destination object, A3 is a new stream at sending side, and A=[] means a unification.

When the destination of the message is the object itself, the merge predicate above is exchanged to append predicate as the message handling sequence must be controlled.

When some object is passed to a destinated object as an argument of message, number of references to the object increases as both sending and receiving objects refer it. Procedure for this increase differs depending on the type of the object, primitive object and instance object. Primitive object is such object as atom and complex term that can be represented by literals. Instance object is such object that is generated from class definition. In case of primitive object, unification is the everything for the increase. For the instance object, "merge" predicate is used to make another branch on the stream which points the object.

So, Fleng++ processor is required to check the type of the value. However, as variable of Fleng++ has no type, we used $s-list structure to represent a stream to send messages of which arguments are instance objects. That is, message sending expression S=[msg(A,B)|S1] is divided into two unifications,

$$S=[MSG|S1], \quad MSG = msg(A,B)$$

where first one is to form a stream by list cell, and second one is to unify the message itself.

As the first one can be done at the instance object side, the list cell can be used to distinguish instance objects from primitive objects. That is, to send some instance object we use the special $s-list structure such as '$s'(msg1,'$s'(msg2,..)) that uses complex term headed with '$s' of which use is limited for system use only. Using this structure, we defined a predicate refer/3 to increase the reference number as follows.

```
refer(A,B,C) :-
        C == '$s'(_,_) -> merge(A,B,C);
                          A = C, B = C.
```

where C is the referred object of which type is checked.

On the other hand, as arguments of message are passed by unification in Fleng, input/output mode of variable should be checked before using the refer/3. We provided a mode-check predicate.

The type check and mode check stated above are done at runtime only for such a case that the type or mode can not be determined at compile time.

4.2 Type/mode analysis

As the type/mode check at run time is not efficient, type/mode analysis is incorporated in compiler. This analysis is also effective for reading and debugging of programs as well as for the compiler optimization. We developed an analyzer for Fleng, on which analyzer for Fleng++ is built. When we limit our attention to the compiler optimization, it is enough for us to distinguish such types as primitive objects, instance objects and any type(unknown or undefined), and such modes as output(marked by -), input(+) and any(?, unknown or undefined).

The Fleng++ compiler is made of two pathes. The first path analyzes the type/mode of arguments of method-head through checking the class definition. For example, the type of the first argument of message-sending expression becomes instance object, and the mode is input-mode. The first argument of method head is of instance type and input mode. The non-temporary variables in the head is of primitive type and input mode ... and so on. For example, when we have a method definition,

```
:p(X,Y) :- :q(Y).
```

the result of analysis is

```
:p(+ins(X), +ins(Y)).
```

The second path compiles the method definitions based on the result of first path and the type/mode table of methods retrieved from library which is already analyzed.

4.3 Access of instance variables

As described earlier, the method is interpreted from left to right and depth-first for the definition. Instance variables are implemented by introducing two special methods and inserting them in appropriate locations of method definition following the scope of instance variable defined by the interpretation sequence. The methods, which are used to refer and rewrite instance variables are

```
:'get$n'(S,Obj), and :'put$n'(S,Obj).
```

For example, consider a method such as

```
:alpha(S) :-
   ...,$n is $n + 1,...,:beta(T,$n),...
```

This is rewritten by inserting the two methods as follows.

```
:alpha(S) :-
   ...,'get$n'(S,N1),:'put$n'(S,N2),
      N2 is N1 + 1,
   ...,'get$n'(S,N3),:beta(S,N3),...
```

4.4 Conditional branch

Conditional branch is macro expanded into two parts. One is to evaluate the condition. The other is to call the subgoal using the result. As the stream is changed into another variable when a message to an object pointed by the stream is sent, transformation is required in such case that there are some message-sending expression inside the conditional part.

For example, when we have a conditional branch

```
..,(A > 0 -> :write(Obj,ok)),...
```

this is transformed into

```
...,greater(A,0,Res),
    sub_0(Res,Obj0,Obj1),...

sub_0(true,Obj0,Obj1) :-
    Obj0 = '$s'(write(Obj1,ok),Obj1).
sub_0(false,Obj0,Obj1) :-
    Obj1 = Obj0.
```

The nesting level of conditional part is managed by compiler.

4.5 Optimization by partial evaluation

Fleng programs which are converted from Fleng++ programs in the unit of every method include redundancy a lot because the interrelationship among methods is not taken into account. This can be reduced by evaluating such predicates as built-in predicates, merge/3 and append/3 whose definitions are known to compiler.

For example, message-sending, which is the operation sequence of using $s-list and instanciation of message, can be optimized by developing almost all of the related unifications into a few one. This method omits most of merge/3 or append/3.

In some cases, static binding of method can be used instead of dynamic binding through partial evaluation.

5 Control of parallel processing

5.1 Static analysis and dynamic control

Fleng is a very simple language and has a role of kernel language for the PIE-language system. However, the language level of Fleng is a little bit too high to be used for the machine language of PIE and for the implementation language of PIE operating system. For this kind of language, we designed a low level language Fleng--, by which programmer can describe some characteristic aspect of code execution which is important from practical point of view.

While programs in Fleng++ are translated into Fleng--, module information derived from the unit of objects is extracted in terms of control information from Fleng++ by compiler and used for load distribution. So the role of compiler is two fold, one is to generate object code, and the other is to extract the control information.

Figure 4 shows the procedure of code execution. The compiled code in the figure is the intermediate code in Figure 2. The code is distributed in parallel processing units(Inference Unit:IU) with such control information as parameter for load distribution and variable allocation by loader. At the time, the loader is given such resource-information as allocated number of Inference Units by operating system. Each loaded

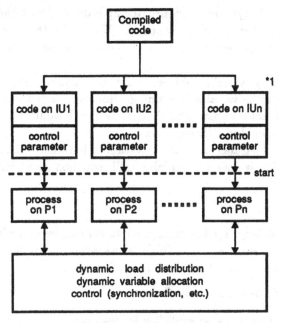

*1 Duplicated allocation is allowed.

Figure 4: Procedure of Code Execution

code is a part of the compiled code and may be duplicated with the code in the other unit for efficient code execution.

Given a start command, each code is executed as a process. Processes communicate each other through message passing for load distribution and execution control among parallel goals.

So far as the load distribution is concerned, dynamic control as well as static allocation are used. The static analysis is used to allocate the compiled code to each IU at the beginning of runtime and to give the suggestive information to dynamic controller at runtime. Dynamic controller which exists on each IU dispatches its local load to some other idle IUs when the local load is heavier than others. The monitoring of other IUs' load is done with the aid of multi-stage interconnection network which has the capability of finding the minimum load IU. Accordingly, each IU can decide locally whether it should distribute the load or not.

We have two choices for load distribution strategy:

1. load minimum

2. designation of a specific IU by a statement such as "To the IU which has the variable X locally."

When a goal refers the variable X many times, (2) is selected. Otherwise, strategy (1) is selected, which is supported by network hardware.

As a matter of fact, dynamic load dispatching is decided with the variables location(in which IU) as a parameter. That is, the specific IU to which the load should be dispatched should be decided by taking the locality of variable access of the dispatched load into account.

Generally speaking, variable address is allocated dynamically to such IU that some activity which needs the variable is running. However, as the load is dispatched to the other IU, remote access becomes needed. Getting the IU address is a simple procedure as variable address is global in PIE machine.

The granularity of parallel execution is controlled in terms of the number of consecutive reductions. Execution is done sequentially until reduction count reaches the number.

5.2 Fleng--

Fleng-- is a low level language by which programmer can designate his intention regarding the behavior of program execution. That is, we added a few features to Fleng. Using these features, we can expect the following results.

- Compiled code becomes more efficient.

- Program can be controlled explicitly for load distribution and efficient execution.

The features introduced are the followings.

1. Active unify annotation (!)

   This annotation is used to designate that the terms attached with this annotation does not cause suspension when head unification is done. Accordingly, the terms can be replaced by variables and the unifications can be moved to the body part. For example, an append program:

   ```
   append([H|X],Y,![H|Z]) :- append(X,Y,Z).
   append([],X,!X).
   ```

   where the third terms of heads are the annotated one, is completely equivalent to the following program.

   ```
   append([H|X],Y,Z1) :-
           append(X,Y,Z), Z1 = [H|Z].
   append([],X,Y) :- Y = X.
   ```

   Through this annotation, we can improve the code execution efficiency by optimizing the unification procedure as the mode and structure of arity is partly known.

2. Non-variable annotation (#)

   This annotation is used to suspend the head unification when the variables in the head attached with this annotation is tested to be unified with variables in a goal. For example, a program

```
a(#X) :- b(X).
```

is suspended its execution when X is tried to be unified with some variable in the goal. However, such unification as between X and f(Y) is not suspended, as f(Y) is not a variable itself but a structure(though it includes a variable Y). This annotation is useful for waiting input and controlling parallelism by specifying additional data dependency.

3. Single reference annotation (')

This annotation is used to designate that the terms attached with this annotation are referenced only once. Generally, memory consumption rate of committed-choice language such as GHC and Fleng is relatively high compared with conventional languages. Accordingly, this annotation is very effective to reduce the frequency of garbage collection by telling to the language system that the memory cell can be collected and reused just after the head unification. It also reduces copying overhead.

For example, in a program

```
append('[H|X],Y,Z1) :-
            append(X,Y,Z), Z1 = [H|Z].
```

the list cell of [H|X] can be reused for generating [H|Z].

4. Load control

A special statement 'local_to' is introduced. This statement is used to designate the locality of activity. For example

```
a :- b,c,d.                           (1)
a :- local(b,c),d.                    (2)
a(X,Y) :- (b(Y),local\_to Y),c(Y,Z).  (3)
```

(1) and (2) have the same semantics. However, local(b,c) in (2) means that literal b and c should be executed locally each other. (3) means that the execution of b(Y) should be done in the IU where the value of Y exists. When the value of Y is of some structure, and the internal part of the structure is tested by such clause as

```
b(Y1) :- ....,
```

the processing of b(Y) had better be executed at the IU that has the value of Y in its local memory, as many access to the elements of Y arises for unification.

5.3 Adding annotations automatically

Though the annotations are very effective, it can be a burden for application programmer to make use of them. Using the mode/type check result, we can attach the single reference annotations automatically. Following is the algorithm.

1. Macro expand all the active unify annotations into the body parts.

2. For all clauses, MR(Multiple Reference) marking is done as follows, where only such variables of which value-type is structure are paid attention.

   - Count the reference times for all variables of which usage mode is input in the body. When the variable appears in the head also, the count is added by one. When a variable appears more than one time in a body-goal, corresponding definition-clauses are checked as well.

   - When the count-number exceeds 3, MR mark is attached at the location of appearance for the variable in both the body-goal and the definition clauses.

   - For MR-marked variables in heads, MR mark is attached to the location of appearance in the definition clauses which correspond to the body-goal in which the variables appear.

3. When some structure is defined in the head without MR, a single reference annotation is attached to the structure.

Though the algorithm above can be used when the variable appears only once in the top-level goal, some provision is required for multiple appearance as follows.

1. Use copy scheme for such structure shared among goals of top-level by providing copy mechanism of structure in the language processor.

2. When the above algorithm decides that the single reference annotation can be attached in a predicate, copy the definition and rename the predicate in the copied program. Of which programs, original or copied one, is used is decided by the analysis of goals.

6 Discussion

6.1 Comparison with other parallel object-oriented languages

In the parallel object-oriented programming language such as ABCL/1[6] and Concurrent Smalltalk[7], consistent state transition is guaranteed by accepting next message only after the completion of a method execution. This resulted in a simple model.

In Fleng++, the next message can be accepted even before the completion of a method execution. This is realized safely through expressing states by single-assignment variables and serialized messages. While the introduction of single-assignment variables brings the needs of efficient garbage collection usually, we can analyze statically almost all of the single reference for Fleng++ and decrease the frequency of garbage collection through collecting and reusing the cell just after the usage.

The objectives of Fleng++ is similar to Vulcan[8] in the meaning that they try to lighten the load of programmer for logic programming. A'UM[9] is a object oriented language based on the stream computation model and uses parallel logic programming language as a mean of implementation. However, Fleng++ supports the argument passing mechanism by unification without the designation of type/mode same as logic programming. Hence, we can get much freedom for argument passing. Moreover, Fleng programs can be rewritten easily into Fleng++ because both the syntax and semantics of Fleng++ are the extension of Fleng.

6.2 Programming environment

As for the programming environment of Fleng++, we are designing following tools.

1. Browser

2. Window programming interface

3. Parallel programming debugger

4. Object library

For (2), we are implementing an interface on X-window. And for (3), the usefulness of conventional trace is limited for parallel programming. On the other hand, declarative model for the debugging of logic programs is not enough for parallel logic programming which uses some committed choice languages, because they are not pure logic programming languages and they need to consider the timing of input/output and causal relationship. Accordingly, it is required to add some operational model. We designed a execution model which can represent the status of parallel execution in terms of communicating processes. Using the model, we are now designing the extension of algorithmic debugging.

7 Conclusion

The language set of Parallel Inference Engine PIE64 is presented. User level language, Fleng++, is a parallel object-oriented programming language based on logic. Fleng-- which is a low level language and has the facility of explicit control feature for parallel execution is also discussed.

8 Acknowledgement

The author would like to thank the members of SIGIE (Special Interest Group of Inference Engine): Hanpei Koike, Eiichi Takahashi, Hiroaki Nakamura, Minoru Yoshida, Xu

Lu, Kentaro Shimada, Takeshi Shimizu, Takeshi Shimoyama, Junichi Tatemura, Yasuo Hidaka, and Akiyoshi Katsumata. This work is supported by Grant-in-Aid for Specially Promoted Research of the Ministry of Education, Science and Culture of Japan (No. 62065002).

References

[1] H.Koike and H.Tanaka: *Multi-Context Processing and Data Balancing Mechanism of the Parallel Inference Machine PIE64*, Proc. Intl. Conf. Fifth Generation Computer Systems 1988, ICOT, pp.970-977, 1988.

[2] M.Kitsuregawa, M.Nakano and M.Takagi: *Query Execution for Large Relations on Functional Disk System*, IEEE Fifth Intl. Conf. Data Engineering, Feb. 1989.

[3] M.Nilsson and H.Tanaka:*Fleng Prolog-The Language which turns Supercomputers into Prolog Machines*,Proc. Japanese Logic Programming '86, in Wada,E.(Ed.), Springer LNCS 264, pp.170-179, 1987.

[4] K.Ueda: *Guarded Horn Clauses*, In Wada,E.(Ed.),Proc.Japanese Logic Programming Conference '85, pp.148-167, Springer LNCS 221, 1986.

[5] T.Chikayama: *Unique Features of ESP*, Proc. Intl. Conf. Fifth Generation Computer Systems, ICOT, pp.292-298, 1984.

[6] A.Yonezawa,J.P.Briot and E.Shibayama: *Object-Oriented Concurrent Programming in ABCL/1*, Proc. Conf. Object Oriented Programming, Systems, Languages and Applications, 1986.

[7] Y.Yokote and M.Tokoro: *The Design and Implementation of Concurrent Smalltalk*, Proc.Conf.Object Oriented Programming,Systems,Languages and Applications, 1986.

[8] K.Kahn, E.D.Tribble, M.S.Miller and D.G.Bobrow: *Vulcan: Logic Concurrent Objects*, In B.Shriber and P.Wegner(Ed.): Research Directions in Object Oriented Programming, MIT Press, 1987.

[9] K.Yoshida and T.Chikayama: *A'UM - A Stream-Based Concurrent Object-Oriented Language -*, Proc. Intl. Conf. Fifth Generation Computer Systems, ICOT, pp.638-649, 1988.

An Operational Semantics of ANDOR-II, A Parallel Logic Programming Language with AND- and OR- Parallelism

Akikazu Takeuchi Kazuko Takahashi

Mitsubishi Electric Corp.

8-1-1, Tsukaguchi honmachi, Amagasaki, Hyogo 661, Japan

Abstract

An operational semantics of AND- and OR- parallel logic programming language, ANDOR-II, is presented. ANDOR-II combines OR-parallel computation of Prolog and AND-parallel computation of committed choice logic programming languages such as PARLOG, Concurrent Prolog and Guarded Horn Clauses.

Starting from a naive semantics suitable for simulation in sequential machines, we develop a new semantics with fine grain parallelism. The semantics is based on the coloring scheme which paints variable substitutions made in each OR-parallel world by distinct colors.

1 Introduction

The ANDOR-II project began in 1986 as part of the Fifth Generation Computer Systems Project. The aims of the ANDOR-II project are 1) to design a language having both AND- and OR- parallelism suitable for parallel problem solving and 2) to find a class of AND- and OR- parallelism which can be efficiently embedded in a parallel logic programming language such as GHC [23]. The second is worth investigating since it might reveal the complexity of small grain parallel and distributed implementation of AND- and OR- parallel computation.

Design and implementation of the ANDOR-II language which meets the two requirements above has already been finished and reported together with its application [20]. Recently, a language with both AND- and OR- parallelism has been of great interest [18] [4] [2] [28] [10] [7] [1] [13] [8]. Like others, ANDOR-II was derived from a current study of parallel logic programming languages such as Concurrent Prolog [16], PARLOG [3] [6] and GHC [22]. Thus the syntax, semantics and implementation of ANDOR-II are heavily influenced by these languages. The syntax of ANDOR-II is similar to one of the parallel logic programming languages, GHC, but in ANDOR-II, predicates are divided into two types : an AND-predicate for description of a determinate or indeterminate component and an OR-predicate for a nondeterministic one. ANDOR-II is now implemented in such a way that an ANDOR-II program is translated into a GHC program first, and then the translated program is executed by a GHC processor. In this paper, an underlying implementation scheme of ANDOR-II which realizes fine grain parallelism is presented.

The paper is organized as follows. First, we define an AND- and OR- parallel logic programming language which is less restrictive than ANDOR-II and give an informal overview of its computation in Section 2. Sketch of operational semantics for that language is given in Section 3. Sections 4 and 5 provide two implementation schemes. Section 4 presents a simple implementation scheme which is well known as *branching world scheme* and is suitable for intuitive understanding of AND- and OR- parallel computation. It can be characterized by the term *eager copying*. The scheme is used in many implementations of AND- and OR- parallel languages because of its simplicity. Section 5 presents a new implementation scheme, called *coloring scheme*, which allows multiple bindings generated to the same variables by independent OR-parallel worlds. The scheme is regarded as *lazy copying*. It also discusses language restriction that simplifies the coloring scheme. Section 6 discusses the differences between the two schemes. Specification of ANDOR-II is given in Section 7. Details of GHC implementation are described in Section 8. Finally, a comparison with related works and the remaining problems are described in Section 9.

2   An Overview of AND- and OR- Parallel Computation

AND-parallel computation model derives its expressive power from committed-choice mechanism which restricts OR-parallel computations. The AND- and OR- parallel computation model considered in this paper is one which combines AND-parallel computation with committed-choice mechanism and OR-parallel computation without commitment. The kernel idea of combining these two is to divide predicates into two classes, *AND-predicates* and *OR-predicates*. An AND-predicate is defined by a set of *guarded clauses* and always makes commitment in resolution. On the contrary, an OR-predicate is defined by a set of *non-guarded clauses* and never makes commitment. All predicates appearing in a program must be classified into one or the other class.

A guarded clause is of the form:

$$G_0 :- G_1, \ldots, G_n \mid B_1, \ldots, B_m.$$

where G_0 and $G_1, \ldots, G_n$ and $B_1, \ldots, B_m$ are called a *head*, a *guard (part)* and a *body (part)*, respectively. An atom in a guard part is restricted to simple and deterministic built-in predicates such as comparison. An atom in a body part can be an AND-predicate or an OR-predicate. A non-guarded clause is of the form:

$$G_0 :- B_1, \ldots, B_m.$$

where G_0 and $B_1, \ldots, B_m$ are called a *head* and a *body*, respectively. An atom in a body part can be an AND-predicate or an OR-predicate.

Informally speaking, a goal reduction with guarded clauses is similar to that of GHC. A goal reduction with non-guarded clauses is similar to that of OR-parallel Prolog except that the reduction which instantiates the goal during the head unification will be suspended until the goal is sufficiently instantiated.

AND- and OR- parallel computation of our logic program starts with a conjunction of atoms. A conjunction of atoms is referred to as *a world*. Atoms in a world are executed in parallel. This corresponds to AND-parallelism. When a nondeterministic atom, (i.e. an atom with an OR-predicate symbol) having several possible actions, is invoked, conceptually the world proliferates into several worlds, each of which corresponds to a world in which one of the actions has been taken. And these worlds are executed in parallel. This corresponds to OR-parallelism. In this model, the most crucial part is the proliferation. Its naive implementation is to make a copy of a conjunction of all atoms, but it seems unacceptable because of its expected overhead. Herein we introduce another implementation scheme called *coloring scheme*. Before formally describing these implementation schemes, first we give an informal overview of AND- and OR- parallel computation using a simple example.

Program 1

```
% AND-predicates

compute(X,Z) :-
     true |
     pickup(X,Y), square(Y,Y2), cube(Y,Y3), add(Y2,Y3,Z).

square(X,Y) :- true | Y:=X*X.
cube(X,Y)   :- true | Y:=X*X*X.
add(X,Y,Z)  :- true | Z:=X+Y.

% An OR-predicate

pickup([X|L],Y) :- Y=X.
pickup([_|L],Y) :- pickup(L,Y).
```

A predicate **compute** picks up an arbitrary element from the input list and returns the sum of its squared value and cubed value. Here, picking up is assumed to be a nondeterministic operation. If the input is [1,2,3], possible solutions are 2 ($1^2 + 1^3$), 12 ($2^2 + 2^3$) and 36 ($3^2 + 3^3$). It is worth noting that the distinction between AND-predicates and OR-predicates is whether a predicate always makes commitment or never makes commitment. It is not directly related to the multiplicity of solutions. This is why **compute** is defined as an AND-predicate.

Figure 1 shows the data flow graph inside **compute**. A node and an edge are regarded as a process and a communication channel, respectively. When **pickup** generates an output value via channel Y, processes **square** and **cube** receive the value and generate squared value via $Y2$ and cubed value via $Y3$, respectively. Then process **add** adds them.

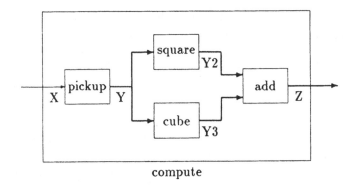

compute

Figure 1: Data flow graph of **compute**

Suppose that **compute** is invoked with the input [1,2,3]. The list is directly sent to **pickup**. **pickup** is a nondeterministic process which finally generates three possible solutions, $1, 2$ and 3.

The naive implementation scheme maintains a data structure corresponding to a world. Thus, when **pickup** generates three solutions, three copies of the structure corresponding to the current world are generated in order to take care of **pickup**'s three possible solutions separately (See Figure 2).

In the coloring scheme, there is no isolated data structure corresponding to just one world. Although worlds share the same data structure, each world is associated with an identifier called a color, and terms owned by a world with a color α are painted by α so that a world never confuses its data with another world's data. Thus when **pickup** generates three solutions, they are painted by distinct colors and packed in arbitrary order in the form $\{v(1, \alpha_1), v(2, \alpha_2), v(3, \alpha_3)\}$, where $\{\ldots\}$ denotes a vector and $v(X, \alpha)$ denotes a value X with a color α. Instead of sending each output value, this vector is sent to **square** and **cube** via Y. For each element of the vector, **square** and **cube** perform their operations and create new vectors, $\{v(1, \alpha_1), v(4, \alpha_2), v(9, \alpha_3)\}$ and $\{v(1, \alpha_1), v(8, \alpha_2), v(27, \alpha_3)\}$, respectively. Note that since **square** and **cube** are determinate they never affect colors. **add** is invoked with these two vectors. Conceptually **add** is requested to add X^2 and Y^3 if X and Y have an identical color. Namely, when they are derived from the same **pickup** action. Otherwise, no addition is applied. Therefore, two vectors are preprocessed to make a set of pairs with the same color, and for each pair **add** operation is applied. Finally, a vector of the solutions $\{v(2, \alpha_1), v(12, \alpha_2), v(36, \alpha_3)\}$ is obtained (See Figure 3).

3 Operational Semantics

AND- and OR- parallel computation of our logic program starts with a conjunction of atoms, that is, a world. Each atom in a world can be resolved in parallel, and as a result of resolution, new worlds are generated to replace the old ones. Thus, computation can be viewed as a world rewriting process. A history of computation forms a tree whose

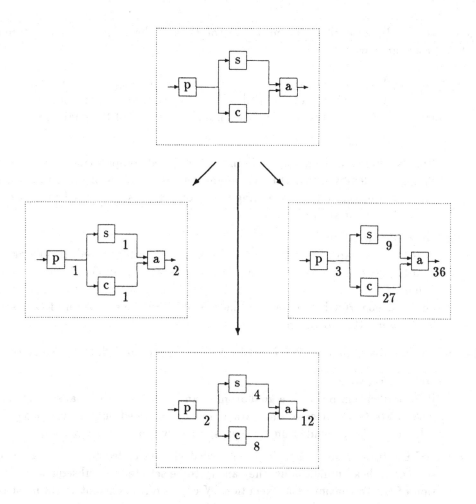

Figure 2: World proliferation

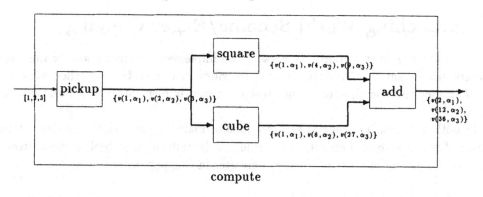

compute

Figure 3: Coloring scheme

nodes are worlds. In resolution, depending on the type of the atom selected, different resolution procedures are taken.

[AND-predicates] Reduction of an AND-predicate must obey the following rules, which are similar to those of GHC [23]. (Here, by the term, *guard computation of a clause C*, we mean both head unification and execution of the guard part.)

Rule of Suspension

Unification invoked directly or indirectly in guard computation of a guarded clause C called by a goal atom G cannot instantiate G. A piece of unification that can succeed only by violating the above rules is suspended until it can succeed without such violation.

Rule of Commitment

When some guarded clause C called by a goal atom G succeeds in solving its guard, C tries to be selected for subsequent execution of G. To be selected, C must first confirm that no other clauses in the program have been selected for G. If confirmed, C is selected indivisibly, and the execution of G is said to be committed to the clause C.

[OR-predicates] Reduction of an OR-predicate must obey the following two rules.

Rule of Suspension

Head unification between a goal atom G and a non-guarded clause C cannot instantiate G. A piece of unification that can succeed only by violating the rules above is suspended until it can succeed without such violation.

Rule of Proliferation
When N non-guarded clauses called by a goal atom G succeed in head unifications, they all try to be selected for subsequent execution of G. To continue the execution, N copies of the current world must be made indivisibly, and the current world is said to proliferate into N worlds.

4 Branching World Scheme/Eager Copying

In this and subsequent sections, we present two implement schemes realizing the above operational semantics. The first scheme, described in this section, is called *branching world scheme* and corresponds to the straightforward implementation of world proliferation.

In both sections, the schemes are described formally as derivation procedure of new worlds. For the sake of simplicity, we consider only unification as built-in predicates.

Here is a listing of all symbols used hereafter in this paper.

A, B, G	:	Atoms
C	:	Clauses
$D(A)$	:	Definitions of an OR-predicate A $(= p(t_1, \ldots, t_n))$
$head(C)$	:	Head of a clause C
$body(C)$	:	Body of a clause C
P	:	Programs
X, Y, Z, U, V	:	Variables
w	:	Worlds
W	:	Sets of worlds
α, β	:	Colors
$\mathcal{A}, \mathcal{B}, \mathcal{G}$	:	Colored atoms or colored disjunctions
θ	:	Unifiers
$domain(\theta)$	:	domain of unifier θ
$range(\theta)$	:	range of unifier θ
Θ	:	Colored unifiers
$\mathcal{W}$	:	Conjunctions of colored atoms

All these symbols may be used with superscripts and/or subscripts. The principle of super(sub)scripting is as follows:

$$\Gamma^{\{\text{disjunctive numbering}\}}_{\{\text{conjunctive numbering}\}}$$

Therefore if Γ is an atom, A^1 and A^2 are in disjunctive relation, and B_1 and B_2 are in conjunctive relation. Also θ^1 and θ^2 indicate that they are logically independent and hence making their composition is useless.

4.1 Non-labelled

Definition 1 *Let A and $G_0 :- G_1, \ldots, G_n \mid B_1, \ldots, B_m$ be a goal atom and a guarded clause, respectively. Assume that $\exists mgu\ \theta$ such that $A = G_0 \cdot \theta$. If $(G_1, \ldots, G_n) \cdot \theta$ has a solution which does not instantiate A, we say $(G_1, \ldots, G_n) \cdot \theta$ has a guarded refutation.*

Note that in our simplified language guard atoms are restricted to a unification atom. Therefore, solvability of a guard part can be easily determined.

Definition 2 *Let W_i be a set of worlds. Assume that $w^j(\in W_i) = A^j_1, \ldots, A^j_a$ and $A^j_k(1 \le k \le a)$ are chosen for reduction by computation rule. Then derivation of W_{i+1} from W_i is defined as follows:*

Case 1 A^j_k *is a unification, $X = t$:*
    W_{i+1} *is defined as $W_{i+1} = (W_i - \{w^j\}) \cup \{w^{j'}\}$,*
    where $w^{j'} = (A^j_1, \ldots, A^j_{k-1}, A^j_{k+1}, \ldots, A^j_a) \cdot \{X/t\}$.

Case 2 A^j_k *is an AND-predicate: If the following conditions are satisfied,*

  1. $\exists G_0 :- G_1, \ldots, G_n \mid B_1, \ldots, B_m$ *such that $\exists mgu\ \theta\ A^j_k = G_0 \cdot \theta$,*

  2. $(G_1, \ldots, G_n) \cdot \theta$ *has guarded refutation and generates θ',*

then execution of A_k^j is committed to the clause and $W_{i+1} = (W_i - \{w^j\}) \cup \{w^{j'}\}$, where $w^{j'} = (A_1^j, \ldots, A_{k-1}^j, B_1, \ldots, B_m, A_{k+1}^j, \ldots, A_a^j) \cdot \theta \cdot \theta'$.

Case 3 A_k^j is an OR-predicate: If there exists a non-empty set of $\{C_1, \ldots, C_t\} \subseteq D(A_k^j)$ such that $\exists mgu\ \theta^l\ A_k^j = head(C_l) \cdot \theta^l, l = 1, \ldots, t$, respectively, then W_{i+1} is defined as

$$W_{i+1} = \begin{cases} (W_i - \{w^j\}) \cup \bigcup_{l=1,\ldots,t} \{w^{jl}\} & \text{if } D_s = \phi \\ (W_i - \{w^j\}) \cup \bigcup_{l=0,\ldots,t} \{w^{jl}\} & \text{otherwise} \end{cases}$$

where

$$w^{jl} = (A_1^{jl}, \ldots, A_{k-1}^{jl}, body(C_l), A_{k+1}^{jl}, \ldots, A_a^{jl}) \cdot \theta^l,\ l = 1, \ldots, t, \text{ respectively},$$

$A_1^{jl}, \ldots, A_{k-1}^{jl}, A_{k+1}^{jl}, \ldots, A_a^{jl}$ is l-th copy of $A_1^j, \ldots, A_{k-1}^j, A_{k+1}^j, \ldots, A_a^j$

$$w^{j0} = (A_1^j, \ldots, A_{k-1}^j, A_k^j|_{D_s}, A_{k+1}^j, \ldots, A_a^j)$$

$A_k^j|_{D_s}$ is an atom with a new definition D_s,

$D_s = D - D_f - \{C_1, \ldots, C_t\}$

$D_f \subset D(A_k^j)$ is a set of clauses which are not unifiable with A_k^j

Note that derivation can be done in parallel as follows. First, different worlds can be executed completely in parallel. Secondly, when more than one atom are selected for reduction simultaneously within a world, the following rules are applied.

1. Arbitrary number of unification atoms and AND-predicates can be reduced in parallel.

2. When an OR-predicate is reduced, it must be the only atom that is going to be reduced.

4.2 Labelled

Labelling each world is considered. A label is a distinct symbol. Intuitively a symbol corresponds to an identifier of a branching event. A label is denoted by ω.

When a world branches into several worlds, variables appearing in the original world are copied. In order to make variable copying explicit, a new structure Θ is introduced. Θ has the following form:

$$\Theta = \{X/\langle X^1|\omega^1, \ldots, X^n|\omega^n \rangle, \ldots\}$$

The form means that a variable X has n copies and X^i is the i-th copy allocated to the world labelled by ω_i.

Definition 3 *Let P be a program and let (W_i, Θ_i) be a set of worlds and history of variable copying. Assume that $w^j(\in W_i) = A_1^j, \ldots, A_a^j$ and $A_k^j(1 \le k \le a)$ are chosen for reduction by computation rule. Then derivation of (W_{i+1}, Θ_{i+1}) from (W_i, Θ_i) is defined as follows.*

Case 1 A_k^j is a unification, $X = t$:
$$W_{i+1} = (W_i - \{w^j\}) \cup \{w^{j'}\}, \Theta_{i+1} = \Theta_i,$$
where $w^{j'} = (A_1^j, \ldots, A_{k-1}^j, A_{k+1}^j, \ldots, A_a^j) \cdot \{X/t\}.$

Case 2 A_k^j is an AND-predicate: If the following conditions are satisfied,

1. $\exists G_0 :- G_1, \ldots, G_n \mid B_1, \ldots, B_m$ such that $\exists mgu\ \theta\ A_k^j = G_0 \cdot \theta,$

2. $(G_1, \ldots, G_n) \cdot \theta$ has guarded refutation and generates $\theta',$

then execution of A_k^j is committed to the clause and
$$W_{i+1} = (W_i - \{w^j\}) \cup \{w^{j'}\}, \Theta_{i+1} = \Theta_i,$$
where $w^{j'} = (A_1^j, \ldots, A_{k-1}^j, B_1, \ldots, B_m, A_{k+1}^j, \ldots, A_a^j) \cdot \theta \cdot \theta'.$

Case 3 A_k^j is an OR-predicate: If there exists a non-empty set $\{C_1, \ldots, C_t\} \subseteq D(A_k^j)$ such that $\exists mgu\ \theta^l\ A_k^j = head(C_l) \cdot \theta^l, l = 1, \ldots, t,$ respectively, then $\Theta_{i+1} = \Theta_i \cup \Theta,$

$$W_{i+1} = \begin{cases} (W_i - \{w^j\}) \cup \bigcup_{l=1,\ldots,t} \{w^{jl}\} & \text{if } D_s = \phi \\ (W_i - \{w^j\}) \cup \bigcup_{l=0,\ldots,t} \{w^{jl}\} & \text{otherwise} \end{cases}$$

where

$$
\begin{aligned}
w^{jl} &= (A_1^{jl}, \ldots, A_{k-1}^{jl}, body(C_l), A_{k+1}^{jl}, \ldots, A_a^{jl}) \cdot \theta^l, \; l = 1, \ldots, t, \text{respectively,} \\
& A_1^{jl}, \ldots, A_{k-1}^{jl}, A_{k+1}^{jl}, \ldots, A_a^{jl} \text{ is } l\text{-th copy of } A_1^j, \ldots, A_{k-1}^j, A_{k+1}^j, \ldots, A_a^j \\
w^{j0} &= (A_1^j, \ldots, A_{k-1}^j, A_k^j|_{D_s}, A_{k+1}^j, \ldots, A_a^j) \\
& A_k^j|_{D_s} \text{ is an atom with a new definition } D_s, \\
& D_s = D - D_f - \{C_1, \ldots, C_t\} \\
& D_f \subset D(A_k^j) \text{ is a set of clauses which are not unifiable with } A_k^j \\
\Theta &= \{X/\langle X^1|\omega^1, \ldots, X^t|\omega^t\rangle \mid \\
& \quad X \text{ appears in } A_1^j, \ldots, A_{k-1}^j, A_k^j, A_{k+1}^j, \ldots, A_a^j, \\
& \quad \text{and } X^l \text{ is its } l\text{-th copy used in } A_1^{jl}, \ldots, A_{k-1}^{jl}, A_{k+1}^{jl}, \ldots, A_a^{jl}\} \\
& \text{where } \omega^1, \ldots, \omega^t \text{ are new distinct symbols.}
\end{aligned}
$$

5 Coloring Scheme/Lazy Copying

The branching scheme is an eager copying scheme. It assumes that atoms belonging to the same world can be collected easily. However under such an environment as distributed execution environment, the assumption is unacceptable because atoms are distributed over multiple resources such as processors and memories.

In this section, yet another implementation scheme, called *a coloring scheme*, is presented. The Coloring scheme is based on lazy copying scheme, where a world is copied part by part incrementally on demand. Coloring scheme can be extended to distributed execution environment. The extension is discussed later.

The scheme is described keeping the resemblance with the labelled branching world scheme. First, we introduce a color and a vector which are similar to a label and history of variable copying, respectively, but have slightly different meanings.

5.1   Colors and vectors

A primitive color identifies one choice made when an OR-predicate is reduced.

Definition 4 *A primitive color is a pair (P, A) of two symbols, where P and A are called a branching point and a branching arc, respectively.*

Two primitive colors are defined to be orthogonal with each other if and only if they share the same branching point, but have different branching arcs. Two primitive colors are defined to be independent if and only if they have different branching points.

A branching point is an identifier of the invocation of an OR-predicate. A branching arc identifies the chosen clause at that invocation.

A color is a record of a history of selections.

Definition 5 *A color is defined to be a set of primitive colors, in which no element is orthogonal with each other. An empty set is regarded as a color.*

Two colors, α, β, are defined to be orthogonal iff $\exists p_1 \in \alpha, p_2 \in \beta$, p_1 and p_2 are orthogonal with each other. Orthogonality of two colors, α, β, is denoted by $\alpha \perp \beta$.

A set of all colors *Col* constitutes a partially ordered set with respect to set inclusion relation $\alpha \subseteq \beta$. For any colors α and β, there always exists a greatest lower bound $\alpha \cup \beta$, while a least upper bound does not always exist. This is because we can not define the least upper bound of two colors when they are orthogonal with each other. Hence a set of all colors is not a lattice. The set of this kind is called a lower semilattice.

Proposition 1 *Let α and β be colors such that $\alpha \perp \beta$. Let α' be a color such that $\alpha \subseteq \alpha'$. Then $\alpha' \perp \beta$.*

In eager copying scheme, all worlds have their own labels at any moment. Labels are identifiers of OR-parallel worlds. On the contrary, in lazy copying scheme, a world is copied part by part incrementally. A color is used to identify a world, however, it is difficult to think about an independent world since at some moment two worlds may still share some part which will be copied later. In order to identify such ongoing copying, a color is attached to a term and an atom, though a label is attached to an isolated world.

Definition 6 (A Vector) *A vector is a finite set of pairs of terms and colors. A vector is denoted by*

$$\langle a^1|\alpha^1, \ldots, a^n|\alpha^n \rangle$$

where n is the size of the set, a^i is a term and α^j's are orthogonal colors.

Due to world proliferation, a variable may have multiple values each of which corresponds to its value in some world. A vector represents such multiple values. For example, if X has a value a^1 in a world with a color α^1 and a^2 in α^2 then X's value is represented by $\langle a^1|\alpha^1, a^2|\alpha^2 \rangle$.

When a non null vector appears in a logical formula, it is interpreted as follows. Suppose that there is an atom including a vector, $p(\langle a^1|\alpha^1, \ldots, a^n|\alpha^n\rangle)$ $n \geq 1$.

$$
\begin{aligned}
p(\langle a^1|\alpha^1, \ldots, a^n|\alpha^n\rangle) &\equiv p(X) \wedge X = \langle a^1|\alpha^1, \ldots, a^n|\alpha^n\rangle \\
&\equiv p(X) \wedge (\boxed{X = a^1}_{\alpha^1} \vee \ldots \vee \boxed{X = a^n}_{\alpha^n}) \\
&\equiv \boxed{p(X) \wedge X = a^1}_{\alpha^1} \vee \ldots \vee \boxed{p(X) \wedge X = a^n}_{\alpha^n} \\
&\equiv \boxed{p(a^1)}_{\alpha^1} \vee \ldots \vee \boxed{p(a^n)}_{\alpha^n}
\end{aligned}
$$

where $\boxed{P}_\alpha$ denotes formula P associated with a color α. Declaratively $\boxed{P}_\alpha$ is equivalent to P. If a vector is a null vector, it is logically interpreted as false. Therefore ,

$$
p(\langle\rangle) \equiv p(X) \wedge false.
$$

There are some works which introduce a set construct or a possibility list into languages and give interpretations similar to the above. In comparison with these, the unique feature of the above interpretation is that each element of a disjunction is associated with an identifier (a color).

For the notational convenience, a colored disjunction is also denoted by a vector term. Thus,

$$
p(\langle a^1|\alpha^1, \ldots, a^n|\alpha^n\rangle) \equiv \langle p(a^1)|\alpha^1, \ldots, p(a^n)|\alpha^n\rangle.
$$

Note that $\langle \cdots \rangle$ forms on both sides represent different things. On the left hand side, $\langle \cdots \rangle$ denotes a data structure while on the opposite side $\langle \cdots \rangle$ denotes a disjunction.

We call an atom including at least one vector *a colored atom*. A colored atom is logically interpreted as *a colored disjunction*. A term is called *a colored term* if and only if it is a vector or it includes at least one vector in it. A unifier is called *a colored unifier* if and only if it has at least one vector in it. Note that a term or a unifier not known to be colored has the possibility to eventually become colored.

Now we define a function which lifts a vector embedded in an atom up to the surface.

Definition 7 *Let A and A' be atoms or colored disjunctions. Let α and Θ be a color and a colored unifier, respectively. A function $f(A, \alpha) = (A', \Theta)$ is defined as follows:*

Case 1 *A is an atom including at least one vector. Let v be a leftmost vector and $v = \langle a^1|\beta^1, \ldots, a^n|\beta^n\rangle$. Let $\beta^{\sigma_1}, \ldots, \beta^{\sigma_m}(\{\sigma_1, \ldots, \sigma_m\} \subseteq \{1, \ldots, n\})$ be all colors not orthogonal with α.*

$$
f(A, \alpha) = (\langle A^1[v/a^{\sigma_1}]|\alpha \cup \beta^{\sigma_1}, \ldots, A^m[v/a^{\sigma_m}]|\alpha \cup \beta^{\sigma_m}\rangle, \Theta)
$$

where $A^i[v/a]$ denotes the i-th copy of A with v replaced by a, and Θ is a colored unifier of the form

$$
\Theta = \{X/\langle X^{\sigma_1}|\beta^{\sigma_1}, \ldots, X^{\sigma_m}|\beta^{\sigma_m}\rangle \mid X \text{ is any variable appearing in } A \text{ except for}
$$
$$
\text{in } v \text{ and } X^i \text{ is the i-th copy of } X\}
$$

Case 2 *A is a colored disjunction, $\langle A^{1''}|\beta^1, \ldots, A^{n''}|\beta^n \rangle$. Let $\{\beta^{\sigma_1} \ldots \beta^{\sigma_m}\}$ be all colors not orthogonal with α.*

$$f(A, \alpha) = (\langle A^{\sigma_1 ''}|\alpha \cup \beta^{\sigma_1}, \ldots, A^{\sigma_m ''}|\alpha \cup \beta^{\sigma_m} \rangle, \phi)$$

Case 3 *A is an atom including no vector.*

$$f(A, \alpha) = (\langle A|\alpha \rangle, \phi)$$

Definition 8 *Let A be an atom, and let F and S be a colored disjunction and a unifier, respectively. A function flatten$(A) = (F, S)$ is defined as follows:*

1. *Let F_0 be $\langle A|\phi \rangle$ and S_0 be ϕ.*

2. *$F_{n+1} = \bigcup_{A''|\alpha \in F_n} f_1(A'', \alpha)$ and*
   $S_{n+1} = S_n \cup \bigcup_{A''|\alpha \in F_n} f_2(A'', \alpha)$
   where f_1 and f_2 are defined as $f_1(A, \alpha) = A'$ and $f_2(A, \alpha) = \Theta$ iff $f(A, \alpha) = (A', \Theta)$.

Since the number of vectors included in A is finite, and the application of f always decreases that number by one, there exists F and S for some N such that $F_N = F_{N+1} = F_{N+2} = \ldots = F$, $S_N = S_{N+1} = S_{N+2} = \ldots = S$. Then

$$\text{flatten}(A) \equiv (F, S)$$

Proposition 2 *Let flatten$(A) = (\langle A^1|\alpha^1, \ldots, A^n|\alpha^n \rangle, \Theta)$. Then*

1. *for any $i(1 \leq i \leq n)$, A^i includes no vector, and*

2. *for any $i, j(1 \leq i < j \leq n)$ A^i and A^j share no variable, and*

3. *for any $i, j(1 \leq i < j \leq n)$, $\alpha^i \perp \alpha^j$.*

Example 2

Let $A = p(\langle a^1|\alpha^1, a^2|\alpha^2 \rangle, \langle b^1|\beta^1, b^2|\beta^2 \rangle, X)$.

$F_0 = \langle A|\phi \rangle$
$S_0 = \phi$

$F_1 = f_1(A, \phi)$
$\quad = \langle p(a^1, \langle b^1|\beta^1, b^2|\beta^2 \rangle, X^1)|\alpha^1, p(a^2, \langle b^1|\beta^1, b^2|\beta^2 \rangle, X^2)|\alpha^2 \rangle$
$S_1 = \{X/\langle X^1|\alpha^1, X^2|\alpha^2 \rangle\}$

$F_2 = f_1(p(a^1, \langle b^1|\beta^1, b^2|\beta^2 \rangle, X^1), \alpha^1) \cup f_1(p(a^2, \langle b^1|\beta^1, b^2|\beta^2 \rangle, X^2), \alpha^2)$
$\quad = \langle p(a^1, b^1, X^{11})|\alpha^1 \cup \beta^1, p(a^1, b^2, X^{12})|\alpha^1 \cup \beta^2,$
$\qquad p(a^2, b^1, X^{21})|\alpha^2 \cup \beta^1, p(a^2, b^2, X^{22})|\alpha^2 \cup \beta^2 \rangle$
$S_2 = S_1 \cup \{X^1/\langle X^{11}|\alpha^1 \cup \beta^1, X^{12}|\alpha^1 \cup \beta^2 \rangle, X^2/\langle X^{21}|\alpha^2 \cup \beta^1, X^{22}|\alpha^2 \cup \beta^2 \rangle\}$

Then

$$\text{flatten}(A) = (F_2, S_2)$$

Given a set of unifiers with associated colors, the following function *compose* makes their composition. To do so, for all variables which come to have multiple substitutions by this composition, *compose* creates vector substitutions.

Definition 9 *Let* $\Theta, \theta^1, \ldots, \theta^n$ *be unifiers, and* $\alpha^1, \ldots, \alpha^n$ *be colors. Let* $S = \{(\theta^i, \alpha^i) \mid i = 1, \ldots, n\}$.

$$compose(S) = \Theta$$

is defined as follows.

If $n = 1$ *then* $\Theta = \theta^1$. *Otherwise* Θ *is defined to be the final value of the following algorithm.*

1. *Let* $\Theta = \phi$.

2. *For each variable* X *such that* $\exists i, j (1 \leq i < j \leq n)$ X *appears in* θ^i *and* θ^j, *let* $\theta^{\sigma_1}, \ldots, \theta^{\sigma_m} (m \geq 2, \{\sigma_1, \ldots, \sigma_m\} \subseteq \{1, \ldots, n\})$ *be all unifiers that share* X,

   - *for* $i = 1, \ldots, m$, *replace* X *in* θ^{σ_i} *by* X^{σ_i} *where* X^{σ_i} *is the* σ_i-*th copy of* X.
   - $\Theta := \Theta \cup \{X / \langle X^{\sigma_1} | \alpha^{\sigma_1}, \ldots, X^{\sigma_m} | \alpha^{\sigma_m} \rangle\}$

3. $\Theta := \Theta \cup \bigcup_{i=1}^{n} \theta^i$

By the introduction of a vector, the most influenced part is the unification.

Definition 10 *Unification between a vector* $\langle a^1 | \alpha^1, \ldots, a^n | \alpha^n \rangle$ *and a term* t *is defined as follows.*

1. *[t is a variable] Unification succeeds with*

   $$\theta = \{t / \langle a^1 | \alpha^1, \ldots, a^n | \alpha^n \rangle\}$$

2. *[t is a non-variable and non-vector term] If no* $a^i (i = 1, \ldots, n)$ *and* t *are unifiable then unification fails. Otherwise, let* $a^{\sigma_1}, \ldots, a^{\sigma_m}$ *be all elements which are unifiable with* t *and* $\theta^{\sigma_j} (j = 1, \ldots, m)$ *be their unifiers. Then unification succeeds with*

   $$\Theta = compose(\{(\theta^{\sigma_1}, \alpha^{\sigma_1}), \ldots, (\theta^{\sigma_m}, \alpha^{\sigma_m})\}).$$

3. *[t is a vector* $\langle b^1 | \beta^1, \ldots, b^l | \beta^l \rangle$*] If any pair of* α^i *and* β^j $(i = 1, \ldots, n, \ j = 1, \ldots, l)$ *is orthogonal with each other, unification terminates without output. If, for any* i, j *such that* $\alpha^i \not\perp \beta^j$, a^i *and* b^j $(i = 1, \ldots, n, \ j = 1, \ldots, l)$ *are not unifiable, unification fails. Otherwise, unification succeeds with*

   $$\Theta = compose(\{(\theta^{ij}, \alpha^i \cup \beta^j) \mid a^i \text{ and } b^j \text{ are unifiable with } \theta^{ij}\})$$

Example 3

1. $h(a, X)$ *and* $\langle h(Y^1, b) | \alpha^1, h(Y^2, c) | \alpha^2 \rangle$ *are unifiable.*

   $$
   \begin{aligned}
   \Theta &= compose(\{(\{Y^1/a, X/b\}, \alpha^1), (\{Y^2/a, X/c\}, \alpha^2)\}) \\
   &= \{X / \langle X^1 | \alpha^1, X^2 | \alpha^2 \rangle, X^1/b, X^2/c, Y^1/a, Y^2/a\}
   \end{aligned}
   $$

2. $\langle X^1|\alpha^1, X^2|\alpha^2\rangle$ and $\langle Y^1|\beta^1, Y^2|\beta^2\rangle$ are unifiable.

$$
\begin{aligned}
\Theta \;=\;& \text{compose}(\{(\{X^1/Y^1\}, \alpha^1 \cup \beta^1), (\{X^1/Y^2\}, \alpha^1 \cup \beta^2), \\
& (\{X^2/Y^1\}, \alpha^2 \cup \beta^1), (\{X^2/Y^2\}, \alpha^2 \cup \beta^2)\}) \\
=\;& \{X^1/\langle X^{11}|\alpha^1 \cup \beta^1, X^{12}|\alpha^1 \cup \beta^2\rangle, X^2/\langle X^{21}|\alpha^2 \cup \beta^1, X^{22}|\alpha^2 \cup \beta^2\rangle, \\
& Y^1/\langle X^{11}|\alpha^1 \cup \beta^1, X^{21}|\alpha^2 \cup \beta^1\rangle, Y^2/\langle X^{12}|\alpha^1 \cup \beta^2, X^{22}|\alpha^2 \cup \beta^2\rangle\}
\end{aligned}
$$

5.2 Derivation

A colored world is defined to be a conjunction of colored atoms and colored disjunctions. Every colored atom $\mathcal{A}$ such that $\mathcal{A} = p(t_1, \ldots, t_n)$ and p is an OR-predicate is associated with a set $D(\mathcal{A})$ of clauses defining p. If $\text{flatten}(\mathcal{A}) = (\langle A^1|\alpha^1, \ldots, A^n|\alpha^n\rangle, \Theta)$, $D(A^i)$ is defined to be equal to $D(\mathcal{A}), i = 1, \ldots, n$.

In the coloring scheme, derivation is defined to be transformation of a colored world. We describe it, assuming that derivation is performed sequentially at first. It is worth noting the following property, which is implied by the sequentiality; All the constructs reflect result of applying substitutions made in the previous derivation. Thus, vectors recognized by *flatten* below are the only vectors which can appear during the current derivation.

Definition 11 *Let $\mathcal{W}_i$ be a colored world, $\mathcal{A}_1, \ldots, \mathcal{A}_a$. Assume that $\text{flatten}(\mathcal{A}_k) = (\langle A_k^1|\alpha^1, \ldots, A_k^s|\alpha^s\rangle, \Theta_0)$ and A_k^j is chosen for reduction by computation rule. Then derivation of $\mathcal{W}_{i+1}$ from $\mathcal{W}_i$ is defined as follows:*

Case 1 A_k^j *is unification, $X = t$:*
$$
\mathcal{W}_{i+1} = ((\mathcal{A}_1, \ldots, \mathcal{A}_{k-1}, \mathcal{A}_{k+1}, \ldots, \mathcal{A}_a) \cdot \Theta_0 \cdot \{X/t\}, \mathcal{A}_k - \langle A_k^j|\alpha^j\rangle)
$$

Case 2 A_k^j *is an AND-predicate: If the following conditions are satisfied,*

   1. $\exists G_0 :\text{-} G_1, \ldots, G_n \mid B_1, \ldots, B_m$ *such that $\exists mgu\ \theta$, $A_k^j = G_0 \cdot \theta$,*

   2. $(G_1, \ldots, G_n) \cdot \theta$ *has guarded refutation and generates θ',*

   then execution of A_k^j is committed to the clause and
$$
\mathcal{W}_{i+1} = ((\mathcal{A}_1, \ldots, \mathcal{A}_{k-1}, \mathcal{A}_{k+1}, \ldots, \mathcal{A}_a) \cdot \Theta_0, \langle (B_1, \ldots, B_m)|\alpha^j\rangle \cdot \theta \cdot \theta', \mathcal{A}_k - \langle A_k^j|\alpha^j\rangle).
$$

Case 3 A_k^j *is an OR-predicate: If there exists a non-empty set $\{C_1, \ldots, C_t\} \subseteq D(A_k^j)$ such that $\exists mgu\ \theta'$, $A_k^j = \text{head}(C_l) \cdot \theta', l = 1, \ldots, t$, respectively, then*

$$
\mathcal{W}_{i+1} = \begin{cases}
\begin{aligned}
&((\mathcal{A}_1, \ldots, \mathcal{A}_{k-1}, \mathcal{A}_{k+1}, \ldots, \mathcal{A}_a) \cdot \Theta_0, & \text{if } D_s = \phi \\
&\langle body(C_1)|\alpha^{j1}, \ldots, body(C_t)|\alpha^{jt}\rangle, \\
&\mathcal{A}_k - \langle A_k^j|\alpha^j\rangle) \cdot \Theta
\end{aligned} \\[2em]
\begin{aligned}
&((\mathcal{A}_1, \ldots, \mathcal{A}_{k-1}, \mathcal{A}_{k+1}, \ldots, \mathcal{A}_a) \cdot \Theta_0, & \text{otherwise} \\
&\langle body(C_1)|\alpha^{j1}, \ldots, body(C_t)|\alpha^{jt}\rangle, \\
&\langle A_k^1|\alpha^1, \ldots, A_k^{j-1}|\alpha^{j-1}, (\overline{A}_k^j|_{D_s})|\alpha^{j(t+1)}, A_k^{j+1}|\alpha^{j+1}, \ldots, A_k^s|\alpha^s\rangle) \cdot \Theta
\end{aligned}
\end{cases}
$$

where

- $\overline{A^j_k}$ is a variant of A^j_k.

- $\overline{A^j_k}|_{D_s}$ and $A^j_k|_{D_s}$ are atoms with a definition D_s where $D_s = D(A^j_k) - D_f - \{C_1, \ldots, C_t\}$ and D_f $(\subset D(A^j_k))$ is a set of clauses which are not unifiable with A^j_k.

- $\Theta = \text{compose}(\{(\theta^j, \alpha^{jl}) \mid l = 1, \ldots, t'\})$ where α^{jl} $(l = 1, \ldots, t')$ are new colors such that $\alpha^{jl} = \alpha^j \cup \{(n, l)\}$ where n is a new symbol identifying this branching[1]. $t' = t$ if $D_s = \phi$, otherwise $t' = t + 1$.
  θ^{t+1} is mgu such that $A^j_k = \overline{A^j_k} \cdot \theta^{t+1}$.

where $\mathcal{A}_k - \langle A^j_k | \alpha^j \rangle = \langle A^1_k | \alpha^1, \ldots, A^{j-1}_k | \alpha^{j-1}, A^{j+1}_k | \alpha^{j+1}, \ldots, A^s_k | \alpha^s \rangle$

Example 4

Suppose that $\mathcal{W}_i = p(\langle 1 | \alpha^1, 2 | \alpha^2 \rangle, Y), q(Y)$ where p is an AND-predicate, and its definition is:

$$p(1, X^1) :- true \mid r_1(X^1)$$
$$p(2, X^2) :- true \mid r_2(X^2)$$

Let the first atom be the selected atom and

$$\begin{aligned} \text{flatten}(p(\langle 1 | \alpha^1, 2 | \alpha^2 \rangle, Y)) &= (\langle p(1, Y^1) | \alpha^1, p(2, Y^2) | \alpha^2 \rangle, \Theta_0) \\ \Theta_0 &= \{Y / \langle Y^1 | \alpha^1, Y^2 | \alpha^2 \rangle\} \end{aligned}$$

Assume that $p(1, Y^1)$ is selected for reduction. Then,

$$\begin{aligned} \mathcal{W}_{i+1} &= q(Y) \cdot \Theta_0, \langle r_1(X^1) | \alpha^1 \rangle \cdot \{X^1 / Y^1\}, \langle p(2, Y2) | \alpha^2 \rangle \\ &\quad q(\langle Y^1 | \alpha^1, Y^2 | \alpha^2 \rangle), \langle r_1(Y^1) | \alpha^1 \rangle \cdot \{X^1 / Y^1\}, \langle p(2, Y^2) | \alpha^2 \rangle \end{aligned}$$

Suppose $p(2, Y^2)$ is selected for next reduction. Then,

$$\mathcal{W}_{i+2} = q(\langle Y^1 | \alpha^1, Y^2 | \alpha^2 \rangle), \langle r_1(Y^1) | \alpha^1 \rangle \cdot \{X^1 / Y^1\}, \langle r_2(Y^2) | \alpha^2 \rangle$$

Example 5

Suppose that $\mathcal{W}_0 = n\text{-merge}([a, b], V, V)$, where n-merge is an OR-predicate with the following definition.

$$\begin{aligned} C_1 &: n\text{-merge}([U^1 | X^1], Y^1, Z^1) :- Z^1 = [U^1 | Z^1_s], n\text{-merge}(X^1, Y^1, Z^1_s) \\ C_2 &: n\text{-merge}(X^2, [U^2 | Y^2], Z^2) :- Z^2 = [U^2 | Z^2_s], n\text{-merge}(X^2, Y^2, Z^2_s) \\ C_3 &: n\text{-merge}([], Y^3, Z^3) :- Z^3 = Y^3 \\ C_4 &: n\text{-merge}(X^4, [], Z^4) :- Z^4 = X^4 \end{aligned}$$

---

[1] As a representation of α^{jl}'s, we can also choose $\{(n, l)\}$. The current decision is based on compatibility with the actual implementation.

$n\text{-}merge([a, b], V, V)$ *is selected for reduction and only* C_1 *can have successful head uni-fication. Let* $A_{01} = n\text{-}merge([a, b], V, V)$. *Then,*

$$
\begin{aligned}
D_f &= \{C_3\}, D_s = \{C_2, C_4\} \\
A_{01} &= head(C_1) \cdot \theta \ where \ \theta = \{U_1^1/a, X_1^1/[b], Y_1^1/V, Z_1^1/V\} \\
\overline{A_{01}} &= n\text{-}merge([a, b], V', V') \ and \ A_{01} = \overline{A_{01}} \cdot \theta' \ where \ \theta' = \{V'/V\} \\
\Theta &= compose(\{(\theta, \alpha^1), (\theta', \alpha^2)\}) \\
&= \{U_1^1/a, X_1^1/[b], Y_1^1/V^1, Z_1^1/V^1, V'/V^2, V/\langle V^1|\alpha^1, V^2|\alpha^2\rangle\}
\end{aligned}
$$

where α^1 *and* α^2 *are new colors and* $\alpha^1 \perp \alpha^2$. $\mathcal{W}_1$ *is:*

$$
\mathcal{W}_1 = \langle (V^1 = [a|Z_{s1}^1], \ n\text{-}merge([b], V^1, Z_{s1}^1))|\alpha^1\rangle, \langle (n\text{-}merge([a, b], V^2, V^2)|_{D_s})|\alpha^2\rangle
$$

If a unification atom is reduced, $\mathcal{W}_2$ *is:*

$$
\mathcal{W}_2 = \langle n\text{-}merge([b], [a|Z_{s1}^1], Z_{s1}^1)|\alpha^1\rangle, \langle (n\text{-}merge([a, b], V^2, V^2)|_{D_s})|\alpha^2\rangle
$$

Suppose that the first atom is chosen for next reduction. C_1 *and* C_2 *have successful head unifications. Let* $A_{21} = n\text{-}merge([b], [a|Z_{s1}^1], Z_{s1}^1)$. *Then,*

$$
\begin{aligned}
D_f &= \{C_3, C_4\}, D_s = \phi \\
A_{21} &= head(C_1) \cdot \theta^1 \ where \ \theta^1 = \{U_2^1/b, X_2^1/[], Y_2^1/[a|Z_{s1}^1], Z_2^1/Z_{s1}^1\} \\
A_{21} &= head(C_2) \cdot \theta^2 \ where \ \theta^2 = \{U_2^2/a, X_2^2/[b], Y_2^2/Z_{s1}^1, Z_2^2/Z_{s1}^1\} \\
\Theta &= compose(\{(\theta^1, \beta^1), (\theta^2, \beta^2)\}) \\
&= \{U_2^1/b, X_2^1/[], Y_2^1/[a|Z_{s1}^1], Z_2^1/Z_{s1}^{11}, U_2^2/a, X_2^2/[b], Y_2^2/Z_{s1}^{12}, Z_2^2/Z_{s1}^{12}, \\
&\qquad Z_{s1}^1/\langle Z_{s1}^{11}|\beta^1, Z_{s1}^{12}|\beta^2\rangle\}
\end{aligned}
$$

where $\beta^1 \perp \beta^2$. $\mathcal{W}_3$ *is:*

$$
\begin{aligned}
\mathcal{W}_3 &= \langle (n\text{-}merge([a, b], V^2, V^2)|_{D_s})|\alpha^2\rangle, \\
&\qquad \langle (Z_{s1}^{11} = [b|Z_{s2}^1], n\text{-}merge([], [a|Z_{s1}^{11}], Z_{s2}^1))|\beta^1, \\
&\qquad (Z_{s1}^{12} = [a|Z_{s2}^2], n\text{-}merge([b], Z_{s1}^{12}, Z_{s2}^2))|\beta^2\rangle.
\end{aligned}
$$

After further reduction of unification atoms, V *becomes the following vector:*

$$
V = \langle [a, b|Z_{s2}^1]|\beta^1 \cup \alpha^1, [a, a|Z_{s2}^2]|\beta^2 \cup \alpha^1, V^2|\alpha^2\rangle
$$

5.3 Optimization and parallelization

Two operations can be considered as sources of its complexity. One is *flatten*, and the other is *compose*. Let us examine them in detail.

Flattening of a colored atom is needed in order to avoid unification between a vector and an ordinary term during head unification. However, flattening of a vector deeply embedded in a term is not necessary if it is not unified with an ordinary term. In fact a deeply embedded vector does not affect the result of head unification. Even if it is flattened and n atoms are generated, n head unifications do the same thing. Furthermore, a deeply embedded vector will eventually be flattened when needed. Thus, it is advantageous to postpone flattening and to share the results of computation. This leads to an idea of *bounded depth flattening*.

Another point of *flatten* is construction of a colored unifier Θ_0. When a colored atom is flattened with respect to a vector, variables outside the vector have to be collected together to make Θ_0. The complexity of this is proportional to the size of the atom. The bounded depth flattening never helps reduction of this complexity. *However if a variable outside the vector is known not to be instantiated during the computation of the atom[2], it is not necessary to take the variable into account, since the purpose of Θ_0 is to prepare for multiple assignments to a variable in a goal atom.* Variables which must be taken into account are those which are not known to be reference-only. This optimization becomes more practical by the introduction of *mode declaration*. For each AND- and OR-predicate, one mode is defined. A mode specifies, for each argument, that it is *reference-only (read)* or *not (write)*. Note that an argument with "write" mode need not be instantiated to a non-variable term. In order to enjoy full advantage of mode declaration, *single producer constraint* must be guaranteed. The single producer constraint means that at most one occurrence of a variable can appear at argument position with "write" mode. If this constraint is kept, it is guaranteed that a term appearing at an argument position with "write" mode is always an unbound variable. Owing to a mode declaration and the single producer constraint, construction of Θ_0 becomes statically predictable.

compose is performed only in the reduction of an OR-predicate. Complexity of *compose* is in construction of vector substitutions for variables which are shared by unifiers with different colors. Its purpose is the preparation of multiple instantiation of a variable in a goal atom by multiple clauses as in the case of Θ_0 of *flatten*. In general, all the variables in a goal atom must be collected to construct vector substitutions. The introduction of mode declaration and the single producer constraint reduces the complexity in this case also. Under these restrictions, vector substitutions can be constructed from terms appearing in argument positions with "write" mode.

In Section 5.2, the derivation procedure was described assuming sequentiality. In other words, the entire procedure was assumed to be an atomic operation. The reason why we need sequentiality is to guarantee firstly that during *flatten* operation its argument never changes, secondly that once an atom is flattened, no new vector appears in a flattened atom until head unification is completed, and thirdly that during *compose* operation its argument never changes. These are obstacles against parallel derivation.

However, the optimization techniques discussed above can contribute to removal of the obstacles here again. First of all, the idea of the bounded depth flattening indicates that we can ignore vectors appearing at a level deeper than some depth. Therefore, the second problem and part of the first problem are resolved. The rest of the first problem and the third problem are solved by the two language restrictions, mode declaration

---

[2]By the term "computation of an atom", we mean the whole tree of computation initiated by that atom.

and single producer constraint. These restrictions make program behavior statically predictable. Therefore *flatten* and *compose* can know final form of their arguments.

As a result, using these optimization techniques, parallel derivation becomes possible and sizes of atomic operations required there become equal to those of atomic operations required by ordinary parallel unification.

6 Comparison

The branching world scheme is an eager copying scheme. When an OR-predicate is reduced, copies of the whole world are created at once.

On the contrary, the coloring scheme is a lazy copying scheme. When an OR-predicate is reduced using, say n clauses, only variables are copied and their copies are then propagated to other atoms sharing the same variables in a vector form. Such a vector will invoke further copying by *flatten* when an atom including the vector is selected for reduction. In this way, copies of a world are created part by part.

Another important difference is that the number of reductions required to solve a problem in the coloring scheme is less than or equal to that in the branching scheme. This is explained using an example. Suppose that there are three atoms,

$$p(X, Y), q(X), r(Y)$$

where p is an AND-predicate which suspends until its two arguments are instantiated, and q and r are OR-predicates. Suppose also that q and r have the following definitions.

$$q(X) \quad :- X = a_1.$$
$$\vdots$$
$$q(X) \quad :- X = a_n.$$

$$r(Y) \quad :- Y = b_1.$$
$$\vdots$$
$$r(Y) \quad :- Y = b_m.$$

In the branching world scheme, if q is executed first, r is executed n times. If r is executed first, q is executed m times. However, in the coloring scheme, q and r are executed only once. Suppose that q is executed first. q generates colored unifier $\{X/\langle a_1|\alpha^1, \ldots, a_n|\alpha^n\rangle\}$ and terminates. Thus the goal atoms become:

$$p(\langle a_1|\alpha^1, \ldots, a_n|\alpha^n\rangle, Y), r(Y)$$

Since p waits for values at the second argument, r is the only atom that can be reduced next. Making colored unifier $\{Y/\langle b_1|\beta^1, \ldots, b_m|\beta^m\rangle\}$, the execution of r terminates. The goals become:

$$p(\langle a_1|\alpha^1, \ldots, a_n|\alpha^n\rangle, \langle b_1|\beta^1, \ldots, b_m|\beta^m\rangle)$$

The whole computation terminates after executing p $n \times m$ times. Clearly q and r are executed only once. This is because q and r invoke copying of only relevant (sharing variables) atoms. The difference is apparent when goal atoms are $q(X), r(Y)$. In the coloring scheme, both goals are executed only once, while in the branching world scheme, q is executed m times or r is executed n times.

The advantage of the coloring scheme with respect to the number of reductions comes from the nature of lazy copying. In lazy copying, copying is performed incrementally. Therefore, the result of computation performed in a position which is not yet copied will be shared later by its copies. The advantage of the coloring scheme is amplified when the number of goal atoms are large and there are many independent sources of OR-parallel branching.

7 Language ANDOR-II

Now it is time to summarize features of our language described so far and present it as ANDOR-II. An ANDOR-II program is a set of AND-predicate definitions and OR-predicate definitions.

An AND-predicate definition is a sequence of a mode declaration and a set of guarded clauses. An OR-predicate definition is a sequence of a mode declaration, an OR-predicate declaration and a set of non-guarded clauses. A predicate defined by an AND(OR)-predicate definition is called an *AND(OR)-predicate*. Note that a clause of either type can contain both AND-predicates and OR-predicates in a body part. An atom in a guard part of a guarded clause is restricted to a test predicate. This is the same restriction as those of flat parallel logic programming languages (see, for example, [22]).

An OR-predicate declaration is of the form:

:- or_predicate P/N.

where P is a predicate symbol and N is its arity.

A mode declaration is of the form:

:- mode $P(m_1, \ldots, m_N)$.

where P, N, m_i are a predicate symbol, its arity and a mode of the i-th argument, respectively. m_i is either + or -, which denote reference-only and write modes, respectively. Their meanings are the same as those explained in Section 5.3. Namely, $m_i = +$ indicates that the i-th argument will never be instantiated during the computation of P. + mode is also referred to as read mode. - mode indicates the complementary case.

As the meaning of reference-only mode indicates, variables appearing at arguments with reference-only mode in a head can only appear at arguments with reference-only mode in guard and body atoms. Furthermore, with respect to mode declarations, a program must satisfy the single producer constraint discussed in Section 5.3.

Definition 12 *We say a program satisfies the single producer constraint if and only if every clause satisfies the single producer constraint. We say a clause satisfies the single* *producer constraint if and only if a variable occurs at most once at arguments with write mode in its right hand side.*

In addition to these, we put the following restriction on unification atoms in body parts.

- It must have the form:

$$X = T$$

where X is a variable and T is a term.

- The left hand side of a unification atom is treated as having write mode. Therefore all the other occurrences of X within a clause must be in reference-only mode.

The following is an ANDOR-II program describing two communicating processes, one is determinate and the other is nondeterministic.

Program 6

```
:- mode cycle.
cycle :- true | p1([2|X],Y), p2(Y,X).

:- mode p1(+,-).
p1([stop],Y) :- true | Y=[].
p1([X|X1],Y) :- true | add(X,1,A), Y=[A|Y1], p1(X1,Y1).

:- mode p2(+,-).
p2([X|X1],Y) :- X > 20  | Y=[stop].
p2([X|X1],Y) :- X =< 20 | multi(X,A), Y=[A|Y1], p2(X1,Y1).

:- mode multi(+,-).
:- or_predicate multi/2.
multi(X,Y) :- square(X,Y).
multi(X,Y) :- cube(X,Y).

:- mode square(+,-).
square(X,Y) :- true | Y:=X*X.

:- mode cube(+,-).
cube(X,Y)   :- true | Y:=X*X*X.

:- mode add(+,+,-).
add(X,Y,Z)  :- true | Z:=X+Y.
```

In the clause defining `cycle`, processes `p1` and `p2` form a cyclic structure with the communication channels X and Y. `p1` receives a stream via its first argument, increments an element of the stream by one, and sends the value to **p2** via its second argument. **p2** receives a stream via its first argument, executes nondeterministic operation **multi** on a received element, and sends the result to **p1**. In this way, simple interaction between determinate and nondeterministic processes is expressed.

8 GHC Implementation

One of the main targets of ANDOR-II project is to find a class of AND- and OR- parallel languages that can be efficiently implemented in parallel logic programming languages. In this section, we briefly explain how ANDOR-II is implemented in GHC. The way to implement ANDOR-II in GHC is the so-called translation approach. Namely an ANDOR-II program is translated into a GHC program. The translation scheme we present here is different from the ones which were already reported in [17] [19] [20]. In those papers, a scheme was presented which intensively analyzed source programs to find possible places in which vectors may appear. In contrast to this, the new scheme is completely dynamic. It does no analysis at translation-time and generates codes which can handle vectors appearing anywhere.

8.1 Implementation of colored worlds

First we give an implementation of a color and a vector. Recall that, in a primitive color (P, A), P is called a branching point identifying an invocation of an OR-predicate, and A is called a branching arc identifying the chosen clause. In our implementation, there exists, in the run-time environment, one special process called *an ID server* which uniquely numbers invocations of OR-predicates starting from 1 up to N. And at translation-time, for each predicate definition D, the translator numbers clauses starting from 1 to $|D|$. Therefore P is represented by an integer between 1 and N, and A is also represented by an integer between 1 and $|D|$.

A color α is implemented as a long string of length N characters,

$$\alpha \quad ::= \quad c_1 \cdots c_N$$

where c_i's are n bits characters. c_i is the field for the primitive color with the branching point $P = i$, and is determined as follows.

$$c_i = \begin{cases} m & \text{if } (i, m) \in \alpha \\ 0 & \text{otherwise} \end{cases}$$

Note that every color is of the same length and has fields for all branching points.

N and n are implementation dependent parameters. N represents the total number of branchings permitted in one execution. n determines the maximum number of clauses in a definition. N is a serious restriction, while n is not. This is because n can be determined so as to be greater than or equal to log of the size of the largest predicate definition.

In relation to a color, we introduce a GHC predicate, $add\_color(C_1, P, A, C_2)$ where P and A are a branching point and a branching arc, respectively, and C_1 and C_2 are colors. *add_color* takes C_1, P and A as input and instantiates a variable C_2 to a color $C_1 \cup \{(P, A)\}$ if C_1 and $\{(P, A)\}$ are not orthogonal with each other.

A vector t $(= \langle a^1|\alpha^1, \ldots, a^n|\alpha^n \rangle)$ is implemented as

$$t \quad ::= \quad \{\mathbf{v}(a^1, \alpha^1), \ldots, \mathbf{v}(a^n, \alpha^n)\}$$

where $\{\cdots\}$ denotes a vector structure[3]. Following KL1 [9], it is assumed that elements of a vector are numbered from 0 and each element is initialized to 0 when a vector is created. In addition to this, we introduce four basic KL1 predicates for vector manipulations.

- *vector(X, L)*
  vector(X, L) tests whether X is a vector or not. If X is a vector it succeeds and L is instantiated to the length of the vector. Otherwise it fails.

- *new_vector(Y, L)*
  new_vector(Y, L) is a predicate which takes an unbound variable Y and an integer L, and instantiates Y to a new vector of length L.

- *vector_element(X, I, E)*
  vector_element(X, I, E) takes a vector X and an integer I, and unifies E with the I-th element.

- *set_vector_element(X, I, E, N, Y)*
  set_vector_element(X, I, E, N, Y) takes a vector X and an integer I, and unifies E with the I-th element. It also creates a new vector Y which is equivalent to X except that the I-th element E is replaced by N.

Given two colors, α and β, it is an elementary procedure to examine whether they are orthogonal with each other or not. The following algorithm does that test as well as computation of the union of two colors when they are not orthogonal.

> **Input:** two colors, α $(= c_1^\alpha \cdots c_N^\alpha)$ and β $(= c_1^\beta \cdots c_N^\beta)$
>
> **Output:** *yes* (orthogonal) or *no(γ)* $(\gamma = \alpha \cup \beta)$
>
> 1. Let $i := 1$ and $\gamma := c_1^\gamma \cdots c_N^\gamma$
>
> 2. While $i \le N$ do
>   If $c_i^\alpha = 0$ then $i := i + 1, c_i^\gamma := c_i^\beta$
>   else if $c_i^\beta = 0$ then $i := i + 1, c_i^\gamma := c_i^\alpha$
>   else if $c_i^\alpha = c_i^\beta$ then $i := i + 1, c_i^\gamma := c_i^\alpha$
>   else exit with output *yes*
>
> 3. Exit with output *no(γ)*

The complexity of this test is $O(N)$. A GHC predicate embodying the above algorithm is denoted by *is_orthogonal($I1, I2, O$)* where $I1$ and $I2$ are input colors and O is an output.

---

[3]Precisely speaking, pure GHC described in, for example, [22] does not have a vector structure. However its practical implementations such as KL1 [9] provide it as the first class data object.

8.2 Translation into GHC

An ANDOR-II program is translated into a GHC program, which includes all codes realizing such operations as *flatten* and *compose*. However, they do not appear explicitly in a code and there is only rough correspondence between Definition 11 and a translated code.

8.2.1 Translation of an AND-predicate

Let us consider the translation of an AND-predicate p with an arity N. Assume that it has the mode declaration:

$$:- \text{ mode } p(\underbrace{+,\ldots,+}_{k},\underbrace{+,\ldots,+}_{l},\underbrace{-,\ldots,-}_{m}).$$

where $k + l + m = N$. Assume also that values of the first k arguments are referred to in at least one clause during head unification or guard computation, and that the next l arguments are directly passed to the body parts in all clauses.

The predicate p is translated into a new predicate p with an arity $N + 2$. Let $\{C_1,\ldots,C_n\}$ be the definition of p/N[4]. Then the definition of $p/(N+2)$ is $\{C_1',\ldots,C_n'\}\cup \{D_1,\ldots,D_{k+1}\}$. With this translation, $k + 1$ new predicates are also introduced. They are $for\_each\_p_i/(N+m+4)$ $(1 \leq i \leq k)$ and $try\_p/(N+2)$. Clauses in $\{C_1',\ldots,C_n'\}$ are basically modifications of corresponding clauses in $\{C_1,\ldots,C_n\}$. The function of *flatten* is realized by the other clauses $D_1,\ldots,D_k$ with the auxiliary predicates $for\_each\_p_i$ and try_p. These clauses handle the case in which a vector is received at an argument with a reference-only mode and is in danger of interfering with head unification. The clause D_{k+1} handles the case in which a goal fails to reduce itself. Figure 4 illustrates how the definition is translated.

Let C_i be

$$C_i = p(X_1,\ldots,X_N) :- G_1,\ldots,G_a \mid B_1,\ldots,B_b, E_1,\ldots,E_c.$$

where B_i $(1 \leq i \leq b)$ is a user defined atom $q_i(Y_1,\ldots,Y_{l_i})$ and E_j $(1 \leq j \leq c)$ is a unification atom. Then C_i' is defined to be

$$C_i' = \begin{cases} p(X_1,\ldots,X_N,Col,Ids) :- & \text{if } b \geq 2 \\ \quad G_1,\ldots,G_a \mid \\ \quad merge(\{Ids_1,\ldots,Ids_b\},Ids), \\ \quad q_1(Y_1,\ldots,Y_{l_1},Col,Ids_1),\ldots,q_b(Z_1,\ldots,Z_{l_b},Col,Ids_b), \\ \quad E_1,\ldots,E_c. \\ p(X_1,\ldots,X_N,Col,Ids) :- & \text{if } b = 1 \\ \quad G_1,\ldots,G_a \mid \\ \quad q_1(Y_1,\ldots,Y_{l_1},Col,Ids), E_1,\ldots,E_c. \\ p(X_1,\ldots,X_N,Col,Ids) :- & \text{if } b = 0 \\ \quad G_1,\ldots,G_a \mid Ids = [],E_1,\ldots,E_c. \end{cases}$$

---

[4] p/N denotes a predicate p with an arity N.

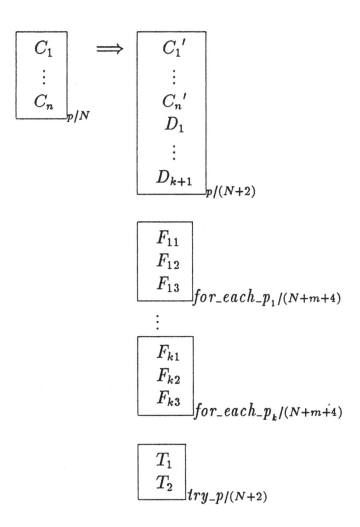

Figure 4: Translation of an AND-predicate

Col and Ids are variables to receive a color from a goal atom and a communication channel to the ID server, respectively. $merge(\{X_1, \ldots, X_n\}, X_0)$ is a merge operator which merges n input streams $X_1, \ldots, X_n$ given at the first argument as a vector to generate one output stream X_0.

D_i $(1 \le i \le k)$ is a clause which monitors the i-th argument and invokes $for\_each\_p_i$ when a vector is detected[5]. At the same time, variables at argument positions with a write mode are instantiated to new vectors of the same size with that vector. D_i is:

$$p(X_1, \ldots, X_N, Col, Ids) :-$$
$$\quad vector(X_i, L) \mid$$
$$\quad new\_vector(Y_1, L),$$
$$\quad \vdots$$
$$\quad new\_vector(Y_m, L),$$
$$\quad for\_each\_p_i(0, L, X_1, \ldots, X_{k+l}, Y_1, \ldots, Y_m, X_{k+l+1}, \ldots, X_N, Col, Ids).$$

In addition to these clauses[6], one more clause, D_{k+1}, is introduced to handle the failure case. D_{k+1} is:

$$p(X_1, \ldots, X_N, Col, Ids) :-$$
$$\quad otherwise \mid$$
$$\quad X_{k+l+1} = \$void\$, \ldots, X_N = \$void\$,$$
$$\quad Ids = [].$$

The meaning of $otherwise$ in the guard part is as follows: it succeeds if and only if all the other clauses defining the same predicate fail to solve their head unifications or guard parts.

The role of the predicate $for\_each\_p_i$ $(1 \le i \le k)$ is to apply the predicate p to each element of the vector received at the i-th argument. This is the point at which the translation and the formal definition of derivation differ. In Definition 11, we concentrated on a derivation of one flattened atom, while in the translation a set of atoms generated by one flattening are considered to be processed in parallel. It is defined by the following three clauses, F_{i1}, F_{i2}, F_{i3}.

$$for\_each\_p_i(J, L, X_1, \ldots, X_N, Z_1, \ldots, Z_m, Col, Ids) :-$$
$$\quad J >= L \mid$$
$$\quad Ids = [],$$

---

[5]In a language like KL1, a term is represented as a vector. Therefore there may be cases in which the goal that should commit to C_i' may commit to D_j and vice versa. There are several ways to inhibit such interference between C_i' and D_j. In this thesis, to make the translation scheme simple, we assume that there is no such interference.

[6]One problem of D_i is that it is insensitive to a vector embedded in a term. A vector deeply nested in a term may cause trouble in head unification. To fix the problem, it is needed to properly realize the bounded depth flatten. However, for simplicity, it is assumed that a vector may appear only in the top level in this section. An extension to full bounded depth flatten needs analysis of the head pattern and enrichment of guard tests, and it is straightforward.

$$Z_1 = X_{k+l+1}, \ldots, Z_m = X_N.$$

$for\_each\_p_i(J, L, X_1, \ldots, X_N, Z_1, \ldots, Z_m, Col, Ids)$:-
$\quad J < L, vector\_element(X_i, J, v(E, R)), E\backslash = \$void\$ \mid$
$\quad merge(\{Ids1, Ids2\}, Ids),$
$\quad is\_orthogonal(R, Col, Answer),$
$\quad set\_vector\_element(X_{k+l+1}, J, \_, Y_1, M_1),$
$\qquad \vdots$
$\quad set\_vector\_element(X_N, J, \_, Y_m, M_m),$
$\quad try\_p(Answer, X_1, \ldots, X_{i-1}, E, X_{i+1}, \ldots, X_{k+l}, Y_1, \ldots, Y_m, Ids1),$
$\quad J1 := J + 1,$
$\quad for\_each\_p_i(J1, L, X_1, \ldots, X_{k+l}, M_1, \ldots, M_m, Z_1, \ldots, Z_m, Col, Ids2).$

$for\_each\_p_i(J, L, X_1, \ldots, X_N, Z_1, \ldots, Z_m, Col, Ids)$:-
$\quad J < L, vector\_element(X_i, J, v(E, R)), E = \$void\$ \mid$
$\quad set\_vector\_element(X_{k+l+1}, J, \_, Y_1, M_1), Y_1 = v(\$void\$, \$void\$),$
$\qquad \vdots$
$\quad set\_vector\_element(X_N, J, \_, Y_m, M_m), Y_m = v(\$void\$, \$void\$),$
$\quad J1 := J + 1,$
$\quad for\_each\_p_i(J1, L, X_1, \ldots, X_{k+l}, M_1, \ldots, M_m, Z_1, \ldots, Z_m, Col, Ids).$

The first clause (F_{i1}) is for stopping the iteration. The second clause (F_{i2}) is a central clause, which picks up the J-th element from the vector, and checks the orthogonality of its color R with respect to Col, and recursively calls itself with J incremented by one. $is\_orthogonal$ uses the same algorithm described in Section 8.1 and computes their union if they are not orthogonal. The result of checking is sent to try_p, which will continue the processing of the J-th element. Note that in the guard it confirms that the J-th element is not $\$void\$$, which denotes useless datum. $\$void\$$ in a vector is skipped by the last clause (F_{i3}).

The role of try_p is to receive the result of the orthogonality test and continue processing. If the result is "orthogonal", the processing of the J-th element is ignored. Otherwise p is applied. try_p is defined by the two clauses, T_1, T_2.

$try\_p(yes, X_1, \ldots, X_N, Ids)$:-
$\quad true \mid$
$\quad X_{k+l+1} = v(\$void\$, \$void\$), \ldots, X_N = v(\$void\$, \$void\$), Ids = [].$
$try\_p(no(UnionColor), X_1, \ldots, X_N, Ids)$:-
$\quad true \mid$
$\quad X_{k+l+1} = v(Y_1, UnionColor), \ldots, X_N = v(Y_m, UnionColor),$
$\quad p(X_1, \ldots, X_{k+l}, Y_1, \ldots, Y_m, UnionColor, Ids).$

3.2.2 Translation of an OR-predicate

Let us consider the translation of an OR-predicate p with an arity N. Let $\{C_1, \ldots, C_n\}$ be the set of clauses defining p. Assume that it has the mode declaration:

$$\text{:- mode } p(\underbrace{+, \ldots, +}_{k}, \underbrace{-, \ldots, -}_{l}).$$

where $k + l = N$. Assume also that, in the i-th clause C_i, values of the σ_{i1}-th, $\ldots$, τ_{ie_i}-th arguments $(\{\sigma_{i1}, \ldots, \sigma_{ie_i}\} \subseteq \{1, \ldots, k\})$ are referred to during head unification and other arguments with a reference-only mode are directly passed to the body part.

The predicate p is translated into a new predicate $p/(N + 2)$, whose definition is $\{C_0'\}$. C_0' plays the role of activating n goal atoms, $p\_1, \ldots, p\_n$, in parallel, where p_i $(1 \leq i \leq n)$ is a predicate with an arity $N + 2$ and corresponds to execution of C_i. p_i is defined by $\{C_i', C_i''\} \cup \{D_{i1}, \ldots, D_{ie_i}\}$. Clauses in $\{C_i', C_i''\}$ $(1 \leq i \leq n)$ are basically modification of C_i. With this translation, for each p_i $(1 \leq i \leq n)$, new predicates $for\_each\_p\_i_j/(N+l+4)$ $(1 \leq j \leq e_i)$ and $try\_p\_i/(N+2)$ are defined. Using $for\_each\_p\_i_j$ $(\leq j \leq e_i)$ and try_p_i as the auxiliary predicates, clauses $D_{i1}, \ldots, D_{ie_i}$ realize flattening of vectors received by a goal atom p_i. Figure 5 illustrates how the definition is translated.

C_0' is defined as follows:

$$p(X_1, \ldots, X_N, Col, Ids) :-$$
$$\quad true \mid$$
$$\quad Ids = [get\_bp(Bp) | Idss],$$
$$\quad merge(\{Ids_1, \ldots, Ids_n\}, Idss),$$
$$\quad new\_vector(Y_{10}, n), \ldots, new\_vector(Y_{l0}, n),$$
$$\quad add\_color(Col, Bp, 1, Col_1), \ldots, add\_color(Col, Bp, n, Col_n),$$
$$\quad set\_vector\_element(Y_{10}, 0, \_, v(Z_{11}, Col_1), Y_{11}),$$
$$\quad set\_vector\_element(Y_{11}, 1, \_, v(Z_{12}, Col_2), Y_{12}),$$
$$\quad \vdots$$
$$\quad set\_vector\_element(Y_{1(n-1)}, n - 1, \_, v(Z_{1n}, Col_n), Y_{1n}),$$
$$\quad \vdots$$
$$\quad \vdots$$
$$\quad set\_vector\_element(Y_{l0}, 0, \_, v(Z_{l1}, Col_1), Y_{l1}),$$
$$\quad set\_vector\_element(Y_{l1}, 1, \_, v(Z_{l2}, Col_2), Y_{l2}),$$
$$\quad \vdots$$
$$\quad set\_vector\_element(Y_{l(n-1)}, n - 1, \_, v(Z_{ln}, Col_n), Y_{ln}),$$
$$\quad p\_1(X_1, \ldots, X_k, Z_{11}, \ldots, Z_{l1}, Col_1, Ids_1),$$
$$\quad \vdots$$
$$\quad p\_n(X_1, \ldots, X_k, Z_{1n}, \ldots, Z_{ln}, Col_n, Ids_n),$$
$$\quad X_{k+1} = Y_{1n}, \ldots, X_N = Y_{ln}.$$

200

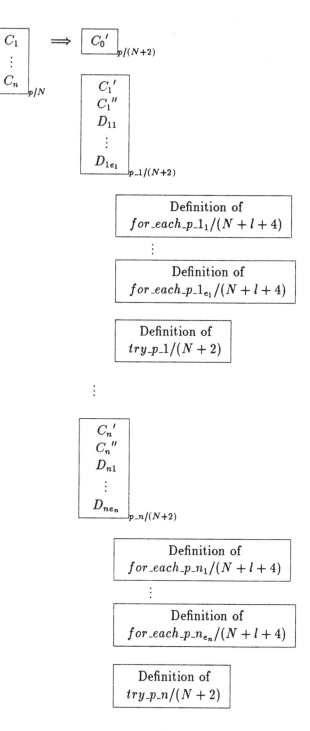

Figure 5: Translation of an OR-predicate

Note that C_0' does in advance what *compose* does. Namely C_0' instantiates variables at argument positions with a write mode to vectors whose sizes are equal to the number of clauses in the original definition. C_0' sends a message $get\_bp(Bp)$ requesting a new identifier of a new invocation of an OR-predicate to the ID server. The value of Bp is used to generate n new colors $Col_1, \ldots, Col_n$.

p_i is defined by C_i' and C_i''. Let C_i be

$$p(X_1, \ldots, X_N) :- q_1(Y_{11}, \ldots, Y_{1l_1}), \ldots, q_b(Y_{b1}, \ldots, Y_{bl_b}), E_1, \ldots, E_c.$$

where E_j $(1 \le j \le c)$ is a unification atom and $b \ge 2$. Then C_i' is defined to be

$$\begin{aligned}
&p\_i(X_1, \ldots, X_N, Col, Ids) :- \\
&\quad true \mid \\
&\quad merge(\{Ids_1, \ldots, Ids_b\}, Ids), \\
&\quad q_1(Y_{11}, \ldots, Y_{1l_1}, Col, Ids_1), \\
&\quad \vdots \\
&\quad q_b(Y_{b1}, \ldots, Y_{bl_b}, Col, Ids_b), \\
&\quad E_1, \ldots, E_c.
\end{aligned}$$

If $b = 1$ or $b = 0$ then C_i' is defined as follows:

$$\begin{aligned}
&p\_i(X_1, \ldots, X_N, Col, Ids) :- \\
&\quad true \mid q_1(Y_{11}, \ldots, Y_{1l_1}, Col, Ids), E_1, \ldots, E_c. \quad \text{when } b = 1 \\
&p\_i(X_1, \ldots, X_N, Col, Ids) :- \\
&\quad true \mid Ids = [\,], E_1, \ldots, E_c. \qquad\qquad\quad \text{when } b = 0
\end{aligned}$$

And C_i'' is defined to be

$$\begin{aligned}
&p\_i(X_1, \ldots, X_N, Col, Ids) :- \\
&\quad otherwise \mid \\
&\quad X_{k+1} = \$void\$, \ldots, X_N = \$void\$, \\
&\quad Ids = [\,].
\end{aligned}$$

C_i' creates a world having chosen the i-th clause C_i when head unification succeeds. Otherwise C_i'' instantiates all the write mode arguments to $\$void\$$.

The roles and definitions of $\{D_{i1}, \ldots, D_{ie_i}\}$, $for\_each\_p\_i_j$ $(1 \le j \le e_i)$ and try_p_i are similar to those of $\{D_1, \ldots, D_k\}$, $for\_each\_p_i$ and try_p which were presented in the description of the translation of an AND-predicate. Therefore we simply present their definitions below.

D_{ij} is:

$$\begin{aligned}
&p\_i(X_1, \ldots, X_N, Col, Ids) :- \\
&\quad vector(X_{\sigma_{ij}}, L) \mid \\
&\quad new\_vector(Y_1, L), \\
&\quad \vdots \\
&\quad new\_vector(Y_l, L), \\
&\quad for\_each\_p\_i_j(0, L, X_1, \ldots, X_k, Y_1, \ldots, Y_l, X_{k+1}, \ldots, X_N, Col, Ids).
\end{aligned}$$

The definition of $for\_each\_p\_i_j$ $(1 \leq j \leq e_i)$ is:

$for\_each\_p\_i_j(J, L, X_1, \ldots, X_N, Z_1, \ldots, Z_l, Col, Ids)$:-
    $J >= L \mid$
    $Ids = [],$
    $Z_1 = X_{k+1}, \ldots, Z_l = X_N.$
$for\_each\_p\_i_j(J, L, X_1, \ldots, X_N, Z_1, \ldots, Z_l, Col, Ids)$:-
    $J < L, vector\_element(X_{\sigma_{ij}}, J, v(E, R)), E\backslash = \$void\$ \mid$
    $merge(\{Ids1, Ids2\}, Ids),$
    $is\_orthogonal(R, Col, Answer),$
    $set\_vector\_element(X_{k+1}, J, \_, Y_1, M_1), \ldots, set\_vector\_element(X_N, J, \_, Y_l, M_l),$
    $try\_p\_i(Answer, X_1, \ldots, X_{\sigma_{ij}-1}, E, X_{\sigma_{ij}+1}, \ldots, X_k, Y_1, \ldots, Y_l, Ids1),$
    $J1 := J + 1,$
    $for\_each\_p\_i_j(J1, L, X_1, \ldots, X_k, M_1, \ldots, M_l, Z_1, \ldots, Z_l, Col, Ids2).$
$for\_each\_p\_i_j(J, L, X_1, \ldots, X_N, Z_1, \ldots, Z_l, Col, Ids)$:-
    $J < L, vector\_element(X_{\sigma_{ij}}, J, v(E, R)), E = \$void\$ \mid$
    $set\_vector\_element(X_{k+1}, J, \_, Y_1, M_1), Y_1 = v(\$void\$, \$void\$),$
    $\vdots$
    $set\_vector\_element(X_N, J, \_, Y_l, M_l), Y_l = v(\$void\$, \$void\$),$
    $J1 := J + 1,$
    $for\_each\_p\_i_j(J1, L, X_1, \ldots, X_k, M_1, \ldots, M_l, Z_1, \ldots, Z_l, Col, Ids).$

The definition of try_p_i is:

    $try\_p\_i(yes, X_1, \ldots, X_N, Ids)$:-
        $true \mid$
        $X_{k+1} = v(\$void\$, \$void\$), \ldots, X_N = v(\$void\$, \$void\$), Ids = [].$
    $try\_p\_i(no(UnionColor), X_1, \ldots, X_N, Ids)$:-
        $true \mid$
        $X_{k+1} = v(Y_1, UnionColor), \ldots, X_N = v(Y_l, UnionColor),$
        $p\_i(X_1, \ldots, X_k, Y_1, \ldots, Y_l, UnionColor, Ids).$

8.2.3   Sizes of translated programs

Now we estimate the size of a translated code. When a predicate p/N is an AND-predicate defined with n clauses, as Figure 4 indicates, the size S_{AND} of the translated code is

$$S_{AND} = (n + k + 1) + 3k + 2$$
$$= n + 4k + 3$$

Let R be the number of arguments with a reference-only mode.

$$S_{AND} \leq n + 4R + 3$$
$$\leq n + 4N + 3$$

On the other hand, when p is an OR-predicate, as Figure 5 indicates, the size S_{OR} of the translated code is,

$$S_{OR} = 1 + \sum_{i=1}^{n}(2 + e_i + 3e_i + 2)$$
$$= 1 + 4n + 4\sum_{i=1}^{n} e_i$$
$$\leq 4n(R + 1) + 1$$
$$\leq 4n(N + 1) + 1$$

For example, the translated code of *merge* has 14 clauses. If *merge* is translated as an OR-predicate the translated code has 33 clauses.

In both cases, the size is proportional to the original size n, and hence it is acceptable. It is also worth noting that another factor controlling the size of the translated code is the number of reference-only mode arguments.

9 Related Work and Future Research

9.1 Comparison with other work

AND-parallel computation and OR-parallel computation of logic programs have been investigated independently for many years. Experience for achievement of each parallelism has been accumulated by many researchers. Outcomes of such research are OR-parallel Prolog systems and parallel logic programming languages. OR-parallel Prolog systems exploit OR-parallelism with AND-sequential computation, while parallel logic programming languages exploit AND-parallelism with OR-sequential or shallow OR-parallel computation.

Recently mixing both parallelism has received much attention and design and implementation of a new language which has both features of AND-parallelism with *indeterminacy* and OR-parallelism (*nondeterminism*) are being studied intensively by many researchers as the ultimate combination of a logic programming language and a committed choice language.

It could be said that PARLOG [3] [6] was the earliest effort to combine committed choice computation and OR-parallel computation. PARLOG predicates are divided into single-solution predicates and all-solution predicates, which are close to AND-predicates and OR-predicates, respectively. However, unlike ANDOR-II, OR-parallel computation in an all-solution predicate is localized and is never propagated over a world. Instead, a set of all solutions is propagated over a world as a stream.

Clark and Gregory proposed the further combination of PARLOG and Prolog [2]. In this combination, although the two languages can comfortably call each other, a truly mixed combination of AND- and OR- parallel execution is not considered.

Yang proposed a language P-Prolog which subsumes both AND- and OR- parallelism and achieves a true mixture of both parallelism [28]. In this respect, P-Prolog is closely related to ANDOR-II. One of the main differences is synchronization mechanism. In P-Prolog, clauses are divided into single-neck and double-neck clauses and for single-neck clauses exclusiveness plays a central role in synchronization, while in ANDOR-II mechanism similar to that of GHC is adopted. Another main difference is implementation. We designed ANDOR-II so that it can be translated into a committed choice language, while P-Prolog seems to be designed together with a new implementation scheme.

Closely related to ANDOR-II, the Andorra model is noteworthy. Andorra is a new parallel computation model proposed by D. H. D. Warren. It is aimed at extracting both dependent AND-parallelism and OR-parallelism from Prolog programs based on the idea that dependent goal atoms can be reduced in parallel if they are reduced deterministically. In Andorra model, execution alternates two phases. In *and-parallel phase*, all deterministic goals are reduced in parallel. When no deterministic goals remain, execution enters into *a nondeterministic phase*. In the nondeterministic phase, the leftmost goal is selected and a world proliferates into several worlds along candidate clauses. Two key features of the Andorra model are: 1) Like P-Prolog, it adopts a determinacy check as a synchronization mechanism. 2) Unlike P-Prolog, it delays OR-forking until no determinacy goals remain.

Based on Andorra model, several languages are proposed. They include Andorra Prolog, Andorra-I and Pandora.

Haridi and Brand proposed the language Andorra Prolog based on Andorra model [7]. Andorra Prolog is aimed at a superset of both OR-parallel Prolog and a committed choice language. Andorra Prolog and ANDOR-II share many features. One of the main differences is that invocations of nondeterministic goals are lazy in Andorra Prolog, while eager in ANDOR-II. Also scheduling of a nondeterministic goal is infinitely unfair in Andorra Prolog, though this is for compatibility to Prolog. Implementation is also different. ANDOR-II adopts a translator approach, while they are designing a new machine for Andorra Prolog.

As Andorra Prolog's successor, Haridi and Janson proposed Kernel Andorra Prolog which has more generality in combination of nondeterministic languages and committed choice languages [8].

Yang implemented the Andorra model as Andorra-I [27]. Andorra-I is now running on a couple of commercial machines. It added a determinacy test code and priority control declaration to the model so that a user can write an efficient code using these impure primitives.

Bahgat and Gregory proposed Pandora, a combination of PARLOG and Andorra [1]. Pandora can be viewed as PARLOG extended with

1. deadlock procedures which are invoked when execution deadlocks and

2. nondeterministic fork.

In Pandora, predicates are divided into AND-parallel relations and deadlock relations. The former is defined by an ordinary PARLOG procedure while the latter is defined by both an ordinary PARLOG procedure and a deadlock procedure. Like Andorra Prolog,

Pandora computation is characterized by lazy nondeterministic computation. In its early implementation, Pandora adopted an eager copying scheme realized by PARLOG meta programming facility.

Among the language family CP proposed by Saraswat, CP[↓,|,&] is closely related to ANDOR-II [13] [14] [12]. The language was proposed as a general-purpose concurrent constraint language. The language has four control primitives. '&'-commit is so-called *don't know commit* and generates the search space in parallel, '|'-commit (*don't care commit*) prunes the search space, '↓', like read-only annotation, enables a process to wait till more information becomes available. The last primitive construct is a block.

Unlike ANDOR-II, on OR-forking invoked by '&', the language basically adopted eager copying scheme. However, to reduce the copying cost, the *block* construct [···] was introduced. A block demarcates the extent to which copying and propagation of bindings is done at &-commit time. The different OR-worlds in two conjunctive blocks are merged into one when there is no more work left to be done in any of the blocks. As far as implementation is concerned, the block construct provides a notion of independent AND-parallelism.

Naish proposed a parallel NU-Prolog which is an extension of NU-Prolog [10]. It can express and-parallelism together with nondeterminism. A nondeterministic code can call an and-parallel code which (in restricted way) can call a nondeterministic code. However, nondeterminism is only handled sequentially.

Program transformation from a nondeterministic program to a determinate program which collects all the solutions is also being intensively studied.

Ueda proposed continuation-based transformation from an exhaustive search program in Prolog into a determinate GHC/Prolog program [24]. OR-parallelism in the original program is realized by AND-parallelism in the transformed program, while the intrinsic AND-parallelism is not considered. He reports that transformed programs are more efficient for a class of programs, and that they do not lose much efficiency for others. In [25], Ueda proposed the extension of continuation-based transformation to a nondeterministic program with coroutine. It is realized by statically determining scheduling of coroutines by compile-time analysis of a source program. However, it is difficult to apply continuation-based scheme to nondeterministic processes communicating with each other since compile-time analysis of process scheduling is generally undecidable.

Tamaki [21] presented stream-based transformation from a logic program with AND- and OR- parallelism into one in a committed choice language. In his system, like our system, a set of solutions from a nondeterministic goal are propagated to other goals in a stream form. Owing to a stream communication, dynamic process scheduling becomes straightforward, and AND- and OR- parallelism in a source program can be naturally realized. In comparison with our language, his language has some restrictions. One is that elements of a stream are processed one by one by a conjunction of goals (called a *block*), that is, only one element can exist in a block at a time, while in our system a conjunction of goals can process any number of elements in parallel. The other is that his language does not allow communication among a conjunction of goals, while our language does allow it and such communication is essential to our applications.

Conversely, in his system these restrictions make an extra mechanism such as coloring unnecessary.

Okumura and Matsumoto proposed another approach called layered-stream programming [11]. It is a kind of programming paradigm in which recursively defined data structure called a layered-stream is used. All the values in the same layer represent alternative solutions to the same subproblem. The program written based on this paradigm provides a high degree of parallelism. However, if we remove associated colors from a nested vector in the translated code of an ANDOR-II program, a similar data structure would be obtained. We believe that our translation-based ANDOR-II is advantageous for the same class of problems, since layered stream programming is not declarative and it seems burdensome for a novice user to describe a problem using this paradigm.

When combining AND- and OR- parallelism, the most important design issues are 1) to exploit both parallelism without restricting either, and 2) to make the size of atomic operations needed for combination as small as possible. The coloring scheme, takes an approach characterized as "eager branching and lazy copying". Eager branching implies "branch whenever you can"; thus, it exploits full OR-parallelism. Lazy copying contributes to reduce the size of an atomic operation. In lazy copying scheme, computation of an atom can proceed without waiting for copying of the whole world being completed, while in eager copying scheme it must wait.

To sum up, our contribution is as follows:

1. We have designed ANDOR-II, a logic programming language with AND- and OR-parallelism, in other words, a parallel programming language with nondeterminism.

2. We have proposed the coloring scheme for an implementation scheme of AND-and OR- parallel computation.

3. We have presented a method to translate an ANDOR-II program into a committed choice language.

9.2 Future research

There are some remaining problems for future research.

The first problem we have to tackle is the comparative study of complexities of various AND- and OR- parallel execution models. We are especially interested in the comparison between ANDOR-II and Pandora, and between ANDOR-II and Kernel Andorra Prolog.

As for the implementation, we should consider the combination with continuation-based translation methods [24], though it was already realized in the system adopting the former translation scheme. Code size optimization is another problem to be solved, but it does not seem so difficult. Implementation on multiprocessor machines such as Multi-PSI and PIM [5] is one of the most interesting experiments to see. It is also interesting to find a new color representation scheme possibly with a hardware support in which orthogonality test of two colors is done in constant time.

Suppression of irrelevant computations is also an important problem to be solved to increase efficiency. If a process fails, then the conjunctive goals need not be computed any more. However, the current scheme completes all the computations.

As for the language-level, one interesting thing is to introduce a mechanism to share the results of computation among worlds. Logically, computations in different worlds are independent. But from the pragmatic point of view, knowledge discovered in one world could benefit other worlds. So it is desirable to program such cross information flow among worlds.

Acknowledgment

We would like to thank Koichi Furukawa and Ryuzou Hasegawa for their various support and encouragement. This research was done as part of the Fifth Generation Computer Project and supported by the Institute for New Generation Computer Technology.

References

[1] R. Bahgat and S. Gregory. Pandora: non-deterministic parallel logic programming. In G. Levi and M. Martelli, editors, *Logic Programming, Proceedings of the Sixth International Conference*, pages 471–486, The MIT Press, 1989.

[2] K. L. Clark and S. Gregory. PARLOG and PROLOG united. In J.-L. Lassez, editor, *Logic Programming, Proceedings of the Fourth International Conference*, pages 927–961, The MIT Press, 1987.

[3] K. L. Clark and S. Gregory. PARLOG: parallel programming in logic. *ACM Transaction on Programming Languages and Systems*, 8(1):1–49, 1986. Also appearing in [15] as Chapter 3.

[4] J. S. Conery and D. F. Kibler. AND parallelism and nondeterminism in logic programs. *New Generation Computing*, 3(1):43–70, 1985.

[5] A. Goto, M. Sato, K. Nakajima, K. Taki, and A. Matsumoto. Overview of the parallel inference machine architecture (PIM). In Institute for New Generation Computer Technology, editor, *Proceedings of the International Conference on Fifth Generation Computer Systems 1988*, pages 208–229, Institute for New Generation Computer Technology, OHMSHA, LTD., 1988.

[6] S. Gregory. *Parallel Logic Programming in PARLOG*. Addison-Wesley, 1987.

[7] S. Haridi and P. Brand. Andorra Prolog, an integration of Prolog and committed choice languages. In Institute for New Generation Computer Technology, editor, *Proceedings of the International Conference on Fifth Generation Computer Systems 1988*, pages 745–754, Institute for New Generation Computer Technology, OHMSHA, LTD., 1988.

[8] S. Haridi and S. Janson. *Kernel Andorra Prolog and its Computation Model.* Research Report, Swedish Institute of Computer Science, 1989.

[9] ICOT PIMOS Development Group. *PIMOS manual.* Institute for New Generation Computer Technology, 1.5 edition, December 1989. (In Japanese).

[10] L. Naish. Parallelizing NU–Prolog. In R. A. Kowalski and K. A. Bowen, editors, *Logic Programming, Proceedings of the Fifth International Conference and Symposium*, pages 1546–1564, The MIT Press, 1988.

[11] A. Okumura and Y. Matsumoto. Parallel programming with layered streams. In *Proceedings of 1987 Symposium on Logic Programming*, pages 224–232, The Computer Society of IEEE, IEEE Computer Society Press, 1987.

[12] V. A. Saraswat. *Concurrent Constraint Programming Languages.* PhD thesis, Carnegie-Mellon University, 1989.

[13] V. A. Saraswat. The concurrent logic programming language CP: definition and operational semantics. In *Proceedings of the Symposium on Principles of Programming Languages*, pages 49–62, ACM, 1987.

[14] V. A. Saraswat. CP as a general-purpose constraint language. In *Proceedings of the AAAI Conference*, AAAI, 1987.

[15] E. Shapiro, editor. *Concurrent Prolog, Collected Papers.* The MIT Press, 1987.

[16] E. Shapiro. *A Subset of Concurrent Prolog and Its Interpreter.* Tech. Report TR-003, Institute for New Generation Computer Technology, 1983. Revised version appearing in [15] as Chapter 2.

[17] K. Takahashi, A. Takeuchi, and T. Yasui. *A Parallel Problem Solving Language ANDOR-II and its Implementation.* Tech. Report TR-558, Institute for New Generation Computer Technology, 1990.

[18] A. Takeuchi. On an extension of stream-based AND-parallel logic programming languages. In *Proceedings of The 1st National Conference of Japan Society for Software Science and Technology*, pages 291–294, Japan Society for Software Science and Technology, 1984. (In Japanese).

[19] A. Takeuchi, K. Takahashi, and H. Shimizu. *A Description Language with AND/OR Parallelism for Concurrent Systems and Its Stream-Based Realization.* Tech. Report TR-229, Institute for New Generation Computer Technology, 1987.

[20] A. Takeuchi, K. Takahashi, and H. Shimizu. A parallel problem solving language for concurrent systems. In M. Tokoro, Y. Anzai, and A. Yonezawa, editors, *Concepts and Characteristics of Knowledge-based Systems*, pages 267–296, North Holland, 1989. Also appearing as ICOT Tech. Report TR-418, 1988.

[21] H. Tamaki. Stream-based compilation of ground I/O Prolog into committed-choice languages. In J.-L. Lassez, editor, *Logic Programming, Proceedings of the Fourth International Conference*, pages 376–393, The MIT Press, 1987.

[22] K. Ueda. *Guarded Horn Clauses*. PhD thesis, The University of Tokyo, 1986.

[23] K. Ueda. *Guarded Horn Clauses: A Parallel Logic Programming Language with the Concept of a Guard*. Tech. Report TR-208, Institute for New Generation Computer Technology, 1986.

[24] K. Ueda. Making exhaustive search programs deterministic. *New Generation Computing*, 5(1):29–44, 1987.

[25] K. Ueda. Making exhaustive search programs deterministic, part II. In J.-L. Lassez, editor, *Logic Programming, Proceedings of the Fourth International Conference*, pages 356–375, The MIT Press, 1987.

[26] E. Wada, editor. *LNCS-221, Logic Programming*. Springer-Verlag, 1986.

[27] R. Yang. Solving simple substitution ciphers in Andorra-I. In G. Levi and M. Martelli, editors, *Logic Programming, Proceedings of the Sixth International Conference*, pages 113–128, The MIT Press, 1989.

[28] R. Yang and H. Aiso. P-Prolog: a parallel logic language based on exclusive relation. In E. Shapiro, editor, *LNCS-225, Third International Conference on Logic Programming*, pages 255–269, Springer-Verlag, 1986.

Premature Return
- Another Interpretation of the Future Construct -
(An Extended Abstract)

Taiichi Yuasa
Department of Information and Computer Science
Toyohashi University of Technology
Toyohashi 440, Japan

Abstract

Several parallel Lisp languages such as MultiLisp[1], MultiScheme[2], and TOP-1 Common Lisp[3] use the *future* construct as the primitive parallel construct. Evaluation of a future expression requires spawning a subprocess. For relatively fine-grained parallel applications, the time for process creation affects the overall performance of the program. In this paper, we propose another interpretation of the future construct, called the *premature-return*, which is useful to reduce the overhead of process creation. With this interpretation, the caller process of a future expression keeps evaluating the expression while another process will be created to execute the program that follows the future expression. Although the premature-return is more efficient than the conventional interpretation in many cases, it is sometimes less efficient. In order to avoid such inefficient situations, we propose the use of an additional construct together with the premature-return.

1   The future construct

The future construct[1] has the following format.

(future E)

where E is an arbitrary form (a Lisp expression). When evaluated, this form immediately returns with an object called *future*, and creates a subprocess that will take care of the task of evaluating E (see Figure 1, where the down arrows indicate the control flow, and the right arrow indicates the process creation). When the value of E is obtained, that value replaces the future object and the execution of the subprocess terminates. In other words, the future is *instantiated* with the value. (The left arrow in Figure 1 indicates the instantiation.) On the other hand, the caller process of the future form keeps going without waiting for the value of E until it needs (or *touches*) the value of E. When the process needs the value of E, if the future is not instantiated yet, then the process will be suspended until the subprocess finishes evaluating E. (The dotted line in Figure 1 indicates the process suspension.) Thus the future construct allows concurrency between the "producer" of a value and the "consumer".

2   The premature-return interpretation

We now introduce our interpretation of the future construct called the *premature-return*. In this interpretation, the subform E in the form (future E) is evaluated by the process which calls

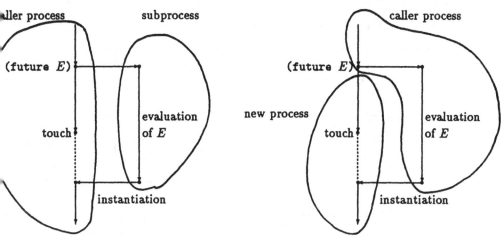

Figure 1: The future construct Figure 2: The premature-return

the future form, and a new process is created to execute the rest of the main task that follows the future form (see Figure 2).

Process creation is a heavy task. In particular, for fine-grained applications, the time for process creation affects the overall performance of the program. In Figure 1 and Figure 2, we ignored the effect of process creation. If we take the overhead of process creation into consideration, we obtain Figure 3(a) from Figure 1 and Figure 3(b) from Figure 2. Here, we assume that a process creation takes a constant time P, in order to simplify the discussion.

In the conventional interpretation of the future construct (Figure 3(a)), the evaluation of E starts at time P after the call of future. Supposing that the evaluation of E takes time t_2, the future object will be instantiated at time $P + t_2$ after the call of future. On the other hand, in the case of the premature-return (Figure 3(b)), the evaluation of E starts immediately after the call of future and thus the future object will be instantiated at time t_2. That is, the instantiation occurs earlier in the case of the premature-return.

Now, suppose in Figure 3(a) that the caller process touches the future object at time t_1. In the case of the premature-return, the execution following the call to future will start at time P, and the future object will be touched at time $P + t_1$. This means that, if $t_1 < t_2$, then the waiting process will resume earlier in the case of the premature-return. The gain is P in this situation. Note that this situation always happens when the main task is suspended for future instantiation.

On the other hand, if the main task is never suspended for future instantiation, i.e., if the subtask finishes its computation before the main task needs the future value, then the main task proceeds faster in the conventional interpretation than in the premature-return. In this case, the loss by the premature-return is P. Therefore, in these simple cases, we cannot say that the premature-return is more efficient than the conventional interpretation.

Let us consider more general cases where several processes are created to perform the computation. Figure 4 illustrates the situation where the main task creates a subtask and the subtask further creates another subtask, assuming that both the main task and the first subtask are suspended for future instantiation. This figure indicates that the gain of using the premature-return is $2P$. In general, if subtasks are nested n levels and if all tasks except the last are suspended for future instantiation, the gain of using the premature-return will be nP. On the other hand, if no tasks are suspended for future instantiation, the loss will be P independently of the nested levels.

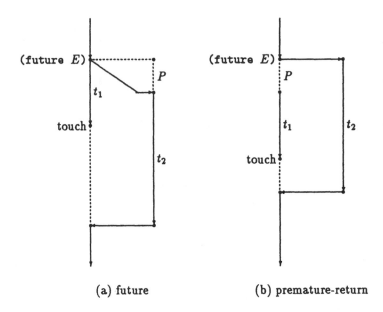

(a) future   (b) premature-return

Figure 3: The effect of process creation overhead

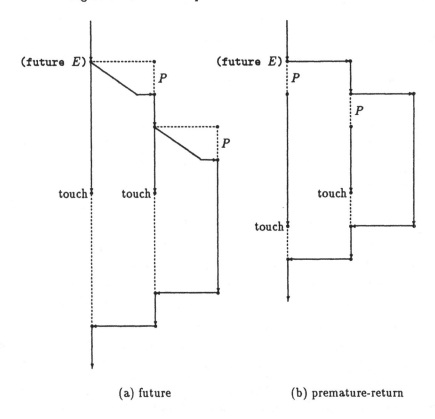

(a) future   (b) premature-return

Figure 4: Nested subtask creation

3 Use of the pcall construct

So far, we have seen that the premature-return is useful when several subtasks are nested. On the other hand, if the main task creates several subtasks, the premature-return may possibly be very inefficient. Consider, for example, the following expression.

(cons (future E_1) (future E_2))

In the conventional interpretation, the second subprocess for E_2 will be created soon after the creation of the first subprocess for E_1 (see Figure 5(a)). In the premature-return, the second subprocess will be created after the main task is resumed, approximately at time P after the call to the first future (see Figure 5(b)). In general, for the expression

(f (future E_1) $\cdots$ (future E_n))

all subprocesses will be created approximately at time P in the conventional interpretation, while the i-th subprocess will be created approximately at time iP in the premature-return. Thus the premature-return is quite inefficient in such situations.

In order to avoid such inefficient situations, we propose the use of the *pcall* construct, which is found in some parallel Lisp languages. Although there are variations of the pcall construct (see [4]), we use the following definition. The pcall construct has the following format.

(pcall f $E_1 \cdots E_n$)

where f is an arbitrary function (precisely speaking, a form whose value is a function object) and each E_i is an arbitrary form which provides the i-th argument to f. When this pcall form is evaluated, it creates one future object for each E_i and calls the function f with these futures as the arguments. When f returns, the pcall form returns immediately with the value of f. At the same time, the pcall form starts evaluating $E_1 \cdots E_n$ to obtain values to instantiate the corresponding futures. Thus the pcall expression is semantically equivalent to

(f (future E_1) $\cdots$ (future E_n))

For example, the above call to cons can be expressed as

(pcall cons E_1 E_2)

The pcall construct can be used to avoid the inefficient situations for the premature-return in the following way. Since the main task knows that several futures will be created for a pcall form, it can proceed to the evaluation of the last subexpression E_n, without waiting for the creation of the processes for the other subexpressions. Thus the evaluation of E_n begins soon after the call of the pcall, whereas the evaluation of each subexpression other than E_n will begin at time P approximately (see Figure 5(c)).

4 Conclusions

We introduced a new interpretation of the future construct and showed that this interpretation is more efficient than the conventional interpretation in many cases. The gain of using the premature-return interpretation depends on the time required to create processes relative to

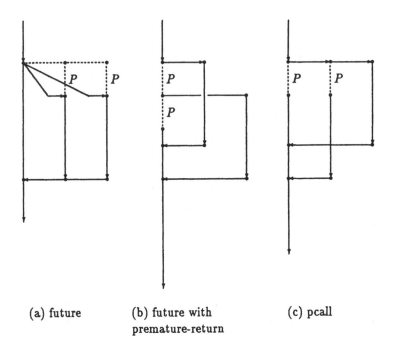

(a) future   (b) future with   (c) pcall
premature-return

Figure 5: Multiple subtask creation by the main task

the granularity of the application. For coerce-grained parallel applications, the time for process creation is negligible and thus the gain will be small. For fine-grained applications, however, the time for process creation affects the performance of the whole program to a great extent, and thus we will obtain a larger gain by using the premature-return.

As explained already, the premature-return is sometimes less efficient than the conventional interpretation. Thus it seems reasonable for the language processor to choose the "appropriate" interpretation, depending on the application or each call to future. However, we are not sure whether such a choice can be done automatically. That will be our future research topic. (It was communicated by Takayasu Ito that some attempts have been made by Gray[5] on this topic.)

References

[1] Halstead, R.: Parallel Computing Using Multilisp. in J. Kowalik, ed., Parallel Computation and Computers for Artificial Intelligence, Kluwer Academic Publishers, 1987.

[2] Miller, J.: MultiScheme: A Parallel Processing System Based on MIT Scheme. TR-402, Laboratory for Computer Science, MIT, 1987.

[3] Tanaka, T. and Uzuhara, S.: Multiprocessor Common Lisp on TOP-1. Proceedings of The Second IEEE Symposium on Parallel and Distributed Processing, Dallas, 1990.

[4] Ito, T. and Matsui, M.: A Parallel Lisp Language PaiLisp and its Kernel Specification. in T. Ito and R. H. Halstead, ed., Parallel Lisp: Languages and Systems, Springer Lecture Notes in Computer Science 441, 1989.

[5] Gray, S.: Using Futures to Exploit Parallelism in Lisp. S.M. thesis, MIT EECS Dept., 1986.

PART III

Parallel Architectures

and

VLSI Logic

Semantic Specifications for the Rewrite Rule Machine

Joseph A. Goguen
Programming Research Group, Oxford University
SRI International, Menlo Park CA 94025

Abstract: This paper presents three semantic specifications for the Rewrite Rule Machine. This machine consists of a large number of parallel rewrite processors operating independently, each implemented as a VLSI chip. The first specification, called **parallel rewriting**, provides an abstract operational semantics for the rewrite processor. The second specification, called the **cell machine** model, provides a more concrete operational semantics for this processor, using algebraic semantics (in OBJ) and set theory. The third specification, called **concurrent rewriting**, gives an abstract semantics for the Rewrite Rule Machine as a whole.

1 Introduction

The goal of the Rewrite Rule Machine (RRM) project is

> to design, build and test a prototype multi-grain, massively parallel computer architecture especially suited for executing non-homogeneous programs written in declarative ultra high level languages.

The RRM architecture is a **multi-grain hierarchy**, with several different levels of organization, each having a different structure. These levels may be described as follows:

1. A **cell** stores one item of data and pointers to two other cells.

2. A **tile** provides shared communication resources for a small number of cells.

3. An **ensemble** consists of many tiles executing instructions broadcast from a common central controller.

4. A **cluster** interconnects many ensembles to cooperate in a larger computation.

5. A **network** interconnects several clusters to give a complete RRM.

This paper concentrates on the third level, the ensemble. A single ensemble consists of a controller which broadcasts microcode instructions to its array of cells; hence it executes in SIMD (Single Instruction Multiple Data) mode. A complete RRM consists of many such ensembles, each executing its own independent instruction stream; hence it operates in MIMD (Multiple Instruction Multiple Data) mode[1]. In this paper, the Rewrite Rule Machine is presented as an *abstract architecture* that is not committed to any particular number or structure for the units at each of these levels, and that deliberately fails to model many lower level details. However, a concrete prototype RRM, which of course does make particular choices for these parameters is being constructed at SRI international, as described in [26, 14] and [2].

---

[1]Actually, the terms MIMD and SIMD are somewhat misleading when applied to the RRM, because of its multi-grain architecture, and also because of its autonomous processes.

The RRM project began in 1985, and its first paper is [11]. An early description of RRM architecture is given in [33], and some early simulation results are reported in [25]. Intermediate stages of the project are documented in [18, 26] and [14], and its current state is described in [1] and [2]. The present paper was drafted in early 1988 to help initiate ensemble design by giving a precise semantics for some basic features, and was put in its present form in 1990. Its style is informal, but its content can (I hope) be made completely precise.

1.1 Models of Computation

A model of computation defines the major interface between the hardware and the software aspects of a computing system. This interface determines both what the hardware must provide, and what the software can rely upon. It therefore plays a basic role in the design of any computing system, even if it is not made explicit. Most current machines are based upon the classical von Neumann model of computation, which is inherently sequential, and is characterized by enormously long streams of fetch/compute/write cycles. We regard a clear statement of desired semantics as essential for design; indeed, the RRM is a *"Semantics First"* machine.

It is important to distinguish the levels of architectural organization that were described above from models of computation. Both may be hierarchically organized, but models of computation should be stratefied by level of abstraction rather than by the aggregation of parts into wholes. In fact, we could develop semantic models for any of the architectural levels, and these models could range from the very abstract to the very concrete. This paper considers the following semantic models:

1. In **concurrent rewriting**, many different rules can be applied simultaneously at many different sites; this is an abstract MIMD operational semantics.

2. In **parallel rewriting**, many instances of the *same* rewrite rule are applied simultaneously at many different sites; this is an abstract SIMD operational semantics.

3. A **cell machine** is an abstract array of cells; it can be used to implement either parallel or concurrent rewriting.

The second and third models are for the third hierarchical level of the RRM, that of ensembles, whereas the first provides a semantics for the RRM as a whole. The first two models are more abstract than the third. More concrete levels would take account of resource limitations, such as the unavailability of cells and communication paths. The present paper does not address these issues. The first two models are especially suitable for the semantics of functional and logic programming languages, because they do not directly model storage; however, the third model does model storage, and is suitable for object oriented languages, as well as for functional and logic programming languages.

1.2 Languages

The languages that we are developing for the RRM include the object-oriented, functional, and logic programming paradigms; they also support parameterized programming, graphical programming, sophisticated error handling, and flexible type systems. The declarative character of these languages makes their programs easier to read, write, debug, verify, modify, and maintain. All of these languages are extensions of OBJ [9, 6, 4, 5], a first order functional language based on (order sorted) equational logic. Eqlog [15, 16] is a logic programming extension of OBJ which also supports so-called constraint based programming. A major discovery of the RRM project is a way to view object oriented programming as a declarative paradigm. This insight is embodied in the language FOOPS [17], which is an object-oriented extension of OBJ, and in FOOPlog [17], which combines all three paradigms. The suitability of OBJ for the RRM is discussed in [13], while a graphical programming interface for FOOPS is described in [7]. See [22] for more on FOOPS and on types.

Rewrite rules provide a link between the abstract mathematical semantics of our languages and the operational semantics of the RRM. For example, the most abstract mathematical semantics of OBJ is initial algebra semantics for order sorted equational logic, but equations in OBJ programs are interpreted operationally as left-to-right rewrite rules [4, 21, 5]. Rewrite rules are the highest level of modelling considered in this paper.

Term rewriting, whether parallel or concurrent, is ideal for implementing functional languages, and can also be used to implement relational languages. But it is not very well suited to the object oriented paradigm. However, the RRM actually implements *graph rewriting*, not just term rewriting, and this provides an excellent way to implement objects and methods. Moreover, extended term rewriting and other techniques greatly extend the expressive capability of even term rewriting. See [18] for further discussion of these issues.

1.3 Architecture

The RRM implements *true concurrent* rewriting, in which many different instances of many different rules can be rewritten asynchronously at many different sites. However, the cell machine model described in this paper implements *parallel* rewriting, in which one rewrite rule at a time is simultaneously applied at many different sites. Compilers can first convert programs into sets of rewrite rules, and then into microcode instruction streams for RRM ensemble execution.

The intended applications of the RRM include symbolic processing, such as: simulation of hardware and other complex systems; software development environments, including specification, rapid prototyping, development, debugging, verification, and testing; and Artificial Intelligence applications, such as natural language processing, planning, expert systems, and reasoning. The RRM can also efficiently implement (arbitrary precision) arithmetic [32], and thus is very suitable for mixed symbolic/numeric computation.

The RRM is a **multi-grain** machine: fine-grain SIMD at the ensemble level, but large-grain MIMD at higher levels of organization. This allows it to take advantage of the fact that many important computations are *locally homogeneous* but not *globally homogeneous*; that is, the data items to which the same operations can be applied tend to occur in local clusters, each of which requires different operations. Neither pure SIMD nor pure MIMD machines can take advantage of this characteristic property of large and complex computations. Another significant architectural property of the RRM is that it does not separate processors from memory, and thus is not subject to the so-called "von Neumann bottleneck," whereby data items must be fetched and stored sequentially over a low bandwidth channel; in fact, an RRM ensemble processes data where it is stored, possibly rearranging storage by a dynamic autonomous process, to ensure that data items that are logically related are also physically contiguous.

The RRM ensemble is an associative processor, but not in the old fashioned sense which required either enormous bandwidth or else was very slow; rather, it is a SIMD machine, whose content addressing is largely internal. The cells in an ensemble only connect to their nearest neighbors[2]. Some cells serve as buffers to the outside world, and there is also a one bit feedback line to the controller, which returns the disjunction across all cells of a special one bit status register. The models in this paper deliberately omit such details, and also avoid commitment to any particular ALU design for cells, except to assume an equality test for tokens. See [14, 2] for architectural details of the SRI prototype.

Our performance estimate[3] for a single ensemble chip is 150 MIPS, based on today's off-the-shelf technology, at a modest 20 MHz, for a 12-by-12 grid of tiles with 8 cells each [26]. Of course, this figure will scale up with improvements in technology, and performance in the penta-op range is expected when a prototype RRM is completed.

In comparison with fine-grain dataflow machines, the RRM avoids the overhead and latency involved in moving many small packets over large distances. In fact, data tends to stay in one place in the RRM. Shared memory machines try to avoid the von Neumann bottleneck with elaborate cache hierarchies and clever caching strategies, but are limited in the number of processors that they can effectively support, and can also be very difficult to program, because they require explicit programming for each processor. Massively parallel SIMD machines are only maximally effective for homogeneous applications that have massive data parallelism; their resources are largely wasted for complex non-homogeneous problems, such as circuit simulations, expert systems, and natural language processing. The RRM combines the advantages of these two classes of machine, because of its multi-grain architecture.

There are some other architecture that resemble the RRM, although they are not yet very well known. These include the ASP machine of Lea [24], and the IUA [31] from Hughes Research Labs, which has a processor called CAAP [30] that plays a role similar to that of the ensemble in the RRM. Both of these machines, like the RRM, have a hierarchical MIMD/SIMD structure, using custom VLSI associative processors. However, these machines were designed for homogeneous applications, particularly signal processing, and cannot be expected to achieve optimum performance for non-homogeneous applications. Also, both machines are programmed with fairly conventional low level languages, and hence can be expected to have difficulties with software reliability, portability and maintenance.

1.4 Summary

Sections 2.1 and 2.2 briefly review the algebra that we need, and then Section 2.3 presents new simplified definitions of parallel and concurrent rewriting. Section 3 gives the cell machine model, including its structure and its instruction set, using OBJ and set theory. Section 4 describes *extended* rewriting, in which variables may match open terms, rather than just ground terms, as in *standard* rewriting. Section 5 describes some topics for future work, including robustness under failures due to resource limitations.

Acknowledgements

I owe an enormous debt to my collegues who have done so much to realize the dreams expressed by the models given in this paper. These include Dr Jose Meseguer, who is now leading the project at SRI, and who has done exciting recent work on the semantics

---

[2]The prototype ensemble being constructed at SRI actually has the topology of a torus; however, many different structures could have been chosen to realize the abstract ideas in this paper.

[3]This is *not* the usual misleading raw peak power estimate, but rather a conservative estimate for realistic problems, about 100 times less than peak power.

of concurrency and on RRM compiler correctness; Dr Sany Leinwand, who is doing the actual VLSI layout, as well as much work on design and simulation; Mr Timothy Winkler, who also has done much work on simulation, as well as on algorithms, compilation and design; Dr Hitashi Aida, who wrote an RRM compiler for (a subset of) OBJ, and who also contributed greatly to the simulators; Mr Patrick Lincoln, who contributed significantly to compiler technology and ensemble design; and Prof Ugo Montanari, for his work on compiler technology and some useful discussions of concurrency. Finally, I wish to thank Healfdene Goguen and Peter Sewell for their careful readings of a draft of this paper, which uncovered several bugs.

2 Parallel and Concurrent Rewriting

For expository simplicity, this section only develops unsorted rewriting; however, order sorted rewriting is needed to fully capture our declarative languages for the RRM. The first two subsections review some basic concepts from algebra. More detail on this material (or its generalizations to many sorted and order sorted algebra) can be found, for example, in [3, 28, 10, 23] and [19].

2.1 Signatures and Terms

Let ω denote the set $\{0, 1, 2, ...\}$ of all natural numbers.

Definition 1 A **signature** is a family Σ_n of sets, for $n \in \omega$. An element $f \in \Sigma_n$ is called a **function symbol** of arity n, and in particular, an element of Σ_0 is called a **constant symbol**.

Given two signatures, Σ and Φ, we say that $\Sigma \subseteq \Phi$ iff $\Sigma_n \subseteq \Phi_n$ for each $n \in \omega$, and we define their **union** by

$$(\Sigma \cup \Phi)_n = \Sigma_n \cup \Phi_n.$$

Given a set X and a disjoint signature Σ, we define the signature $\Sigma(X)$ by

$$\Sigma(X)_0 = \Sigma_0 \cup X, \text{ and}$$
$$\Sigma(X)_n = \Sigma_n \text{ for } n > 0.$$

This notation views X as a ground signature of variable symbols. □

Definition 2 The set T_Σ of all (**ground**) Σ-**terms** is the smallest set of *strings* over the alphabet $\Sigma \cup \{(,)\}$ (where $($ and $)$ are special symbols disjoint from Σ) such that

- $\Sigma_0 \subseteq T_\Sigma$ and

- given $t_1, ..., t_n \in T_\Sigma$ and $\sigma \in \Sigma$, then $\sigma \underline{(} t_1 ... t_n \underline{)} \in T_\Sigma$.

The underlined parantheses are a pedagogical device that is only used occasionally to improve clarity. □

Terms that have variables, e.g., $t \in T_{\Sigma(X)}$, will be called **open terms**.

2.2 Algebras, Initiality and Substitution

We first show that the Σ-terms form a Σ-algebra, and then state a simple property that characterizes this algebra.

A Σ-algebra is a set A with a function $A_\sigma: A^n \to A$ for each $\sigma \in \Sigma_n$; note that if $\sigma \in \Sigma_0$, then A_σ is essentially an element of A, since A^0 is a one point set. Given Σ-algebras A and B, a Σ-**homomorphism** $h: A \to B$ is a function h such that

$$h(A_\sigma(a_1, ..., a_n)) = B_\sigma(h(a_1), ..., h(a_n)),$$

for all $a_1, ..., a_n \in A$. We may view T_Σ as a Σ-algebra as follows:

- For $\sigma \in \Sigma_0$, let $(T_\Sigma)_\sigma$ be the string σ.

- For $\sigma \in \Sigma_n$ with $n > 0$, let $(T_\Sigma)_\sigma$ be the function that sends $t_1, ..., t_n \in T_\Sigma$ to the string $\sigma(t_1 \ldots t_n)$.

Thus, $\sigma(t_1, ..., t_n) = \sigma(t_1 \ldots t_n)$, and from here on we prefer to use the first notation. The key property of T_Σ is its *initiality*:

Theorem 3 For any Σ-algebra A, there is a unique Σ-homomorphism $T_\Sigma \to A$. $\square$

Definition 4 Given a set X of variable symbols and a Σ-algebra A, an **interpretation** of X in A is a function $a: X \to A$. Notice that any such function a determines a unique $\Sigma(X)$-homomorphism $\overline{a}: T_{\Sigma(X)} \to A$ by Theorem 3 for $\Sigma(X)$-algebras, i.e., a unique Σ-homomorphism that extends a. When $A = T_{\Sigma(Y)}$ such an a is called a **substitution**, and if $X = \{x_1, ..., x_n\}$, then the notation

$$t[x_1 \leftarrow t_1, \ldots, x_n \leftarrow t_n]$$

is used for $\overline{a}(t)$ when $a(x_i) = t_i$ for $i = 1, ..., n$; this is called the **result of substituting** t_i for x_i in t. $\square$

Notice that the order in which the variables x_i are substituted for does not matter, as long as they are distinct.

2.3 Rewriting

Definition 5 Given a signature Σ, a Σ-**rewrite rule** is a triple $\langle X, l, r \rangle$ where X is a set of **matching variables** disjoint from Σ, and l and r are $\Sigma(X)$-terms. We write such rules in the form

$$(\forall X) \, l \to r$$

and more concretely in forms like

$$(\forall x, y) \, l \to r$$

when (for example) $X = \{x, y\}$. $\square$

The following definition captures the semantics of rewriting multiple instances of a single rule in parallel. In the formula for t_1 below, $y_1, ..., y_n$ mark n sites where the rule $(\forall X) \, l \to r$ applies, and the corresponding formula for t_2 gives the result of applying this rule at all n sites in parallel.

Definition 6 A **parallel rewrite** using the Σ-rule $(\forall X) \, l \to r$ is a pair $\langle t_1, t_2 \rangle$ of ground Σ-terms, where

$$t_1 = t_0[y_1 \leftarrow \overline{a_1}(l)] \ldots [y_n \leftarrow \overline{a_n}(l)]$$

for some $n > 0$, where $t_0 \in T_{\Sigma(X \cup Y)}$ with $Y = \{y_1, ..., y_n\}$ disjoint from $\Sigma(X)$, where $a_i: X \to T_{\Sigma(X \cup Y)}$ for $i = 1, ..., n$, where each term $t_0[y_1 \leftarrow \overline{a_1}(l)] \ldots [y_k \leftarrow \overline{a_k}(l)]$ for $k = 1, ..., n$ has at most one occurrence of each y_i, and where

$$t_2 = t_0[y_1 \leftarrow \overline{a_1}(r)] \ldots [y_n \leftarrow \overline{a_n}(r)].$$

In this case, we may write $t_1 \overset{P}{\to} t_2$. Ordinary, i.e., sequential, rewriting is the special case where $n = 1$. $\square$

It is easy to generalize Definition 6 to any number of rules applied at any number of sites; parallel rewriting is then the special case where just one rule is involved. Let us assume that we are given a finite set R of Σ-rewrite rules, say $(\forall X)\ l_i \to r_i$ for $i = 1, ..., N$, where we may assume without loss of generality that all rules are quantified over the same set of variables, say X.

Definition 7 A **concurrent rewrite** using a rule set R as above is a pair $\langle t_1, t_2 \rangle$ of ground Σ-terms, where
$$t_1 = t_0[y_1 \leftarrow \overline{a_1}(l_{j_1})] \ldots [y_n \leftarrow \overline{a_n}(l_{j_n})]$$
for some $n > 0$, with $t_0 \in T_{\Sigma(X \cup Y)}$ where $Y = \{y_1, ..., y_n\}$ is disjoint from $\Sigma(X)$, where $a_i : X \to T_{\Sigma(X \cup Y)}$ for $i = 1, ..., n$, where each term $t_0[y_1 \leftarrow \overline{a_1}(l_{j_1})] \ldots [y_k \leftarrow \overline{a_k}(l_{j_k})]$ for $k = 1, ..., n$ has at most one occurrence of each y_i, where $1 \leq j_i \leq N$ for $i = 1, ..., n$, and where
$$t_2 = t_0[y_1 \leftarrow \overline{a_1}(r_{j_1})] \ldots [y_n \leftarrow \overline{a_n}(r_{j_n})].$$
In this case, we may write $t_1 \xrightarrow{C} t_2$. $\square$

A more complex explication of these two concepts appears in the appendix of [12]. Everything in this section generalizes easily to the many sorted case, and the order sorted case is only slightly more difficult.

2.4 An Example

Here is a simple rule set R for computing Fibonacci numbers in the Peano representation[4] for the natural numbers:

```
f(0) = 0
f(s 0) = s 0
f(s s N) = f(N) + f(s N)
```

(Some further rules are needed for addition.)

A sequential implementation of this functional program takes time exponential in N to compute f(N), whereas a parallel rewriting execution takes only linear time. Of course, one can write a different functional program for Fibonacci numbers that does run in linear time. But the point of this simple example is that even naive programs can often be executed in optimal or near optimal time on the RRM, so that it really is reasonable to use ultra high level declarative languages in a straightforward way with this machine and model of computation; see [13, 18] for further discussion and more substantial examples.

3 Cell Machines

The cell machine models an RRM ensemble as an array of (small) processors, each of which can contain a token, two pointers to other cells, and some (Boolean) flags. Rewriting is implemented on a cell machine by broadcasting microcode which initiates elementary actions in parallel in each cell. This level of description is more concrete than parallel rewriting, and indeed is a form of graph rewriting. The models in this section ignore resource limitations, assuming that an unbounded number of cells is available, and that communication always succeeds.

---

[4]That is, the constructors are 0 and s, with 1 represented by s 0, with 2 represented by s s 0, etc.

3.1 Cells, States and Terms

We first describe cells and cell machine states without flags, using set theory; the main result characterizes when a cell machine state represents a term. Let Σ be a fixed unsorted signature with $\Sigma_n = \emptyset$ for $n > 2$; this is no loss of generality because an n-ary operation with $n > 2$ can be expressed as a composition of n binary operations. (Also, note that high arity operations are rare in practice.) We use natural numbers for the addresses of cells, and hence also as pointers to cells; $\bot$ represents the null pointer. Let $\omega_\bot = \omega \cup \{\bot\}$.

Definition 8 A **cell state** c is a triple $\langle op, lpt, rpt \rangle$, where $op \in \Sigma$ and $lpt, rpt \in \omega_\bot$. If $c = \langle o, l, r \rangle$ then $op(c) = o$, $lpt(c) = l$ and $rpt(c) = r$. Call c **nullary** and write $\#c = 0$ if $lpt(c) = rpt(c) = \bot$; call c **unary** and write $\#c = 1$ if $lpt(c) \neq \bot$ and $rpt(c) = \bot$; call c **binary** and write $\#c = 2$ if $lpt(c) \neq \bot$ and $rpt(c) \neq \bot$; otherwise, let $\#(c) = \bot$. Let C denote the set of all cell states. $\square$

Definition 9 A **cell machine state** is a partial function $s \colon \omega \to C$. The **domain** of s is $D(s) = \{n \in \omega \mid s(n) \text{ is defined}\}$. Given a cell machine state s and $n \in D(s)$, let $op(n) = op(s(n))$, let $lpt(n) = lpt(s(n))$, and let $rpt(n) = rpt(s(n))$. $\square$

Definition 10 The **graph** of a cell machine state s is defined as follows:

1. Its **node set** is the domain of s.

2. Its **edges** are the pairs $\langle m, n \rangle$ with $m, n \in D(s)$ such that $lpt(m) = n$ or $rpt(m) = n$.

3. Node n is labelled by $op(n)$.

This is a directed labelled graph whose edges are not ordered. $\square$

Definition 11 A cell machine state s is **well formed** iff

1. its domain $D(s)$ is finite,

2. if $n \in D(s)$, then $lpt(n) = \bot$ implies $rpt(n) = \bot$,

3. if $n \in D(s)$, then $op(n) \in \Sigma_{\#s(n)}$, and

4. the graph of s is acyclic, with a single root node from which all other nodes are reachable.

$\square$

Definition 12 The **term** of a well formed cell machine state s at node $n \in D(s)$ is defined as follows:

0. $term(s, n) = op(n)$ if $\#s(n) = 0$.

1. $term(s, n) = op(n)\langle term(s, lpt(n)) \rangle$ if $\#s(n) = 1$.

2. $term(s, n) = op(n)\langle term(s, lpt(n)), term(s, rpt(n)) \rangle$ if $\#s(n) = 2$.

Here $\langle$ and $\rangle$ are the special symbols used in the strings that represent terms.) $\square$

Fact 13 The term of a well formed cell machine state is a ground Σ-term. $\square$

3.2   Cells and States

The following algebraic specification for cell machines assumes familiarity with OBJ; see
[21, 4, 5] for more information on OBJ. We first describe the structure of cell machines; the
instruction set is described in Section 3.3. The ARRAY and 5TUPLE data types used here are
standard, and are defined in Appendix A. The first specification defines two auxiliary data
types, representing tokens as (quoted) identifiers and addresses as natural numbers; 0 is used
as a null address, so that proper addresses are positive numbers.

```
obj DATA is
  dfn Tkn is QID .
  dfn Adr is NAT *(sort NzNat to PAdr, op 0 to null).
endo
```

We will define flags as an array of Booleans, and cells as 5-tuples with components for a
token, a flag array, two addresses (i.e., pointers to other cells), and a reference count. The
constant "*" names the default value in an array (see the Appendix); for the flag array, its
value is false. The operations that end with "*" are selectors for the four components of
cells (except for just "*" by itself). nullc will serve as the default value for cells in the
cell machine, when it is defined as an array of cells. The line "psort Cell" says that the
"principal sort" of CELL is Cell; this is needed to make the default view in the second line
of CELLMO come out as intended.

```
obj CELL is ex DATA .
  dfn FlagA is ARRAY[NAT,view from TRIV* to BOOL is op * to false . endv].
  dfn Cell is 5TUPLE[Tkn,FlagA,Adr,Adr,INT] *(op (1*_) to (tkn*_),
      op (3*_) to (lpt*_), op (4*_) to (rpt*_), op (5*_) to (rfc*_)).
  let nullc = << 'null ; initial ; null ; null ; 0 >> .
  op flag* : Nat Cell -> Bool .
  var N : Nat . var C : Cell .
  eq flag*(N,C) = (2* C)[N] .
  psort Cell .
endo
```

```
obj CELLMO is ex DATA .
  dfn Cellm is (ARRAY *(op initial to initialCm, op * to nullc))[Adr,CELL].
  var A1 : PAdr . var T : Tkn . vars A2 A3 : Adr .
  var Cm : Cellm . var N : Nat .
  op mkcell : PAdr Tkn Adr Adr Cellm Nat -> Cellm .
  eq mkcell(A1,T,A2,A3,Cm,N) = put(<< T ; initial ; A2 ; A3 ; N >>,A1,Cm) .
endo
```

The mkcell operation is for initializing a cell machine. Note that the cell machine model
given here omits the details needed for allocating and deallocating cells; this facility is not
difficult to specify, but the details would cloud the overall picture. Also note that reference
counts must be explicitly incremented and decremented, as illustrated in the program in
Section 3.4.

3.3 Cell Instructions

The cell machine is an abstraction of the ensemble chip. Hence, it does not have the complete instruction set of the real RRM ensemble, but rather a smaller set sufficient to show the principles involved, given by the following BNF grammar:

$$
\begin{array}{lll}
Pgm & := & Act \mid Ins \mid Act \;;\; Pgm \mid Ins \;;\; Pgm \\
Ins & := & \text{if } Cond \text{ then } Act \\
Cond & := & Acond \mid Acond \text{ \& } Cond \mid Bool \\
Acond & := & Tkn \text{ eq } Tkn \mid \text{flag}(Nat, Path) \\
Tkn & := & \text{tkn}(Path) \mid Id \\
Path & := & \text{nil} \mid 1 \mid r \mid 1\ Path \mid r\ Path \\
Act & := & \text{settkn}(Tkn, Path) \mid \text{setflag}(Nat, Path) \mid \text{unsetflag}(Nat, Path) \mid \\
& & \text{skip} \mid \text{clear}(Path) \mid \text{clear} \mid \text{reset} \mid \text{setlpt}(Path, Path) \mid \\
& & \text{setrpt}(Path, Path) \mid \text{inc}(Path) \mid \text{dec}(Path)
\end{array}
$$

Programs in this language are streams of actions and instructions. An instruction is a condition-action pair, written with if_then_ syntax. This way of structuring the grammar prevents the recursive nesting of condition-action pairs. Conditions may be conjoined using _&_, and they include the Booleans, equality testing on tokens, and testing whether a given flag, accessed down a given path, is "up" (i.e., has value true). A path is a string of 1 and r symbols, indicating whether a left or right branch should be taken in passing from a cell where the instruction is executed to the designated cell; the empty path is nil. The token in the cell down the path P is indicated tkn(P).

There are eleven actions: settkn(T,P) sets the token of the cell down the path P to the value T, setflag(N,P) sets the Nth flag of the cell down path P to true, unsetflag(N,P) sets the Nth flag down path P to false, skip has no effect, clear(P) clears all the flags in the cell down the path P, clear clears every flag in the machine, and reset returns the entire machine to its initial state. Also, setlpt(P,P') and setrpt(P,P') respectively set the value of the left and the right pointers of the cell down the path P' to the address of the cell down the path P, while inc(P) and dec(P) respectively increment and decrement the reference count of the cell down the path P.

The OBJ version of this grammar is more satisfactory, because it allows the declaration of associative syntactic operations, and it also conveys some semantic information, including that the skip instruction has no effect, that nil obeys the identity law, and that _&_ and _;_ obey the associative law. This OBJ code could be used to drive an ensemble simulator, by using OBJ's facility for "building in" Lisp code to attach efficient underlying implementations to the high level syntax. Here, it is used as the initial part of a specification for the RRM ensemble chip.

```
obj PGM is sorts Cond Pgm Act Path .
  including DATA + NAT .
  subsort Bool < Cond .
  subsorts Act < Pgm .
  ops skip clear reset : -> Act .
  op _;_ : Pgm Pgm -> Pgm [assoc idr: skip prec 50] .
  op if_then_ : Cond Act -> Pgm .
  op _&_ : Cond Cond -> Cond [assoc idr: true] .
  op flag : Nat Path -> Cond .
```

```
    op tkn : Path -> Tkn .
    op _eq_ : Tkn Tkn -> Cond .
    op nil : -> Path .
    op __ : Path Path -> Path [assoc idr: nil] .
    ops l r : -> Path .
    op settkn : Tkn Path -> Act .
    ops inc dec : Path -> Act .
    ops setflag unsetflag : Nat Path -> Act .
    ops setlpt setrpt : Path Path -> Act .
    op clear : Path -> Act .
  endo
```

The following specification for instructions builds on the cell machine and program specifications given above. In it, **ev** is the main evaluation function, specifying the effects of
programs on cell machines. As usual in denotational definitions, there are several auxiliary
denotation functions: **Cev** evaluates a condition at a given cell in a cell machine, **Pev** returns
the address of the cell pointed to by a path, starting from a given cell, and **Tev** returns the
token at the end of a path from a cell at a given address.

```
  obj CELLM is ex CELLMO + PGM .
    op ev : Pgm Cellm -> Cellm .
    var A : Act . var P P1 : Pgm . var Cm : Cellm . var B : Bool .
    var Ad : PAdr . var N : Nat . vars Pa Pa1 : Path . vars C C1 C2 : Cond .
    vars T T1 T2 : Tkn .  var I : Tkn . *** was Id
    eq ev(P1 ; P,Cm) = ev(P,ev(P1,Cm)) .
    eq ev(skip,Cm) = Cm .
    eq ev(reset,Cm) = initialCm .
    op Cev : Cond Adr Cellm -> Bool .
    op Pev : Path Adr Cellm -> Adr .
    op Tev : Tkn Adr Cellm -> Tkn . *** was Id
    eq Cev(B,Ad,Cm) = B .
    eq Cev(flag(N,Pa),Ad,Cm) = flag*(N,Cm[Pev(Pa,Ad,Cm)]) .
    eq Cev(C1 & C2,Ad,Cm) = Cev(C1,Ad,Cm) and Cev(C2,Ad,Cm) .
    eq Cev(T1 eq T2,Ad,Cm) = Tev(T1,Ad,Cm) == Tev(T2,Ad,Cm) .
    cq ev(if C then A,Cm)[Ad] = ev(A,Cm)[Ad] if Cev(C,Ad,Cm).
    cq ev(if C then A,Cm)[Ad] = Cm[Ad] if not Cev(C,Ad,Cm).
    eq Pev(nil,Ad,Cm) = Ad .
    eq Pev(l Pa,Ad,Cm) = lpt*(Cm[Pev(Pa,Ad,Cm)]) .
    eq Pev(r Pa,Ad,Cm) = rpt*(Cm[Pev(Pa,Ad,Cm)]) .
    eq Tev(I,Ad,Cm) = I .
    eq Tev(tkn(Pa),Ad,Cm) = tkn*(Cm[Pev(Pa,Ad,Cm)]) .
    eq tkn*(ev(settkn(T,Pa),Cm)[Pev(Pa,Ad,Cm)]) = T .
    eq rfc*(ev(inc(Pa),Cm)[Pev(Pa,Ad,Cm)]) = rfc*(Cm[Ad]) + 1 .
    eq rfc*(ev(dec(Pa),Cm)[Pev(Pa,Ad,Cm)]) = rfc*(Cm[Ad]) - 1 .
    eq flag*(N,ev(setflag(N,Pa),Cm)[Pev(Pa,Ad,Cm)]) = true .
    eq flag*(N,ev(unsetflag(N,Pa),Cm)[Pev(Pa,Ad,Cm)]) = false .
    cq lpt*(ev(setlpt(Pa,Pa1),Cm)[Pev(Pa1,Ad,Cm)]) = Pev(Pa,Ad,Cm)
        if Pa =/= nil and Pa1 =/= nil .
```

```
cq rpt*(ev(setrpt(Pa,Pa1),Cm)[Pev(Pa1,Ad,Cm)]) = Pev(Pa,Ad,Cm)
    if Pa =/= nil and Pa1 =/= nil .
eq lpt*(ev(setlpt(nil,nil),Cm)[Pev(nil,Ad,Cm)]) = null .
eq rpt*(ev(setrpt(nil,nil),Cm)[Pev(nil,Ad,Cm)]) = null .
eq 2*(ev(clear,Cm)[Ad]) = initial .
cq ev(clear,Cm)[Ad] = nullc if rfc*(Cm[Ad]) == (0).Nat .
eq 2*(ev(clear(Pa),Cm)[Pev(Pa,Ad,Cm)]) = initial .
endo
```

For example, the third to last equation says that after a clear instruction has been broadcast, the flag component of each cell in the machine is the initial flag array (in which all flags are "down", i.e., false). The last equation says that after a clear(Pa) instruction, the cell which is down the path Pa from a cell at address Ad has its flag array cleared (i.e., set to initial). This equation may begin to look a little strange; the fourth from last equation may show more clearly why. It says that after a setrpt(Pa,Pa1) instruction has been broadcast, the right pointer of the cell down the path Pa1 from a cell at address Ad will have the address of the cell down the path Pa from Ad. Although this will usually occur as part of a condition-action pair, it is still possible that a given cell will be down the Pa1 path of more than one other cell, and consequently there can be contention about which address it gets. Note that the instructions setlpt(nil,nil) and setrpt(nil,nil) are used to set a (left or right) pointer in the current cell to null.

It should not be surprising that this specification is not Church-Rosser, because it defines a non-deterministic process. However, this means that initial algebra semantics cannot be used to give a standard denotation in the usual way, as in [20]. Also, it cannot be fully animated using just term rewriting, because of the need to determine for each cell which other cells are pointing at it down a given path. However, the "rewriting logic" of Meseguer [27] can be used to give a standard denotation for this specification. This logic admits non-determinism by dropping the symmetry law from equational logic, and it has an initial category of proofs instead of an initial model. Unification and backwards chaining could be used to animate this specification, as in the Eqlog system [15, 16], instead of just forward chaining, as in the rewriting operational semantics for abstract intial algebra semantics. Despite all this, the code given above is syntactically correct OBJ3, which has been run and tested, to the extent that this is possible without using unification.

It is exciting that ordinary equational deduction can be used, plus induction over the data type constructors, to prove things about this cell machine model. For example, we could prove that a given microcode sequence correctly implements a given rewrite rule, or that a given compiler always produces correct microcode. No such proofs are given here, but [1] and [29] (which builds on the 1988 draft version of this paper) show correctness of compilers for more realistic models of the RRM.

3.4 Fibonacci Numbers on the Cell Machine

This subsection gives a program for computing the Fibonacci numbers (in Peano notation) on the cell machine given in Sections 3.2 and 3.3 above. This code does not use all the power of cell machines, in order to be more like the programs that are needed for the real RRM.

```
if tkn(nil) eq 'z then setflag(0,nil);
if tkn(nil) eq 's then setflag(1,nil);
if tkn(nil) eq 'f then setflag(2,nil);
```

```
if flag(2,nil) & flag(0,1) then settkn('z,nil);
if flag(2,nil) & flag(0,1) then dec(1);
if flag(2,nil) & flag(0,1) then setlpt(nil,nil);
if flag(2,nil) & flag(0,1 1) then settkn('z,nil);
if flag(2,nil) & flag(0,1 1) then dec(1);
if flag(2,nil) & flag(0,1 1) then setlpt(nil,nil);
if flag(2,nil) & flag(1,1) then setflag(3,nil);
if flag(2,nil) & flag(1,1) then dec(1);
if flag(3,nil) then settkn('p,nil);
if flag(3,nil) then setlpt(1 1,nil);
if flag(3,nil) then inc(1 1);
if flag(3,nil) then dec(1);
if flag(3,nil) then setrpt(1 1 1,nil);
if flag(3,nil) then inc(1 1 1);
clear .
```

Here 'z, 's, 'f and 'a indicate 0, successor, Fibonacci and addition, respectively. (This code has been checked using OBJ3.)

3.5   Associative Search

This subsection indicates how associative search can be implemented on the RRM. Given an alphabet A, we can represent its elements as functions $a \colon A^* \to A^*$ which append the given element on the left of a list; then we can represent the list $a_1 a_2 ... a_n$ as the term

$$a_1(a_2(...(a_n(nil))...)),$$

and by using prefix notation for the a_i we can even get the usual list notation,

$$a_1 a_2 \ldots a_n \; nil.$$

The fact that concatenation in A^* is associative corresponds to the fact the composition of unary functions is associative.

On the cell machine, this term representation leads to the linked list data representation, in which each a_i is a cell with a pointer to a_{i+1}, and a_n finally points to nil. Using this data representation, we can program the cell machine to do an associative search[5] for a given element, by setting a certain flag in each cell if it contains the given element; on the RRM, the disjunction of all these bits can then be read out of the machine, or used internally. This gives a *constant time* search algorithm that is very natural on the RRM.

4   Extended Rewriting

We now discusses *extended term rewriting*, in which variables can match open terms as well as ground terms. This extension can be very useful in practice, e.g., in verifying VLSI circuits [8]. Although it is a special case of second order rewriting, it should be seen as taking first order rewriting to its limit, rather than as a part of proper second order rewriting; for the terms themselves are first order, and so is the associated equational logic [10].

An example of extended rewriting arises in giving a denotational style semantics for expressions, where one can avoid having to write many rules of the form

$$(\forall e, e') \; [[e + e']](\rho) \to [[e]](\rho) + [[e']](\rho)$$

---

[5]It is amusing that the associativity of composition is so closely related to associative search; in Section 4, we will see that it is also related to rewriting modulo associativity!

$$(\forall e, e') \; [[e - e']](\rho) \to [[e]](\rho) - [[e']](\rho)$$
$$(\forall e, e') \; [[e \times e']](\rho) \to [[e]](\rho) \times [[e']](\rho)$$
....

by instead writing the following much simpler rule which uses matching over the binary function symbol $*$,

$$(\forall e, e') \; (\forall\!\!\!/ *) \; [[e * e']](\rho) \to [[e]](\rho) * [[e']](\rho).$$

There is a somewhat subtle point here. Although it is easy to implement the matching of function symbol variables to function symbols, it can be hard to implement the matching of function symbol variables to open terms, as is required by full second order rewriting. Let us use the symbol $\forall$ to indicate the variables that match terms, whether open or ground, and let us use $\forall\!\!\!/$ to indicate the variables that only match individual function symbols. The latter can be regarded as a special case of the former by imposing a conditional equation (provided the signature is finite).

Definition 14 Given a signature Σ, then an **extended rewrite rule** is a quadruple $\langle \Phi, \Psi, l, r \rangle$ where Φ and Ψ are signatures of **matching variables**, and where l and r are $(\Sigma \cup \Phi \cup \Psi)$-terms. Let us write such rules abstractly in the form

$$(\forall \Phi) \, (\forall\!\!\!/ \Psi) \, l \to r$$
and concretely in forms like

$$(\forall x, y, f, g) \, (\forall\!\!\!/ h) \, l \to r$$
where (for example) $\Phi = \{x, y, f, g\}$ and $\Psi = \{h\}$ and the arities of f, g, h can (presumably) be inferred from their uses in l and r. (No ordering of the matching process is implied by the ordering of the quantifiers.) $\square$

Standard rewriting is the special case where only Φ_0 is non-empty. In many cases, we can get the effect of second order rewriting using just $\forall\!\!\!/$ and first order $\forall$; one such case is homomorphic equations like those given above for $[[\ ]]$.

We can now give definitions similar to those in Section 2.3 for sequential, parallel and concurrent extended rewriting. However, the details are somewhat complex, and are omitted here[6]. Instead, let us consider the example of Section 3.5. The following extended rewrite rules produce *true* iff the character $a \in A$ occurs in a list in the unary function representation:

$(\forall \Phi) \; searcha(f \, a \, f' \, nil) \to true$
$(\forall \Phi) \; searcha(a \, f' \, nil) \to true$
$(\forall \Phi) \; searcha(f \, a \, nil) \to true$
$(\forall \Phi) \; searcha(a \, nil) \to true,$

where $\Phi_1 = \{f, f'\}$ and $\Phi_i = \emptyset$ for $i \neq 1$. The essential idea is that the variables in Φ match open unary terms. For example, if $A = \{a, b, c, d, e\}$, then $searcha(b \, c \, a \, d \, nil)$ rewrites to *true* by the first rule with f matching $b \, c$ and f' matching d. This shows how rewriting modulo associativity can be implemented with extended rewriting[7].

We might well prefer to treat lists as objects, so that they are not destructively rewritten by the *searcha* function; this can by done, for example, in FOOPS [17].

---

[6]This is because notation is needed for substituting open terms into other open terms.

[7]By allowing the identity function to match a variable, we can also implement rewriting modulo associativity and identity; then only the first rule above for *searcha* is needed. This case is actually the most natural to implement on the RRM

5 Discussion and Future Research

The models in this paper do not address the resource limitations that necessarily occur in real machines. One important limitation is that a given cell can connect directly to only a relatively small number of other cells. Fortunately, our choice of rewriting as a model of computation guarantees that the required communications are largely local; but unfortunately, communication cannot be entirely local, particularly when executing an object-oriented language. The systematic exploitation of the locality of communication involved in the rewriting model of computation allows us to get more computational power from a given amount of silicon than is possible with conventional designs.

An important topic that could be studied using more detailed models of computation is the *robustness* of various ways to implement rewriting: we would like to guarantee that if a rewrite is aborted because of resource failure (e.g., if there is no free communication link), then the machine is still in a correct state, and will be able to execute that rewrite at some future time. This goes beyond the compiler correctness issues discussed in Section 3.3.

A Auxiliary Specifications

The following specifications are used in Section 3.2. The first two define interfaces for the two parameterized objects that follow, defining arrays and 4-tuples, respectively.

```
th TRIV is sort Elt .
endth

th TRIV* is sort Elt .
  op * : -> Elt .
endth

obj ARRAY[INDEX :: TRIV, VAL :: TRIV*] is sort Array .
  op initial : -> Array .
  op put : Elt.VAL Elt.INDEX Array -> Array .
  op _[_] : Array Elt.INDEX -> Elt.VAL .
  var V : Elt.VAL . var I I' : Elt.INDEX . var A : Array .
  eq put(V,I,A)[I'] = if I == I' then V else A[I'] fi .
  eq initial[I] = * .
endo

obj 5TUPLE[C1 C2 C3 C4 C5 :: TRIV] is sort 5Tuple .
  op <<_;_;_;_;_>> : Elt.C1 Elt.C2 Elt.C3 Elt.C4 Elt.C5 -> 5Tuple .
  op 1*_: 5Tuple -> Elt.C1 .
  op 2*_: 5Tuple -> Elt.C2 .
  op 3*_: 5Tuple -> Elt.C3 .
  op 4*_: 5Tuple -> Elt.C4 .
  op 5*_: 5Tuple -> Elt.C5 .
  var e1 : Elt.C1 . var e2 : Elt.C2 . var e3 : Elt.C3 .
  var e4 : Elt.C4 . var e5 : Elt.C5 .
  eq 1* << e1 ; e2 ; e3 ; e4 ; e5 >> = e1 .
  eq 2* << e1 ; e2 ; e3 ; e4 ; e5 >> = e2 .
```

```
eq 3* << e1 ; e2 ; e3 ; e4 ; e5 >> = e3 .
eq 4* << e1 ; e2 ; e3 ; e4 ; e5 >> = e4 .
eq 5* << e1 ; e2 ; e3 ; e4 ; e5 >> = e5 .
endo
```

The modules 5TUPLE and ARRAY are from the library, while the natural numbers (NAT), the Booleans (BOOL), and quoted identifiers (QID) are part of the standard prelude. (The standard prelude includes 2-, 3- and 4-tuples, but not 5-tuples.)

References

[1] Hitoshi Aida, Joseph Goguen, and Josè Meseguer. Compiling concurrent rewriting onto the Rewrite Rule Machine. Technical Report SRI-CSL-90-03, Computer Science Lab, SRI International, February 1990. To appear in *Proceedings, International Workshop on Conditional and Typed Rewriting Systems*, Montreal, Canada, 1990.

[2] Hitoshi Aida, Sany Leinwand, and Josè Meseguer. Architectural design of the Rewrite Rule Machine ensemble. Technical Report to appear, Computer Science Lab, SRI International, 1990. Also, to appear in *Proceedings, International Workshop on VLSI for Artificial Intelligence and Neural Nets*, edited by Will Moore and A. Delgado-Frias, Oxford University Press, 1990.

[3] Rod Burstall and Joseph Goguen. Algebras, theories and freeness: An introduction for computer scientists. In Martin Wirsing and Gunther Schmidt, editors, *Theoretical Foundations of Programming Methodology*, pages 329–350. Reidel, 1982. Proceedings, 1981 Marktoberdorf NATO Summer School, NATO Advanced Study Institute Series, Volume C91.

[4] Kokichi Futatsugi, Joseph Goguen, Jean-Pierre Jouannaud, and José Meseguer. Principles of OBJ2. In Brian Reid, editor, *Proceedings, Twelfth ACM Symposium on Principles of Programming Languages*, pages 52–66. Association for Computing Machinery, 1985.

[5] Kokichi Futatsugi, Joseph Goguen, José Meseguer, and Koji Okada. Parameterized programming in OBJ2. In Robert Balzer, editor, *Proceedings, Ninth International Conference on Software Engineering*, pages 51–60. IEEE Computer Society Press, March 1987.

[6] Joseph Goguen. Parameterized programming. *Transactions on Software Engineering*, SE-10(5):528–543, September 1984.

[7] Joseph Goguen. Graphical programming by generic example. In Steven Kartashev and Svetlana Kartashev, editors, *Proceedings, Second International Supercomputing Conference, Volume I*, pages 209–216. International Supercomputing Institute, Inc. (St. Petersburg FL), 1987.

[8] Joseph Goguen. OBJ as a theorem prover, with application to hardware verification. In V.P. Subramanyan and Graham Birtwhistle, editors, *Current Trends in Hardware Verification and Automated Theorem Proving*, pages 218–267. Springer, 1989. Also Technical Report SRI-CSL-88-4R2, SRI International, Computer Science Lab, August 1988.

[9] Joseph Goguen. Principles of parameterized programming. In Ted Biggerstaff and Alan Perlis, editors, *Software Reusability, Volume I: Concepts and Models*, pages 159–225. Addison-Wesley, 1989.

[10] Joseph Goguen. Proving and rewriting. In *Proceedings, Second International Conference on Algebraic and Logic Programming*, pages 1–24. Springer, 1990. Lecture Notes in Computer Science, Volume 463.

[11] Joseph Goguen, Claude Kirchner, Sany Leinwand, José Meseguer, and Timothy Winkler. Progress report on the Rewrite Rule Machine. *IEEE Computer Architecture Technical Committee Newsletter*, March:7–21, 1986.

[12] Joseph Goguen, Claude Kirchner, and José Meseguer. Concurrent term rewriting as a model of computation. In Robert Keller and Joseph Fasel, editors, *Proceedings, Graph Reduction Workshop*, pages 53–93. Springer, 1987. Lecture Notes in Computer Science, Volume 279.

[13] Joseph Goguen, Claude Kirchner, José Meseguer, and Timothy Winkler. OBJ as a language for concurrent programming. In Steven Kartashev and Svetlana Kartashev, editors, *Proceedings, Second International Supercomputing Conference, Volume I*, pages 195–198. International Supercomputing Institute, Inc. (St. Petersburg FL), 1987.

[14] Joseph Goguen, Sany Leinwand, José Meseguer, and Timothy Winkler. The Rewrite Rule Machine, 1989. Technical Report Technical Monograph PRG-76, Programming Research Group, Oxford University, 1989.

[15] Joseph Goguen and José Meseguer. Eqlog: Equality, types, and generic modules for logic programming. In Douglas DeGroot and Gary Lindstrom, editors, *Logic Programming: Functions, Relations and Equations*, pages 295–363. Prentice-Hall, 1986. An earlier version appears in *Journal of Logic Programming*, Volume 1, Number 2, pages 179–210, September 1984.

[16] Joseph Goguen and José Meseguer. Models and equality for logical programming. In Hartmut Ehrig, Giorgio Levi, Robert Kowalski, and Ugo Montanari, editors, *Proceedings, 1987 TAPSOFT*, pages 1–22. Springer, 1987. Lecture Notes in Computer Science, Volume 250.

[17] Joseph Goguen and José Meseguer. Unifying functional, object-oriented and relational programming, with logical semantics. In Bruce Shriver and Peter Wegner, editors, *Research Directions in Object-Oriented Programming*, pages 417–477. MIT Press, 1987. Preliminary version in *SIGPLAN Notices*, Volume 21, Number 10, pages 153–162, October 1986.

[18] Joseph Goguen and José Meseguer. Software for the Rewrite Rule Machine. In *Proceedings, International Conference on Fifth Generation Computer Systems 1988*, pages 628–637. Institute for New Generation Computer Technology (ICOT), 1988.

[19] Joseph Goguen and José Meseguer. Order-sorted algebra I: Equational deduction for multiple inheritance, overloading, exceptions and partial operations. Technical Report SRI-CSL-89-10, SRI International, Computer Science Lab, July 1989. Given as lecture at Seminar on Types, Carnegie-Mellon University, June 1983; many draft versions exist.

[20] Joseph Goguen, James Thatcher, and Eric Wagner. An initial algebra approach to the specification, correctness and implementation of abstract data types. Technical Report RC 6487, IBM T.J. Watson Research Center, October 1976. In *Current Trends in Programming Methodology, IV*, Raymond Yeh, editor, Prentice-Hall, 1978, pages 80–149.

[21] Joseph Goguen and Timothy Winkler. Introducing OBJ3. Technical Report SRI-CSL-88-9, SRI International, Computer Science Lab, August 1988. Revised version to appear with additional authors José Meseguer, Kokichi Futatsugi and Jean-Pierre Jouannaud in *Applications of Algebraic Specification using OBJ*, edited by Joseph Goguen, Derek Coleman and Robin Gallimore, Cambridge University Press, 1990.

[22] Joseph Goguen and David Wolfram. On types and FOOPS. In *Proceedings, IFIP TC2 Conference on Object Oriented Databases*. IFIP, to appear 1990.

[23] Gérard Huet and Derek Oppen. Equations and rewrite rules: A survey. In Ron Book, editor, *Formal Language Theory: Perspectives and Open Problems*, pages 349–405. Academic Press, 1980.

[24] R.M. Lea. ASP: A cost-effective parallel microcomputer. *IEEE Micro*, 8(5):10–29, 1988.

[25] Sany Leinwand and Joseph Goguen. Architectural options for the Rewrite Rule Machine. In Steven Kartashev and Svetlana Kartashev, editors, *Proceedings, Second International Supercomputing Conference, Volume I*, pages 63–70. International Supercomputing Institute, Inc. (St. Petersburg FL), 1987.

[26] Sany Leinwand, Joseph Goguen, and Timothy Winkler. Cell and ensemble architecture of the Rewrite Rule Machine. In *Proceedings, International Conference on Fifth Generation Computer Systems 1988*, pages 869–878. Institute for New Generation Computer Technology (ICOT), 1988.

[27] José Meseguer. Rewriting as a unified model of concurrency. In *Proceedings, Concur'90 Conference*, number 458 in Lecture Notes in Computer Science, pages 384–400, Amsterdam, August 1990. Springer. Also, Technical Report SRI-CSL-90-02R, Computer Science Lab, SRI International.

[28] José Meseguer and Joseph Goguen. Initiality, induction and computability. In Maurice Nivat and John Reynolds, editors, *Algebraic Methods in Semantics*, pages 459–541. Cambridge University Press, 1985.

[29] Peter M. Sewell. Cell machine correctness via parallel jungle rewriting, 1990. MSc Thesis, Programming Research Group, University of Oxford.

[30] David Shu, Lap-Wai Chow, Greg Nash, and Charles Weems. A content addressable, bit-serial associative processor. In *Proceedings, IEEE Workshop on VLSI Signal Processing*, pages 120–128. IEEE Computer Society Press, 1988.

[31] David Shu, Greg Nash, and Charles Weems. Image understanding architecture and applications. In Jorge Sanz, editor, *Machine Vision*. Springer, 1988.

[32] Timothy Winkler. Numerical computation on the RRM. Technical report, SRI International, Computer Science Lab, November 1988. Technical Note SRI-CSL-TN88-3.

[33] Timothy Winkler, Sany Leinwand, and Joseph Goguen. Simulation of concurrent term rewriting. In Steven Kartashev and Svetlana Kartashev, editors, *Proceedings, Second International Supercomputing Conference, Volume I*, pages 199–208. International Supercomputing Institute, Inc. (St. Petersburg FL), 1987.

Graph Rewriting as a Computational Model

D.L.McBurney   M.R.Sleep

Declarative Systems Project, University of East Anglia
Norwich NR4 7TJ, England

ABSTRACT

Graph Rewriting can be viewed as a rather general framework which encompasses a variety of 'New generation' computational models, ranging from functional languages through logic languages of the commited choice variety to actor (object) languages.

The language Concurrent Clean is a graph rewriting language augmented with annotations for expressing control of offloading and synchronisation in a distributed architecture. ZAPP is a simple work diffusion architecture which works well for suitable divide and conquer algorithms.

In this paper we describe a scheme for extending ZAPP to support Concurrent Clean. An early experimental implementation on transputers is described, together with some preliminary performance measurements of basic kernel functions. A distinctive feature of our implementation is the use of the transputer process instructions to support concurrent graph rewriting directly. Our results show definite benefit from this approach. In addition, we demonstrate the expressive power of Concurrent Clean with respect to pipelining and programmer control of granularity.

BACKGROUND

Term (or tree) rewriting systems have proved useful both as specifications and — though less commonly — as practical systems for symbolic computation (see [HO82] for a practical system with a sound theoretical underpining). Klop [Klo90] and Dershowitz and Jouannaud [Der89] provide comprehensive treatments of term rewriting theory, which is now reasonably well understood.

The idea of studying transformation systems based on graphs (as opposed to trees) dates back at least to [Ros72], and a significant body of theory has been developed, most notably by the Berlin school of Ehrig and others: [Ehr79] gives an authoritative overview.

Practical uses of 'graph rewriting' date back at least to Wadsworth [Wad71], who develops a graph based representation of lambda terms and an associated implementation method for normal order evaluation of lambda calculus expressions. The relation between tree and graph rewriting has been studied in some detail [Sta80a, Sta80b, Bar87, Hof88, Far90]. The main result is that sharing implementations produce the correct semantics at least for *orthogonal* term rewrite systems[1].

New generation Logic languages of the committed choice variety (for example Concurrent Prolog [Sha86] and Parlog [Gre87]) may be viewed as specialised graph rewriting languages, as may actor models such as DyNe [Ken85]. More recently Lafont [Laf89] has proposed an interaction net model of computation which again may be viewed as specialised graph rewriting, whose constraints are inspired by Girard's work on Linear Logic.

Graph Rewriting has been the basis of a number of sequential and parallel implementation projects during recent years, mainly in the context of functional languages[Tur79a, PJ87, Gog87, PCS87, Gla87, WSWW87]. The work described in this paper is in that tradition: we seek an efficient compilation scheme which harnesses the power of RISC technology to deliver fast execution of

---

[1]An orthogonal Term Rewrite System is both left linear, and non-overlapping.

functional programs. Our work brings together an efficient distributed execution mechanism (called ZAPP) and an annotated functional notation (called Concurrent Clean).

ZAPP is a work distribution scheme for distributed memory architectures which is designed to exploit the 'divide and conquer' principle. It was originally proposed in [BuSl82], and experiments with ZAPP based on transputer implementations are described in [McBSl87]. They show that good speedups can be obtained for suitable applications.

Clean [PES90,PLEK90] is a graph rewriting intermediate language based on the term graph rewriting notation introduced in [BELP87]. *Concurrent Clean* is Clean extended to support a variety of annotations which specify control information, such as when to create new parallel reducers, when to copy subgraphs, and when to synchronise computations.

In this paper we present an experimental scheme designed to support Concurrency in Clean using ZAPP as the basis for distributing work. The scheme is called CCOZ (Concurrent Clean On ZAPP). The overall aim is to make ZAPP performance more programmable.

BACKGROUND

In 1982 Burton and Sleep[BuSl82] proposed a work distribution mechanism (ZAPP) for exploiting *divide and conquer* parallelism on a distributed memory parallel architecture. In 1987, McBurney and Sleep[McBSl87] demonstrated the effectiveness of the ZAPP mechanism for a number of simple applications, using transputer arrays.

This work demonstrated that very good performance could be obtained via ZAPP mechanisms. However, it did not do so in a truly programmable way because slight modifications to the basic 'ZAPP kernel' were made for each new application.

To extend this work to a programmable form, we began collaborating with the Dutch Parallel Reduction Machine project led by H.P.Barendregt and M.J.Plasmeijer. This project gave us the Modula2 source of a prototype compiler for a functional language (called **Clean**). In July 1989, we began developing the parallel compiler technology required to tie together the Dutch work on Clean and the British work on ZAPP. This collaborative work was supported by ESPRIT Basic Research Action 3074 (Semagraph).

This paper gives an introduction to both ZAPP and concurrent Clean, and describes technical details of the compilation scheme currently under development. In addition, it gives performance measurements for some of the offloading and copying primitives.

The paper is organised as follows. First, we give introductions to the language and architecture we are attempting to combine. We then descibe our approach, and report the results of some preliminary experiments. Finally, we draw some conclusions, most notably:

A.   Even in its present rudimentary form, our compiler technology exhibits the main results of earlier ZAPP experiments, namely that for suitable applications good speedups are observed.

B.   Concurrent Clean can express a wide range of parallel programming paradigms, ranging from ZAPP's 'Divide and Conquer' through pipelining to programmer control of grain size in a distributed execution environment.

C.   Our experiments suggest that direct use of the transputer instruction set to handle the creation of, and communication between, a dynamically varying number of reduction agents definitely pays off.

DESCRIPTION OF THE COMPONENTS

Our work attempts to combine a simple architectural mechanism (ZAPP) with an annotated graph rewriting language called Concurrent Clean. In this section we describe both components.

OVERVIEW OF ZAPP

This section of the paper introduces the essential features of ZAPP as originally proposed in BuSl82 and modified in McBSl87 and McBSl88. Later sections of the paper describe the modifications necessary to support distributed execution of annotated graph rewriting programs.

Consider the function definition:

Nfib (n) = if n < 2 then 1 else (Nfib (n-1) + Nfib (n-2)) + 1

In this function the problem of calculating Nfib (n) where n is greater than 1 is divided into two simpler problems which once solved are combined to form the overall result. Note that this is a very inefficient way to calculate Nfib but it does serve as a simple way of demonstrating the principles of divide and conquer.

More generally, the divide and conquer paradigm for solving problems can be expressed[2] as a higher order function D_C as follows:

<pre>
        def   D_C (primitive,divide,combine,solve) = f
        where

            f(x)=   if primitive(x)
                       then solve(x)
                       else combine(map(f, divide(x)))
                       fi
</pre>

x	is a problem description.
primitive (x)	returns true if x can be solved directly, otherwise it returns false.
solve (x)	solves a primitive problem.
divide (x)	splits a non-primitive problem into a list of smaller ones.
combine [s1...sk]	combines a set of solutions of subproblems into a single solution.

For example, if we define:

primitive(n)	= if n<2 then true else false
solve(n)	= 1
divide(n)	= [(n-1),(n-2)]
combine(L)	= if null (L) then 1 else ((head (L))+(combine (tail (L)))

then the naive Nfib function may be defined by:

Nfib = D_C (primitive,divide,combine,solve).

Parallelism in the D_C Function

The referential transparency property of functional languages ensures that the elements of the list generated by the divide function can be evaluated in any order *or even in parallel* without affecting the outcome. To exploit this we could implement the functional expression:

(combine (map (f, divide (x))))

as a (parent) process which spawns a number of child processes, one for each element of the list, together with a blocked parent process which waits until the results of the child processes are available. The parent process then combines the results from its children and forms the overall result which it passes back to its parent.

Reduction using the D_C function can be viewed as growing a tree of processes from the single process evaluating the initial complex problem. If we had an infinite tree of real processors, we could allocate one physical processor to each process arising from the divide and conquer 'process tree'. Given only a finite number of processes, we need some scheme which can map a dynamically varying number of divide and conquer processes onto a fixed number of real processors. This is what ZAPP does. It is a *virtual tree* architecture.

When only a single processor is available, ZAPP must simulate all the logical processes in the divide and conquer process tree. When more processors are available, the logical processes can be distributed over a network to the individual processors and evaluated in parallel.

The sort of parallelism generated by the pure form of divide and conquer embodied in the D_C function has several important properties:

1. Communication is *only* between parent and child. The child process is given data to work on when it is created. The child then works on the problem without further communication from the parent until the child has computed the result. The child notifies the parent that the result is available, and then dies.

2. Throughout the lifetime of the child, its parent is suspended awaiting the results from all its children.

The ZAPP architecture exploits both these properties.

---
[2] The notation used here is based on [Burge75]

ZAPP Architecture Overview

A ZAPP machine consists of a number of connected processors (called *ZAPP elements*) each consisting of a von Neumann processor with its own private memory. There is *no* shared memory. The ZAPP elements communicate with one and other by message passing.

Each ZAPP element executes a *ZAPP kernel* which supports a virtual tree of processes and implements the D_C function as a virtual tree generator. ZAPP kernels balance the distribution of the process tree between them dynamically using local loading information.

The user encodes a particular application by defining the four functions primitive, solve, divide and combine. The three steps to applying ZAPP to perform a calculation are:

1. Initialise the ZAPP elements by broadcasting the user program (that is, the code which defines the functions *primitive, solve, divide*, and *combine*) to all of them.
2. Inject the initial problem and data into a single ZAPP element.
3. Extract and report the final result from the ZAPP element chosen for 2.

Main Principles of ZAPP Execution

Each ZAPP element evaluates the nodes of the process tree in a sequential depth first manner. Thus, with a single ZAPP element the nodes of the process tree are visited in the same order as a sequential recursive evaluation strategy.

The depth first strategy avoids the obvious space explosion problems of breadth first evaluation.

Task Pools

The processes of the process tree are held in one of three task pools called the *Pending*, *Fixed* and *Blocked* pools. Processes are placed in the Pending pool when they are spawned by the divide function. Pending processes are processes which have not started executing, they can be executed on the same processor or offloaded and executed on a different processor. Pending processes are the only processes whch can be offloaded. The Fixed pool contains processes which have started executing on this processor together with those which have been offloaded. Fixed processes *cannot* be offloaded. The Blocked pool contains processes which have been suspended while they wait for the results of their child processes. Processes start in the Pending pool, move to some Fixed pool, and (if they generate children) may visit the Blocked pool.

Load Balancing

Load balancing is performed by all the ZAPP elements, each acting on local loading information. When a ZAPP element determines that it has too few active (Pending or Fixed) processes it requests tasks from its immediate neighbours. By immediate we mean processors directly connected by a physical link. A neighbour can choose to either respond by sending a task from its Pending pool or it can refuse the request. The neighbour does *not* pass such a request for more work to other ZAPP elements in the network. This restricts offloading to immediate neighbours, and is a key design decision in ZAPP.

Offloading and copying

Because ZAPP is a distributed memory architecture with no support for physically shared store, offloading a task actually means sending a complete descriptor of a task as a message from one processing element to another. In keeping with ZAPP's search for simplicity, only *pending* tasks may be offloaded. By design, these tasks are always of the form 'apply the divide and conquer function to the following data', and consequently such tasks are defined by the data alone. In contrast a Fixed task, usually an executing process, would have some amount of state associated with it and would invlove more work to offload. Returning a result to a parent on a different processor similarly requires a copy of the result being made and sent to the parent.

Programming grain size

The ZAPP architecture has been modelled in occam and run on transputers for specific applications. For suitably large process trees real absolute speedups were frequently observed[McBsl87]. In fact the key issue is not the *size* of the process tree, but the ratio (time to execute a primitive task sequentially)/(time to communicate a task descriptor) which we can reasonably call the *granularity* of the computation.

In the original ZAPP experiments, each new application required major modifications to the ZAPP kernel. A key aim of the experiments reported below is to access ZAPP technology in a more programmable manner (via the Concurrent Clean notation and an appropriate compliation scheme). One of the natural benefits of adopting this new approach is that the programmer can control the granularity of a parallel computation. This seems an important feature, so we highlight it here. The basic idea is that the programmer writes two versions of key functions. One version runs purely sequentially, even when there are other idle processors in the system. The second version applies (at run time) some programmer defined test of grain size. True concurrent execution is possible if, *and only if*, this test is passed.

We illustrate this programmer control of granularity using the Nfib function. Recall that the ZAPP kernel supports parallel implementation of the higher order function D_C, whose definition is given earlier: To define a 'coarser grain' version of the Nfib function, we can write:

```
primitive(n) = (if n<grainsize then true else false) where grainsize=10
solve(n)     = seqNfib(n)
             where seqNfib(n)    =       if n<2
                                         then 1
                                         else  1+seqNfib(n-1)+seqNfib(n-2)
divide(n)    =   [(n-1),(n-2)]
combine(L)   = if null (L) then 1 else ((head (L))+(combine (tail (L)))
```

and our coarse grain Nfib function may be defined by:

$$Nfib = D\_C \ (primitive, divide, combine, solve).$$

The understanding is that the ZAPP kernel support for the parallel interpretation of the D_C combinator is the *only* source of parallelism, and that all the individual codes for the user functions will operate in fast sequential mode. Hence the definition above of seqNfib may be compiled to generate fast uniprocessor code.

Summary of ZAPP design decisions

What to offload:	complete data defining a subproblem for the D_C function
When to offload:	on request from relatively idle immediate neighbour
How to offoad:	by complete copy
Where to offload:	immediate neighbours only
How to distribute program:	complete copy in every physical Processor/Memory Element at start of computation.

CONCURRENT CLEAN

The language Clean[BELP87] is a term graph rewriting language which was developed at the University of Nijmegen as the 'clean' subset of the generalised graph rewriting LEAN[BEGKPS87]. This was designed as an intermediate code between a functional language with much richer syntax and a range of target machines (for example the G-machine[Aug84]). As with the graph rewriting language LEAN sharing of subterms can be expressed explicitly in Clean. However, the freedom to define context dependent graph rewriting which is available in LEAN is not available in Clean, and this enables a compiler for Clean to take advantage of the implementation techniques developed for the G-Machine[Aug84].

A compiler for a sequential implementation of Clean has been developed at Nijmengen. It produces G-machine like abstract code which is compiled into assembly code for a range of machines. The Modula2 source of this compiler was kindly made available to us by the Dutch Reduction Machine project, and was adopted as a basis for the concurrent clean compiler developed in this project.

Concurrent Clean was developed by the University of Nijmegen from Clean. It has the same syntax but with extensions to the set of annotations which allow the programmer to express which actions to perform in parallel. The semantics of Clean are extended to handle parallel rewriting. For a detailed description of Concurrent Clean the reader is referred to [PES90,PLEK90].

Using ZAPP to execute concurrent Clean

ZAPP is a techniques for executing a process tree of varying size on a finite distributed memory architecture. One way of defining the growth of the process tree is by some specific divide and conquer function (for example Fib). Early experiments [McBS187] made appropriate modifications to the ZAPP kernel for each new application, and required considerable expertise to exploit.

To make ZAPP more programmable we retain the notion of exploiting divide and conquer parallelism, but we apply the divide and conquer technique to the very general problem of evaluating an expression in an annotated functional notation (Concurrent Clean in our case). We evaluate expressions by simplifying them using a set of *rewriting* or *reduction* rules, for example:

if TRUE then E1 else E2 fi	->	E1
if FALSE then E1 else E2 fi	->	E2
5=5	->	TRUE
...		

The central notion is that there is initially a single rewriting engine which applies the rewrite rules of a program to the data graph to reduce it to normal form. Within a single rewriting engine, rewriting is performed sequentially on a single processor. However, the programmer can annotate the functional expression at key points to - for example - suggest that new rewriting engines (or reducers) might be created and offloaded to neighbouring processors to evaluate parts of the expression in parallel. Instead of having to rewrite parts of the ZAPP kernel for each new program, the user writes and annotated functional expression.

Annotations for Parallelism

Concurrent Clean as defined in [PES90,PLEK90] supports a number of control annotations. The semantics of these annotations are complex, and their experimental nature makes them subject to change. At present we are investigating the use of just *two* primitive process annotations. Other more specialised annotations may be introduced in future. The system can choose to *ignore* such annotations if it sees fit, but the system will not add its own annotations to a program.

Fixed Annotation

The Fixed or {F} annotation is used by the programmer to create a new Fixed reducer which will execute on the same processor. Hence it does not generate genuine parallelism, but rather creates reducers whose execution can be interleaved on the same processor. The main use of this annotation is when creating data streams between reducers to implement pipelined paradigms.

Mobile Annotation

The Mobile or {M} annotation is used to create a new reducer which is mobile in the sense that it can execute on a different processor or oh the same processor. The final choice is left to the system. If it executes on a new processor, the reducer rewrites a copy of the annotated subgraph, not the subgraph itself. *In contrast, if the work is done on the same processor, no copy is made, and graph sharing takes place.* Note that this differs from the Concurrent Clean definitions in [PES90,PLEK90] which (strictly) insists on copying semantics even when no offload takes place. Our implementation takes a similar approach to the passing back of results: within a processor, we do this by pointer sharing whereas across interprocessor boundaries true copying takes place.

Our design decisions might be summarised as: *use pointer sharing within a processor, but copy structures across processors.*

Why copy as a graph?

Having decided to offload by copying, there remains the question of how to copy graph structures. There are two extreme approaches to this problem:

a.   copy as a graph, preserving all the sharing.
b.   copy as a tree, generating no sharing at all.

The advantage of (b) is that it is easier and usually faster to implement. However, it fails for cyclic graphs (because it generates infinite trees). Both techniques require exploration. Our initial implementation uses a graph copying algorithm.

Properties of Reducers

Reducers generated by the Mobile and Fixed annotations exhibit the following properties :-

-   a reducer rewrites its subgraph to weak head normal form[3] (WHNF) and then terminates.
-   a reducer can execute interleaved with the execution of other reducers on the same processor including its parent.
-   if any reducer R attempts to evaluate a node already being evaluated by some other reducer S, R suspends until the node has been reduced by S to weak head normal form at which point R reactivates and uses the reduced form of the node.

Lazy and Eager Copying

The Concurrent Clean model uses two varietes of graph copying, *eager* copying and *lazy* copying. When copying a subgraph to be rewritten by a *Mobile* reducer the subgraph is copied in full immediately (eagerly). When copying the subgraph generated as the results of a reducer, copying does not take place until the node is in WHNF, and it only takes place if the result is actually needed. This is called lazy copying: it allows 'producer-consumer' (pipeline) concurrency to be expressed, where for example the producer function generates elements of a list, and some other function consumes these elements in a node at a time fashion.

The semantics of lazy copying can be described operationally using DEFER and COPYING_DEFER nodes in the data graph. DEFER nodes prevent copying of the subgraph which they are the root of, until the subgraph is in WHNF, at which point the DEFER node is removed from the graph. COPYING_DEFER nodes, are like DEFER nodes except that in addition they take a copy of the weak head normal form graph.

The two types of DEFER node can be expressed as rewrite rules which are :-

```
DEFER           {!} g ->      g;
COPYING_DEFER   {!} g ->      {C}g;
```

The annotation {!} expresses the constranint that g must be evaluated to WHNF before matching can take place.

The annotation {C} indicates that a copy of g should be taken and used as the result. Note that{C} is not part of the actual language.

IMPLEMENTING CONCURRENT CLEAN ON ZAPP (CCOZ)

Concurrent Clean On ZAPP (CCOZ) is an experimental implementation of Concurrent Clean on transputers which extends the dynamic process scheduling mechanisms of ZAPP to support the expressive power of Concurrent Clean.

OUTLINE OF MODEL

CCOZ is implemented on a network of transputers each of which executes an extended ZAPP kernel which handles the local scheduling of reducers, together with load balancing and communications. Additionally, every transputer typically executes a number of reducers which rewrite subgraphs of the data graph (a task) to weak head normal form (WHNF).

Rewriting is initially performed by a single reducer executing on a transputer which has access to the outside world. If the program executed contains no process creation annotations then rewriting to normal form is performed entirely sequentially by the one reducer.

Normal operation of a reducer is to execute G-machine like reduction code to rewrite its subgraph to WHNF. Occasionally, as a result of applying a rule containing process annotations, a reducer will spawn new tasks (subgraphs to be evaluated by reducers). On other occasions, by evaluating a COPYING_DEFER node, a reducer will initiate communication with a neighbouring transputer to obtain a copy of the WHNF subgraph.

---

[3] a subgraph is in WHNF if it is fully evaluated (in normal form), OR has a constructor at its root. For example, (Cons (1+2) Nil) is in WHNF because it has the constuctor Cons at its root.

Tasks are assigned to reducers (scheduled) for execution by the ZAPP kernel code which follows a depth first scheduling strategy (last in first out).

Tasks can be transferred from one transputer to another (offloaded) by the ZAPP kernel to achieve load balancing. The load balancing mechanism employed is simple: ZAPP kernels request tasks from neighbours when they have too few, according to a simple heuristic measure.

All communication between transputers is by message passing and is performed through the ZAPP kernels. A subgraph is copied from transputer to transputer by taking a copy on the same transputer as the original, and packaging the copy as a message which is communicated to the other transputer.

USING THE TRANSPUTERS PROCESS INSTRUCTIONS

A critical design decision is how to represent concurrent communicating reducers. One possibility, adopted in earlier ZAPP experiments [McBS187] is to write the kernel as a small fixed number of transputer processes which would simulate the creation, destruction and interprocess communication between a dynamically varying number of ZAPP processes. This approach was mainly chosen because we were working in Occam, rather than at the machine code level.

For this series of experiments we decided to implement reducers as real transputer processes. The transputer instruction set contains special provision for synchronized process communication via point-to-point channels.

Our choice was made mainly to explore the potential of the transputer's support for processes rather than any definite quantitative argument. However, there is some hope that the overheads in modelling dynamic reducers might be reduced if the scheduling and communication primitives of the transputer could be used.

COMPILATION ROUTE

Concurrent Clean programs are compiled by a Concurrent Clean compiler written in Modula2, producing transputer assembly code as output. The output is then combined with the runtime system and assembled into a library file which is invoked from an occam harness program which contains details of the machine configuration. The runtime system consists of the ZAPP kernel and code for such things as delta rules, node building, evaluation and input/output. The occam harness program is finally run on a transputer based machine called a Meiko computing surface.

SEQUENTIAL REWRITING CODE

The majority of code executed by a reducer is concerned with sequentially rewriting its task to WHNF. The rewriting code implements an abstract machine model similar to the G–machine. The model uses three stacks and one heap. The heap is used to store a representation of the data graph. The system stack holds return addresses for functions and various other system values. The argument and basic value stacks perform an optimising role by acting as graph node caches for the heap. The argument stack holds pointer values (into the heap) whilst the basic value stack holds non pointer values like integers and booleans. The three stacks contain part of the state of the rewriting of the data graph (activation record stack, local variables etc.) the rest being held in the graph itself.

The rewrite rules are compiled into functions consisting of a matching section and a rewriting section. The matching part of a function tries to match parts of the data graph against the left hand side pattern of the related rewrite rule. On successful matching the rewriting code rewrites the matching piece of graph according to the right hand side pattern of the rule. The order in which matching and hence rewriting is performed, is determined by the reduction strategy which for Concurrent Clean is the pattern driven functional rewriting strategy of lazy functional languages.

CCOZ ELEMENT COMPONENTS

The major components of each CCOZ element implemented on a transputer are a heap, rewriting and system code, reducers, task pools, a ZAPP scheduler, and Input and Output processes. The heap is shared by all the reducers within an element and contains a representation of the data graph. All code is similarly shared. The diagram shows the overall structure of a CCOZ element.

DESCRIPTION OF COMPONENT PROCESSES

Reducer

A reducer is implemented as a low priority transputer process. It consists of a unique workspace and a code pointer. The workspace acts like the activation record stack of conventional architectures, the traditional stack pointer being represented by the workspace pointer (Wptr).

The contents of the three stacks used by a reducer in rewriting a subgraph are unique to that reducer. To prevent reducers corrupting the stack contents of one and other, each reducer combines the three stacks and implements the combined stack in its private workspace. Using the workspace for the combined stack allows the stack elements to be accessed in a uniform way using the fast local memory addressing instructions of the transputer. As a consequence of holding both basic values and heap pointers in the same stack, the garbage collector needs some extra information about the nature of each entry in the stack if it is to perform its function. In the present model the status flags are represented by a bit mapped image of the stack contents, stored as a word on the stack

Reducer processes are created dynamically with workspaces being assigned from a pool of preallocated stacks. All the stacks in the pool are of a fixed size but can be chained together allowing stacks to grow to the required size. This means that it is not necessary to know how large a stack will be needed by a particular reducer, which is generally impossible to predetermine.

A reducer process is initially scheduled by creating a work descriptor (bitwise OR of the Wptr and process priority) and adding it to the low priority scheduling queue of the microcoded transputer scheduler. Once in the transputers' scheduling lists the reducer is scheduled for execution by the transputer scheduler and it is subject to descheduling and interruption by high priority processes.

Synchronizing Reducers

The suspension and reactivation of reducers, for example when a reducer tries to rewrite a subgraph already being evaluated by another reducer, is achieved through the use of the communications primitives of the transputer (in, out). DEFER nodes are implemented as nodes containing a channel. When a reducer evaluates such a node it tries to input on the channel, the communication succeeds when the reducer evaluating the subgraph completes its rewriting and outputs a value on the channel.

Synchronising reducers which evaluate COPYING_DEFER nodes is also achieved using the in and out primitives. The evaluating reducer sends a message to the appropriate transputer requesting a copy of the result graph and then tries to input on the channel in the COPYING_DEFER node. The multiplexing input and output processes deliver the message and send a value down the appropriate channel to wake the reducer when the copy has been received.

ZAPP Scheduler

The ZAPP scheduler exists to regulate space consumption and to perform load balancing. The ZAPP scheduler is implemented as a low priority transputer process which cycles, scheduling reducers and performing load balancing. After each cycle it inserts itself in the low priority process queue and deschedules itself to allow reducers to execute and perform some constructive work.

Creating Tasks and Scheduling Reducers

The model of spawning reducers of Concurrent Clean is implemented as a two phase operation. When a rule is applied, each process annotation in the rule spawns a task which contains a pointer to a representation of the annotated subgraph, and a DEFER node containing a reference to the task is inserted into the contractum. Tasks spawned by the Fixed annotation are inserted into the FIXED pool, whilst those spawned by the MOBILE annotation are put in the MOBILE pool.

When the ZAPP scheduler determines that there are no active reducer processes on its transputer, it takes a task out of one of the task pools, gets a stack out of the stack pool, initialises it as a reducer process and assigns the task to it and then enters it into the transputers low priority process queue, thus scheduling the reducer.

The scheduler assigns FIXED tasks to reducers in preference to MOBILE tasks, and it applies a depth first scheduling strategy to each pool, so the last task created is the first to be scheduled.

Load Balancing

The ZAPP scheduler is also responsible for balancing the distribution of tasks between the transputers. When a scheduler detects that there are no tasks in its task pools and that there are no active reducers running on its transputer, it requests a task from the ZAPP scheduler of a neighbouring transputer. If successful, a task is offloaded and immediately assigned to a reducer for rewriting. The mechanism by which schedulers decide where to ask for work and whether to offload is shown below :-

The Unemployed Scheduler

0   all neighbours are initially eligible as potential suppliers of work

1   choose an eligible neighbour, and send it a work_request message. If there are no eligible neighbours the scheduler repeats 1.

2   if the neighbour replies with a task, it assigns it to a reducer and schedules it, otherwise, on receiving the do_not_disturb message it flags the neighbour as ineligible for request and returns to 1.

3   when it receives a try_again message from a neighbour it flags the neighbour as eligible.

The Neighbour

1   when a scheduler receives a work_request message, if it has sufficient (as determined by some heuristic) MOBILE tasks it offloads one to the requester, but if it has insufficient it sends a do_not_disturb message.

2   when the scheduler determines that it has sufficient MOBILE tasks to offload one, it sends a try_again message to each neighbour to which it has sent a do_not_disturb but has not sent a try_again to cancel it.

Offloading

Only tasks in the MOBILE pool (PENDING pool in the ZAPP model) can be offloaded to a neighbouring transputer. To offload a MOBILE task, the scheduler makes a complete copy of the task and the subgraph it refers to and packages it up as a message, which it passes onto the input and output processes. At the destination of the message, a stack is initialised as a reducer, assigned the transferred task and then scheduled as a reducer process.

Pre-emptive Scheduling

When a reducer evaluates a DEFER node which still refers to a task in one of the task pools (ie. a reducer has not been scheduled to rewrite it), it removes the task from the pool and proceeds to evaluate the subgraph itself. This benefits performance since a reducer does not have to be spawned to rewrite the task, and more efficient code can be produced for part of the rewriting. The only drawback is that it if the task is a MOBILE task it reduces the number of tasks that are eligible for offloading. However, if the reducer evaluating the DEFER node is the only one able to run, then on suspending it the scheduler would schedule another task which might itself be a MOBILE task, so there would be no net loss.

Input and Output Processes

The Input and Output processes control communications on the links connecting each transputer to neighbours. On every tranputer, each used link has an input and an output process multiplexing messages on it. Since a tranputer has 4 links it can have upto four input and four output processes running.

Operation

Each output process has associated with it a FIFO message buffer. Reducers, and the ZAPP scheduler place messages for neighbouring transputers into the appropriate message buffer. An Output process takes messages out of its buffer and sends them down the appropriate link to be picked up by the corresponding Input process on the neighbouring transputer. An Input process accepts messages from a link and performs whatever action is appropriate. This could be updating a variable, spawning a reducer or signalling a process.

Input and Output processes are run at high priority. When run at low priority the communications delay was found to be greater. The reason for this appears to be that, at high priority the input and output processes can interrupt execution and communicate as soon as they are ready to. But at low priority they cannot interrupt and have to wait their turn.

Atomicity

In an environment where multiple reducers share and modify the same data graph it is necessary to ensure that operations which modify the graph, like evaluating a node and copying, are performed as atomic actions. Otherwise, reducers could try to update the same node, or a reducer might see a node in an invalid state whilst being updated by another reducer. In the implementation, atomicity is achieved by making all processes which access the data graph low priority processes which cannot interrupt, and ensuring that the code for atomic actions does not contain instructions which allow a reducer to be descheduled. Once a reducer starts an update no other process which accesses the graph can execute until the update is complete.

GRAPH COPYING

The algorithm used for copying graphs is relatively simple based on a two space copying garbage collector. The algorithm has two phases. First, the original graph is copied into a continuous block of memory. To maintain sharing in the copy the original is modified during copying so that each node contains a pointer to its image in the copy. In the second phase, the original graph is traversed again resetting the pointers to the copy to their original value. In total the original graph is traversed twice during the copying process. The copy produced is a relatively addressed version of the original, occupying a continuous block of memory. Such a copy is suitable for communicating between transputers, but before it can be used in the rewriting process it has to be converted to absolute addressed form, which simply requires the addition of a constant to each relative pointer.

CONCURRENT CLEAN EXECUTION

A CCOZ network is connected to the users environment through a special element which can interact with the environment and has access to the initial data graph. A Concurrent Clean program begins execution on this element when the intial graph is assigned to a reducer by the system. The reducer is different from other reducers in that it rewrites its task to normal form not WHNF. As the normal form graph is produced the system outputs it to the users environment. The other elements in the network initially have no work and simply cycle, requesting work from one another. Parallelism is only possible once the normal form reducer has spawned some mobile tasks.

Spawning Tasks

To help explain parallel rewriting in the Concurrent Clean implementation we will use a simple encoding of the Nfib function as given below :-

```
Nfib   0     ->     1                                                          |
Nfib   1     ->     1                                                          |
Nfib   n     ->     ++I ( +I {M}( Nfib ( --I n)) {M}( Nfib ( -I n 2)));
```

When a reducer (call it R) rewrites using the third Nfib rule, two mobile tasks are spawned and added to the mobile pool, DEFER nodes referring to the mobile tasks are built and pointers to them are put onto the stack of reducer R.The two tasks are for the graphs (Nfib (--I n)) and (Nfib (-I n 2)).

For the figures in this section we assume Nfib is called initially with the value 4. In all the figures DEFER and COPYING_DEFER nodes are represented by D and C_D nodes respectively.

The tasks in the Mobile pool can be assigned to reducers for rewriting in three ways. They can be assigned to a reducer on the same element, copied and the copy offloaded to a neighbour or they can be removed from the pool and evaluated by their parent reducer.

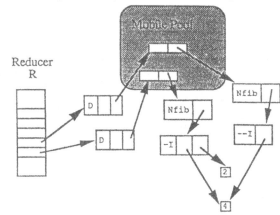

Creating Fixed Reducers

If a Mobile task is assigned to a reducer on the same element as its parent the mechanism employed is the same as for assigning Fixed tasks to reducers. The new reducer is created by the ZAPP scheduler which removes the task from the task pool, initialises a new reducer (call it F) with a reference to the relevant DEFER node, and assigns the task to the reducer which it then schedules as a reducer process.

Creating Mobile Reducers

Mobile reducers are created when tasks are offloaded. A Mobile task is offloaded by the ZAPP scheduler on request from a neighbouring ZAPP scheduler. The ZAPP scheduler takes the task

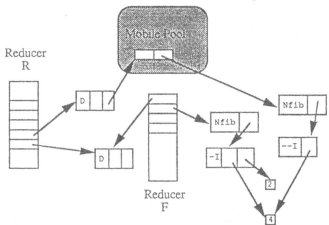

out of the Mobile pool, copies the associated subgraph and packages the result as a message which it sends to the neighbour. On the neighbouring element, the appropriate Input process receives the message, initialises a reducer (call it M), assigns it the copied task contained in the message and then schedules it. The DEFER node on the previous element is converted into a COPYING_DEFER node which refers to the new reducer which in turn refers to the COPYING_DEFER node. The first act of the new Mobile reducer is to convert the copied graph into an absolute addressed graph which it can then rewrite.

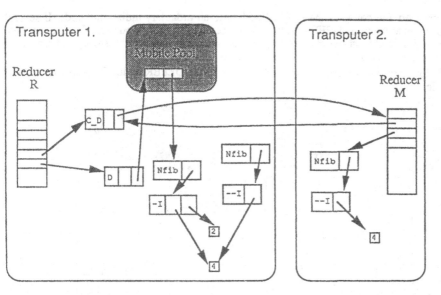

Rewriting DEFER Nodes

According to the rewriting strategy, after spawning the Mobile tasks the next action in rewriting Nfib is to rewrite the ++I node, which being strict in its argument requires it to be in WHNF. Its argument is +I and to rewrite it to WHNF both its arguments have to be in WHNF. The choice of which one to rewrite first is left to the system. At present it chooses to rewrite the rightmost argument first. All this has been determined at compile time: what the code for Nfib does at this point is to try and evaluate the DEFER node which is the second argument to +I in the contractum.

Note that if the second argument to +I had not been annotated the code for Nfib would have simply rewritten (-I n 2), and recursively invoked the code for Nfib on the result.

When reducer R rewriting Nfib, tries to rewrite a DEFER node there are two possibilities, either the task associated with the DEFER has been assigned to a reducer or it is still in the Mobile pool.

Preemptive Evaluation

If the task is still in the Mobile pool, the reducer removes the task from the pool and rewrites the relevant subgraph itself. In this instance it can ignore the DEFER node once it starts rewriting the subgraph, but if the DEFER node were shared the reducer would have to take care to synchronise with any reducers that might have suspended on the DEFER whilst it was evaluating the subgraph.

Suspending On DEFER Nodes

If the task has been assigned to a reducer on the same element it is treated like a Fixed task. When the reducer tries to rewrite the DEFER node it tries to communicate on the channel in the DEFER node and becomes suspended until the reducer rewriting the subgraph has 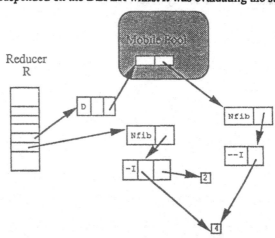 completed, and synchronises on the channel in the DEFER node. After synchronising, the suspended reducer is reactivated and converts the DEFER node into an ordainary indirection node. If several reducers try to evaluate the same DEFER node they all become suspended and their identities are held in a linked list maintained by the first reducer to be suspended. When the first suspended reducer is reactivated, it has to reactivate all the reducers in its suspended list.

In the figure below the I Node in the right hand diagram is the DEFER node after conversion to an Indirection node.

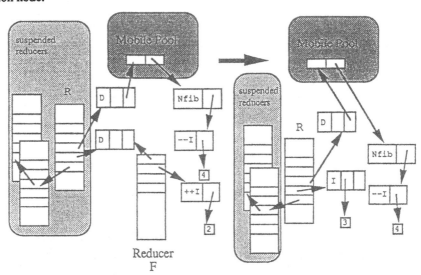

Suspending On COPYING_DEFER Nodes

If the task has been assigned to a Mobile reducer on a neighbouring element then reducer R first sends a message to the new Mobile reducer to inform it that the result is requested. Reducer R then suspends by communicating on the channel in the COPYING_DEFER node. When the message arrives at the neighbouring element, the receiving Input process flags the arrival of the request message. When the Mobile reducer completes rewriting, it waits until the flag indicating the arrival of its result request message is set, and then copies its result and sends it back as a message to reducer R. When the result message is received by the Input process on reducer R's element, the Input process communicates on the channel in the COPYING_DEFER node thus reactivating R, which then converts the copy of the result to absolute addressing form and converts the COPYING_DEFER node into an indirection node.Fig 6. Multiple reducers trying to evaluate the same COPYING_DEFER node are treated in the same way as for DEFER nodes.

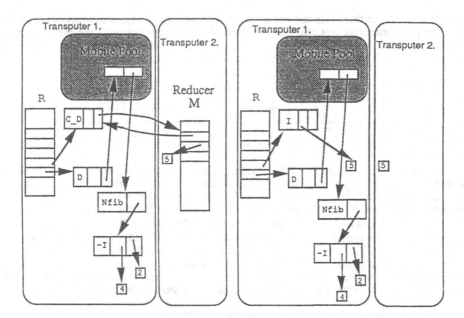

Copying DEFER and COPYING_DEFER Nodes

Whilst copying a graph, if DEFER or COPYING_DEFER nodes are encountered the copying algorithm inserts a COPYING_DEFER node into the copy, and spawns a copying reducer to rewrite the original DEFER or COPYING_DEFER node. The copying reducer only attempts to rewrite the original node once it receives notification that a reducer has tried to evaluate the new COPYING_DEFER node. After the copying reducer has evaluated the relevant DEFER or COPYING_DEFER node it takes a copy of the WHNF graph produced and sends it as a message to the reducer which tried to evaluate the new COPYING_DEFER node.

CURRENT STATUS AND PRELIMINARY EXPERIMENTS

The current implementation of Concurrent Clean is preliminary. At present only a few of the delta rules have been implemented and user input and output are very limited so the compilation route is not yet completely general. The implementation also lacks a number of optimisations, most significantly the use of a basic value stack. As a result arithmetic and boolean logic are relatively slow. Also, there is as yet no garbage collection hence it is possible only to run relatively small example programs. However, all the concurrency aspects of the model have been implemented, and we are able to report preliminary measures of some fundamental parameters.

When a compiled Concurrent Clean program is executed, certain functions like node building, garbage collection and user IO are provided for by the runtime system. The parallel runtime system provides those functions associated with concurrent execution, including task spawning, graph copying, reducer scheduling and load balancing. We will examine the performance of the parallel runtime system in the context of a few simple programs.

TASK SPAWNING WITH A SINGLE PROCESSOR

We use a program calculating the nfib function to examine the performance of task spawning. The program, which we refer to as parallel Nfib, is shown below:-

```
Nfib 0 -> 1 |
Nfib 1 -> 1 |
Nfib n -> ++I(+I {M}(Nfib (--I n))(Nfib (-I n 2)));


Start -> Nfib 15;
```

Each application of the third rule spawns a new mobile process. To asses the cost of spawning we compare the performance of this program running on a single transputer with the performance of an almost identical sequential program. The only difference in fact is that the sequential program does not contain any {M} or {F} annotations. We refer to the second program as sequential Nfib.

Table 1.

Program	Result Nfib 15	Execution time in milli seconds	Function calls per second
sequential Nfib	1973	53.44	36920
parallel Nfib	1973	66.5	29671

Note that the performance of the sequential Nfib program will improve significantly when the basic value stack is implemented.

The execution time for the parallel Nfib program includes the cost of spawning tasks by the {M} annotation, and their subsequent removal from the Mobile pool and evaluation by their parent reducer. No new reducer processes are created. Because of preemptive evaluation of tasks, the initial reducer can perform all the rewriting. New reducers are only generated to achieve real parallel execution which was not possible in this case because the programs were run on a single transputer.

The number of tasks spawned in the example is 986, which accounts for 13.06 milli seconds of the execution time or 13.25 micro seconds per task. For this simple example spawning tasks causes a 24.44% degradation in performance compared to the sequenital program. We expect this figure to improve significantly with further implementation effort, but whatever the final overhead figure, the user can write code which prevents offloading of small tasks, thus controlling the losses.

TASK SPAWNING WITH MULTIPLE PROCESSORS

The cost of offloading a task is dependent on several factors including the cost of copying the relevant subgraph, communicating the task to its new home and creating a new reducer to rewrite the task. Here we will examine the total cost of offloading a task and retrieving the result, with another simple program.

```
TwoTrees   -> +I {M}Tree10 Tree10;

Tree10 -> Tree 10;
Tree 0 -> 1 |
Tree n -> +I (Tree (--I n)) (Tree (--I n));


Start -> TwoTrees;
```

Tree10 grows a binary tree of depth 10, with integer 1 as leaves, and sums the leaf values. Note that the rules for Tree10 and Tree contain no annotations, and therefore will lead to sequential execution.

TwoTrees creates two identical Tree10 tasks, one of which may be offloaded because of its M (mobile) annotation. If TwoTrees is run with just 1 transputer, no offloading occurs and both of the Tree10 tasks are run in 'fast sequential' mode. When run on 2 transputers, the Tree10 task with the M annotation is offloaded. Because the task descriptor (which is just the term Tree10) is very small, and the result (an integer) is also very small, the difference in time taken to execute the program on 1 transputer and on 2, is close to the cost of offloading the task when structure copying costs are ignored. For larger subgraphs the cost of copying and communication have to be added to this minimum figure.

The total cost of offloading a task in the example is 0.48 milli seconds. This figure represents the total cost of requesting work from

Number of processors	Result	Execution time milli seconds	Offloading overhead ms
1	2048	84.8	-
2	2048	42.88	0.48

a neighbour, copying the (small) task, creating a new reducer and eventually sending back the result. Sending the result back actually requires two messages to be sent, one to request the result and the other the result itself. This could be optimised so that a result is automatically sent back if it is known to be strict, thus saving a message. A number of other optimisations to the coding of offloading and returning results are being considered.

GRAPH COPYING

To examine the cost of graph copying we use another program shown below.

```
Start -> Cons (Last (RevTwoLists (Rev (FromTo 1 20) Nil))) '\n';
Rev (Cons x r) list -> Rev r (Cons x list) |
Rev Nil list -> list;
FromTo a b -> IF (=I a b) (Cons b Nil) (Cons a (FromTo (++I a) b));
RevTwoLists Nil -> Nil |
RevTwoLists x -> Merge (Revn 40 x) {M}(Revn 40 x);
Revn 1 x -> x |
Revn n x -> Revn (--I n) (Rev x Nil);
Merge Nil b -> b |
Merge (Cons h t) b -> Cons h (Merge t b);
Last Nil -> -1 |
Last (Cons x Nil) -> x |
Last (Cons h t) -> Last t;
ListLast Nil -> Nil |
ListLast b:(Cons x Nil) -> b |
ListLast (Cons h t) -> ListLast t;
```

The program generates a list of 20 numbers which it then reverses n times on one processor in parallel with a second processor which reverses a copy of the list the same number of times. If the program is run on a single processor the list is reversed n times and then it is reversed n times again. No copying takes place. By running the program on 1 and 2 transputers we can examine the relative cost of graph copying. We also estimate the actual time taken to perform the copying.

Table 3.

Problem size	Time on 1	Time on 2	Relative speedup	Adj time on 1	Adj time on 2	Adj speedup	Overhead time	Copying time
n = 20	338	261	1.295	288	211	1.365	67	47.8
n = 40	628	405	1.55	578	355	1.628	66	46.8
n = 60	917	550	1.667	867	500	1.734	66.5	47.3
n = 80	1206	694	1.738	1156	644	1.795	66	46.8
n = 100	1493	839	1.779	1443	789	1.829	67.5	48.3

All times are measured in units of 64 micro seconds.

The program contains two sequential sections, generating the list of numbers initially and merging the two reversed lists, we estimate that this sequential portion takes 50 units of execution time. The figures in columns 5 and 6 are calculated by subtracting the sequential execution component (50 units) from the corresponding execution time in columns 2 and 3 respectively. The entries in the adjusted speedup column are calculated from the figures in columns 5 and 6. The adjusted speedup figures, are the actual speedup obtained during the portions of the program that can be performed in parallel.

The figures in column 6 are effectively the time taken to reverse a list of 20 integers n times and then reverse it a further n times. Halving the figures in column 6 gives the time taken to reverse the list n times, which ideally would be the same as the figures in column 7 but because of the overheads of offloading they are not, the difference between the two is shown in column 8. The overhead times in column 8 consist of 3 components, the cost of offloading a task which we estimated earlier to be 7.5 time units, the additional cost of communicating the list of integers which accounts for approximately 11.7 units, and the time taken to copy the list of integers. The copying time is given in column 9. The copying and communications times actually consist of the times taken to copy and communicate the initial list for offloading and converting the copy to absolute addressing after communicating, and then copying, communicating and converting the reversed list at the end. Halving the copying figures gives the time taken to copy a list of 20 integers and convert the list to absolute addressing form, this works out at approximately 23.7units.

The figures in the Table 3 are approximate, the purrpose of presenting them is to show the relative costs of the various components which contribute to the overhead of offloading a task with a non-trivial subgraph. The table does however show that graph copying is a relatively expensive operation in the current implementation, although it is linearly proportional to the size of subgraph to be copied. A number of optimisations have yet to be applied to the copying code.

Table 3 also demonstrates the effect of increasing the grain size in the list reversing program. We define grain size here as: the time taken to rewrite a task / the overhead time associated with offloading the task. In the list reversal program, as the value of n (number of times list is reversed) is increased the time taken to rewrite the offloaded task increases but the total offloading overhead time remains constant, the relative cost of offloading therefore diminishes and the relative speedup increases.

LAZY COPYING OF DATA STREAMS

To examine the performance of lazy copying of streams of data we use three runs of two programs. The parallel program is shown below :

```
ConsumeList n num -> Consume {M}(ListofN n num);


Consume Nil -> Nil |
Consume (Cons h t) -> Consume t;


ListofN 0 num -> Nil |
ListofN n num -> Cons num {F}(ListofN (--I n) (++I num));


Start -> ConsumeList 20 1;
```

This program is a simple producer consumer type program. A list of n integers is generated on one processor and consumed on another. Each element of the list is generated by a different reducer. The first element is generated by a Mobile reducer, the rest are generated by Fixed reducers. The elements are copied to the consumers processor on demand, the number of separate communications required to copy the whole list is proportional to the length of the list. The parallel program was run on one and on two transputers whilst the sequential version was run on just one transputer. The performance of the sequential program excludes the cost of spawning tasks.

Table 4

Program name	Time on 1 transputer	Time on 2 transputers	Stream overhead
Sequential Consumer list of 20	32	-	-
Parallel Consumer list of 20	40	135	95
Sequential Consumer list of 40	63	-	-
Parallel Consumer list of 40	79	265	186

The Table shows that lazy copying in the current implementation is considerably more expensive than eager copying which was examined in the previous table. Lazy copying is in fact approximately 4 times as expensive. Given the importance of streams for general parallel programming the performance needs improving. A number of optimisations are being developed and will soon be implemented.

GENERAL PARALLEL PERFORMANCE

Here we analyze the performance of the implementation on two simple highly parallel programs. The two programs we use are Split whch is shown below, and the Nfib program which was given earlier in this section.

In these programs we would expect a linear improvement in performance for a linear increase in the number of processors used. Also, when running one of the programs on P processors we would expect it to run almost P times faster than it does on 1 processor. In reality however there are a number of factors which inevitably reduce the parallel performance of these programs on our implementation.

```
Split 0 -> 1 |
Split n -> ++I (+I {M}(Split (--I n)) (Split (--I n)));

Start -> Split n;
```

The performance of the two programs is given in the tables below.

Results for the Nfib program run on 1,2,3,4,8 and 16 transputers

Problem size n=	Result nfib(n)	Time on 1	fc/s on 1	RS on 2	RS on 3	Rs on 4	Rs on 8	Rs on 16	fc/s on 16
15	1973	1039	29671	1.820	2.456	3.020	4.577	6.259	185712
20	21891	11529	29668	1.970	2.931	3.840	7.297	13.07	387808
21	35421	18655	29668	1.985	2.961	3.890	7.483	13.86	411184

Results for the Split program run on 1,2,3,4,8 and 16 transputers.

Problem size n=	Result Split(n)	Time on 1	RS on 2	Rs on 3	RS on 4	Rs on 8	Rs on 16
10	2047	1008	1.965	2.632	3.733	6.340	6.857
14	32767	16145	1.998	2.959	3.982	7.887	13.906
15	65535	32290	1.999	2.977	3.991	7.943	14.771

In tables 5 and 6 fc/s stands for function calls per second. All times are in units of 64 micro seconds. RS stands for Relative Speedup, that is

RS = the time taken using 1 transputer / time taken using p transputers.

The two programs are very similar, they are both divide and conquer programs which generate a binary tree of tasks. The size of the tree is the same as the result produced which in turn increases as the initial value of n increases. In ZAPP terms the four functions primitive, solve, divide and combine are relatively trivial for both programs. However, the tree generated by Split is a balanced tree whilst that generated by Nfib is unbalanced, the effects of this are noticeable in the difference in speedup figures for the two programs when generating trees of similar size.

Both sets of figures exhibit a trend which was evident in the earlier ZAPP experiments. As the size of task tree increases so too does the speedup figure for the same network of transputers. Also, for a tree of a given size the efficiency decreases as the number of transputers in the network increases.

The speedup and efficiency figures for the Nfib program are worse than those for the Split program for problems of similar complexity and networks of the same size, although the same trends are evident.

The major difference between Split and Nfib is that Split generates a well-balanced binary tree of processes, whilst Nfib does not. Balancing the work load on the transputers is more difficult with an unbalanced task tree than with a balanced one. More tasks need offloading to keep all the transputers occupied, thus increasing the total offloading overhead. Also, in its efforts to balance the work small grains of work (even (Nfib (-I n 2))) will get offloaded thus increasing the overhead of parallel evaluation. The overheads associated with these two effects are the main reason for the poorer performance of the Nfib program.

PROGRAMMING CONTROL OVER GRAIN SIZE

The problem of offloading small grains of work in the Nfib program can be alleviated by the programmer by modifying the program. An example of the programmability of grain size is shown in the Nfib program below.

```
Nfib 0 --> 1 |
Nfib 1 --> 1 |
Nfib n -> IF    (<I n Threshold)
                (SeqNfib n)
                (ParNfib n);


ParNfib n -> ++I (+I (M)(Nfib (--I n)) (Nfib (-I n 2)));


SeqNfib 0 -> 1 |
SeqNfib 1 -> 1 |
SeqNfib n -> ++I (+I (SeqNfib (--I n)) (SeqNfib (-I n 2)));


Threshold -> 5;
```

Essentially, if a problem is smaller than a threshold value then no task is spawned for the problem, instead it is solved sequentially. The figures below show that even a fairly small threshold value (5) leads to a measurable improvement.

Results for programmer controlled restriction of Nfib grain size									
Problem size	Result Nfib(n)	Time on 1	fc/s on 1	RS on 2	RS on 3	RS on 4	RS on 8	RS on 16	fc/s on 16
n = 21	35421	16494	33555	1.985	2.951	3.888	7.487	14.05	471425

All times are in units of 64 micro seconds.

CONCLUSIONS

A detailed scheme for programming and implementing parallel graph rewriting code has been described, and some performance figures for an early implementation given. Although these performance figures should not be taken too seriously given the incomplete nature of the present implementation, we can attempt to draw some preliminary conclusions.

i.   The raw function call rate for Nfib (about 30000 fc/s per transputer) and other simple functions is encouraging: even without the use of 'grain control programming', and before introducing the constant stack, the performance is already greater than that reported for the original hand coded ZAPP experiments. This result supports continued direct use of the process handling instructions in the transputer.

ii.   For simple divide and conquer functions, good relative and absolute speedups were observed.

iii.   Our examples have illustrated the expressive power of the annotations M and F. Besides the usual divide and conquer examples a producer-consumer (pipelined) example was given.

iv.   We also illustrated how the programmer could achieve considerable control of the grain size of offloaded work using the annotations. This is particularly important as whilst coarse grain MIMD parallelism can make things go faster, very fine grain parallelism can make things go much slower.

WORK TO BE DONE

We are currently introducing the use of a basic value stack into our implementation, and generally modifying the sequential code to make it more efficient. The graph copying code is being rewritten to take advantage of some of the improvements in the sequential code model. Once the basic value stack is complete garbage collection will be added.

ACKNOWLEDGEMENTS

This work was partially supported by SERC grants GR/E/36173 and GR/F/37719, and also by ESPRIT Basic Research Action 3074 (Semagraph), and ESPRIT project 2025. We are particularly grateful to the Dutch Reduction Machine project led by Henk Barendregt, Rinus Plasmeijer and Marco van Eekelen for providing us with the source of their Clean compiler, and explaining Concurrent Clean to us. Members of the Declarative Systems Project at UEA made many helpful comments and suggestions.

REFERENCES

Aug84   Augustsson L., "A compiler for lazy ML", Proc. ACM Symposium on Lisp and Functional Programming, Austin 1984.

Bar87   Barendregt, H.P., van Eekelen, M.C.J.D., Glauert, J.R.W., Kennaway, J.R., Plasmeijer, M.J., and Sleep, M.R., 1987, "Term graph rewriting", Proc. PARLE conference, Lecture Notes in Computer Science, 259, 141–158, Springer.

BEGKPS87   BARENDREGT H.P., EEKELEN M.C.J.D. van, GLAUERT J.R.W., KENNAWAY J.R.,PLASMEIJER M.J. and SLEEP M.R., "Towards an Intermediate Language based on Graph Rewriting", Journal of Parallel Computing 9, North Holland, 1989., also in Proc. PARLE conference, June 1987 LNCS 259, Springer-Verlag. pp 159-177

BELP87   Brus T., Eekelen M.C.J.D. van, Leer M. van, Plasmeijer M.J., "Clean - a language of functional graph rewriting", Proc. 3rd. Int. Conf. on Functional Programming Languages and Computer Architecture (FPCA '87) Portland, Oregon, USA., Springer-Verlag LNCS 274, pp364-384

Burge75   Burge W.H., "Recursive Programming Techniques", Addison Wesley 1975

BuSl82   Burton F.W. and Sleep M.R., "Executing functional programs on a virtual tree of processors", Proc. ACM Conf. Functional Programming Languages and Computer Architecture, Portsmouth, New Hampshire, Oct. 1982 pp187-194

Der89   Dershowitz, N., and Jouannaud, J.P., 1989, "Rewrite Systems", Chap. 15. in Handbook of Theoretical Computer Science, B, North-Holland.

Ehr79   Ehrig H, "Tutorial introduction to the algebraic approach of graph grammars", in Lecture Notes in Computer Science, 73, 83–94, Springer

Far90   Farmer, W.M., Ramsdell, J.D., and Watro, R.J., 1990 "A correctness proof for combinator reduction with cycles", ACM TOPLAS, 12, 123-134

Gla87   J.R.W. Glauert, J.R. Kennaway, M.R. Sleep, N.P.Holt, M.J.Reeve and I.Watson. "Specification of Core Dactl 1". Internal report, UEA SYS-C87-09, University of East Anglia, 1987.

Gog87   J.Goguen, C.Kirchner, J.Messeguer. "Concurrent term rewriting as a model of computation". in Proc. Workshop on Graph Reduction, LNCS 279, 54-93. (Springer, 1987).

Gre87   Gregory, S., 1987, "Parallel Logic Programming in PARLOG – The Language and its Implementation", Addison-Wesley, London.

HO82   Hoffmann C. and O'Donnell M.J., 1982, "Programming with equations", ACM Transactions on Programming Languages and Systems, 83-112.

Hof88   Hoffmann, B., and Plump, D., 1988, "Jungle Evaluation for Efficient Term Rewriting", Proc. Joint Workshop on Algebraic and Logic Programming, Mathematical Research, 49, 191-203, Akademie-Verlag, Berlin.

Ken85   Kennaway,J.R. and Sleep,M.R. "Syntax and informal semantics of DyNe". in The Analysis of Concurrent Systems, LNCS207, Springer-Verlag 1985.

Klo90   Klop, J.W., 1990, "Term rewriting systems", Chap. 6. in Handbook of Logic in Computer Science, 1, (eds. Abramsky, S., Gabbay, D., and Maibaum, T.), Oxford University Press.

Laf89   Lafont Y, "Interaction Nets", LIENS report, Paris 1989 (also 1990 POPL).

McBSl87 McBURNEY D.L. and SLEEP M.R., "Transputer based Experiments with the ZAPP architecture"., Proc. PARLE conference, Vol.1, June 1987 LNCS 259, Springer-Verlag. pp242-259

McBSl87 McBURNEY D.L. and SLEEP M.R., "Experiments with a transputer-based diffusion architecture"., Proc.7th OUG and workshop on Parallel Programming of Transputer-based Machines , Univ. Grenoble, Sept. 1987.

McBSl88   McBURNEY D.L. and SLEEP M.R., "Transputers + Virtual Tree Kernel = Real Speedups", *Proc. 3rd Hypercube Conference, Caltech Pasedena, Jan 88.*

PCS87   Peyton Jones, S.L., Clack, C.D., and Salkild, J., 1987, "GRIP: a parallel graph reduction machine", ICL Technical Journal, 5, 595–599.

PES90   Plasmeijer M.J., van Eekelen M.C.J.D. and Smetsers J.E.W., "Parallel Graph Rewriting on Loosely Coupled Machine Architectures", proc. 2nd International Workshop on Conditional and Typed Rewriting Systems, June 1990, Montreal, Canada.

PJ87   Peyton Jones, S.L., 1987, "The Implementation of Functional Languages", Prentice-Hall, London.

PlEk90   Plasmeijer M.J. and van Eekelen M.C.J.D., "Concurrent Functional Programming", NLUUG Conference on Unix and Parallelism. Mei 1990, Ede, The Netherlands.

Ros72   Rosenfeld A and Milgram D.L., "Web automata and web grammars", Machine Intelligence 7 (1972), 307-324.

Sha86   Shapiro, E.Y., 1986, "Concurrent Prolog: A Progress Report", Fundamentals of Artificial Intelligence - An Advanced Course, Lecture Notes in Computer Science, 232, Springer.

Sta80a   Staples, J., 1980, "Computation on graph-like expressions", Theor. Comp. Sci., 10, 171-185.

Sta80b   Staples, J., 1980, "Optimal evaluations of graph-like expressions", Theor. Comp. Sci., 10, 297-316.

Tur79a   D.A. Turner, "A new implementation technique for applicative languages", *Software: Practice and Experience*, 9, 31–49 (1979).

Wad71   Wadsworth, C.P., 1971, "Semantics and pragmatics of the lambda-calculus", Ph.D. thesis, University of Oxford.

WSWW87   Watson, I, Sargeant, J., Watson, P., and Woods, V., 1987, "Flagship computational models and machine architecture", ICL Technical Journal, 5, 555–594.

An Ultra-Multiprocessing Machine Architecture
for
Efficient Parallel Execution of Functional Languages

Makoto Amamiya   **Rin-ichiro Taniguchi**

Department of Information Systems
Graduate School of Engineering Sciences
Kyushu University
6-1 Kasugakoen Kasuga-shi Fukuoka 816, Japan
e-mail: amamiya@is.kyushu-u.ac.jp

Abstract

In the execution of a functional program, a large number of function instances are dynamically created, and these created function instances are executed as fine grain concurrent processes. In order to implement massively parallel execution of such fine grain concurrent processes, ultra-multiprocessing mechanism must be designed in parallel machine architecture.

This paper proposes a machine architecture for massively parallel execution of functional programs. The machine performs parallel execution along a multithread control flow, which is called datarol. First, the datarol concept is discussed in comparison with the dataflow model. Next, a method to extract datarol program from a functional program is described through a dependency analysis. Then, a datarol machine architecture is described. The datarol processor offers a parallel execution mechanism for ultra-multiprocessing based on the continuation-based execution control mechanism. Finally, the evaluation of the datarol architecture is shown.

Keyword: Functional language, Dataflow ananlysis, Multiprocessing, Massively parallel machine architecture, Dataflow machine.

1. INTRODUCTION

Functional programming languages have various attractive features, due to their pure formal semantics, for writing short and clear programs, as well as verifying and transforming programs automatically. These merits of functional programs are more explicit in writing programs for massively parallel processing. Several parallel machines are proposed and implemented based on dataflow and reduction models, for the efficient execution of functional programs[1-6].

We have proposed a machine architecture for implementing a parallel reduction model on the basis of the dataflow model[7,8]. In the proposed machine architecture, the parallel reduction process is treated as a mixture of data driven and demand driven computations. The philosophy behind the architecture design is that the processor should have an ultra-multiprocessing facility in order to execute a large number of fine grain processes in highly concurrent way. In functional programs, a number of functions are defined and their instances are executed as concurrent processes. Bodies of such defined functions are rather small, and therefore their instances are tiny processes, i.e. a large number of fine grain concurrent processes should be executed efficiently.

The dataflow architecture offers a basis for ultra-multiprocessing in a natural way. In the data-flow-based computation control, all operations are executed in parallel according to data dependency, whether they are executed in the same process instance or not. The dynamic dataflow architecture offers an efficient multiprocessing environment, because the process switching is performed efficiently at the hardware mechanism[9].

Although the dataflow computing scheme offers the beneficial points, it has several drawbacks which should be overcome, and it is needed to develop a new massively parallel architecture that will solve the problems in the dataflow architecture.

This paper proposes a machine architecture for ultra-multiprocessing, which will overcome the drawbacks in the conventional dataflow machine architecture. The machine is designed to perform parallel executions along a multithread control flow, which is called *datarol*. First, the datarol concept is introduced so as to solve several problems in the dataflow machine. The datarol program is shown to be an optimization of a data flow program: Although the datarol reflects the underlying dataflow structure in the given functional program, it eliminates the need for redundant dataflow operations such as switch and gate controls, and the overhead in operand matching. Then, a dataflow analysis and compilation method is presented, in which a multithread control flow is extracted from a given functional program and a datarol machine code is generated.

Next, a datarol machine architecture for ultra-multiprocessing is described. The machine is constructed with a number of datarol processors, which are connected with a packet switching network. The datarol processor offers a highly parallel execution mechanism for ultra-multiprocessing. Execution control in datarol processor is based on a concept of continuation, in which instructions to be executed next are specified explicitly by the currently executed instruction, instead of using the program counter. The continuation-based execution control mechanism of the datarol processor solves problems such as the dataflow control overhead in the dataflow machine and the process switching overhead in the von Neumann type sequential machine.

Finally, several evaluations of the datarol architecture are shown. The datarol architecture is evaluated from the viewpoints of the efficiency of the datarol program and the performance of the datarol multiprocessor system. The efficiency of datarol programs is shown in comparison with dataflow and conventional sequential programs. The dynamic behavior of a datarol mutiprocessor is simulated at the instruction execution level using an N-queen problem as a sample program.

2. DATAROL MACHINE ARCHITECTURE

2.1 Massisvely Parallel Computation of Functional Program

Massively parallel computation can be extracted from functional programs, which are composed of a number of prmitive and user-defined functions. In the parallel computation of functional program, several function instances are activated, and executed concurrently.

Since function bodies are small and almost all of functional programs are highly recursive, and a large number of such tiny function instances are executed in highly concurrent way, the computing system is required to support the execution environment for such a large number of tiny concurrent processes efficiently.

The hardware of massively parallel computing system will consist of multiple processing elements (PEs); hundreds or thousands of PEs. Activated instances are allocated to PEs at run time, and any number of instances should be allocated to PEs dynamically. Therefore, PE has to have a facility to execute efficiently such a large number of tiny concurrent processes. We call this *Ultra-MultiProcessing* facility.

2.2 Dataflow versus Control Flow

Important points in designing a practical functional language machine are: (1) how to extract the parallelism inherent in the functional program, and (2) how to reduce the overhead in massively parallel computation for evaluating the functional language.

The massively parallel functional language machine, which implements an ultra-multiprocessing facility, should be designed on the following philosophy:

(1) The dataflow computation scheme is inevitable as a basis for implementing the massively parallel execution environment. One of the most important features of dataflow architecture is that it implements a high speed process switching mechanism at the hardware level.

(2) The architecture should overcome several drawbacks inherent in the conventional dataflow architecture, e.g., overhead caused by the low level redundant dataflow control and overhead for senquential computation inherent in the circular pipeline processor construction.

(a) Features of dataflow architecture

Dataflow architecture offers several beneficial features for massively parallel machine[9,10]:

(1) The data driven control mechanism is quite natural for parallel execution. It can maximally exploit the parallelism inherent in a given functional program.

(2) The tagged token mechanism, with which multiprocess execution environments are managed on the hardware level, can efficiently control the parallel and concurrent execution of multiple function instances.

(3) The packet-communications-based circular pipeline architecture realizes both of pipeline and parallel operations among hardware modules, which are basic mechanisms for massively parallel MIMD (Multiple-Instruction and Multiple-Data Stream) machine architectures.

(b) Problems in dataflow machine

Although the dataflow architecture offers these beneficial points, it has several drawbacks which must be overcome in order to implement a massively parallel high performance machine:

(1) Communications overhead: There exists an overhead in communications that occurs within a processor and between processors. Low level communications are essential in dataflow architecture, since all operations explicitly transfer data to their successors as tokens. Even though a circular pipeline execution mechanism obtains high through-put operations within a dataflow processor, it increases the turn-around time for less parallel computations because of its communications overhead. One solution to this problem is to eliminate redundant data transfers.

(2) Overhead of fine grain dataflow control: If the process granularity is set at a finer level, a larger number of switch and gate operations will be required. This results in an increase in dataflow control overhead.

(3) Demerits of by-value data driven mechanism: The pure by-value data driven control mechanism produces needless data copies and redundant operations. A by-reference data sharing mechanism, on the other hand, never produces needless data, and therefore only the demanded operations are activated, since data are accessed only when they are needed[9].

(4) Although the circular pipeline construction of a processor is effective for getting high through-put in parallel computation programs, it is not effective for programs which is inherentlly sequential. Moreover, the circular pipeline structure makes lower the computation speed for such sequential programs, because the advance instruction execution is difficult to implement in the circular pipeline mechanism.

2.3 Datarol and Its Execution Mechanism

A new architecture which solves the problems sataed in Section 2.2 is called *datarol*. The idea of *datarol* is in eliminating redundant dataflows by introducing by-reference concept, which uses operand registers.

The datarol machine code is a mult-ithread control flow program, which reflects the dataflow inherent in its source program. A datarol instruction is a three-address instruction (two sources and one destination) in the case of a two-operand instruction, or a two-address instruction (one source and one destination) in the case of a one-operand instruction. Every datarol instruction has a continuation field which specifies the instructions to be executed next. Sequencing of execution is managed by this explicitly specified continuation information instead of a program counter. This continuation information method implements effectively the mutithread control flow execution in a circular pipeline architecture.

Datarol instructions are executed logically in four phases: (1) fetch instruction from instruction memory, (2) fetch operand from register cell, (3) execute, and (4) write result value in a register cell. The important point is that this execution cycle is performed in a circular pipeline. In the practical implementation, this circular pipeline can be constructed in a two-stage pipeline, in which instruction fetch and operand fetch are done at one time in parallel with the result data write of the previous instruction. The implementation of datarol processor is described in Section 4.

The datarol architecture has good features compared with the conventional dataflow architecture:

(1) Even if a result value produced by an operation is referred to by several operations, the result value is not necessary to be copied, since a register strores the result value.

(2) By introducing registers, an operand data of some instruction is assured to exist when the data is fetched by the instruction, since the operand data has been written into a register just when the data is produced by a preceding instruction. Therefore, if one of the two operands of an instruction is a dependent of the other operand, the availability of the partner operand need not be checked. This reduces the overhead of checking the availability of pair token for detecting enabled instructions.

(3) The address of a register, which is shared by two consecutive operations, can be determined and allocated at the compilation time, and thus be free from the run time memory allocation.

(4) By using continuation information included in the token packet, both instruction fetch and operand fetch can be done in parallel. This parallel fetch method, in combination with the dual port memory mechanism for register files, reduces the circular pipeline stage from four to two.

The general format of datarol instruction is

$$l : [*](w \; op \; u \; v) \rightarrow D.$$

Where l is a label of this instruction and D is a set of instructions which should be executed next to this instruction. D is called continuation points. Two instructions l and $e \in D$ are in the relation $\rightarrow$. This format means the operation op operates on two operands u and v, and writes its result to w. Operands u, v and result w are variables. In general, u, v and w denotes register name. But, if special variable name ♮ is used in place of u, v, it means data value is contained in an op-token, and no need to fetch operand from a register. If ♮ is used in palce of w, the result value need not be written to a register.

Other instructions are switch and link instructions. Switch instruction, $l : (sw \; b) \rightarrow D_t, D_f$, transfers control to continuations D_t or D_f depending on the Boolean value b. Link and rlink instructions, which is used for function application, are represented as $l : (link \; n \; f_i \; v)$ and $l : (w \; rlink \; n \; f_i)$. The meaning of these instructions are described later.

The tag * shows that the operand of this instruction is not assured to exist in the specified register when an op-token triggers this instruction. [*] means that the tag * is optional. When the tag * is indicated, it is needed to check the existence of the partner operand. If the operand has not been written in the register, the execution of this instruction will wait for the arrival of this operand.

It should be noted that datarol instructions are position independent, i.e. any instruction may be placed in any position of an instruction mermory.

[Execution of Datarol Program]

We will describe the execution mechanism of the datarol program by using examples.

(1) Simple expression: $(x + y) * x$

$$l_0 : (\natural + x \ y) \rightarrow (l_v),$$
$$l_v : (v * \natural \ x) \rightarrow (l),$$
$$l :$$

When the instruction l_w is driven by op-token l_w, only one operand x (or y) is fetched from the register because the op-token contains operand data y (or x). After the $+$ operation, its result is contained in the op-token l_v and transferred to the instruction l_v. In this case, this result value need not be written to a register since it is referred to only by the instruction l_v.

(2) Conditional expression: $if \ x > y \ then \ x - y \ else \ x$

$$l_p : *(\natural > x \ y) \rightarrow (l_b),$$
$$l_b : (sw \ \natural) \rightarrow (l_t), (l_f),$$
$$l_f : (z \ move \ x) \rightarrow (l),$$
$$l_t : (\natural \ move \ x) \rightarrow (l_1),$$
$$l_1 : (z - \natural \ y) \rightarrow (l),$$
$$l :$$

The result of the predicate $>$ is a Boolean value, and l_b is a sw-token. The sw instruction l_b transfers control to the instruction l_t or l_f, according to the Boolean value contained in the sw-token l_b.

(3) Function application: $z = f(x, y)$

$$l_{w1} : (w_1 \ call \ f) \rightarrow (l_{w2}, l_{w3}, l_{w4}),$$
$$l_{w2} : *(link \ 1 \ w_1 \ x),$$
$$l_{w3} : *(link \ 2 \ w_1 \ y),$$
$$l_{w4} : *(z \ rlink \ 3 \ w_1) \rightarrow l$$

There are three special operations concerning the function application, $(w \ call \ f)$, $(link \ n \ x \ y)$, and $(w \ rlink \ n \ x)$. First, a sw-token triggers the call instruction $(w \ call \ f)$. This operation instantiates the function f. The instance of this function will be allocated to its own processor or other processor. In any cases, the result of this operation is an instance name of the activated function f. The operation $(link \ n \ f_i \ x)$ passes the argument x to the n-th entry of the function instance f_i. The value of this operation is an acknowledge signal returned from the function instance f_i. The operation $(w \ rlink \ n \ f_i)$ gets a return value from function instance f_i. This return value is referred to by the variable w.

(4) Function body: $function \ f(a, b) = a + b$.

$$la : (a\ receive\ 1) \rightarrow (l_v),$$
$$l_b : (b\ receive\ 2) \rightarrow (l_v),$$
$$l_r : (c\ receive\ 3) \rightarrow (l_{w1}),$$
$$l_v : *(v\ +\ a\ b) \rightarrow (l_{w1}),$$
$$l_{w1} : *(return\ c\ v),$$

Function head has argument value receivers, $(w\ receive\ n)$, which receives actual argument via the n-th entry. This instruction is triggered by the hardware mechanism, when the argument value has arrived. Instructions which refer to these argument in function body access to these registers.

The mechanism of parameter passing is as follows. Each of actual arguments and return value acceptors is sent to the function instance via the 1-st to (n+1)-th entries by link and rlink operations. The function instance can identify the rlink operation name, to which the evaluation result is returned, via the (n+1)-th entry, where n is the number of arguments.

The result of the evaluation of function body is returned to the caller by the return operation $(return\ ret\ v)$, which returns the value v to rlink operation of the caller that is specified by ret.

Basic idea of this parameter passing mechanism is similar to the dynamic dataflow computing model[9,10].

2.4 Function Instances and Register Sets

Whenever a function is activated, a new function instance is created for that function. These function instances are executed as concurrent processes. These function instances share the same function code, while a register set is used as a working memory for each function instance, and is allocated to each activated function instance. All data, which are used in a function instance, are stored in the allocated register set.

A unique instance name is assigned to each function activation in order to identify each activated function instance. In general, this instance name is considered to represent a name of register set which is allocated to the activated function instance.

Each register in the allocated register set is accessed as a local displacement address in the register set. This local displacement can be obtained at the compilation time for each function body. At run time, access to a register is done by two-level addressing mechanism; the dynamically specified register set name and statically decided register name.

3. GENERATION OF DATAROL PROGRAM

Functional programs never specify the control flow of execution explicitly, but the execution sequence will be determined by data dependency. At compilation of functional language, control flow will be extracted by analyzing the data dependency. The datarol is defined as a multithread control flow, which is extracted from a given functional program.

We assume the functional program, e.g., Valid[11], is transformed into the following internal representation by preprocessing, to which the datarol extraction is applied.

(a) Simple expression:

(Operator Expression-1 Expression-2),

(b) Conditional expression:

(if Expression-p Expression-t Expression-f),

(c) Value definition:

(= Variable-name Expression),

(d) Block expression:

(let Value-definition-1 ... Value-definition-n in Expression),

(e) Function definition:

($func$ Function-name (Argument-name-1 ... Argument-name-n) Expression),

(f) Function application:

(Function-name Expression-1 ... Expression-n),

Source program is translated into datarol code in three phases:

(A) Transform a source program into an intermediate form, which is a set of instructions (w op u v). Here u, v and w are variable names newly introduced in the transformation. This intermediate form represents a dataflow structure in the source program.

(B) Extract a multithread control flow from the dataflow obtained in step (A).

(C) Allocate registers to each variable appeared in the set of instructions obtained in step (A).

In the following, we denote a set of all instructions in a transformed form of expression E by $node(E)$, and we call the form of (w op u v) as instruction w.

3.1 Definitions of Dependency Relations

Let us define several concepts, which are used for analyzing a dependency relation among instructions.

[Direct dependency between instructions: $<$]

If instructions p and q are in a set of instructions S, and (p op q w) or (p op w q), where w is any instruction in S, then p is said to be a direct dependent of q. We describe this $p < q$.

[Dependency relation between two instructions: $<<$]

(1) For any instructions p, $p << p$.

(2) For any instructions p, q and r, if $p < q$ and $q << r$, then $p << r$.

Next, we define a dependent and a governor for each instruction.

[Dependents of instruction: Dep]

$$Dep(p) = \{q | q << p\}$$

[Governor of instruction: Gov]

$$Gov(p) = \{q | p << q\}$$

[Least upper dependent: Lud]

An instruction $q \in Lud(p)$ assures that all instructions which refer to p have already finished their execution when the execution of q finishes.

$$Lud(p) = \{q | q \in ud(p) \quad and \quad Gov(q) \cap ud(p) = \{q\}\ \},$$

$$ud(p) = \{q | for\ \forall w < p,\ q \in Dep(w)\}.$$

[Least upper governor: Lug]
An instruction $q \in Lug(p)$ generates necessary and sufficient data for the execution of instruction p.

$$Lug(p) = \{q | q \in Gov(p) \quad and \quad Gov(q) = \{q\}\ \}$$

[Head of expression: $head$]
$head(E)$ is a set of instructions which have no governors in E.

$$head(E) = \{p | p \in node(E) \quad and \quad Gov(p) \cap node(E) = \{p\}\}$$

[Tail of expression: $tail$]
$tail(E)$ is a set of instructions which have no dependents in E.

$$tail(E) = \{p | p \in node(E) \quad and \quad Dep(p) \cap node(E) = \{p\}\ \}$$

3.2 Control Fow Extraction

Datarol is extracted from the intermediate form using dependency relations defined above. Datarol graph is a directed acyclic graph $G = (N, L)$, where N is a set of datarol instructions, and L is a partial set of directed arc defined between elements of N. We describe $p \rightarrow q$ when a node p has a directed arc to a node q. $p \rightarrow q$ means that q is a continuation point of p.

Datarol extraction is done by the following rules.

(1) Simple expression: $E = (op\ E_1\ E_2)$
Suppose $w \in tail(E), u \in tail(E_1), v \in tail(E_2)$, then

$$u \rightarrow w \quad and \quad v \rightarrow w \quad if \quad not(u << v \quad or \quad v << u,)$$
$$u \rightarrow w \quad if \quad u << v,$$
$$v \rightarrow w \quad if \quad v << u.$$

The translated datarol code of the simple expression is

$$l_u : (u\ op\ x_1\ x_2) \rightarrow (l_w),$$
$$l_v : (v\ op\ y_1\ y_2) \rightarrow (l_w),$$
$$l_w : (w\ op\ u\ v) \rightarrow D.$$

Here x_1, x_2, y_1, y_2 are variable names, and D is a set of destinations of instruction l_w.

The head and tail of simple expression E are defined as,

$$head(E) = head(E_1) \cup head(E_2), \quad tail(E) = w.$$

(2) Conditional expression: $E = (if\ E_p\ E_t\ E_f)$

Suppose $b = tail(E_p)$, $x = tail(E_t)$, $y = tail(E_f)$, then

$$b \to w, \quad w \to u \in D_x \quad if \quad b \quad is \quad true$$
$$w \to v \in D_y \quad if \quad b \quad is \quad false.$$

Here w is a sw instruction, and $D_x = Lug(x)$ and $D_y = Lug(y)$.
The translated datarol code is

$$l_b : (b\ op\ a_1\ a_2) \to (l_w),$$
$$l_w : (sw\ b) \to D_x, D_y,$$
$$\cdots\cdots$$
$$l_u : (u\ op\ u_1\ u_2) \to D_u,$$
$$l_v : (v\ op\ v_1\ v_2) \to D_v,$$
$$\cdots\cdots$$
$$l_x : (z\ op\ x_1\ x_2) \to D,$$
$$l_y : (z\ op\ y_1\ y_2) \to D.$$

Here $a_1, a_2, u_1, u_2, v_1, v_2, w, x_1, x_2, y_1, y_2, z$ are variable names, and $l_u \in D_x$ and $l_v \in D_y$ are continuation points following the sw instruction. D_u, D_v, D are sets of continuation points.

The head and tail of the conditional expression are defined as,

$$head(E) = head(Ep), \quad tail(E) = tail(E_t)\ (= tail(E_f)).$$

3.3 Register Allocation

A variables appeared in the datarol instruction will be allocated to a register which holds an execution result. Life interval concept is used for this allocation.

[Life interval of variable]

Life interval of an variable x, $Iv(x)$, is defined as an interval: $[birth(x), death(x)]$. The $birth(x)$ is the name of instruction which generates the variable x, and $death(x)$ is a set of instructions which is the last reference to x, i.e.

$$birth(x) = l_x \quad such \quad that \quad l_x : (x\ op\ u\ v),$$
$$death(x) = Lud(x).$$

A variable x is said to be alive in $Iv(x)$. A register which is allocated to the variable x can not be made free in the interval. Or conversely, outside the $Iv(x)$, the register which is allocated to x is free for re-allocation to other result value.

If the last reference of the variable x occurs in true part Et or false part E_f of a conditional expression, the $death(x)$ is defined both in E_t and E_f. In this case $death(x)$ is expressed as $death(x) = (Lud(x) \cap E_t; Lud(x) \cap E_f)$, and this expression of life interval is used by distributing to the true part and false part in the register allocation process. For example, when a life interval is expressed as $[a, (b, c; d, e, f)]$, the life intervals $[a, (b, c)]$ and $[a, (d, e, f)]$ are used in the true part analysis and the false part ananlysis, respectively.

Register allocation is calculated independently for each function body. A brief description of allocation algorithm is shown in the following.

[Allocation algorithm for function body E]

(1) Calculate life interval for all variables in $node(E)$.

(2) Let $RS = \{$ all registers in a Register set $\}$.
Set $Rvar = \{$all variables in $node(E)\}$ and $Var = head(E)$.

(3) Let $Rvar = Rvar - Var$.
Assign distinct registers to each of Var.
Let R be the set of allocated registers, and let $RS = RS - R$.

(4) For some $y \in Var$, if there exists $x \in Rvar$ such that $l_x \in death(y)$ then allocate to x the register r_i which is allocated to variable y.
Let $Rvar = Rvar - \{x\}$ and $Var = Var \cup \{x\} - \{y\}$.

(5) If there are no variables that satisfy the condition in step (4), then allocate a new register $r_j \in RS$ to a variable $x \in Rvar$.
Let $Rvar = Rvar - \{x\}$, $Var = Var \cup \{x\}$, $RS = RS - \{r_j\}$

(6) Repeat step (4) or (5) until $Rvar = \emptyset$.

3.4 Example of Datarol Code

An example of datarol programs which is translated from Fibonacci function and Summation function is shown in figure 1.

(a) Fibonacci Function $fibo(n)$

$(func\ fibo\ (n)$
$\quad (if\ (<\ n\ 1)\ 1\ (+\ (fibo\ (-\ n\ 1))\ (fibo\ (-\ n\ 2)))))$
$\Rightarrow\quad c_0 : (r_0\ receive\ 1) \rightarrow (l_1),$
$\quad e_1 : (r_1\ receive\ 2) \rightarrow (l_9),$
$\quad l_1 : (b\ <\ r_0\ 1) \rightarrow (l_2),$
$\quad l_2 : (sw\ b) \rightarrow (l_3), (l_{21}),$
$\quad l_{21} : (\sharp\ move\ r_0) \rightarrow (l_4, l_6),$
$\quad l_3 : (r_0\ move\ 1) \rightarrow (l_9),$
$\quad l_4 : (r_2 - \sharp\ 1) \rightarrow (l_6),$
$\quad l_5 : (r_3 - \sharp\ 2) \rightarrow (l_7),$
$\quad l_6 : (\sharp\ call\ fibo) \rightarrow (l_{61}, l_{62}),$
$\quad l_{61} : (link\ 1\ \sharp\ r_2),$
$\quad l_{62} : (r_2\ rlink\ 2\ \sharp) \rightarrow (l_8),$
$\quad l_7 : (\sharp\ call\ fibo) \rightarrow (l_{71}, l_{72}),$
$\quad l_{71} : (link\ 1\ \sharp\ r_3),$
$\quad l_{72} : (r_3\ rlink\ 2\ \sharp) \rightarrow (l_8),$
$\quad l_8 : \bullet(r_0 + r_2\ r_3) \rightarrow (l_9),$
$\quad l_9 : \bullet(return\ r_1\ r_0),$

(b) Summation Function $sum(i, j)$

$(func\ sum\ (i\ j)$
$\quad (if\ (=\ i\ j)\ j$
$\quad\quad (let\ (=\ k\ (\div\ (+\ i\ j)\ 2)$
$\quad\quad in\ (+\ (sum\ i\ k)\ (sum\ (+\ k\ 1)\ j)))))$
$\Rightarrow\quad c_0 : (r_0\ receive\ 1) \rightarrow (l_1),$
$\quad e_1 : (r_1\ receive\ 2) \rightarrow (l_1),$
$\quad e_2 : (r_2\ receive\ 3) \rightarrow (l_9),$
$\quad l_1 : \bullet(b = r_0\ r_1) \rightarrow (l_2),$
$\quad l_2 : (sw\ b) \rightarrow (l_{21}), (l_{22}),$
$\quad l_{21} : (\sharp\ move\ r_2) \rightarrow (l_9),$
$\quad l_{22} : (\sharp\ move\ r_0) \rightarrow (l_3),$
$\quad l_3 : (\sharp + \sharp\ r_1) \rightarrow (l_4),$
$\quad l_4 : (r_3 + \sharp\ 2) \rightarrow (l_5, l_6),$
$\quad l_5 : (\sharp\ call\ sum) \rightarrow (l_{51}, l_{52}, l_{53}),$
$\quad l_{51} : (link\ 1\ \sharp\ r_1),$
$\quad l_{52} : (link\ 2\ \sharp\ r_3),$
$\quad l_{53} : (r_4\ rlink\ 3\ \sharp) \rightarrow (l_6),$
$\quad l_6 : (r_5 + r_3\ 1) \rightarrow (l_7),$
$\quad l_7 : (\sharp\ call\ sum) \rightarrow (l_{71}, l_{72}, l_{73}),$
$\quad l_{71} : (link\ 1\ \sharp\ r_5),$
$\quad l_{72} : (link\ 2\ \sharp\ r_1),$
$\quad l_{73} : (r_5\ rlink\ 3\ \sharp) \rightarrow (l_8),$
$\quad l_8 : \bullet(r_1 + r_4\ r_5) \rightarrow (l_9),$
$\quad l_9 : \bullet(return\ r_2\ r_1),$

Figure 1 Example of Datarol Program

4. DATAROL MACHINE ARCHITECTURE

4.1 Parallel and Pipeline Multiprocessor System

The datarol machine is constructed with a thousand processing elements and structure memory banks. An overview of the datarol machine is shown in figure 2. Processors and memory banks are connected with a multistage packet switching network. Processing elements, called PEs, execute datarol programs. The program codes and operand data are stored in Instruction Memory and Operand Memory in the PE. Structure data such as lists and arrays are stored in Structure Memory, called SM, and pointers to structure data are treated as operand data within a PE. This mechanism of handling structure data is the same as that in the data flow machine DFM[4,10].

The inter-processor connection network, called PE-net, implements a flexible tree structure in logical connection, while its physical connection remains regular and local. The PE-net also controls the processors' work load, distributing it evenly among different processors, watches the work load of each processor, and allocates an activated function instance to the least loaded PE so as to distribute the work load evenly over PEs.

The PE-SM connection network, called PS-net, realizes equi-distant packet communications for any PE-SM pairs.

Since the system construction and network configuration are described and discussed in another paper[12], we focus the discussion on the datarol processor construction and the function linkage mechanism.

4.2 Construction of Datarol Processor

The datarol processor is constructed as a two-stage circular pipeline with a Fetch module and an Execution module, as shown in figure 3. The Fetch module consists of an Instruction Memory unit (IM), an Activation Control unit (AC), and an Operand Memory unit (OM). The Execution unit consists of a Function Unit (FU) and a Communication Control unit (CC). The IM stores datarol instructions and manages instruction fetching. The OM stores operand data, and manages operand fetching and result-data writing. The FU executes datarol instructions. The continuation linkage to following instructions is specified in the preceding instruction, stored in IM as a pointer chain.

The general instruction format of datarol code is

$label$: [*] opc res $cont$ opr_1 [, opr_2].

Where opc is an operation code. opr_1 and opr_2 are register addresses of the first and second operands. If opr_1 or opr_2 is ♮, this operand is contained in a token packet and does not need to be fetched from a register. opr_2 is omitted for one-operand instructions. res is a register address in which an operation result is stored. If res is ♮, the result data do not need to be written into a register. $cont$ is a set of continuation points, which specifies a linkage to following instructions. If the two operands have no dependency relation, the instruction has a tag *.

A switch operation has the following form.

$label$: sw $cont_t, cont_f$ [opr_1 [, opr_2]].

In a switch operation, a Boolean operation is first performed on operands; continuation points, $cont_t$ or $cont_f$, are selected according to the value of the Boolean operation.

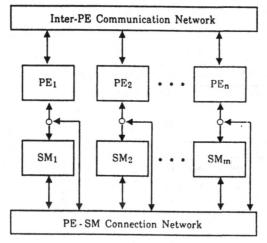

PE : Processing Element
SM : Structure Memory

Figure 2 Datarol Machine Architecture
(Parallel and Pipeline Multi-Processor System)

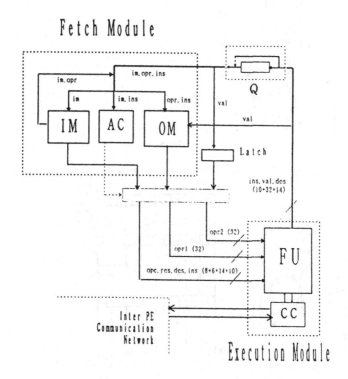

Figure 3 Datarol Processor

IM Format

(1) Two operand Instruction   (total 58 bits)

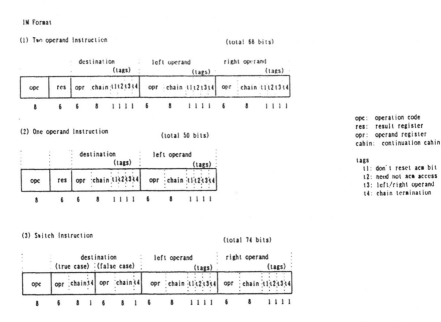

opc: operation code
res: result register
opr: operand register
cahin: continuation cahin

tags
 t1: don't reset acm bit
 t2: need not acm access
 t3: left/right operand
 t4: chain termination

Figure 4 IM Field Configuration

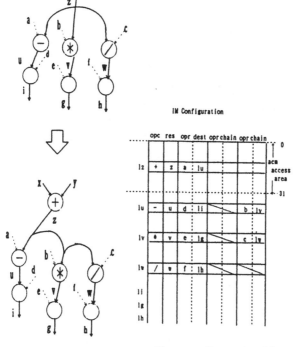

Figure 5 Example of Continuation Chaining

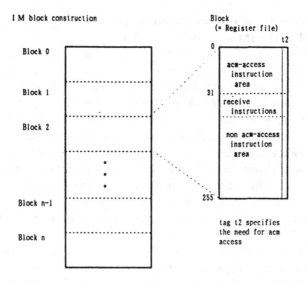

Figure 6 IM Block Configuration

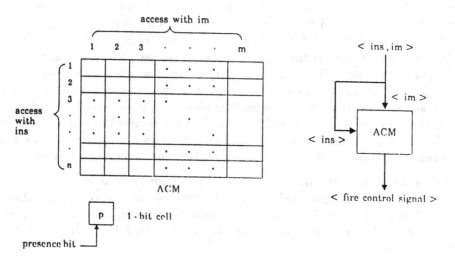

Figure 7 Construction of Activation Control Unit

A datarol assembler translates the assembly code of the above format into machine code, which is stored in the IM by a datarol loader.

A configuration of IM field is shown in figure 4. Two coding techniques are designed in the IM configuration for implementing a two-stage circular pipeline. One is the chaining of the multiple continuation points, and the other is advanced parallel fetching control. In the machine code, one of the continuation points, i.e., one of the addresses of the next instructions, is specified in the destination field of the current instruction, and the remaining continuation points are chained in the operand field of subsequent instructions. For advanced parallel fetching, the register address of the partner operand of the next instructions is specified either in the destination field, or in the operand field of chained instructions. Thus, both the instruction address and the operand register address are specified in advance in the continuation chain.

For example, if l_1, l_2 and l_3 are continuation points of an instruction l_0, when a result of the instruction l_0 is used as the first operand of instruction l_1, the second operand of instruction l_2 and the first operand of instruction l_3, and the regiters of their partner operands are r_1, r_2, and r_3 respectively, then, the operand and instruction address pairs, $< r_1, l_1 >$, $< r_2, l_2 >$ and $< r_3, l_3 >$ are specified in the destination field of the instruction l_0, the first operand field of the instruction l_1 and the second operand field of instruction l_2 respectively. This chain terminates at the first operand field of instruction l_3. A more precise example is shown in figure 5.

Every instruction of a function body is assigned to a local address relative to each function body. Each function body has its own entry address, and instructions in the function body are assigned to each local address starting from each entry address. It should also be noted that all instructions are position free in each function body.

Instructions which need the activation control are assigned to a local address from 0 to 3, specified by tag t_2. The address area from 0 to 31 is called the acm-access area. If the tag $t2$ is not on, no activation control is needed, even if an instruction is assigned to the acm-access area. It should be noted that almost all two-operand instructions need no activation control, and less than 32 instructions are assumed to require an activation control. Therefore, instructions which need no activation control may also be assigned to the acm-access area, and tag t_2 is set off for these instructions (see figure 6).

Execution of an instruction in the datarol processor proceeds as follows (See figure 3). In the following description, *ins* denotes an instance name. *opc* is an operation code *opr*1, *opr*2 and *res* are register names. *des* spceifies an entry address of IM, which is the starting point of a continuation chain. *im* specifies both IM address and AC table entry.

(1) Instruction Packet, IP= $\langle ins, opc, res, des, opr1, [opr2] \rangle$ is put into FU. FU performs the operation specified by the *opc*. The execution result, *val*, is written into the register *res* in OM. For switch instructions, FU evaluates a Boolean value and selects for *des* either a true case destination or a false case destination, according to the Boolean value. Instructions which concern inter-PE function linkages are executed in Communication Control unit (CC). Details of function linkage are described in Section 4.

(2) Result Packet RP= $\langle ins, val, des \rangle$ is sent to the queue Q. IF Q is empty, this packet is sent directly to the Fetch module. If a program has no parellelism, Q will be empty, and in this case, the Q unit will be by-passed, so as to reduce the pipeline stage.

(3-1) RP is dequeued from Q and sent to the Fetch module. The Fetch module accesses IM, OM and AC in parallel. At the same time, the *val*, which is held in RP, is set into a latch register. The data held in the latch register is used as an operand data. IM and AC is accessed through the same address *im*, specified in the chain field of *des* in RP. IM fetches *opc*, *res* and *des*. If more than one continuation points are chained, the Fetch module repeats the cycle of parallel IM-AC-OM fetching while tracing the chain of continuation points.

(3-2) The Activation control unit (AC) checks whether or not the partner operand has been written in OM for two-operand instructions with tag *. AC memory is divided into multiple blocks, each of which is assigned to each function instance. AC memory cell consists of only one bit, which is used as a tag to show the presence of a partner operand. The AC memory cell is accessed through a two level address: the block address specified by *ins*, and *im*, which is a local block address (see figure 7). If a presence bit is off, it means that the partner operand has not yet been written. In this case, the instruction is not fired, but the presence bit is switched on. If the presence bit is on, the instruction is fired, and the presence bit is cleared. If an operand is specified as sticky by the tag *t1*, its presence bit is not cleared until the execution of the function instance terminates and its AC memory block is garbage collected.

(3-3) A partner operand is fetched from OM. An Example of OM construction is shown in figure 8. The OM cell is accessed through two level addressing: the name of the register file specified by *ins*, and the register address in the register file specified by *opr*. OM access contention will be a problem, since OM access occurs at the time of result data writing and operand data fetching, which are performed in concurrent way. However, this problem can fortunately be solved by designing a multiport memory device which enables high speed parallel access of reading and writing.

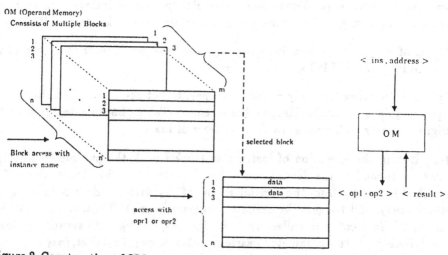

Figure 8 Construction of OM

4.3 Function Linkage Mechanism

Two kinds of function linkage mechanisms are designed. One is an intra-PE function linkage and the other is an inter-PE function linkage. Intra-PE function linkage simply creates a new instance and transfers parameters from the current instance to the newly created instance. The inter-PE function linkage gets a new instance from some other PE and sends/returns parameters/return-value to/from the newly created instance of the newly allocated PE, through inter-PE communications.

(a) Intra-PE function linkage

When a call instruction, $(w\ call\ f)$, is executed, a new instance, i.e., register set, is allocated, and its name, say ins_2, is written into the register w of current instance, say ins_1. The entry address, say im_f, of the function im_f is also written in the register w, so that w's content is $< ins_2, im_f >$. The execution of a link instruction, $(link\ i\ w\ y)$, writes the i-th parameter to the register i of the new register set, and transfers control to the $im_f + 31 + i$, where the receive instruction is located. The execution of an rlink instruction, $(v\ rlink\ j\ w)$, is the same as that of the link instruction, except that the caller information $< ins_1, v, dest >$ is passed to the callee as a parameter, where $dest$ is a destination address of this rlink instruction.

The callee's execution of a receive instruction, $(x\ receive\ i)$, simply fetches the parameter from the register i of ins_2. The execution of a return instruction, $(return\ ret\ v)$, writes the data value of the register v of ins_2 to the register w of ins_1, and transfers control to the instruction with address $instr$. It should be noted that ins_1, w and $instr$ have been sent through the rlink instruction executed by the caller, and are held in the register ret.

(b) Inter-PE function linkage

Inter-PE function linkage is rather complicated since it requires inter-PE communications. A protocol of function linkage between PEs is shown in figure 9.

The following is an example of function linkage protocol:

(1) A call instruction of function f_1 in pe_1 delivers a message packet to the inter-PE communication network, demanding a new PE and a new instance, to be assigned to the callee function f_2. The inter-PE communication network selects a PE, say pe_2.

(2) CC of pe_2 creates a new instance, say ins_2, and sends back the name of this new instance ins_2 and self PE name pe_2 to pe_1.

(3) When receiving the reply packet from pe_2, CC of pe_1 writes the callee information $< pe_2, fn_2, ins_2 >$ in the Linkage Management Table (LMT) integrated in CC, and assigns this entry address, k, to the register r of ins_1.

(4-5) During the execution of instruction $(link\ i\ r\ v)$, the parameter passing packet $< data >$ is send to the destination $< pe_2, fn_2, ins_2 >$. This destination information is fetched indirectly from the register r. CC of pe_2 writes $< data >$ into register r_1 of instance ins_2, and triggers the execution of $(receive\ r_1)$. Thus, the parameter data is transferred from caller to callee. In a similar way, during the execution of instruction $(w:\ rlink\ j\ r)$, the parameter passing packet $< pe_1, fn_1, dest, ins_1, w >$ is sent to the destination $< pe_2, fn_2.ins_2 >$, where $dest$ is the destination address of this rlink instruction. On receiving the parameter packet, CC of pe_2 writes this return information in LMT, and assigns the entry address of LMT, l , to register r_j.

(6) When the instruction $(return\ r_j\ v)$ is executed, the return value $< data' >$ held in v and the return information $< fn_1, dest, ins_1, w >$ are sent to pe_1. On receiving the return value packet, CC of pe_1 writes the $data'$ in register w of ins_1, and transfers control to the instruction located at $dest$ of fn_1. Thus the return value is transferred from callee to caller.

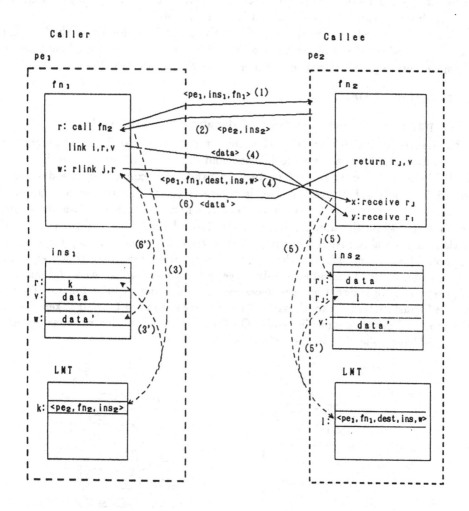

LMT: Linkage Management Table
LMT is in Communication Control Unit
in FU.

Figure 9 Inter-PE Function Linkage Protocol

5. EVALUATION

In this section, we show evaluations of the datarol architecture. We developed a datarol compiler[13], which analizes data dependency in a given source program and translates it into datarol code. The source programs are written in a functional language, *Valid*. Compiled codes of several benchmark programs are compared with dataflow codes of DFM[10]. Furthermore, the datarol codes are compared with compiled codes of the same benchmark programs which are written in Lisp and C. The benchmark programs used for evaluation include factorial function, Fibonacci function, integer summation, set manipulation, matrix calculation and N-queen problem.

We also developed a software simulator of the datarol machine described in Section 3 and 4, and evaluated the datarol machine architecture by simulating load balancing, and a speeding up proportional to the increase in the number of PEs.

5.1 Evaluation of Datarol Code

(a) Comparison between datarol and dataflow machine codes

The datarol program is shown to be more efficient than the dataflow program with regard to the memory space for storing operand data, and the number of instructions needed to check the exsistence of partner operand. An example of the datarol code compiled from a *Valid* source program is shown in figure 10, in comparison with the DFM machine code. This figure shows that the number of instructions is 25 in the dataflow code, while the number is 17 in the datarol code. It should also be noticed that there are six sink instructions in the dataflow code, although they are omitted in the figure. The number of instructions required for pair operand matching is eight in the dataflow code, while the number is only three in the datarol code. Although omitted in the figure, six more instructions are necessary for collecting garbage tokens. Therefore, there are 31 instructions in total, with 14 instructions required for pair token matching, in the practical dataflow machine code. On the other hand, no instructions are needed for such garbage collection in the datarol machine.

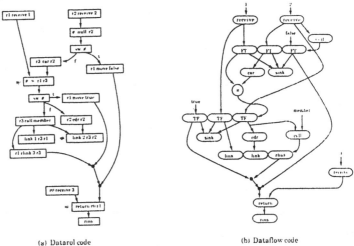

(a) Datarol code   (b) Dataflow code

Figure 10 Example of Datarol Program
(Member Function in Set Operations)

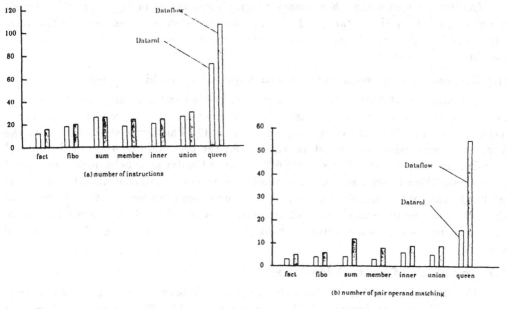

Figure 11   Comparison between Datarol and Dataflow Codes

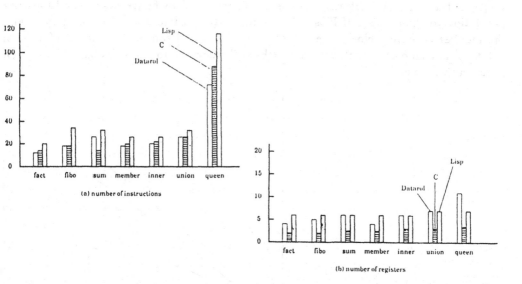

Figure 12   Comparison between Datarol and Sequential Machine Codes

Comparisons on several benchmark programs are shown in figure 11. These comparisons show that the datarol code is superior to dataflow codes because the total number of instructions is lower and the number of instructions required for pair operand matching is also lower.

(b) Comparison between datarol and sequential machine codes

The same benchmark programs are written in Lisp and C in procedural style, and they are compiled into the sequential MC68020 machine code. A comparison between datarol codes and M68020 codes is shown in figure 12. This figure shows that both the number of instructions and registers required for the program execution of the datarol machine are comparable to those of MC68020. Since the dynamic behavior of procedural programs of these benchmark, e.g., the number of iterations and conditional branches, is similar to that of functional programs, these comparison data for a static structure will show the same features in the case of dynamic behavior. Therefore, the compiled code extracted from a functional program through dataflow analysis is feasible for practical use.

5.2 Simulation of Datarol Machine

The software simulator simulates the datarol machine system at the register transfer level, extracting the performance of the datarol machine[14]. The extracted performance data include execution clocks, FU working ratio, the number of created instances, and the length of the queue Q. Several benchmark programs are executed and evaluated on the simulator. The result of a simulation of the N-queen problem, which searches all solutions for N-queen positions, is shown in figure 13. This figure shows good linearity in relation to the number of PEs. FU working ratio, distribution of working ratio and the number execution clocks are shown in Table. 5.1. Using a clock speed of 100 ns, a datarol machine constructed with 32 PEs will calculate all the solutions of a 7-queen problem in 3.7 ms.

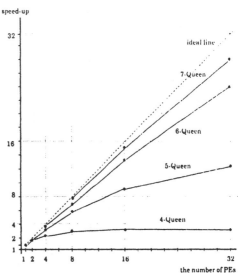

Figure 13   Speed-up to the number of PE
(N-Queen Problem)

6. RELATED WORK

Similar works are pursued in MIT[15] and ETL[16]. These works are also motivated from optimizing the dataflow architecture by using control flow information and locality in the dataflow program. The architecture of MIT is designed to execute multithread control flow by introducing fork and join operations as hardware primitives. The join operation checks whether the n threads of computation meet at the join point by inspecting a memory cell which is cleared when all threads have joined, and if not, the join operation decreases the value. The problem of this join operation is that, since all operations access to the same memory module, all operations which access to the memory must wait until the join operation completes, and therefore the concurrent execution by circular pipeline cannot be exploited maximally because of the memory access contention.

The ETL architecture uses the concept of strongly connected block, in which all operations are executed exclusively within a sequential control processor. However, how to extract the strongly connected block is the problem yet to be solved.

Our datarol architecture, on the other hand, is designed from a different approach. First, datarol architecture is designed from top-down, that is, the compiler algorithm, which automatically extracts a multithread control flow from a functional program, is designed at first, and then the datarol architecture, which executes the extracted multithread control flow efficiently, is designed by introducing the concepts of continuation point and circular pipeline mechanism. Second, the ACM is introduced for firing the enabled operations. The introduction of ACM solves the memory contention problem, which will occur if the join operation is introduced such as in the MIT architecture.

7. CONCLUSIONS

A machine architecture for ultra-multiprocessing of functional programs was proposed, which overcomes several drawbacks in conventional dataflow machines. The proposed machine performs parallel executions along a multithread control flow, which is called *datarol*.

First, several merits of this dataflow architecture were pointed out, especially from the viewpoint of process switching, that is the most important issue for ultra-multiprocessing. Then, the datarol concept was proposed in order to eliminate the drawbacks of conventional dataflow architecture, while preserving the merits of the dataflow architecture. The datarol program is an optimized version of a dataflow program, which reflects the underlying dataflow structure in a given functional program, and yet eliminates redundant dataflow operations such as switch and gate controls, and overhead in operand matching.

Next, a datarol machine architecture for an ultra-multiprocessing function linkage mechanism in the datarol machine was described. The machine is constructed with a number of datarol processors, connected by a packet switching network. The datarol processor was designed as a two-stage circular pipeline, capable of executing a large number of activated function instances in a highly concurrent way due to its pipeline structure.

Last, evaluations of datarol architecture were shown. Datarol codes are superior to dataflow codes with regard to the memory space required for storing operand data, and the number of instructions required for pair operand matching. Datarol codes are comparable to sequential codes of conventional machines with regard to the number of instructions and registers. Software simulation of the datarol machine showed good linearity in relation to the number of datarol processors and balanced work load distribution.

REFERENCES

[1] Dennis,J.B: A Preliminary Architecture for a Basic Data Flow Processor, Proc. 2nd Ann. Symp. on Computer Architecture, 1975, pp.126-132.

[2] Arvind, Gostelow,K.P. and Plouffe,W.: An Asynchronous Programming Language and Computing Machine, Report TR114a, Dept. Inf. and Comp. Science, Univ. California, Irvine, 1978.

[3] Watson,I. and Gurd,J.: A Prototype Data Flow Computer with Token Labeling, Proc. NCC, pp.623-628, 1979.

[4] Amamiya,M., Hasegawa,R.,Nakamura,O. and Mikami,H.: A list-processing-oriented data flow machine architecture, Proc. NCC, AFIPS, 1982, pp.143-151.

[5] Darlington,J. and Reeve,M.J.: "ALICE": A multiprocessor Reduction Machine, Proc. Conf. Functional Programming Languages and Computer Architecture, 1982, pp.65-75.

[6] Vegdahl,S.: A survey of proposed architecture for the execution of functional languages, IEEE Trans. on Computer, 33, 1984, pp.1050-1071.

[7] Amamiya,M.: A New Parallel Graph Reduction Model and Its Machine Architecture, Proc. ICPP, 1987, pp.47-50.

[8] Amamiya,M.: Data Flow Computing and Parallel Reduction Machine, Future Generations Computer Systems, Vol.4, No.1, 1988, pp.53-67.

[9] Amamiya,M.: Dataflow computing and eager and lazy evaluations, New Generation Computing, Vol.2, 1984, pp.105-129.

[10] Amamiya,M., Takesue,M., Hasegawa,R. and Mikami,H.: Implementation and evaluation of a list-processing-oriented data flow machine, Proc. 13th Ann.Int. Conf. on Computer Architecture, 1986, pp.10-19.

[11] Amamiya,M. Hasegawa,R. and Ono,S.: Valid: A High-Level Functional Language for Data Flow Machine, Rev. ECL, Vol.32, No.5, pp.793-802, NTT, 1984.

[12] Sonoda,K., Ueda,T., Taniguchi,R. and Amamiya,M.: Processor Optimization and Load Control in Datarol Architecture, to appear in Proc. Joint Symposium on Parallel Processing, in Japanese, May, 1990.

[13] Tachibana,T., Taniguchi,R. and Amamiya,M.: Compiling Method of Functional Programming Language Valid by Data Flow Analysis - Extraction of Datarol Program -, Journal of Information Processing, Vol.30, No.12, pp.1628-1638, in Japanese, 1989.

[14] Ueda,T., Taniguchi,R. and Amamiya,M.: Datarol Processor: Its Design and Performance Evaluation, Proc. Computer System Workshop, CPSY 89-15, The Institute of Electronics, Information and Communication Engineers, in Japanese, 1989.

[15] Nikhil,R.S. and Arvind: Can Dataflow Subsume von Neumann Computing?, Proc. Ann. Int. Symp. on Computer Architecture, pp.262-272, 1989.

[16] Sakai,S., Yamaguchi,Y., Hiraki,K., Kodama,Y. and Yuba,T.: An Architecture of a Dataflow Single Chip Processor, Proc. Ann. Int. Symp. on Computer Architecture, pp.46-53, 1989.

A Hierarchical Approach to Hardware Design

J. W. Sanders

Programming Research Group, Oxford

Abstract

It is proposed that hierarchical hardware development can benefit from techniques inspired by the hierarchical development of software, and that claim is supported with an example.

A series of levels of abstraction are indicated, the most interesting of which deal with timing of device observables, and criteria are given for moving between them. One of the techniques considered, *temporal decoding*, enables an event to be refined by a sequence of smaller events. Use of the hierarchy is sketched for a stack array of Mead and Conway.

1 Introduction

The development of a hardware design involves a subtle blend of logical and intuitive (usually time-related) reasoning. Currently much effort is being spent in the attempt to formalise that process.

In this paper we outline a hierarchy of levels of abstraction that we have found to be useful in studying the more abstract regions of hardware design. The levels are based on the traditional two-valued logical model and incorporate drive and time—both continuous and discrete. To perform development is to move between such levels; for that purpose we employ criteria for system refinement. Our ideas are sketched on the much-studied stack array of Mead and Conway.

In contrast to some recent work our description language is that of mathematical logic. As a consequence it is an easy language for formulation and reasoning but it is not directly executable. Work of similar outlook, but using more stringent refinement criteria and targeted towards executable notation, appears in [12].

2 Background: Software Development

In this section we consider the sort of hierarchical software development to be exploited later in the paper. We consider separately sequential systems and concurrent systems because they are traditionally quite different disciplines, using quite different techniques. However we try to present them so as to make apparent a uniform approach; it is the approach advocated here for hardware development.

2.1 Development of Sequential Systems

The (formal) development of a sequential system may be viewed as follows.

Requirements. First the functional (and other) *requirements* of the system are outlined: in part explicitly, in part implicitly and in part by analogy and example. Natural language is the main vehicle for the resulting document which is, unavoidably, frequently incomplete and ambiguous.

Specification. From the requirements document is distilled a (formal, functional) *specification*, which aims to capture the entire functionality of the system. The system is viewed as a data type (or abstract machine, or action system) exhibiting states and operations on them. The resulting document is expressed in some mathematical language (like Z, [21], or VDM, [9]) which is capable of expressing nondeterminism and of structuring complex predicates. It is hoped that ambiguities and much incompleteness are identified here and can be dealt with before the costly task of development proper begins; the result is usually a reiteration of the requirements-to-specification step. Behaviour of the system is derived, mathematically, from the specification.

Series of refinements. Next begins a sequence of design decisions. Each is embodied in a new system that is proved (either by verification or development) to meet the previous design. To begin the sequence, the specification is viewed as an abstract design.

Criteria for refinement ensure that each concrete design implements the abstract one which spawned it. Such criteria leave input and output unchanged but show how the system state is refined. Examples of refinement criteria are: upwards and downwards simulation (see [5]). Since the latter suffices for present purposes let us summarise it here (in the context of predicate transformers it is in fact complete (see [16]) so only downwards simulation need be considered).

Firstly, an operation (perhaps nondeterministic) is defined by the predicate that describes how it relates the system state in which it starts, input, output and the state in which it leaves the system. In this paper we write a predicate as a boolean-valued function (to enable functional replacement to be used for substitution of variables). Thus we write

$$Op(s, in?, out!, s')$$

for the operation that starts in state s, accepts input $in?$, delivers output $out!$ and terminates in state s'. Its precondition is the predicate that is true of those s and $in?$ for which termination is possible; it is defined:

$$preOp(s, in?) \; \widehat{=} \; \exists \, out!, s' \bullet Op(s, in?, out!, s').$$

Secondly, a data type (for simplicity we ignore initialisation and finalisation) is a pair $(States, Operations)$ consisting of states, and operations on those states. We consider here data types with only a single operation; otherwise what we say must be repeated with each operation.

Finally a data type $C := (CS, \{Cop\})$ is said to be a *downwards simulation* of a data type $A = (AS, \{Aop\})$ if there is a relation

$$R \subseteq AS \times CS$$

satisfying the following conditions for *weakening the precondition* and *strengthening the postcondition* respectively:

$$aRc \land preAop(a, in?) \rightarrow preCop(c, in?)$$

$$aRc \land preAop(a, in?) \land Cop(c, in?, out!, c') \rightarrow$$
$$\exists\, a' : AS \bullet Aop(a, in?, out!, a') \land a'Rc'.$$

Downcode to executable language. The overall development is designed to that the final step results in efficient, executable code. If the language is chosen appropriately the last step consists of manual 'downcoding'; for example from Dijkstra's language of guarded commands to modula 2 (see [17]).

2.2 Development of Concurrent Systems

Seen in the light of the previous section, the approach to development of concurrent systems is analogous to that for sequential systems.

Requirements. A requirements document is compiled much as before. Because of the bewildering wealth of structure confronting the person describing the system, it is often stressed that interactions across natural boundaries be described (see [7]).

Specification. A (formal) specification is constructed much as before. Now the system is viewed as a process (or agent) and the notation used (for example CSP, [4] or CCS, [15]) must be able to express concurrency (typically synchronous) as well as the features mentioned in section 2.1.

The level of abstraction of the description is captured in the set of events—called the alphabet—in which the modelling process may engage. The events which process P can perform on its first interaction with its environment are called the initials of P and written $inits(P)$. The sequences of events that P can perform are called its traces and written $traces(P)$. A process may be described using a combination of process algebra and semantics. In the former a process is constructed by combining its events algebraically; in the latter its traces and degrees of nondeterminism are described.

Series of refinements. A sequence of design decisions is made much as before. A refining design now shows how to factor its more abstract description into communicating components. However the standard definition of process refinement (see [4]) requires the processes to have the same alphabets: process Q *refines* process P, written $P \sqsubseteq Q$, iff they have identical alphabets: $\alpha P = \alpha Q$; and if Q is at least as deterministic as P.

Yet during a step in system development the more concrete process has lower level of abstraction—and hence more events—than the more abstract one. In simple cases the alphabet of the concrete process Q is a superset of that of the abstract one, P. Then Q is a valid development from P if

$$P \sqsubseteq Q \text{ hide } (\alpha Q \setminus \alpha P).$$

However in general there is some process renaming, f, such that P is refined by a relabelled version of Q with its new events concealed:

$$P \sqsubseteq (f^{-1}Q) \text{ hide } (\alpha(f^{-1}Q) \setminus \alpha P).$$

That is our touchstone for saying that Q is a valid development of P (with respect to f). When f is the identity the previous special case of refinement is regained.

More workable criteria, sufficient for refinement of processes, can be obtained from those for data types by viewing a process as a data type. Consider first the case of processes having equal alphabets.

The states of the data type are the states of the process as it evolves; and the operations of the data type are the events of the process, including one for internal transition. The set of states of a process P thus consists of all processes at least as deterministic as an evolution, P after t, of P after it has engaged in trace a t:

$$states(P) \triangleq \{p \mid \exists t \in traces(P) \bullet p \sqsupseteq (P \text{ after } t)\}.$$

(Aside: In automata theory, states can be identified with equivalence classes of traces. In CSP that simple result needs extension to incorporate the extra semantic components.)

A process (or state) is *stable* if it is deterministic on its initials; otherwise it is *unstable*. Progress from a state is made by either the single internal operation *int*, or by one of the external, event-indexed operations. In this paper we consider only processes with external operations. The external, event-indexed, operation *eop* is defined, for $e \in \alpha(P)$:

$$eop(p, e, p') \triangleq e \in inits(p) \land p' \sqsupseteq (p \text{ after } \langle e \rangle).$$

State p can be either stable or unstable. Because we consider only stable states the refinement rules can be simplified.

Now *downwards simulation* from P to Q translates (cf [3]) (again for simplicity we ignore initialisation and finalisation): there is a relation between the (stable) states of P and Q

$$R \subseteq states(P) \times states(Q)$$

that satisfies:

$$aRc \land e \in inits(a) \land \rightarrow e \in inits(c)$$

$$aRc \land e \in inits(a) \land c' \sqsupseteq (c \text{ after } \langle e \rangle) \rightarrow$$
$$\exists a' : states(Q) \bullet a' \sqsupseteq (a \text{ after } \langle e \rangle) \land a'Rc'.$$

From the first condition we see that, an external choice offered in a (stable) state must again be offered in any refinement.

That criterion preserves the alphabets of the two processes, but leads to the following one which is only slightly more complicated but permits the refining process to have alphabet at a lower level of abstraction.

Suppose that P and Q are processes with $\alpha P \subseteq \alpha Q$. A *downwards event simulation* from P to Q (cf [18]) is a relation

$$R \subseteq states(P) \times states(Q)$$

that satisfies (again ignoring initialisation and finalisation):

$$\forall e : \alpha Q \setminus \alpha P \bullet aRc \wedge c' \sqsupseteq (c \text{ after } \langle e \rangle) \rightarrow aRc'$$

$$\forall e : \alpha P \bullet aRc \wedge \wedge e \in \text{inits}(a) \rightarrow$$
$$\exists b : (\alpha Q \setminus \alpha P)^* \bullet e \in \text{inits}(c \text{ after } b)$$

$$\forall e : \alpha Q \bullet aRc \wedge e \in \text{inits}(a) \wedge c' \sqsupseteq (c \text{ after } \langle e \rangle) \rightarrow$$
$$\exists a' : \text{states}(Q) \bullet a' \sqsupseteq (a \text{ after } \langle e \rangle) \wedge a'Rc'.$$

When $\alpha Q = \alpha P$ the granularity of the two processes coincides and that definition reduces to the one in section 2.1, but translated to processes (see [3] and [10]).

For example, according to the previous criterion (and a relabelling), the process P which performs a then b then terminates

$$\alpha P = \{a, b\}$$
$$P = a \rightarrow b \rightarrow Skip$$

is refined by the process Q in which a is split into $a1$ followed by $a2$, but in which $a2$ and b can occur simultaneously

$$\alpha Q = \{a1, a2, b\}$$
$$Q = a1 \rightarrow (a2 \rightarrow b \rightarrow Skip$$
$$\mid b \rightarrow a2 \rightarrow Skip).$$

A relation R establishing downwards event simulation is:

P	R	Q
$(P \text{ after } \langle a \rangle)$	R	$(Q \text{ after } \langle a1 \rangle)$
$(P \text{ after } \langle a \rangle)$	R	$(Q \text{ after } \langle a1, a2 \rangle)$
$(P \text{ after } \langle a, b \rangle)$	R	$(Q \text{ after } \langle a1, b \rangle)$
$(P \text{ after } \langle a, b \rangle)$	R	$(Q \text{ after } \langle a1, b, a2 \rangle)$
$(P \text{ after } \langle a, b \rangle)$	R	$(Q \text{ after } \langle a1, a2, b \rangle).$

In fact:

$$P = Q[a/a1] \text{ hide } \{a2\},$$

where $Q[a/a1]$ denotes the relabelled process that results from the substitution of a for $a1$ in process Q.

It is unfortunate that, because CSP captures simultaneity of events by interleaving, the CSP syntax for process Q conceals the simple nature of that particular event refinement. It is more evident if we employ nonstandard, but occam-like, syntax:

$$P = a \rightarrow b \rightarrow Skip$$

$$Q = a1 \rightarrow (a2 \| b) \rightarrow Skip.$$

There,

$$(e \| f) \rightarrow \cdots$$

stands for

$$(e \rightarrow f \rightarrow Skip$$
$$| f \rightarrow e \rightarrow Skip)\,; \ \ldots$$

or, equivalently,

$$((e \rightarrow Skip)\|(f \rightarrow Skip))\,; \ \ldots \ .$$

Further useful and typical refinement criteria appear in [8], [3], [18] and [1]. Again either development or calculation is possible.

Downcode to executable language. Again the final development step results in downcoding to efficient, executable code; for example from CSP to occam 2.

3 Foreground: Generic Steps in Hardware Development

The levels of abstraction through which development passes depend on the system being designed and on the technology avaliable for its target implementation. In this section we briefly review some of the levels encountered when the system is to be implemented in hardware. The hierarchy is far from complete; here we concentrate on the more abstract reaches (that is perhaps justified because the lower ones are amenable to silicon compilation (see [13])). Thus development is curtailed above the layout level. Some further details appear in [19].

3.1 Device Complexity

The traditional bottom-up view of hardware construction identifies the following strata of device complexity.

1. Atomic Devices: power; ground; n and p-type transistor; capacitor; clock.

2. Gates: inverter; transmission gate; nand; and; exor; etc.

3. Combinational Devices: multiplexor; decoder; logic array; shifter; adder; etc.

4. Sequential Devices: static and dynamic latches; register; memory array; etc.

5. Register Transfer Design.

6. Microprocessor, systolic array, pipeline, and other dedicated architectures.

3.2 Models

Our choice of levels of abstraction supports that hierarchy. But we find it convenient to expand the lower levels by considering: 2-valued devices; driven devices; discretely-timed devices; then continuously-timed devices.

Let us indicate those levels by following the description of an n-type transistor through several of them. First some more notation.

Common to all our levels is the decision to use *classical* logic. That results in the choice to model observables as having boolean values. Thus the type of *booleans* is defined to have values 0 (low, or zero) and 1 (high, or one)

$$\mathbf{B} ::= 0\ |\ 1$$

and to include all logical and arithmetic operations (modulo two).

Two-valued model [2]. An n-type transistor is modelled by a predicate with three free boolean variables, g, s and d, that represent the voltages observed at the gate, source and drain respectively when the transistor is in a stable state. The predicate reflects the fact that when the gate is high the source and drain equilibrate. Thus predicate $ntran(g, s, d)$ is defined:

$$g, s, d : \mathbf{B}$$
$$g \rightarrow (s = d).$$

More generally, in the two-valued model a circuit is represented by a predicate T whose free variables, like those of $ntran$, are the boolean values at observable places in the device (typically input and output). We say that one device, c, refines or implements another device, a, and we write $a \sqsubseteq c$, iff

$$T_c = T_a.$$

That simplistic, symmetric, definition is necessary in view of the fact that were the condition

$$T_c \rightarrow T_a$$

used instead, a short circuit (which is described by predicate false) would implement any device!

Driven model [6]. The 2-valued model fails to reflect the fact that an n-type transistor passes 0's well and 1's poorly (that is, with a threshold-voltage drop) between source and drain. We wish to express the fact that if the gate is driven high and either source or drain is driven low then so too is the other; but when the gate is high but not driven, source and drain merely equilibrate. Thus we wish to extend the two-valued predicate $ntran$ by conjoining with it a new predicate incorporating drive.

For each of the three variables $x : \mathbf{B}$ of $ntran$ we introduce a new variable $\delta x : \mathbf{B}$ which is interpreted to be high iff signal x is driven. The previous description is now extended to obtain a predicate having six free variables.

$$g, s, d, \delta g, \delta s, \delta d : \mathbf{B}$$
$$g \rightarrow (s = d)$$
$$(g \wedge \delta g \wedge \neg s \wedge \neg d) \rightarrow (\delta s = \delta d).$$

More generally in the driven model a circuit is represented by a predicate D whose free variables are either observable signals $x : \mathbf{B}$ or their driven component $\delta x : \mathbf{B}$ and which is the conjunction of a two-valued predicate T (involving only undriven variables) and a driven one Δ (involving both driven and undriven variables). In the driven model a circuit c refines a circuit a, again written $a \sqsubseteq c$, iff

$$(T_c = T_a) \wedge (\Delta_c \rightarrow \Delta_a).$$

Continuous-signal model [19]. The driven model is static—it expresses no time dependence. At the signal level each observable is defined to be a function from $\mathbf{R}$ to $\mathbf{B}$. The set of such functions, which are called signals, is thus defined:

$$\mathbf{S} \triangleq \mathbf{R} \rightarrow \mathbf{B}.$$

Time impinges on signals by the delay operation:

$$delay_\tau : S \to S$$
$$(delay_\tau s)(r) \triangleq s(r - \tau).$$

In an n-type transistor with transit time τ the previous, driven, relationship holds only after the gate has been high for time τ. Thus:

$$\tau : R$$
$$g, s, d, \delta g, \delta s, \delta d : S$$

$$g \to (delay_\tau s = delay_\tau d)$$
$$(g \wedge \delta g \wedge \neg s \wedge \neg d) \to (delay_\tau \delta s = delay_\tau \delta d).$$

More generally in the signal model a circuit is represented by a predicate S whose free variables include time delays together with the free variables of the driven description D but now changed to have type S rather than B. Now refinement is defined to hold pointwise between signals in such a way that no greater delay is incurred in the refinement.

Another combinational example—to be used later—is provided by a *transmission gate*. After its control c goes high there is a delay of time τ before its observables x and y equilibrate; if control is driven then x and y are equidriven—but only after time τ. Predicate $TG(\tau, c, x, y)$ (in which driven variables are implicit) is defined:

$$\tau : R$$
$$c, x, y, \delta c, \delta x, \delta y : S$$

$$delay_{-\tau} c \to (x = y)$$
$$delay_{-\tau}(\delta c \wedge c) \to (\delta x = \delta y).$$

A transmission gate can be implemented using an n-type transistor, a p-type transistor and an inverter. A p-type transistor is like an n-type transistor except that it switches when its gate is low rather than high:

$$ptran(\tau, g, s, d) \triangleq ntran(\tau, \neg g, s, d).$$

An inverter transfers its input's drive and the complement of its input's value to output after delay τ. Thus $inverter(\tau, in, out)$ is defined:

$$\tau : R$$
$$in, out, \delta in, \delta out : S$$

$$out = delay_\tau \neg in$$
$$\delta out = delay_\tau \delta in.$$

Correctness of a CMOS inverter using power (always driven high), ground (always driven low), an n-type transistor and a p-type transistor is embodied in:

$$inverter(\tau, x, y) \sqsubseteq \exists c, d : S \bullet \; power(c)$$
$$\wedge$$
$$ground(d)$$
$$\wedge$$
$$ptran(\tau, x, c, y)$$
$$\wedge$$
$$ntran(\tau, x, d, y)$$

Finally correctness of a transmission gate using those components is:

$$TG(\tau, c, x, y) \sqsubseteq \exists d : S \bullet \; ntran(\tau, c, x, y)$$
$$\wedge$$
$$ptran(\tau, d, x, y)$$
$$\wedge$$
$$inverter(\tau, c, d).$$

Discrete-signal model [19], [20]. With signals it is possible to describe and reason about general synchronous circuits. But most synchronous circuits, if correctly designed, do not warrant the use of a continuous variable. They are accurately described using discrete time. For example in a pipeline signals are latched when control goes high, and that is permitted to occur only after a delay sufficient to enable hazards and transients to subside.

Thus introduction of continuous signals is necessary in order to reason about hazads and transients and to design a clocking sheme; in short, to justify movement to the simpler discrete model. In that model a continuous signal $x : S$ is replaced by a member of the set of discrete signals:

$$S(Z) \; \hat{=} \; Z \to B.$$

The values of the discrete signal are given by the locally constant values of the continuous signal; if the continuous signal is not locally constant then movement from level S to level $S(Z)$ is not justified. Furthermore that movement is justified only when the environment of the device keeps signals constant when control is high, thus banishing all signal change to the times when control is low.

The simplest example is a clock. Modelled at level S, a clock which is high on the interval $[0,\frac{3}{4})$, low on the interval $[\frac{3}{4},1)$ and periodic with period 1 is defined:

$$clock : S$$
$$clock(r) = 1 \quad \text{iff} \quad \exists n : Z \bullet n \leq r < n + \tfrac{3}{4}.$$

At level $S(Z)$ if values are sampled when $clock$ is high, the clock itself is represented by the constant function 1 on Z.

Systolic arrays are conveniently described at this level; traces may be determined algebraically using CSP (see [20], [11]).

Finite-state model [19]. An even-more-drastic simplification is available for devices that have a finite number of internal states. For then a state variable can be used to describe the relationship between observables. For example a controlled T latch has a control input c, input and output bits in and out respectively, and a boolean state component whose value before interaction is written st and whose value after interaction is written st'; when control is low no change occurs in the state, which is available for output; and when control is high the transition predicate of a T latch holds:

$$c, in, out, st, st' : B$$
$$st' \; = \; out \; = \; [(st \bigtriangledown in) \triangleleft c \triangleright st].$$

There $\bigtriangledown$ denotes *exclusive or* and $a \triangleleft c \triangleright b$ denotes infix conditional (that is, *if c then a else b*). The notation Z (see [21]) is evidently well suited to such device descriptions. By way of comparison the description at level $S(Z)$ of that device is:

$c, in, out, st : S(Z)$
$st(n+1) = out(n+1) = [(st(n) \triangledown in(n)) \triangleleft c(n) \triangleright st(n)].$

The natural implementation language at this level is Register Transfer Language, RTL.

4 Example: A Stack Array

In this section the preceding ideas are applied to the stack array of Mead and Conway [14], section 3.7.

It is required to implement a stack in hardware. For convenience we suppose the stack to be unbounded (the bounded version is treated in [20]).

4.1 Specification

We start at the level of discrete time, by describing those sequences of interactions the stack may have with its environment. That is achieved by giving an algebraic description (see [4]) of the stack as a finite-state machine.

In CSP the stack is a process with alphabet

$\{push, pop, in?, out!\}.$

Here *in* and *out* are channels that convey values of type *Data* and *push* and *pop* are events which the stack is able to perform in synchrony with its environment.

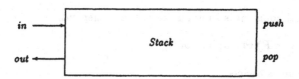

The stack is initially empty. At any time it can, at the direction of its environment, engage in *push*; in that case it accepts the value provided by the environment on channel *in* and appends it to the stack. Alternatively at any time when it is not empty the stack can, at the direction of its environment, engage in the event *pop*; in that case it outputs to channel *out* the value on top of the stack.

Writing angle braces for trace comprehension and colon for append, that requirement is expressed algebraically:

$$
\begin{aligned}
Stack &= S_{()} \\
&= push \to in?x \to S_{(x)},
\end{aligned}
$$

$$
\begin{aligned}
S_{x:l} = \ &push \to in?y \to S_{y:x:l} \\
&[] \\
&pop \to out!x \to S_{l}.
\end{aligned}
$$

4.2   Design Decision: Replication

Our first design decision is to achieve the specification by replicating a single cell. In order to interconnect copies of the cell we need to give its channels indexed names. Suppose cell C_i has alphabet

$$\alpha C_i = \{push, pop, in_i?, out_i!, in_{i+1}!, out_{i+1}?\}.$$

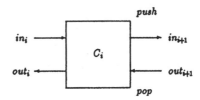

It is to perform *push* and *pop* events as follows. After a *push* cell C_i simultaneously outputs its contents to channel in_{i+1} and inputs the value y from channel in_i. After a *pop* it simultaneously outputs its contents to channel out_i and inputs a new value y from channel out_{i+1}. Initially, like the stack, each cell C_i can perform only a push and its input.

In CSP cell C_i is defined:

$$C_i = push \rightarrow in_i?x \rightarrow C_i(x)$$

$$C_i(x) = push \rightarrow (in_i?y\|in_{i+1}!x) \rightarrow C_i(y)$$
$$\square$$
$$pop \rightarrow (out_{i+1}?y\|out_i!x) \rightarrow C_i(y).$$

Validity of that first development is summarised in the refinement:

$$Stack \sqsubseteq (\|_i C_i \text{ hide } F)[in, out/in_0, out_0],$$

where the set F of events is defined:

$$F \triangleq \bigcup_i \alpha(C_i) \setminus \{in_0, out_0, push, pop\};$$

and where multiple substitution of events a for x and b for y is denoted

$$[a, b/x, y].$$

That refinement is messy to demonstrate from first principles; but it is exactly the type for which downwards simulation is useful. Indeed the process

$$push \rightarrow in_i?y \rightarrow Skip$$

is simulated by the process

$$push \rightarrow (in_i?y\|in_{i+1}!x) \rightarrow Skip,$$

as in section 2.2; that enables the downwards event simulation to be defined recursively.

4.3 Design Decision: Temporal Decoding

We must now decide how to implement the concurrent input and output in cell C_i. Both after a *push* and after a *pop* the cell's state, x, is output and its new state, y, input. To perform that in parallel requires a master-slave configuration with master x and slave y. To control movement of data between the master and slave we double the pair of events

$$push, pop$$

to obtain

$$push1, push2, pop1, pop2.$$

The resulting cell, D_i, is defined as follows.

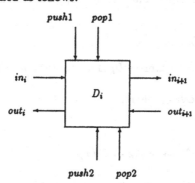

$$\alpha D_i = \{push1, push2, pop1, pop2, in_i?, in_{i+1}!, out_i!, out_{i+1}?\}$$

$$D_i = push1 \rightarrow in_i?x \rightarrow push2 \rightarrow D_i(x)$$

$$D_i(x) = push1 \rightarrow (in_i?y\|in_{i+1}!x) \rightarrow push2 \rightarrow D_i(y)$$
$$\square$$
$$pop1 \rightarrow pop2 \rightarrow (out_{i+1}?y\|out_i!x) \rightarrow D_i(y)$$
$$\square$$
$$pop1 \rightarrow push2 \rightarrow D_i(x).$$

Validity of that second development is summarised in the refinement:

$$C_i \sqsubseteq (D_i \text{ hide } G)[push, pop/push1, pop1]$$

where the set G of events is defined:

$$G \triangleq \{push2, pop2\}.$$

D_i is capable of offering a new event, *refresh*, to its environment to perform; it consists of *pop1* followed by *push2*. Its purpose will be to enable fast, dynamic memory to be used in the implementation of master and slave.

We call such downwards event simulations *temporal decodings*. The pairs of new events are to occur on the phases of a non-overlapping two-phase clocking scheme. Of course the scheme must be designed so that the signals are constant while the clock is high; but at the discrete level it satisfies:

$$Clock = (push \rightarrow push1 \rightarrow push2 \rightarrow Clock$$
$$| pop \rightarrow pop1 \rightarrow pop2 \rightarrow Clock$$
$$| refresh \rightarrow pop1 \rightarrow push2 \rightarrow Clock).$$

4.4 Design Decision: Basic Devices

Finally we head towards an implementation in which each D_i has two memory elements, master x_i and slave y_i.

The parallel pair

$$in_i?y \| in_{i+1}!x$$

results in

$$(y_i := x_{i-1}) \to (x_i := y_i).$$

(Such transformations are formalised and used in [11].) Expressed at the register-transfer level, for $i \geq 1$,

$$(y_i \longleftarrow x_{i-1}) \,; (x_i \longleftarrow y_i).$$

Similarly for *pop*. That leads us to express D_i in a form that matches the description of memory elements.

Thus cell D_i is refined by cell E_i where:

$$\alpha E_i \;=\; \alpha D_i$$

$$E_i \;=\; push1 \to in_i?x \to push2 \to E_i(x)$$

$$E_i(x) \;=\; \mu X \bullet \; (push1 \to (in_i?y \| in_{i+1}!x) \to push2 \to (x := y) \to X$$
$$\mathbb{0}$$
$$pop1 \to (y := x) \to pop2 \to (out_{i+1}?y \| out_i!x) \to X$$
$$\mathbb{0}$$
$$pop1 \to (y := x) \to push2 \to (x := y) \to X).$$

An implementation of E_i in terms of four transmission gates and two dynamic latches (y on the left and x on the right) is:

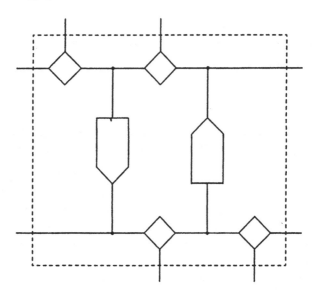

Discrete events are protracted using the continuous-signal model and then the cell is verified in terms of basic gates and the clocking scheme involving *push*1, *push*2, *pop*1 and *pop*2. Correctness is thus subject to the event relabelling:

$$push \rightsquigarrow push1 \rightarrow push2$$

$$pop \rightsquigarrow pop1 \rightarrow pop2.$$

References

[1] G. Barrett, *The Semantics and Implementation of* occam, draft book, 1990.

[2] M. J. C. Gordon, *HOL: A Proof Generating System for Higher Order Logic*, in G. Birtwistle and P. A. Subrahmanyam (eds.) *VLSI Specification, Verification and Synthesis*, Kluwer, 1987.

[3] He, Jifeng *Process Refinement*, Preprint, Oxford University, January 1987, 24 pages.

[4] C. A. R. Hoare, *Communicating Sequential Processes*, Prentice-Hall International, 1985.

[5] C. A. R. Hoare, He, Jifeng and J. W. Sanders, *Prespecification in Data Refinement*, Information Processing Letters, 25, 71-76, 1987.

[6] C. A. R. Hoare, *A Calculus for the Derivation of CMOS Switching Circuits*, Preprint, Oxford University, 1988.

[7] M. A. Jackson, *System Development*, Prentice-Hall International, 1983.

[8] J. L. Jacob, *On Shared Systems*, DPhil Thesis, Oxford University, January 1988.

[9] C. B. Jones, *Systematic Software Development using VDM*, Prentice-Hall International, 1986.

[10] M. B. Josephs, *A State-Based Approach to Communicating Processes*, Preprint, Oxford University, 1988, 19 pages.

[11] C. Lengauer and J. W. Sanders, *The Projection of Systolic Programs*, SLNCS, 375, 307-324.

[12] W. Luk, *Parametrised Design of Regular Processor Arrays*, DPhil Thesis, Oxford University, October 1988.

[13] D. May and C. Keane, *Compiling* occam *into Silicon*, Chapter 4 in *Communicating Process Architecture*, inmos, Prentice-Hall, 1988.

[14] C. Mead and L. Conway, *Introduction to VLSI Systems*, Addison Wesley, 1980.

[15] A. J. R. G. Milner, *Communication and Concurrency*, Prentice-Hall International, 1989.

[16] C. C. Morgan and P. H. B. Gardiner, *A single complete rule for data refinement*, Internal preprint, Oxford University, November, 1989.

[17] C. C. Morgan, *Programming from Specifications*, Prentice-Hall International, 1990.

[18] Xu Qiwen, *Towards a General CSP Process Refinement Theory*, Transfer of Status Dissertation, Oxford University, September 1988, 36 pages.

[19] J. W. Sanders, *Lectures on the Foundations of Hardware Design*, Oxford University, 1989-90, 175 pages.

[20] J. W. Sanders, *Lectures on VLSI Design*, Oxford University, 1989, 211 pages.

[21] J. M. Spivey, *The Z Reference Manual*, Prentice-Hall International, 1988.

Transformational Derivation of Systolic Arrays

Norihiko Yoshida

Department of Computer Science and Communication Engineering
Kyushu University
Hakozaki, Fukuoka 812, JAPAN

Abstract

We propose a novel approach to derivation of systolic arrays from their specifications. This approach is based on a program transformation technique. The specifications are described in recurrence equations. A certain sub-class of systolic array architectures can be derived following this approach.

In order to apply program transformation to systolic array derivation, we first introduce a subset of concurrent logic language to represent a systolic array architecture as well as a recurrence equation in a uniform program. This subset is named *relational representation*. We then introduce some transformation rules, tactics and a strategy for the derivation.

Given a recurrence equation for a specification, we first translate it to a program in relational representation, and then transform this program into a semantically-equivalent *systolic* program using the rules, tactics and a strategy. We have succeeded in deriving several kind of systolic arrays such as convolution filters and matrix multipliers.

1. Introduction

The advance in VLSI technology has made so-called hardware algorithms realistic, which are algorithms implemented in hardware instead of software to get much higher performance [1]. Most of hardware algorithms are now not designed systematically, but are just invented. A formal design method for hardware algorithms is desired so as to make them practically available, since they are based on the cellular automaton model unlike conventional software-implemented algorithms, and correction of their design errors after fabrication is impossible.

One of the most promising among formal design methods for software-implemented algorithms is program transformation [2]. This is, in its essence, a technique to rewrite one program into another semantically-equivalent one, and a program implementation is derived from its respective abstract specification in a semantics-preserving manner.

Our research aims at developing a systematic technique for aiding hardware algorithm design. Here we choose a major class of hardware algorithms, systolic arrays, in particular, and propose a novel approach to their formal derivation [3, 4]. It is based on a program transformation technique.

A certain sub-class of systolic arrays can be derived in the following manner. Given a recurrence equation for a specification, we first translate it to a program, and transform this program into a semantically-equivalent *systolic* program using some transformation rules, tactics and a strategy.

In order to represent a systolic array architectures as well as a recurrence equations in a uniform program, we also introduce a subset of concurrent logic language [5], which is named *relational representation*.

In the rest, Chapter 2 reviews systolic arrays, and specifies a sub-class of them for the derivation target. Chapter 3 introduces relational representation. Chapter 4 describes transformation rules for relational programs, and provides some transformation tactics and a strategy for the systolic array derivation. Chapter 5 shows an example of the derivation. Chapter 6 contains some discussions and concluding remarks.

2. Systolic Arrays

Systolic arrays are a major class of hardware algorithms. There are two reasons for choosing them to apply our technique to. One is that specifications for most systolic arrays can be represented in recurrence equations ; the other is that some systolic array computer systems have been released commercially, in particular for signal processing [6].

There is, in fact, no strict definition of systolic arrays. They are processor arrays with the following features :

- a regular configuration ;
- local connections of processor cells by channels ;

- lock-step synchronization of the whole system ;
- deterministic operations of processor cells.

Some systematic techniques for systolic array design have been proposed so far [7, 8], but few are widely used.

We specify a certain sub-class of systolic arrays for the derivation target. It includes linear (one-dimensional) pipelines and SIMD's, N-dimensional orthogonal grids and trees, with their channels parallel or orthogonal ; it excludes, for example, hexagonal grids, arrays with counter channels or arrays with feedback

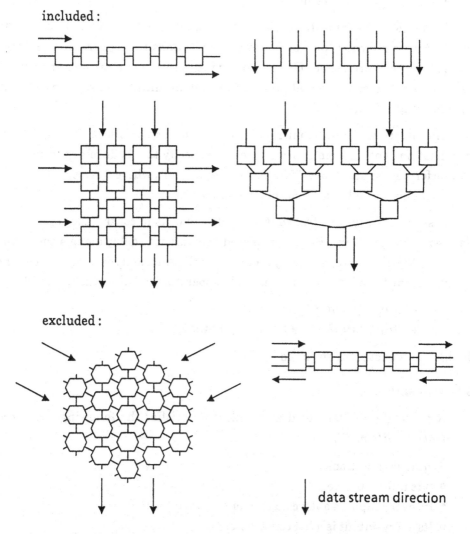

Fig.1. A Target Sub-Class of Systolic Arrays

channels. This is a basic sub-class of systolic arrays. Figure 1 shows it in a schematic manner.

3. Relational Representation

3.1 Basic Concepts

In order to represent inner-cell operations and cell configurations of a systolic array and a recurrence equation as well in a uniform program, we introduce relational representation. It is a subset of concurrent logic language with the following restrictions so as to have a necessary and sufficient describability :

- It specifies the input / output mode of arguments ;
- It allows no nondeterminacy.

In relational representation, like in concurrent logic languages, predicates have a uniform format, but have two interpretations : procedure interpretation and process interpretation. Under process interpretation, a tail-recursive predicate represents a cell (a perpetual process), and an infinite list represents a data stream along a channel.

The notation of relational representation basically follows Prolog. A sole modification is of an atomic formula so as to specify the mode of arguments. An atomic formula is denoted as "$P(I_1, ..., I_m ; O_1, ..., O_n)$", where P is a symbol, I_i's are input arguments and O_j's are output arguments.

A systolic array uses transmission delay in cells to control the flow rates of data streams. Delay in a cell is considered equivalent to delay along a succeeding channel. We, therefore, put delay along every channel, and represent the channel delay by a shift of a list. We introduce a list operator " + " to denote this shift :

$$+ \text{Strm} \equiv [\perp \,|\, \text{Strm}] ;$$
$$+ [\text{Strm1}, \text{Strm2}, ...] \equiv [+ \text{Strm1}, + \text{Strm2}, ...]$$

In this, "$\perp$" denotes the so-called bottom.

3.2 Translation

A predicate is interpreted as a cell, if it satisfies the following set of *cell-predicate conditions* :

Syntactic conditions :
- It is tail-recursive ;
- Its every input is a list constructor or a variable ;
- Its every output is a list constructor.

Semantic condition :

• It reads in the first elements of input lists, do some operations, and writes out the first elements of output lists ; and it passes the rest of the lists to itself which is recursively called.

For example, a cell cellP doing an operation opF with a stream StrmX along an input channel, StrmY along an output channel and an internal state transition State → NextState is represented as :

cellP(State, [X | StrmX] ; [Y | StrmY]) :-
    opF(State, X ; NextState, Y), cellP(NextState, StrmX ; StrmY).

A predicate with its body composed of cell-interpreted predicates is interpreted as a cell configuration, in which shared variables represent channels to connect cells. For example, a pipeline pipelinePQ of two cells cellP and cellQ connected by a channel StrmY with an input channel StrmX and an output channel StrmZ is represented as :

pipelinePQ(StrmX ; StrmZ) :-
    cellP(StrmX ; StrmY), cellQ(+ StrmY ; StrmZ).

A recurrence equation can be translated into a relational program in a straightforward manner, since both are of an inductive nature. A relational program can be translated into a systolic array architecture, if it satisfies the following set of *systolic conditions* (which are necessary but not sufficient yet) :

• It has a nested loop structure ;
• Clauses of each predicate never *overlap* ;
• It contains one or more cell predicates ;
• In its cell-configuration predicates, every internal variable appears twice, and an internal variable appeared in an input argument has more than zero "+" operators.

By executing a relational program for a systolic array architecture, we can simulate the behavior of the array.

4. Transformation of Relational Programs

4.1 Basic Principles

For transformation of logic programs, the *unfold / fold* transformation rules have been established [9]. They can be applied also to relational programs which have well-formed causality.

Transformation of a program is done by applying these rules to the given program in a stepwise manner. But these rules are so primitive and minute that structuring a rule sequence is required for practical applications. We introduce some transformation *tactics*, each of which is a combination of transformation rules corresponding to a specific situation. We also introduce a transformation *strategy*, which specifies combination of tactics for the systolic array derivation.

The transformation tactics for the systolic array derivation are of three kinds : ones for deriving cell configurations, ones for cascading channels and ones for introducing delay. We show them in the following sections using a notation of "initial program schema → final program schema."

4.2 Tactics for Deriving Cell Configurations

Configuration-deriving tactics are at the heart of the systolic array derivation. Their essence is in decomposing a cell into a configuration of smaller cells, which is achieved by mapping an inner-cell operation in the initial program to a cell configuration in the final program.

(1) Tactics for Deriving Pipelines

Figure 2(a) shows a tactic for deriving a pipeline of two cells. In the initial program, cellPP represents a cell, and opFF represents an inner-cell operation as a sequence of opF1 and opF2. In the final program, cellP1 and cellP2 represent cells respectively, and cellPP represents a cell configuration as a pipeline of them. The sequence of opF1 and opF2 is mapped to the pipeline of cellP1 and cellP2.

A tactic for deriving a pipeline of identical cells has the same framework. It is as follows :

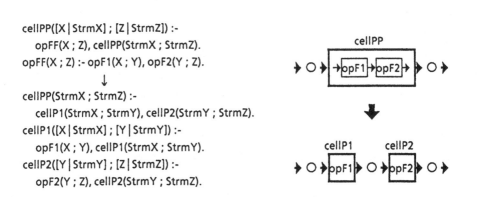

```
cellPP([X | StrmX] ; [Z | StrmZ]) :-
    opFF(X ; Z), cellPP(StrmX ; StrmZ).
opFF(X ; Z) :- opF1(X ; Y), opF2(Y ; Z).
                    ↓
cellPP(StrmX ; StrmZ) :-
    cellP1(StrmX ; StrmY), cellP2(StrmY ; StrmZ).
cellP1([X | StrmX] ; [Y | StrmY]) :-
    opF1(X ; Y), cellP1(StrmX ; StrmY).
cellP2([Y | StrmY] ; [Z | StrmZ]) :-
    opF2(Y ; Z), cellP2(StrmY ; StrmZ).
```

(a) Pipeline-Deriving Tactic

Fig.2. Tactics for Deriving Cell Configurations

cellPP([X | StrmX] ; [Z | StrmZ]) :- opFF(X ; Z), cellPP(StrmX ; StrmZ).
opFF(X ; Z) :- opF(X ; Y), opFF(Y ; Z).

↓

cellPP(StrmX ; StrmZ) :- cellP(StrmX ; StrmY), cellPP(StrmY ; StrmZ).
cellP([X | StrmX] ; [Y | StrmY]) :- opF(X ; Y), cellP(StrmX ; StrmY).

(2) Tactics for Deriving SIMD's

Figure 2(b) shows a tactic for deriving an SIMD of two cells, in which the predicate trans transposes a list of lists :

$$trans([[1, 2], [3, 4], [5, 6]] ; [[1, 3, 5], [2, 4, 6]])$$

A tactic for deriving an SIMD of identical cells has the same framework.

(3) Tactics for Deriving Orthogonal Grids

A tactic for deriving an orthogonal grid is a combination of a pipeline-deriving tactic and an SIMD-deriving tactic.

(4) Tactics for Deriving Trees

The base technique for deriving a tree of cells is called recursive doubling, which introduces a bi-linear recursion. Figure 2(c) shows this transformation, in which e is the identity of the operation opF, and the operator "[@]" is to divide a list into two :

$$[1, 2, 3, 4, 5, 6] = [[1, 2, 3] @ [4, 5, 6]]$$

cellPP([ListX | StrmListX] ; [ListZ | StrmListZ]) :-
    opFF(ListX ; ListZ), cellPP(StrmListX ; StrmListZ).
opFF([X1, X2] ; [Z1, Z2]) :- opF1(X1 ; Z1), opF2(X2 ; Z2).

↓

cellPP(StrmListX ; StrmListZ) :-
    trans(StrmListX ; ListStrmX),
    cellPP'(ListStrmX ; ListStrmZ),
    trans(ListStrmZ ; StrmListZ).
cellPP'([StrmX1, StrmX2] ; [StrmZ1, StrmZ2]) :-
    cellP1(StrmX1 ; StrmZ1), cellP2(StrmX2 ; StrmZ2).
cellP1([X | StrmX] ; [Z | StrmZ]) :-
    opF1(X ; Z), cellP1(StrmX ; StrmZ).
cellP2([X | StrmX] ; [Z | StrmZ]) :-
    opF2(X ; Z), cellP2(StrmX ; StrmZ).

(b) SIMD-Deriving Tactic
Fig.2. Tactics for Deriving Cell Configurations (cont'd)

This tactic is applicable only if opF is associative.

4.3 Tactics for Cascading Channels

The essence of channel-cascading tactics is in making every channel local, which is achieved by making every internal variable appear twice in cell-configuration predicates.

Figure 3(a) shows a tactic for cascading outflow channels, in which e is some value in the domain of opF. This tactic is applicable only if opF is associative (The predicate is named pseudocell, since its output is, in fact, not a stream.)

Figure 3(b) shows a tactic for cascading branch channels. It is quite straight-forward.

4.4 Tactics for Introducing Delay

A cell with the same amount of additional delay along every input and output channel is equivalent to the original cell. We hereafter make an assumption that we may remove delay (or the "+" operators) on the last output channels. Figure 4 shows a tactic for introducing delay to a cell pipeline, in which a "+" on the last output variable, StrmZ, is removed. This transformation is, in fact, not seman-tics-preserving, but we assume it to be correct.

```
opFF([] ; e).
opFF([X | ListX] ; Z) :-
    opFF(ListX ; Y),
    opG(X ; X'), opF(X', Y ; Z).
                ↓
opFF([X] ; Z) :- opG(X ; Z).
opFF([ListX1 @ ListX2] ; Z) :-
    opFF(ListX1 ; Y1), opFF(ListX2 ; Y2),
    opF(Y1, Y2 ; Z).
```

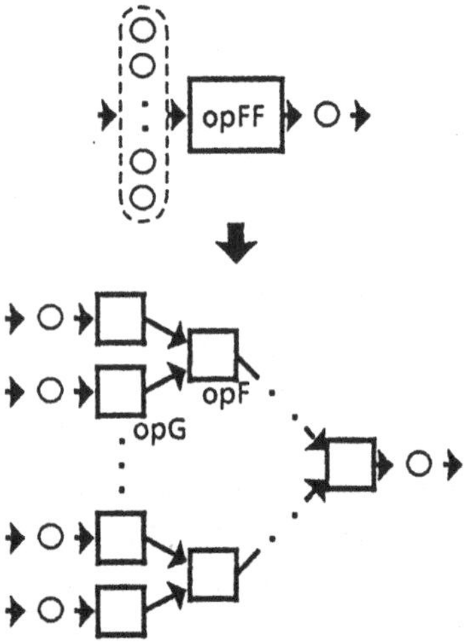

(c) Tree-Deriving Tactic.
Fig.2. Tactics for Deriving Cell Configurations (cont'd)

4.5 Transformation Strategy

In transformation for the systolic array derivation, the initial program represents a recurrence equation, while the final program represents a systolic array architecture. The former has a nested loop structure, and has clauses which never overlap ; while the latter has to satisfy the systolic conditions, and should have cell predicates as inner of the nest as possible.

A transformation strategy is to specify combination of tactics to achieve this transformation, which has the following procedure :

① Find the innermost cell predicate, p, in the initial program ; predicates outer than p are interpreted as cell configurations, while predicates inner than p are interpreted as inner-cell operations.

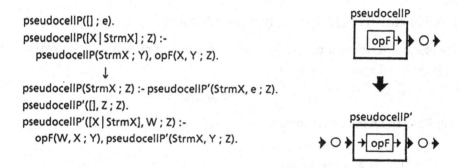

```
pseudocellP([] ; e).
pseudocellP([X | StrmX] ; Z) :-
    pseudocellP(StrmX ; Y), opF(X, Y ; Z).
                    ↓
pseudocellP(StrmX ; Z) :- pseudocellP'(StrmX, e ; Z).
pseudocellP'([], Z ; Z).
pseudocellP'([X | StrmX], W ; Z) :-
    opF(W, X ; Y), pseudocellP'(StrmX, Y ; Z).
```

(a) Outflow-to-Cascade Tactic

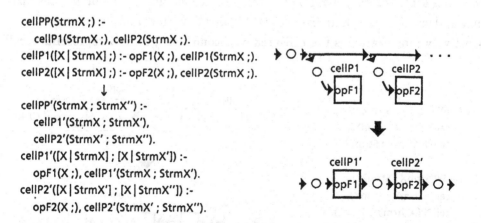

```
cellPP(StrmX ;) :-
    cellP1(StrmX ;), cellP2(StrmX ;).
cellP1([X | StrmX] ;) :- opF1(X ;), cellP1(StrmX ;).
cellP2([X | StrmX] ;) :- opF2(X ;), cellP2(StrmX ;).
                    ↓
cellPP'(StrmX ; StrmX'') :-
    cellP1'(StrmX ; StrmX'),
    cellP2'(StrmX' ; StrmX'').
cellP1'([X | StrmX] ; [X | StrmX']) :-
    opF1(X ;), cellP1'(StrmX ; StrmX').
cellP2'([X | StrmX'] ; [X | StrmX'']) :-
    opF2(X ;), cellP2'(StrmX' ; StrmX'').
```

(b) Branch-to-Cascade Tactic
Fig.3. Tactics for Cascading Channels

② Apply a configuration-deriving tactic to p. Before this, apply outflow-to-cascade tactics so as to make every predicate tail-recursive if needed ; and after this, apply branch-to-cascade tactics so as to make every channel local if needed.

③ By configuration-deriving tactics, a cell predicate is now not p but an inner one, so a cell represented by p is decomposed into a configuration of smaller cells. Then, do the same procedure recursively to a new cell predicate until a predicate as inner of the nest as possible becomes a cell predicate.

④ Last, apply delay-introducing tactics to every cell-configuration predicates so that every channel has delay.

There may be a case in which more than one configuration-deriving tactics can be applied to a single program, and some final programs are obtained respectively. In such case, we should choose one following some criterion.

5. Derivation Example of Systolic Arrays

We show a derivation process using an example of matrix multiplication. It is expressed in an abstract form as :

$$Z \equiv X \cdot Y \qquad \text{or} \qquad z_{ij} \equiv \Sigma x_{ik} y_{kj}$$

"Σ" is defined in an inductive form as :

$$\Sigma^0 a_k \equiv 0$$
$$\Sigma^{n+1} a_k \equiv a_{n+1} + \Sigma^n a_k$$

Figure 5(a) shows a relational program which computes matrix multiplication. In it, a matrix is represented by a column list of row lists. The predicates mxm, mxv and vxv compute "matrix · matrix", "matrix · vector" and "vector · vector" respectively ; mxv satisfies the cell-predicate conditions, so mxv represents a cell,

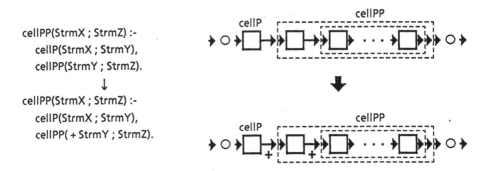

Fig.4. Tactics for Introducing Delay

while mxm represents a cell configuration, and vxv represents an inner-cell operation.

We transform this initial program to derive a corresponding matrix multiplier array :

mult(ListStrmX, ListListY ; ListStrmZ) :-   (a) Initial Program
   trans(ListStrmX ; StrmListX),
   mxm(StrmListX, ListListY ; ListStrmZ).
mxm(StrmListXin, [] ; []).
mxm(StrmListXin, [ListY | ListListY] ; [StrmZout | ListStrmZout]) :-
   mxv(StrmListXin, ListY ; StrmZout),
   mxm(StrmListXin, ListListY ; ListStrmZout).
mxv([], ListY ; []).
mxv([ListXin | StrmListXin], ListY ; [Zout | StrmZout]) :-
   vxv(ListXin, ListY ; Zout),
   mxv(StrmListXin, ListY ; StrmZout).
vxv([], [] ; 0).
vxv([Xin | ListXin], [Y | ListY] ; Zout) :-
   vxv(ListXin, ListY ; Zmid),
   f(Xin, Y, Zmid ; Zout).
f(Xin, Y, Zin ; Zout) :- Zout = Xin * Y + Zin.

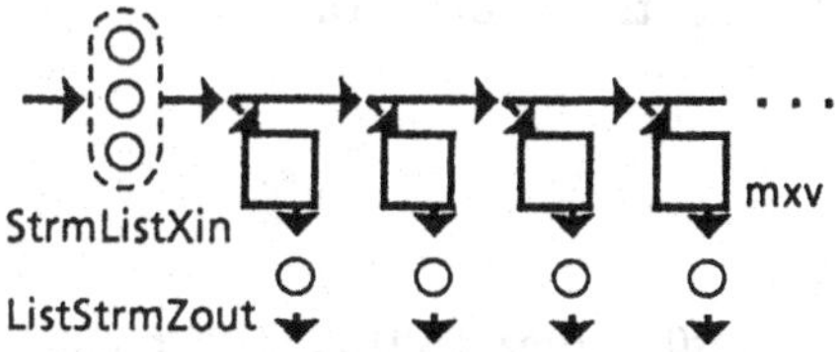

StrmListXin
ListStrmZout

mult(ListStrmX, ListListY ; ListStrmZ) :-   (b) Outflow Channels Cascaded
   trans(ListStrmX ; StrmListX),
   mxm(StrmListX, ListListY, [[0, 0, ···], ···] ; ListStrmZ).
mxm(StrmListXin, [], [] ; []).
mxm(StrmListXin, [ListY | ListListY], [StrmZin | ListStrmZin] ;
   [StrmZout | ListStrmZout]) :-
   mxv(StrmListXin, ListY, StrmZin ; StrmZout),
   mxm(StrmListXin, ListListY, ListStrmZin ; ListStrmZout).
mxv([], ListY, [] ; []).
mxv([ListXin | StrmListXin], ListY, [Zin | StrmZin] ;
   [Zout | StrmZout]) :-
   vxv(ListXin, ListY, Zin ; Zout),
   mxv(StrmListXin, ListY, StrmZin ; StrmZout).
vxv([], [], Zin ; Zin).
vxv([Xin | ListXin], [Y | ListY], Zin ; Zout) :-
   f(Xin, Y, Zin ; Zmid),
   vxv(ListXin, ListY, Zmid ; Zout).
f(Xin, Y, Zin ; Zout) :- Zout = Zin + Xin * Y.

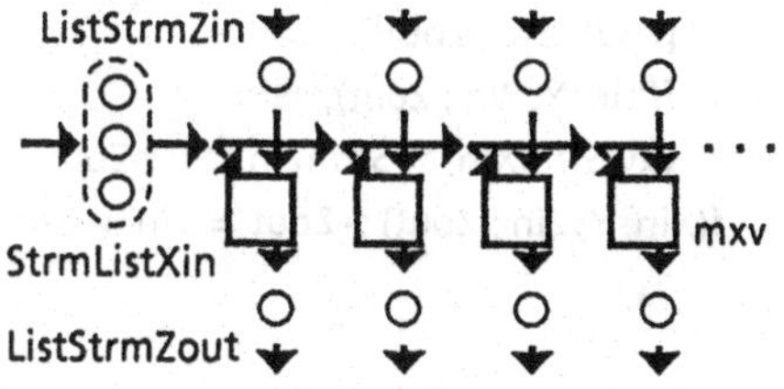

ListStrmZin
StrmListXin
ListStrmZout

Fig.5. A Derivation Process of a Matrix Multiplier Array

① Apply a channel-cascading tactic to StrmZ so as to transform vxv into a tail-recursive predicate. Figure 5(b) shows the result.

② Apply a pipeline-deriving tactic (an SIMD-deriving tactic at the same time) to mxv and vxv. Figure 5(c) shows the result.

③ The innermost predicate vxv satisfies cell-predicate conditions, so no more configuration-deriving tactics can be applied. Then apply a channel-cascading tactic to ListStrmX so as to transform it into a cascade channel. Figure 5(d) shows the result.

④ Apply delay-introducing tactics twice to mxm and mxv so as to make channels ListStrmX and ListStrmZ have one or more "+'s" (ListStrmXout and ListStrmZout are the last output channels, so "+'s" along them are removed.) Figure 5(e) shows the result.

Now we obtain a final program. In it, vxv satisfies the cell-predicate conditions, so vxv represents a cell, mxv represents a column of the cells, and mxm represents the whole array.

(c) Pipelines Derived

```
mult(ListStrmX, ListListY ; ListStrmZ) :-
    mxm(ListStrmX, ListListY, [[0, 0, ···], ···] ; ListStrmZ).
mxm(ListStrmXin, [], [] ; []).
mxm(ListStrmXin, [ListY | ListListY], [StrmZin | ListStrmZin] ;
    [StrmZout | ListStrmZout]) :-
    mxv(ListStrmXin, ListY, StrmZin ; StrmZout),
    mxm(ListStrmXin, ListListY, ListStrmZin ; ListStrmZout).
mxv([], [], StrmZin ; StrmZin).
mxv([StrmXin | ListStrmXin], [Y | ListY], StrmZin ; StrmZout) :-
    vxv(StrmXin, Y, StrmZin ; StrmZmid),
    mxv(ListStrmXin, ListY, StrmZmid ;
        StrmZout).
vxv([], Y, [] ; []).
vxv([Xin | StrmXin], Y, [Zin | StrmZin] ;
    [Zout | StrmZout]) :-
    f(Xin, Y, Zin ; Zout),
    vxv(StrmXin, Y, StrmZin ; StrmZout).
f(Xin, Y, Zin ; Zout) :- Zout = Zin + Xin * Y.
```

Fig.5. A Derivation Process of a Matrix Multiplier Array (cont'd)

6. Concluding Remarks

We proposed a novel approach, which is based on program transformation, to the derivation of systolic arrays from their specifications. We have succeeded in deriving several kind of arrays such as convolution filters and matrix multipliers. We are now building a system for aiding systolic array design based on this derivation technique.

Our derivation target excludes arrays with counter channels or arrays with feedback channels, which are some major class of systolic arrays. They contain loops of causality (mutual dependencies), so we need some refined transformation rules in order to manage them without any possibility of deadlock. Our target also excludes hexagonal grid arrays, since they do not fit orthogonal dimensions well. We may need some augmented representation form in order to manage

```
mult(ListStrmX, ListListY ; ListStrmZ) :-
    mxm(ListStrmX, ListListY, [[0, 0, ···], ···] ; __ , ListStrmZ).
mxm(ListStrmXin, [], [] ; ListStrmXin, []).
mxm(ListStrmXin, [ListY | ListListY], [StrmZin | ListStrmZin] ;
    ListStrmXout, [StrmZout | ListStrmZout]) :-
    mxv(ListStrmXin, ListY, StrmZin ; ListStrmXmid, StrmZout),
    mxm(ListStrmXmid, ListListY, ListStrmZin ; ListStrmXout, ListStrmZout).
mxv([], [], StrmZin ; [], StrmZin).
mxv([StrmXin | ListStrmXin], [Y | ListY], StrmZin ;
    [StrmXout | ListStrmXout], StrmZout) :-
    vxv(StrmXin, Y, StrmZin ; StrmXout, StrmZmid),
    mxv(ListStrmXin, ListY, StrmZmid ; ListStrmXout, StrmZout).
vxv([], Y, [] ; [], []).
vxv([Xin | StrmXin], Y, [Zin | StrmZin] ; [Xin | StrmXout], [Zout | StrmZout]) :-
    f(Xin, Y, Zin ; Zout), vxv(StrmXin, Y, StrmZin ; StrmXout, StrmZout).
f(Xin, Y, Zin ; Zout) :-
    Zout = Zin + Xin * Y.
```

(d) Branch Channels Cascaded

Fig.5. A Derivation Process of a Matrix Multiplier Array (cont'd)

them. We need a strict formalism (both syntactic and semantic) in order to specify definitely which recurrence equations can be transformed into systolic arrays, and which systolic arrays can be transformed from recurrence equations.

We are now just at the starting point. Some kind of heuristics are still required in applying this derivation technique. A strict formalism has to be introduced to specify recurrence equations and systolic arrays. We will expand the target sub-class of systolic arrays by providing more tactics and a more general strategy.

```
mult(ListStrmX, ListListY ; ListStrmZ) :-
    mxm(ListStrmX, ListListY, [[0, 0, ···], ···] ; _, ListStrmZ).
mxm(ListStrmXin, [], [] ; ListStrmXin, []).
mxm(ListStrmXin, [ListY | ListListY], [StrmZin | ListStrmZin] ;
    ListStrmXout, [StrmZout | ListStrmZout]) :-
    mxv(ListStrmXin, ListY, StrmZin ; ListStrmXmid, StrmZout),
    mxm( + ListStrmXmid, ListListY, + ListStrmZin ; ListStrmXout, ListStrmZout).
mxv([], [], StrmZin ; [], StrmZin).
mxv([StrmXin | ListStrmXin], [Y | ListY], StrmZin ;
    [StrmXout | ListStrmXout], StrmZout) :-
    vxv(StrmXin, Y, StrmZin ; StrmXout, StrmZmid),
    mxv( + ListStrmXin, ListY, + StrmZmid ; + ListStrmXout, StrmZout).
vxv([], Y, [] ; [], []).
vxv([Xin | StrmXin], Y, [Zin | StrmZin] ; [Xin | StrmXout], [Zout | StrmZout]) :-
    f(Xin, Y, Zin ; Zout),
    vxv(StrmXin, Y, StrmZin ; StrmXout, StrmZout).
f(Xin, Y, Zin ; Zout) :-
    Zout = Zin + Xin * Y.
```

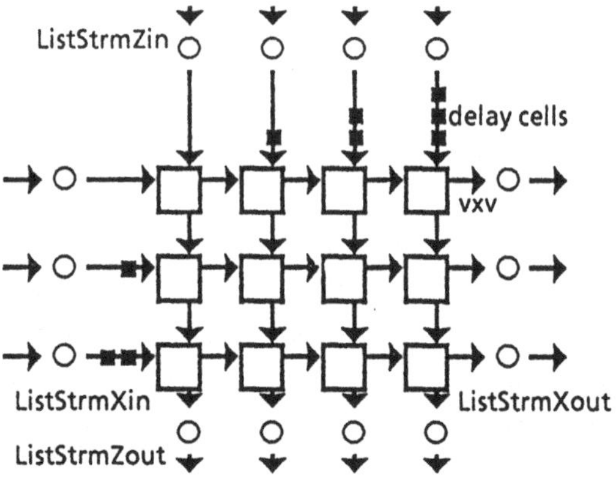

(e) Delay Introduced
↓
Final Program

Fig.5. A Derivation Process of a Matrix Multiplier Array (cont'd)

Acknowledgments

The author would like to thank Professor Kazuo Ushijima and Professor Shinji Tomita of Kyushu University for their valuable support and encouragement.

References

[1]   C. Mead and L. Conway. *Introduction to VLSI Systems*. Addison-Wesley (1980).

[2]   J. Darlington. Program Transformation. in *Functional Programming and Its Application* (J. Darlington et al. eds.), Cambridge Univ. Press (1982).

[3]   N. Yoshida. A Transformational Approach to the Derivation of Hardware Algorithms from Recurrence Equations. in *Proceedings of Supercomputing '88* (1988), 433-440.

[4]   N. Yoshida. Program Transformation Applied to the Derivation of Systolic Arrays. in *Proceedings of the International Conference on Fifth Generation Computer Systems* (1988), Vol.2, 565-572.

[5]   E. Y. Shapiro ed. *Concurrent Prolog*. MIT Press (1988).

[6]   J. A. B. Fortes and B. W. Wah eds. Special Issue on Systolic Arrays. *IEEE Computer* 20,7 (1987).

[7]   D. I. Moldovan. On the Design of Algorithms for VLSI Systolic Arrays. *Proceedings of IEEE* 71,1 (1983), 113-120.

[8]   M. S. Lam and J. Mostow. A Transformational Model of VLSI Systolic Design. *IEEE Computer* 18,2 (1985), 42-52.

[9]   H. Tamaki and T. Sato. Unfold / Fold Transformation of Logic Programs. in *Proceedings of 2nd Logic Programming Conference* (1984), 127-138.

Locally Computable Coding for Unary Operations

Hiroto Yasuura

Department of Electronics
Kyoto University
Kyoto 606, Japan
Email yasuura%kuee.kyoto-u.ac.jp@jpnkyoto.bitnet

Abstract

Coding plays an important role in the design of parallel algorithms. When each digit of a result of a desired operation depends only on a part of digits of operands under a coding scheme, we say the operation is locally computable under the coding scheme. There is a closed relation between local computability and redundancy of codes. Several excellent algorithms utilizing local computability by redundant coding schemes are developed and used practically. The problem to examine the relation among coding schemes, local computability and algebraic structures of target operations is a basic problem on the design of parallel algorithms. In this paper, we discuss a relation between redundancy of coding schemes and local computability of unary operations defined on finite sets. We show that it is generally impossible to realize local computability by nonredundant coding schemes. If we introduce redundancy into coding, we can construct a coding under which every digit of a result depends only on 2 digits of an operand for any unary operations. These results are closely related with a state assignment problem of finite state machines. The above 2-locally computable coding derives a state assignment of a pipelined sequential circuit for an arbitrary sequential machine.

1 Introduction

In parallel algorithm design, it is important problem how to extract parallelism and compute partial computations independently each other. If we can design an algorithm in which each partial computation depends only on a local information, the partial computations should be simple and overhead of communication in the algorithm must be reduced. In other words, if we can construct a parallel algorithm by simple partial computation with local communication, we can reduce time and resources for communication and computation.

Based on the above idea, we proposed a concept of "local computability" and we showed that redundant coding schemes are useful for realizing local computability [YASUT87]. For a given finite set S and a given operation f defined on S, if there is a computation rule of f under a coding scheme C such that every digit of a result of f is computable from only l digits of operands of f, we say that f is l-locally computable under the coding scheme C. In [YASUT87], we showed that any binary operations of Abelian (commutative) groups are 28-locally computable under a binary coding. This result is a mathematical generalization of SD(Signed Digit)-representation [AVIZ61][SPAN81] or redundant binary coding [TAKAY85] which are used in efficient practical parallel algorithms. The key feature of a coding realizing local computability is redundancy in the above examples.

It is expected that there is a trade-off between redundancy of code and local computability. It is also an interesting problem in both practically and mathematically to show a relation between algebraic structure of operations and local computability. In this paper, we will examine the relation between redundancy of code and local computability for unary operations defined on a finite set.

This problem is closely related with a state assignment problem of sequential circuits, which is discussed so often in the area of logic synthesis. Namely, a definition of a sequential machine is just a definition of unary operations specified by input symbols defined on a set of states. A coding under which the unary operations are locally computable is corresponding a state assignment reducing circuit size and depth (speed of computation). In other words, a state assignment by a local computable coding derives a pipelining realization for a given sequential machine.

In this paper, we examine local computability under single coding schemes and multiple coding schemes. In multiple coding scheme, we can assign two or more code words for an element of a given set. It is shown that arbitrary set of unary operation can be 2-locally computable using a redundancy of multiple coding. This result induces that all sequential machines have pipelining realizations.

2 Definitions

2.1 Redundant Coding Scheme

Let S be a finite set and n be a number of elements in S. $\{OP_1, OP_2, ..., OP_m\}$ is a set of unary operations defined on S. Let Σ be a finite alphabet with a symbols. A coding C for S on Σ is defined as a surjection (onto-mapping) from a subset of Σ^k to S. Here, we only consider fixed-length codes. k is called the code length.

For $c \in \Sigma^k$, if $C(c) = s$ for $s \in S$, c is called a code word of s. A code word c can be represented a vector form such as $(x_1, x_2, ..., x_k)$ where $x_i \in \Sigma$ is called the i-th digit. If $C(c)$ is not defined for $c \in \Sigma^k$, c is called a non-code word. If $k = \lceil \log_a n \rceil$, we say that C is a minimum coding scheme. If each element s in S has only one code word, the coding scheme is called a single coding. If an element s has two or more code words, we call it a multiple coding scheme. We say that a single and minimum coding scheme is a nonredundant coding scheme and others are redundant ones. For simplicity, we discuss only a binary coding (i.e. $\Sigma = \{0, 1\}$) but the result of this paper can easily extend to the cases of $a > 2$.

2.2 Local Computability

For $f : \Sigma^k \to \Sigma^k$, we say that f realizes a unary operation OP under a coding scheme C, if $C(f(c)) = OP(C(c))$ for all code words c's. In this case, f can be expressed as

$$(z_1, z_2, ..., z_k) = f(x_1, x_2, ..., x_k) = (g_1(x_1, x_2, ..., x_k), ..., g_k(x_1, x_2, ..., x_k))$$

Namely, we can write

$$z_j = g_j(x_1, x_2, ..., x_k)$$

If each g_j $(j = 1, 2, ..., k)$ depends on at most l input variables, f is said to be l-local computable. A unary operation OP on S is said to be l-local computable under a coding scheme C, when there exists a l-local computable function f realizing OP.

[**Definition 1**] A set of unary operations $\{OP_1, OP_2, ..., OP_m\}$ is weakly l-locally computable under a coding scheme C, if each unary operation OP_i is l-locally computable.

[**Definition 2**] Suppose that a set of unary operations $\{OP_1, OP_2, ..., OP_m\}$ is weakly l-locally computable under a coding scheme C. For each f_i realizing OP_i, if z_j $(j = 1, 2, ..., k)$ depends on the same l inputs, we say that the set of unary operations is strongly l-locally computable under C.

2.3 State Assignment of Sequential Circuits

A sequential machine is defined by a set of states S and state transitions on the set. A definition of state transitions for m inputs is just the definition of m unary operations on S. For implementation of a sequential machine as a sequential circuit, we assign binary codes to states in S. Thus a state assignment corresponds to a definition of a coding scheme for unary operations.

We consider a sequential circuit with a single phase clock constructed of a combinational circuit and D-type flipflops. The combinational circuit consists of fanin restricted logic gates and lines connecting the gates. The size and clock cycle of the sequential circuit depends on the size and depth (or delay) of the combinational part which computes a next state function. Generally, the complexity of a combinational circuit depends on the number of input variables of a logic function realized by the circuit. It is known that for almost all n variable functions require $\Theta(2^n/n)$ logic gates and depth of $\Theta(n)$. Thus if we find a coding scheme under which the next state function is strongly locally computable, we can drastically reduce the size and depth of the combinational part.

Pipelining is known as an effective method for designing a high-performance system. Basic idea of pipelining is to divide a circuit into small subcircuits and decided the next state of each subcircuit only from small numbers of neighbor subcircuits. Namely, designing a pipeline circuit is just finding locally computable coding. If the next state function is locally computable under a coding scheme, the next value of each state variable can be computed by a small depth circuit and then the clock period can be minimized. Locally computable coding may derive a new design concept for high-speed sequential circuits that is a generalization of pipelining.

3   Nonredundant Coding Scheme

A nonredundant coding scheme is a single and minimum coding scheme and most popular in the practical use. According to the tight restrictions on coding, we can't achieve local computability by the nonredundant coding scheme.

[Theorem 1] There exists a set of unary operations such that l must equal to $k(=\lceil \log_2 n \rceil)$ on the weakly local computability under nonredundant coding schemes.
(Proof) Assume $n = 2^k$. Consider a set of operations as shown in Table 1. By an operation OP, s_0 is mapped to itself and other elements are mapped to s_1. Suppose that $l < k$. Without loss of generality, we assume that $(0, 0, ..., 0)$ is the code word of s_0. Let $(a_1, a_2, ..., a_k)$ be the code word of s_1 and $a_i = 1$. From the assumption, there is at least one digit x_j such that x_i does not depend on it. Consider a code such that only the j-th digit is one and others are all 0. The code is the code word of an element s. Since x_i does not depend on the x_j, the i-th digit of s_0, the image of s_0 of OP, must be equal to one of s_1, the image of s. It contradicts the assumption of $a_i = 1$. Q.E.D.

ele- ments	operations .. OP...	code word x_1 x_2 x_i x_j x_k				
s_0	s_0	0	0 ...0	...0	...0	
s_1	s_1	a_1	a_2...1	...a_j...	a_k	
s_2	s_1					
s_i	s_1	0	0 ...0	...1	...0	
s_{n-1}	s_1					

Table 1. Proof of Theorem 1

Since strongly local computability is stronger restriction than weakly local computability, the above result also stands up for strongly local computability. This result shows that there exists a unary operation such that at least one digit must depend on all digits of a operand under any nonredundant coding scheme. we can conclude that redundancy is essentially required to realize local computability. In the next section, we introduce redundancy into single coding schemes.

4 Single Coding Scheme

There is two kinds of redundancy of code. One is redundancy by introducing non-code words. The other is redundancy by multiple coding, i.e., each element has two or more code words. Using the former kind of approach, we can introduce redundancy into a single coding scheme. Single coding schemes with redundancy have been utilized practically as a one hot coding and so on. Here we examine a relation of single coding schemes and local computability.

First we discussed on the simplest case.

[Theorem 2] For a unary operation OP defined on S, we can construct a single coding scheme under which OP is 1-locally computable and the code length is n, where n is the number of element of S.

(Proof) For an element s of S, if $s = OP^p(s)$ for some p, s is called a cyclic element, where OP^p denotes p times applications of OP. An element which is not a cyclic element is called a transient element. Let $\{s_1, s_2, ..., s_r\}$ be a set of cyclic elements of S, and $\{s_{r+1}, ..., s_n\}$ be a set of transient elements. For elements of S, we define a binary relation as follows:

$$s_i \sim s_j \text{ iff } OP^n(s_i) = OP^n(s_j)$$

This relation $\sim$ is an equivalence relation on S, and S can be partitioned by the relation. We have r equivalent classes and each equivalence class includes a cyclic element. So we chose the cyclic element s_i as a representative element of each class S_i for $i = 1, 2, ..., r$. For transient elements, we can construct trees in which vertices are transient elements and there is an edge (s_i, s_j) iff $s_i = OP(s_j)$. The direction of edges is from leaves to roots. In each tree, we select a longest path from leaves to the root, and call the path a trunk. Transient elements in each tree can be partitioned into equivalent classes by the distance to the root. Since each class includes just one element t_i on the trunk, we chose the element t_i as a representative element of the class. We denote the class including t_i T_i. The elements which are not on trunks also constructs a collection of trees. Thus we chose trunks recursively and partitioned the elements into equivalent classes by the same manner. A code word $(x_1, x_2, ..., x_n)$ of an element s is defined as follows:

$$x_i = 1(i = 1, 2, ..., r) \text{ iff } s \in S_i$$

$$x_i = 1(i = r + 1, ..., n) \text{ iff } s \in T_i$$

In this coding, only one digit is 1 for a cyclic element and more than two digits are 1 for a transient element. For the i-th digit $x_i(i \leq r)$, there is one digit x_j $(j \leq r)$ such that x_i depends only on x_j. x_i $(r + 1 \leq i \leq n)$ also depends only on one of $\{x_{r+1}, ..., x_n\}$. Then OP is 1-locally computable under the coding scheme. Q.E.D.

We can obtain a similar result, when the number of operations increases.

[Theorem 3] For a finite set S with arbitrary numbers of operations, we can construct a single coding scheme with length $O(2^n)$ under which all operations are weakly 1-locally computable.

(Proof) Under a single coding scheme, each digit of a code corresponds to a two block partition of S. For every two block partition $\{S_1, S_2\}$ and a unary operation OP, there is a two block partition $\{S_3, S_4\}$, such that elements in S_3 and S_4 are mapped into S_1 and S_2 by OP respectively. We can construct a coding scheme containing all digits corresponding all two block partition on S. The code length is $2^{n-1} - 1$. In this coding, for any digit x_i there is a digit x_j such that $x_i = g(x_j)$. Practically, we can construct a coding scheme shorter than above construction for given set and operations. Q.E.D.

In Theorem 3, we show that redundancy by introducing non-code word derives 1-local computability in the weak sense. When we consider strongly local computability, we can't, however, achieve it by a single coding scheme.

[Theorem 4] For any finite set with m unary operations, we can construct a single coding scheme under which the operations are strongly $\min(m, \lceil \log_2 n \rceil)$-locally computable. On the other hand, there exists a finite set S with m operations such that $\min(m, \lceil \log_2 n \rceil)$ is the greatest lower bound of l for any single coding schemes.

(Proof) By the similar discussion of Theorem 3, we can construct a coding in which

$$z_i = g_i(x_1, x_2...., x_k) = OP_1 x_{i1}^* + OP_2 x_{i2}^*, + \cdot + OP_m x_{im}^*$$

where x^* means x or $\bar{x}$. When $m < \lceil \log_2 n \rceil$, we use the above coding and get m-locally computability. When $m \geq \lceil \log_2 n \rceil$, we use an arbitrary minimum coding scheme. The lower bound is proved as follows.

Case 1: Assume $m \geq \lceil \log_2 \rceil$ and $n = 2^p$ (p is a positive integer). Consider the following operations (See Table 2). Each element s_j ($j = 0, 1, ..., n-1$) is mapped to s_0 (s_1) by a operation OP_i ($i = 0, 1, ..., \lceil \log_2 \rceil - 1$), when the i-th bit of binary representation of j is 0 (1, respectively). There is at least one digit z of code such that the value of z for s_0 and s_1 is different. Since image of two different elements is different each other by some operation, z must depend on at least $\lceil \log_2 n \rceil$ digits required for distinguishing n elements.

Case 2: Assume $m < \lceil \log_2 n \rceil$ and $n = 2^p$. Consider the similar coding of case 1 and digit z as same as case 1. S is partitioned into 2^m subsets such that two elements in different subsets has different image by some operation. Namely, z must depend on at least m digits which requires for distinguishing 2^m subsets. Q.E.D.

Then it is generally impossible that l is a constant independent of n under single coding schemes in the sense of strongly local computability.

ele- ments	unary operations $OP_0 OP_1 OP_2 .. OP_{p-1} .. OP_m$	code word ... z ...
S_0	$S_0 \ S_0 \ S_0 ... S_0$	0
S_1	$S_1 \ S_0 \ S_0 ... S_0$	1
S_2	$S_0 \ S_1 \ S_0 ... S_0$	
S_3	$S_1 \ S_1 \ S_0 ... S_0$	
S_n	$S_1 \ S_1 \ S_1 ... S_1$	

Table 2. Proof of Theorem 4

5 Multiple Coding Scheme

In a multiple coding scheme, we can assign two or more code words to an element. The freedom of the coding increases drastically. Utilizing the freedom of the coding, we can achieve strongly 2-local computability for an arbitrary finite set with unary operations.

[**Theorem 5**] For a finite set of n elements with m unary operations defined on it, we can construct a multiple coding scheme with the length of $O((m+n)n\log_2 n)$ under which the operations are strongly 2-locally computable.

(Proof) For the coding, we use an idea of prefix computation [UNGE77] [LADNF80]. Here we consider a construction of a coding scheme for unary operations as a state assignment problem of a sequential circuit. For a given set S and unary operations, consider a sequential machine (S, I, δ) where S is a set of states, I is a set of input symbols and δ is a mapping $S \times I \to S$. Each element in I just corresponds to a unary operation and δ is defined as a collection of the operations. We assume that we use logic gates with one or two inputs and D-flipflop for the construction of a sequential circuit.

(1) For S, consider a set M of all mappings from S into S. A unary operation defined on S is a member of M. We consider a composition of operations as a binary operation between the unary operations. M becomes a monoid by the binary operation. Since the number of elements of M is n^n, we can construct a minimum coding for M with the length of $n \log_2 n$. We adopt a simple coding $(X_0, X_1, ..., X_{n-1})$, where X_i is the image of s_i by the unary operation and X_i is represented by a minimum coding of S.

(2) Construct a combinational circuit (called I-circuit) realizing the binary operation of M. From the definition of the binary operation, if an image of s_i is s_j in the first operand, then an image of s_i in the result is equal to an image of s_j in the second operand. So I-circuit can be implemented by n selectors as shown Fig.1. Each selector has depth $O(\log_2 n)$ and size $(O(n\log_2 n))$. Insert buffers to make all path from inputs to outputs of I-circuit have the same number of gates (Synchronization). By this synchronization, the order of depth and size do not change. Let D be a depth of I-circuit. For the sake of simplicity, we assume $D = 2^p$ for some positive integer p.

(3) Construct a combinational circuit (called Ip-circuit) which convert OP's to corre-

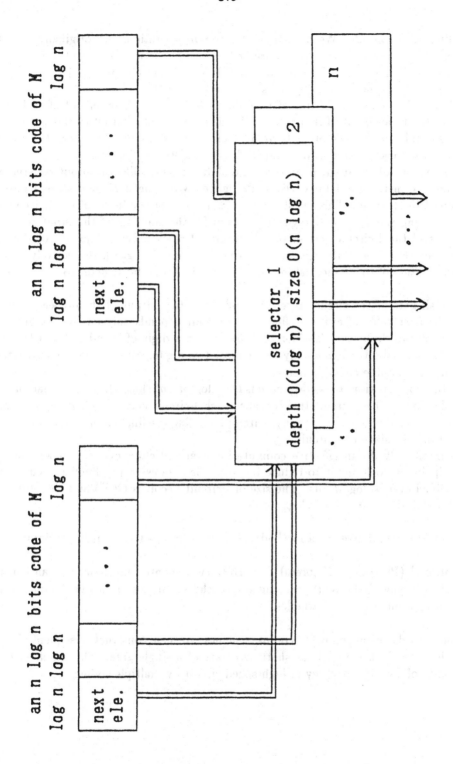

Fig.1 I-Circuit

sponding codes on M. We assume that given m operations are originally coded by $\lceil \log_2 m \rceil$ bits. Ip-circuit is also constructed by a selector whose control inputs are the binary code of operations. Size and depth of Ip-circuit are $O(mn \log_2 n)$ and $O(\log_2 m)$. Ip-circuit is also synchronized by the same manner in (2).

(4) Make a complete binary tree of I-circuit with D leaves. The output of each circuit is connected to an input of its parent node. The output of the root circuit is connected to the second input of the other I-circuit, called a final circuit. The output of the final circuit is fed back to the first input of itself (See Fig.2).

(5) The output of Ip-circuit is entered to a shift register, called an input register, with length D. Construct a 1 bit cyclic shift register with length D, and store 1 only one portion of the register. This register works as a clock for the input of the I-circuit tree. Namely, using the 1-bit shift register, we transfer the contents of the input register to all leaves of the I-circuit tree in parallel every D clock cycles. The size of the input register and the 1-bit shift register are $O(n \log_2 n)$ and $O(\log_2 n)$, respectively. For the implementation of the sequential machine, we need a $\log_2 n$ bit register to store an initial state.

(6) For all gate of the circuit, insert D-flipflops to the output of them (See Fig.2 (b)). Then the next value of every flipflop in the circuit depends only on the present values of at most two flipflops. Consider each flipflop as a digit of a code. From the above property, every digit depends only on at most two digits. So we have realized strongly 2-locally computable coding scheme.

(7) In this construction, the code length is $O(n^2 \log_2^2 n + mn \log_2 n)$. The first factor comes from the size of the I-circuit tree, because each I-circuit contains $O(n^2 \log_2 n)$ flipflops and the tree contains $D = O(\log_2 n)$ I-circuit including the final circuit. The second term comes from the size of Ip-circuit.

(8) I-circuit only do an effective computation every D clock cycles. So we can introduce pipelining to I-circuit to reduce its size. Fig.3 shows a pipelined I-circuit. Input is pipelined ever $n/\log_2 n$ bits. The size of I-circuit becomes $O(n^2)$ and then total code length reduced to $O((m+n)n \log_2 n)$. Q.E.D.

Proof of Theorem 5 gives us a method to construct a pipelined sequential circuit.

[Corollary] (Pipelining Theorem) For arbitrary sequential machine, we can construct a pipelined sequential circuit realizing the machine. In this circuit each state variable depends only on two state variables.

In other words, using multiple coding schemes, we can construct a sequential circuit such that the clock period is as short as delays of a single gate. This result suggest a possibility of a design strategy of high-speed circuit by multiple coding.

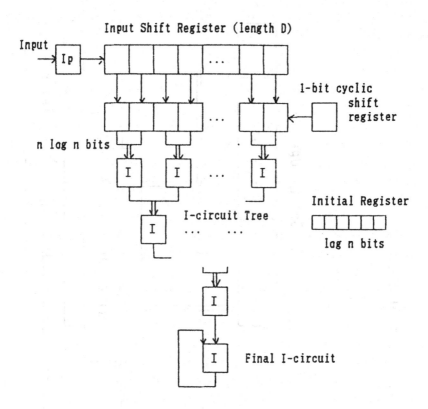

Input Shift Register (length D)

Input

Ip

1-bit cyclic
shift
register

n log n bits

I-circuit Tree

Initial Register

log n bits

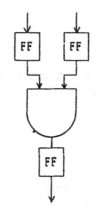

I

I   Final I-circuit

(a) Block Diagram

FF   FF

FF

(b) Gate and Flipflops in the circuit

Fig.2 Construction of a Sequential Circuit

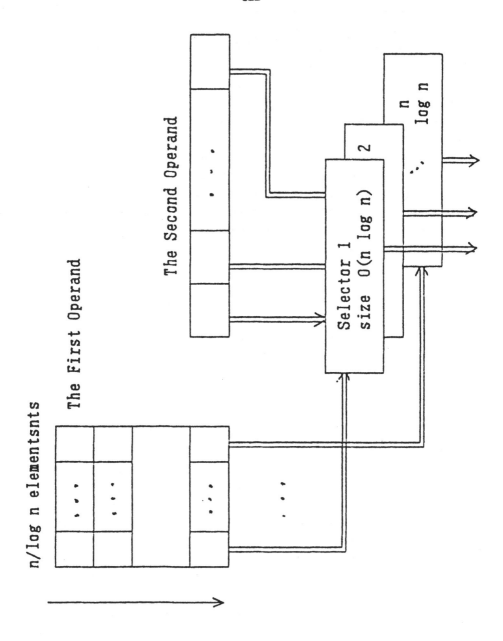

Fig.3 Pipelined I-Circuit

6   Conclusion

In this paper, we showed a relation between local computability and redundancy of codes for unary operations defined on finite sets. By nonredundant coding schemes, we cannot achieve local computability. Introducing redundancy to single coding schemes, we can realize weakly 1-local computability, but it is impossible to make a strongly locally computable coding. By multiple coding schemes, we can construct a coding under which any unary operations are strongly 2-local computable. This result can be directly apply to the design of high-speed sequential circuits.

The lower bounds of the code length to realizing local computability are still open. In [YASUT87], we discussed local computability of binary operations. There is a close relation between local computability of unary and binary operations.

References

[AVIZ61] Avizienis, A: Signed-Digit Number Representation for Fast Parallel Arithmetic, *IRE Trans. Elec. Comput. vol.EC-10, no.3, pp.389-400, Sept. 1961.*

[LADNF80] Ladner, R.E. and Fischer, M.J.: Parallel Prefix Computation, *J. of ACM, vol.27, no.4, pp.831-838, Oct.1980.*

[SPAN81] Spaniol, O.: Computer Arithmetic, *John Wiley Sons, p.194 1981.*

[TAKAY85] Takagi, N., Yasuura, H. and Yajima, S.: High-speed VLSI Multiplication Algorithm with a Redundant Binary Addition Tree, *IEEE Trans. on Comput. vol.C-34, no.9, pp.789-796, Sept. 1985.*

[UNGE77] Unger S.H.: Tree Realization of Iterative Circuits, *IEEE Trans. on Comput. vol.C-26, no.4, pp.365-383, April 1977.*

[YASUT87] Yasuura H., Takagi N. and Yajima, S.: Redundant Coding for Local Computation, *in Discrete Algorithms and Complexity, Proceedings of the Japan-U.S. Joint Seminar, Academic Press, pp.145-159, 1987.*

PART IV

Overview

of

UK/Japan Workshop, Oxford

September 25-27, 1989

Overview of the Workshop

The second UK/Japan Workshop in Computer Science was organized by R. M. Burstall, T. Ito, and A. Yonezawa under the support of SERC and JSPS. The topic of the workshop was focused on Cocnurrency, which has been one of the most active research areas in both countries. Dr. W. F. McColl was in charge of the local arrangements of the workshop and he arranged for the workshop participants to stay at Wadham College, one of the oldest colleges in Oxford. The workshop participants had a plenty of chances for informal discussions on computer science, one of the newest scientific areas, under Wadham's old academic atomosphre and English cultural tradition. All the Japanese participants were very much impressed with the old and academic atomosphere of Oxford. It is worth mentioning how they enjoyed the social events held at the Hall and the Old Library at Wadham College. They had wonderful times to talk with Wadham residences at breakfast, lunch, and dinner. Professor E. W. Mitchell (President of SERC and the college fellow of Wadham) kindly joined the worhshop banquet at the Hall of the college.

Programme

Sunday 24th September

19.30 Reception in Old Library

Monday 25th September

9.00 Workshop - Opening Remarks : R. M. Burstall, A. Yonezawa, W. F. McColl

9.10 Session 1 - Theory : Chaired by A. Yonezawa and R. M. Burstall

- *The Imperative Future and Concurrent Temporal Processes*
  D. Gabbay
- *Logic of Execution*
  T. Ito
- *Local Model Checking*
  C. P. Stirling
- *Semantics of a Hardware Design Language with Nondeterminism*
  H. Yasuura

14.15 Session 2 - Theory and Models : Chaired by T. Ito and D. Gabbay

- *Probabilistic Powerdomains*
  G. D. Plotkin
- *Reflection in an Object-Oriented Concurrent Language*
  A. Yonezawa

- *Algorithmic Challenges in General Purpose Parallel Computing*
  W. F. McColl
- *Analyzing Flat GHC Programs for Sophistocated Optimization*
  K. Ueda
- *An Overview of the Gigalips Project*
  D. H. D. Warren

19.15 Dinner in Old Library

Tuesday 26th September

9.00 Session 3 - Models : Chaired by H. Yasuura and J. A. Goguen

- *Ways of Observing Processes*
  I. Phillips
- *The Computational Model of A'UM*
  K. Yoshida
- *A Calculus of Mobile Processes*
  D. J. Walker
- *Modelling Real Time CSP*
  A. W. Roscoe (joint work with G. M. Reed)
- *An Operational Semantics of And-Or-Parallel Logic Programming Language ANDOR-II*
  A. Takeuchi
- *Concurrent Program Specification using Conditional Equations*
  R. Milne

14.15 Session 4 - Software : Chaired by M. Tokoro and M. R. Sleep

- *A Pure Applicative Implementation of Object Oriented Computation System*
  M. Amamiya
- *The VSA Portable Compiler Code-Generation System for Parallel Computers*
  I. McNally
- *Synchronization and Communication for Concurrent COB*
  T. Kamimura
- *Sharing Concurrent Object Descriptions - Towards Reuse of Synchronization Codes*
  E. Shibayama
- *Application Programming Environments on Multi-Computers for Image Processing and Synthesis*
  P. M. Dew

- *Premature Return - An Alternative Construct for Parallel Lisp Languages*
  T. Yuasa

19.45 Reception in Old Library

20.15 Banquet in Hall

Wednesday 27th September

9.00 Session 5 - Architecture : Chaired by M. Amamiya and W. F. McColl

- *Towards General Purpose Parallel Computers*
  D. May
- *A Parallel Object Oriented Language Fleng++ and its Control System on the Parallel Machine PIE64*
  H. Tanaka
- *Hardware Developments Involving Time*
  J. W. Sanders
- *Some Experiments in Dual Paradigm Parallelism*
  I. Page
- *Transformational Derivation of Systolic Arrays*
  N. Yoshida
- *Applications Experienced from the Edinburgh Concurrent Supercomputer Project*
  D. Roweth

14.15 Session 6 - Concurrency and Rewriting :
                              Chaired by H. Tanaka and G. D. Plotkin

- *On Object-Oriented Concurrent Computing*
  M. Tokoro
- *Graph Rewriting as a Computational Model*
  M. R. Sleep
- *Concurrent Rewriting Models of Computation for the Rewrite Rule Machine*
  J. A. Goguen
- *Compiled Parallel Graph Reduction on the GRIP Multiprocessor*
  S. L. Peyton-Jones

17.15 Closing Remarks : T. Ito and R. M. Burstall

17.30 End of Workshop

List of Participants

UK Participants

R. M. Burstall	University of Edinburgh
P.M. Dew	Leeds University
D. Gabbay	University of London (Imperial College)
J. A. Goguen	Oxford University
K. Jackson	System Designers, Cambridge
C. B. Jones	Manchester University
D. May	INMOS Bristol
W. F. McColl	Oxford University
I. McNally	University of Southampton
R. Milne	STC Technology Ltd., Harlow
I. Page	Oxford University
S. L. Peyton-Jones	University of London (UCL)
I. Phillips	University of London (Imperial College)
G. D. Plotkin	University of Edinburgh
A. W. Roscoe	Oxford University
D. Roweth	University of Edinburgh and Meiko Ltd.
J. W. Sanders	Oxford University
M. R. Sleep	University of East Anglia
C. P. Stirling	University of Edinburgh
D. J. Walker	University of Edinburgh
D. H. D. Warren	University of Bristol

Japanese Participants

M. Amamiya	Kyushu University
T. Ito	Tohoku University
T. Kamimura	Tokyo Research Laboratory, IBM Japan
E. Shibayama	Ryukoku University
A. Takeuchi	Central Research Laboratory, Mitsubishi Electric Corporation
H. Tanaka	University of Tokyo
M. Tokoro	Keio University
K. Ueda	Institute of New Generation Computer Technology
H. Yasuura	Kyoto University
A. Yonezawa	University of Tokyo
K. Yoshida	Institute of New Generation Computer Technology
N. Yoshida	Kyushu University
T. Yuasa	Toyohashi University of Technology

Abstracts of Talks

What follows is the list of titles and abstracts of the talks given at the workshop. Those that are included in the main body of this volume are excluded.

Application Programming Environments on Multi-Computers for Image Processing and Synthesis

P. Dew, Dept. of Computer Studies, University of Leeds

The talk outlines recent work at Leeds directed towards the development of application programming environments to support computations as in the manufacturing industries. The talk concentrates on application programming environment being developed to support solid geometry computations and look towards future research directions.

Towards General Purpose Parallel Computers

D. May, INMOS, Bristol

One of the major successes of computer science has been the development of an efficient *general purpose* architecture for sequential computers. This has allowed the construction of standard languages and portable software which have been a primary factor in increasing the pervasiveness of the sequential computer. One of the major questions of current computer science research is whether a similar success can be achieved for highly parallel general purpose *parallel* computers.

A wide range of specialized parallel architectures can already be found in applications such as real-time control, image processing, graphics and supercomputing. Experience with these machines and theoretical considerations suggest several promising approaches to the architecture of scalable general purpose parallel computers. How efficiently such architectures can be implemented in current and future technology remains an open question.

Algorithmic Challenges in General Purpose Parallel Computing

W.F. McColl, Programming Research Group, Oxford University

The Parallel Random Access Machine (PRAM) provides a standard, architecture-independent model of parallel computation. By adopting the PRAM as the standard model we can begin the long overdue separation of software from hardware considerations in parallel computing. This separation should encourage the growth of a large and diverse parallel software industry and help provide a focus for future hardware developments (The von Neumann model has provided such a separation for sequential computing for at least the last three decades.)

The efficient implementation of PRAMs on distributed memory architectures is now well understood. We also have a large set of "efficient" PRAM algorithms for important problems, i.e. algorithms which require only polylog parallel time on a polynomial number of processors. Many of these so-called "NC algorithms" do, however, have a number of shortcomings with respect to practical implementation which are now becoming apparent.

This talk discusses some of the issues involved, and highlights some of the challenges.

The VSA Portable Compiler Code-Generation System for Parallel Computers

. McNally, Dept. of Electronics and Computer Science, University of Southampton

The Virtual Systems Architecture defines the architecture and a programming interface of a virtual machine. This definition facilitates the creation of portable compilers for computers with widely different parallel (or even serial) architectures, by writing the compilers for the virtual machine and implementing the virtual machine on real architectures. This talk outlines the virtual machine and its portable compiler code-generation system.

Concurrent Program Specification Using Conditional Equations

R. Milne, STC Technology Ltd., Harlow

Techniques for formal specification are many and varied, but they are typically limited to dealing with one aspect of the problem. This may be, say, the data typing, the sequential control structuring, or the time ordering of communication events. This limitation can make the techniques awkward to exploit in a development process which is meant to cover the development of complete systems.

The talk indicates how an approach to specification based on conditional equational axioms can allow the applicative, sequential imperative, and concurrent imperative aspects of programming to be considered in a uniform manner. The resulting styles of specification and of proof are outlined and related to others, such as those based on pre-conditions and post-conditions.

Some Experiments with Dual-Paradigm Parallelism

. Page, Computing Laboratory, Oxford University

Many computer applications are amenable to huge increases in execution speed through the deployment of parallel processing. Two of the most powerful paradigms of parallel processing which have so far seen extensive use are the MIMD and SIMD models. These models are often considered as suitable implementation vehicles for control-parallel algorithms and data-parallel algorithms, respectively. However, many applications, particularly in the areas of computer graphics and vision, use a number of algorithms at different stages, where some of the algorithms are naturally control-parallel and others data-parallel. The algorithms of early vision and those late in the graphics pipeline typically deal with large rectangular arrays of pixels and they extensively exploit spatial coherence in the data. Such algorithms are best considered as data-parallel and a SIMD computational environment may well be the most cost effectively for high speed execution. The algorithms in higher-level vision and those close to the display data structures in graphics are probably best considered as control parallel and best suited to a MIMD environment, although progress in developing parallel algorithms has so far been slower in these areas.

In order to provide an environment in which highly complex vision and graphics algorithms can run at high speed, we have constructed a computing engine (the Disputer) which encompasses both a data-parallel computing paradigm in a 256 processor SIMD array, and also a control-parallel paradigm in a MIMD network of transputers. The two parallel machines are closely coupled and the entire system is controlled by a single program in the Occam 2 parallel processing language. This system allows us to investigate dual paradigm algorithms and we report some of the early results from using this novel parallel processor for applications in both graphics and vision.

Compiled Parallel Graph Reduction on the GRIP Multiprocessor

S. L. Peyton-Jones, Dept. of Computer Science, University College London

Parallel graph reduction is an attractive implementation for functional languages, because of its simplicity and inherently distributed nature.

Over the past few years, highly effective compilation methods have been developed for graph reduction on sequential architectures. This talk sketches how to adapt these techniques to a parallel machine, and discusses some of the new questions raised by parallelism.

In particular, the talk discusses management of the storage hierarchy to achieve locality, and methods for dynamically determining granularity.

Ways of Observing Processes

I. Phillips, Dept. of Computing, Imperial College

We aim to contribute to the debate about what equivalence of processes should mean by examining the territory between failures equivalence of CSP and bisimulation of CCS through means of varying the power of an outside observer of processes.

Probabilistic Powerdomains

G. D. Plotkin, Dept. of Computer Science, University of Edinburgh

Probabilistic powerdomains are intended to handle the semantics of programming languages with probabilistic nondeterminism, just as powerdomains do ordinary nondeterminism. We present a construction which works for general complete partial orders using evaluation (rather than the more expected measures). We motivate the work with the example of proving properties of a simple imperative language with a fair coin tossing construct. Then the general theory is presented, guided by Moggi's lambda-c calculus framework. The work is joint with Claire Jones.

Applications Experienced from the Edinburgh Concurrent Supercomputer Project

D. Roweth, Dept. of Physics, University of Edinburgh, and Meiko Ltd.

We discuss the range of applications that have been ported to the Edinburgh Concurrent Supercomputer, a 500 processor Meiko computer surface, highlighting applications suitable and unsuitable for this machine architecture.

Analyzing Flat GHC Programs for Sophisticated Optimization

K. Ueda, Institute of New Generation Computer Technology

Compile-time program analysis based on mode analysis and type inference may greatly help optimization. This approach is applied to the optimization of Flat GHC. We first show how simple mode (or dataflow) analysis helps the optimization of unification, the basic operation of Flat GHC. The mode system is based on the notion of constraints, and the mode analysis means to solve a system of mode (in)equations. The mode system can handle complex dataflow such as incomplete messages and streams of streams under certain conditions. Second, we extend the above mode analysis to be used for the optimization of programs in which processes are almost always dormant (suspended). Programs using demand-driven computation and those in which processes are used for programming storage rather than computation fall into this category. Conventional implementation schemes, which are tuned for programs that do not suspend often, are inappropriate for those programs. We found that the analysis of interprocess communication enables us to take a quite different scheduling policy by which process switching overhead is reduced and message buffering is suppressed.

An Overview of the Gigalips Project

D. H. D. Warren, Dept. of Computer Science, University of Bristol

The Gigalips project is an informal research collaboration between a number of parties concerned with developing parallel logic programming systems. The main original parties were groups from Argonne National Laboratory, the University of Bristol, and the Swedish Institute of Computer Science. Recently started Esprit projects have extended the collaboration to include the Belgian Institute of Management, the European Computer Industry Research Centre, Meiko Limited, and the Universities of Leuven and Madrid. The research in general is aimed at exploiting parallelism transparently, to enable advanced applications to run faster on parallel hardware with little or no extra programming effort.

The main development to date has been the Aurora system, a prototype or-parallel implementation of the full Prolog language for shard memory multiprocessors. Other work is concerned with designing and implementing a more general parallel execution model, the Andorra model, which combines an or-parallelism with dependent and-parallelism. Using the Andorra model as a basis, we are also defining a new language, Andorra Prolog, intended to subsume both Prolog and the committed choice languages (especially GHC). The new language combines nondeterminacy with implicit coroutining. Also being developed is the Data Diffusion Machine, a general-purpose, scalable, shared address space machine. The design is believed to provide particularly good support for Aurora and Andorra, and is being emulated on the transputer-based Meiko Computing Surface.

This talk reviews the project's achievements and future plans.

The Computational Model of A'UM

K. Yoshida, Institute of New Generation Computer Technology

When a computation system is decomposed into possibly fine pieces, finally left are events. The major difference between concurrent systems and sequential systems is whether events are partially ordered or totally ordered. A'UM is a concurrent programming language designed in pursuit of highly parallel and highly abstract computation. It treats messages as events, and regards a concurrent system as the ordering of messages. The computational model is characterized by two features: stream computation and object-oriented abstraction. The computational space consists of objects which communicate with each other via streams. Stream manipulation operations enable to produce totally ordered sets of events for sequential computation and partially ordered sets of events for concurrent computation.

APPENDIX

A Brief Report

of

First UK/Japan Workshop

in

Computer Science

Sendai, 6-10 July 1987

List of Participants

UK Participants

R. M. Burstall	University of Edinburgh
J. Darlington	Imperial College
T. Hagino	University of Edinburgh
J. Hughes	Glasgow University
C. Jones	Manchester University
D. May	Inmos
B. Roscoe	Oxford University
D. Sannella	University of Edinburgh
M. Spivey	Oxford University
D. Turner	University of Kent

Japanese Participants

K. Furukawa	ICOT
S. Goto	NTT
S. Hayashi	Kyoto University (currently at Ryukoku University)
T. Ito	Tohoku University
Y. Kameyama	Tohoku University
T. Matsuyama	Tohoku University (currently at Okayama University)
M. Murakami	ICOT
T. Sakuragawa	Kyoto University
T. Sakurai	Tokyo Metropolitan University
M. Sato	Tohoku University
E. Shibayama	Tokyo Institute of Technology (currently at Ryukoku University)
Y. Takayama	ICOT (currently at Oki Electric Co.)
A. Togashi	Tohoku University
H. Yokouchi	IBM Japan
N. Yoneda	University of Tokyo
A. Yonezawa	Tokyo Institute of Technology (currently at University of Tokyo)

Overview of the Workshop

The first UK/Japan Workshop in Computer Science was organized by R. M. Burstall and T. Ito on July 6-10, 1987 under the support of SERC and Tohoku University. The topics of the workshop were focused on Logic, Proof, and Specification in Computer Science. This appendix gives a brief report of the first workshop, containing its programme and the list of the workshop participants.

Programme

Sunday 5th July

18.00 Reception at the Olive Room of Washington Hotel

Monday 6th July

9.00 Session A - Logic and Type Theory : Chaired by R. Burstall
- *Reasoning about Partial Functions*
  C. Jones
- *Quty : A Concurrent Language Based on Logic and Function*
  M. Sato
- *A New Formulation of Constructive Type Theory*
  D. Turner

13.00 Session B - Concurrency : Chaired by M. Sato
- *Unified Message Send : Representing Different Execution Models in Objects*
  N. Suzuki
- *An Alternative Partial Order for the Failures Model*
  A. Roscoe
- *Theory of Forcing and Recovery from Deadlock*
  T. Ito
- *Temporal Prolog*
  T. Sakuragawa

Tuesday 7th July

9.00 Session C - Proof and Logic(I) : Chaired by C. Jones
- *Interactive Proof Editors*
  R. Burstall
- *PX : A Computational Logic*
  S. Hayashi

- *Programming System Based on QJ*
  Y. Takayama

Lunch Time Panel : Chaired by A. Yonezawa

13.00 Session D - Proof and Logic(II) : Chaired by S. Goto
- *Mechanized Reasoning about Z Specifications*
  M. Spivey
- *Three Approaches to Infinitely Long Lists in Constructive Logic*
  S. Goto
- *Toward Formal Development of ML Program from Algebraic Specifications*
  D. Sannella
- *Categorical Programming Language*
  T. Hagino
- *(Short Talk) Proving Partial Correctness of Guarded Horn Clauses Programs*
  M. Murakami
- *(Short Talk) Axiomatic System for Concurrent Logic Programming*
  Y. Kameyama

Wednesday 8th July

9.30 Session E - Program Transformation : Chaired by T. Matsuyama
- *Functional Programming*
  J. Darlington
- *Unfolding Rules for FGHC Programs*
  K. Furukawa

11.00 Bus Tour to Hiraizumi and Matsushima

18.30 Banquet at Matsushima (Taritu-An)

Thursday 9th July

9.00 Session F - Program Development and Analysis : Chaired by J Darlington
- *Object-Oriented Concurrent Programming in ABCL/1*
  A. Yonezawa
- *Program Transformation in an Object-Based Parallel Computing Model*
  E. Shibayama
- *Backward Analysis of Functional Programs*
  J. Hughes
- *Use of Formal Methods by a Silicon Manufacturer*
  D. May

13.30 Session G - "Short Talk" : Chaired by J. Hughes

- *(Short Talk) A Functional Language with String Pattern Unification*
  T. Matsuyama
- *(Short Talk) Proof and Types*
  T. Sakurai

14.15 Panel Discussion : Chaired by R. Burstall

15.10 Session H - "Short Talk" : Chaired by S. Goto

- *(Short Talk) Structured Theories in B*
  M. Spivey
- *(Short Talk) Specifying User Interface with Windows and a Mouse*
  T. Hagino
- *(Short Talk) RACCO : A Model Logic Programming Language for Writing Models of Realtime Process Control Systems*
  T. Sakuragawa
- *(Short Talk) Transformation of Logic Programs into Rewriting Programs*
  A. Togashi
- *(Short Talk) On CCC Computation by CCM*
  H. Yokouchi

Friday 10th July

9.30 Demo Events on Sun-3 and Symbolics-3670 at Ito's Laboratory.

(1) R. Burstall and T. Hagino	: Interactive Proof Editing Environment for Formal Systems
(2) D. Turner	: Miranda (Functional Programming System)
(3) M. Spivey	: B
(4) A. Yonezawa and E. Shibayama	: ABCL/1
(5) T. Ito and T. Matsuyama	: A Parallel Lisp Interpreter
(6) S. Hayashi	: PX

13.30 Public Lectures

- *Interactive Proof Editing : Friendliness and Generality*
  B. Burstall
- *The VDM Program Development Methodology*
  C. Jones
- *Research in Parallel Computing*
  N. Suzuki

Vol. 437: D. Kumar (Ed.), Current Trends in SNePS – Semantic Network Processing System. Proceedings, 1989. VII, 162 pages. 1990. (Subseries LNAI).

Vol. 438: D. H. Norrie, H.-W. Six (Eds.), Computer Assisted Learning – ICCAL '90. Proceedings, 1990. VII, 467 pages. 1990.

Vol. 439: P. Gorny, M. Tauber (Eds.), Visualization in Human-Computer Interaction. Proceedings, 1988. VI, 274 pages. 1990.

Vol. 440: E.Börger, H. Kleine Büning, M. M. Richter (Eds.), CSL '89. Proceedings, 1989. VI, 437 pages. 1990.

Vol. 441: T. Ito, R. H. Halstead, Jr. (Eds.), Parallel Lisp: Languages and Systems. Proceedings, 1989. XII, 364 pages. 1990.

Vol. 442: M. Main, A. Melton, M. Mislove, D. Schmidt (Eds.), Mathematical Foundations of Programming Semantics. Proceedings, 1989. VI, 439 pages. 1990.

Vol. 443: M. S. Paterson (Ed.), Automata, Languages and Programming. Proceedings, 1990. IX, 781 pages. 1990.

Vol. 444: S. Ramani, R. Chandrasekar, K. S. R. Anjaneyulu (Eds.), Knowledge Based Computer Systems. Proceedings, 1989. X, 546 pages. 1990. (Subseries LNAI).

Vol. 445: A. J. M. van Gasteren, On the Shape of Mathematical Arguments. VIII, 181 pages. 1990.

Vol. 446: L. Plümer, Termination Proofs for Logic Programs. VIII, 142 pages. 1990. (Subseries LNAI).

Vol. 447: J. R. Gilbert, R. Karlsson (Eds.), SWAT 90. 2nd Scandinavian Workshop on Algorithm Theory. Proceedings, 1990. VI, 417 pages. 1990.

Vol. 448: B. Simons, A. Spector (Eds.), Fault-Tolerant Distributed Computing. VI, 298 pages. 1990.

Vol. 449: M. E. Stickel (Ed.), 10th International Conference on Automated Deduction. Proceedings, 1990. XVI, 688 pages. 1990. (Subseries LNAI).

Vol. 450: T. Asano, T. Ibaraki, H. Imai, T. Nishizeki (Eds.), Algorithms. Proceedings, 1990. VIII, 479 pages. 1990.

Vol. 451: V. Mařík, O. Štěpánková, Z. Zdráhal (Eds.), Artificial Intelligence in Higher Education. Proceedings, 1989. IX, 247 pages. 1990. (Subseries LNAI).

Vol. 452: B. Rovan (Ed.), Mathematical Foundations of Computer Science 1990. Proceedings, 1990. VIII, 544 pages. 1990.

Vol. 453: J. Seberry, J. Pieprzyk (Eds.), Advances in Cryptology – AUSCRYPT '90. Proceedings, 1990. IX, 462 pages. 1990.

Vol. 454: V. Diekert, Combinatorics on Traces. XII, 165 pages. 1990.

Vol. 455: C. A. Floudas, P. M. Pardalos, A Collection of Test Problems for Constrained Global Optimization Algorithms. XIV, 180 pages. 1990.

Vol. 456: P. Deransart, J. Maluszyński (Eds.), Programming Language Implementation and Logic Programming. Proceedings, 1990. VIII, 401 pages. 1990.

Vol. 457: H. Burkhart (Ed.), CONPAR '90 – VAPP IV. Proceedings, 1990. XIV, 900 pages. 1990.

Vol. 458: J. C. M. Baeten, J. W. Klop (Eds.), CONCUR '90. Proceedings, 1990. VII, 537 pages. 1990.

Vol. 459: R. Studer (Ed.), Natural Language and Logic. Proceedings, 1989. VII, 252 pages. 1990. (Subseries LNAI).

Vol. 460: J. Uhl, H. A. Schmid, A Systematic Catalogue of Reusable Abstract Data Types. XII, 344 pages. 1990.

Vol. 461: P. Deransart, M. Jourdan (Eds.), Attribute Grammars and their Applications. Proceedings, 1990. VIII, 358 pages. 1990.

Vol. 462: G. Gottlob, W. Nejdl (Eds.), Expert Systems in Engineering. Proceedings, 1990. IX, 260 pages. 1990. (Subseries LNAI).

Vol. 463: H. Kirchner, W. Wechler (Eds.), Algebraic and Logic Programming. Proceedings, 1990. VII, 386 pages. 1990.

Vol. 464: J. Dassow, J. Kelemen (Eds.), Aspects and Prospects of Theoretical Computer Science. Proceedings, 1990. VI, 298 pages. 1990.

Vol. 465: A. Fuhrmann, M. Morreau (Eds.), The Logic of Theory Change. Proceedings, 1989. X, 334 pages. 1991. (Subseries LNAI).

Vol. 466: A. Blaser (Ed.), Database Systems of the 90s. Proceedings, 1990. VIII, 334 pages. 1990.

Vol. 467: F. Long (Ed.), Software Engineering Environments. Proceedings, 1989. VI, 313 pages. 1990.

Vol. 468: S. G. Akl, F. Fiala, W. W. Koczkodaj (Eds.), Advances in Computing and Information – ICCI '90. Proceedings, 1990. VII, 529 pages. 1990.

Vol. 469: I. Guessarian (Ed.), Semantics of Systems of Concurrent Processes. Proceedings, 1990. V, 456 pages. 1990.

Vol. 470: S. Abiteboul, P. C. Kanellakis (Eds.), ICDT '90. Proceedings, 1990. VII, 528 pages. 1990.

Vol. 471: B. C. Ooi, Efficient Query Processing in Geographic Information Systems. VIII, 208 pages. 1990.

Vol. 472: K. V. Nori, C. E. Veni Madhavan (Eds.), Foundations of Software Technology and Theoretical Computer Science. Proceedings, 1990. X, 420 pages. 1990.

Vol. 473: I. B. Damgård (Ed.), Advances in Cryptology – EUROCRYPT '90. Proceedings, 1990. VIII, 500 pages. 1991.

Vol. 474: D. Karagiannis (Ed.), Information Systems and Artificial Intelligence: Integration Aspects. Proceedings, 1990. X, 293 pages. 1991.

Vol. 475: P. Schroeder-Heister (Ed.), Extensions of Logic Programming. Proceedings, 1989. VIII, 364 pages. 1991. (Subseries LNAI).

Vol. 476: M. Filgueiras, L. Damas, N. Moreira, A. P. Tomás (Eds.), Natural Language Processing. Proceedings, 1990. VII, 253 pages. 1991. (Subseries LNAI).

Vol. 477: D. Hammer (Ed.), Compiler Compilers. Proceedings, 1990. VI, 227 pages. 1991.

Vol. 478: J. van Eijck (Ed.), Logics in AI. Proceedings, 1990. IX, 562 pages. 1991. (Subseries LNAI).

Vol. 479: H. Schmidt, Meta-Level Control for Deductive Database Systems. VI, 155 pages. 1991.

Vol. 480: C. Choffrut, M. Jantzen (Eds.), STACS 91. Proceedings, 1991. X, 549 pages. 1991.

Vol. 481: E. Lang, K.-U. Carstensen, G. Simmons, Modelling Spatial Knowledge on a Linguistic Basis. IX, 138 pages. 1991. (Subseries LNAI).

Vol. 482: Y. Kodratoff (Ed.), Machine Learning – EWSL-91. Proceedings, 1991. XI, 537 pages. 1991. (Subseries LNAI).

Vol. 483: G. Rozenberg (Ed.), Advances in Petri Nets 1990. VI, 515 pages. 1991.

Vol. 484: R. H. Möhring (Ed.), Graph-Theoretic Concepts in Computer Science. Proceedings, 1990. IX, 360 pages. 1991.

Vol. 485: K. Furukawa, H. Tanaka, T. Fujisaki (Eds.), Logic Programming '89. Proceedings, 1989. IX, 183 pages. 1991. (Subseries LNAI).

Vol. 487: A. Bode (Ed.), Distributed Memory Computing. Proceedings, 1991. XI, 506 pages. 1991.

Vol. 488: R. V. Book (Ed.), Rewriting Techniques and Applications. Proceedings, 1991. VII, 458 pages. 1991.

Vol. 489: J. W. de Bakker, W. P. de Roever, G. Rozenberg (Eds.), Foundations of Object-Oriented Languages. Proceedings, 1990. VIII, 442 pages. 1991.

Vol. 490: J. A. Bergstra, L. M. G. Feijs (Eds.), Algebraic Methods II: Theory, Tools and Applications. VI, 434 pages. 1991.

Vol. 491: A. Yonezawa, T. Ito (Eds.), Concurrency: Theory, Language, and Architecture. Proceedings, 1989. VIII, 339 pages. 1991.

This series reports new developments in computer science research and teaching – quickly, informally and at a high level. The type of material considered for publication includes preliminary drafts of original papers and monographs, technical reports of high quality and broad interest, advanced level lectures, reports of meetings, provided they are of exceptional interest and focused on a single topic. The timeliness of a manuscript is more important than its form which may be unfinished or tentative. If possible, a subject index should be included. Publication of Lecture Notes is intended as a service to the international computer science community, in that a commercial publisher, Springer-Verlag, can offer a wide distribution of documents which would otherwise have a restricted readership. Once published and copyrighted, they can be documented in the scientific literature.

Manuscripts

Manuscripts should be no less than 100 and preferably no more than 500 pages in length.
They are reproduced by a photographic process and therefore must be typed with extreme care. Symbols not on the typewriter should be inserted by hand in indelible black ink. Corrections to the typescript should be made by pasting in the new text or painting out errors with white correction fluid. Authors receive 75 free copies and are free to use the material in other publications. The typescript is reduced slightly in size during reproduction; best results will not be obtained unless the text on any one page is kept within the overall limit of 18 x 26.5 cm (7 x 10½ inches). On request, the publisher will supply special paper with the typing area outlined.
Manuscripts should be sent to Prof. G. Goos, GMD Forschungsstelle an der Universität Karlsruhe, Haid- und Neu-Str. 7, 7500 Karlsruhe 1, Germany, Prof. J. Hartmanis, Cornell University, Dept. of Computer Science, Ithaca, NY/USA 14853, or directly to Springer-Verlag Heidelberg.

Springer-Verlag, Heidelberger Platz 3, D-1000 Berlin 33
Springer-Verlag, Tiergartenstraße 17, D-6900 Heidelberg 1
Springer-Verlag, 175 Fifth Avenue, New York, NY 10010/USA
Springer-Verlag, 37-3, Hongo 3-chome, Bunkyo-ku, Tokyo 113, Japan

ISBN 3-540-53932-8
ISBN 0-387-53932-8